Teaching the African Novel

Modern Language Association of America
Options for Teaching

For a complete listing of titles,
see the last pages of this book.

Teaching the African Novel

Edited by

Gaurav Desai

The Modern Language Association of America
New York 2009

Library of Congress Cataloging-in-Publication Data

Teaching the African novel / edited by Gaurav Desai.
p. cm.—(Options for teaching; 24)
Includes bibliographical references and index.
ISBN 978-1-60329-037-1 (hardcover : alk. paper)
ISBN 978-1-60329-038-8 (pbk. : alk. paper)
1. African fiction—Study and teaching. 2. African fiction (English)—Study and teaching. 3. Africa—In literature. I. Desai, Gaurav Gajanan.
PL8010.6.T43 2009
809.3'008996—dc22 2009017792

Options for Teaching 24
ISSN 1079-2562

Cover illustration: *Rhythms of Prayer*, by Obiora Udechukwu. Watercolor, 1985. An example of Uli painting of the Nsukka school. Reproduced with permission of the artist

Published by The Modern Language Association of America
26 Broadway, New York, New York 10004-1789
www.mla.org

Contents

Part IV: Resources

Acknowledgments

Most of the work of editing this volume was conducted in the fall of 2005, when my family and I had evacuated from New Orleans in the aftermath of Hurricane Katrina. We left the city with very few of our academic belongings, fully expecting to be back home in a few days. As it turns out, our stay in Austin, Texas, was to last for an entire semester—a time during which we were warmly welcomed by the Department of English at the University of Texas, Austin. I thank James Garrison, then chair of the department, for his support and my friends and colleagues Barbara Harlow, Bernth Lindfors, and Neville Hoad for making us feel at home. I also thank Thomas F. Staley, director of the Harry Ransom Center, for making me part of the community of scholars visiting that very rich archive.

Back in New Orleans, my colleagues in the English department and at Tulane University as a whole continue to impress on me why, despite so many challenges, we love this city that we call home. I am grateful for their continued camaraderie and support. I thank as well all the contributors to this volume, who have shown an enormous amount of patience as the manuscript has been vetted by a number of external reviewers. I think they will agree that the review process has resulted in a stronger collection and will join me in thanking the reviewers as well as the MLA Publications Committee, which had oversight over its development. Joseph Gibaldi, who first acquired the manuscript; David Nicholls and James Hatch, who both worked on editing it; and Michael Kandel, our meticulous copyeditor, all deserve a great round of applause. I am very grateful to them for their keen advice and for moving the project along. Thanks as well to Samantha Bruner, who prepared the index for this volume.

Supriya Nair and Sameer Nair-Desai are two of the best companions one could ever ask for. As always, I remain in their debt—a debt that with each project only grows.

Gaurav Desai

Introduction: Teaching the African Novel

What we have created is another hybrid tradition, a tradition in transition, a minority tradition that can only be termed as Afro-European literature; that is the literature written by Africans in European languages.

—Ngũgĩ wa Thiong'o, *Decolonising the Mind*

What I am saying really boils down to a simple plea for the African novel. Don't fence me in.

—Chinua Achebe, "Thoughts on the African Novel"

I would submit that the study of Africa demands nothing less than a reconsideration of all the terms of literary analysis, starting with the word "literature" itself, and that such a reconsideration is the best thing that can happen to the field.

—Christopher Miller, *Nationalists and Nomads*

I would be most pleased if those who read this book should never again say casually of an African novel, "Well, of course it's like that. That's the oral tradition for you."

—Eileen Julien,
African Novels and the Question of Orality

These four passages serve as important signposts in the debates around the definition of the African novel, the institutional locations they address, and the appropriate protocols for reading them. When Ngũgĩ wa Thiong'o writes that the tradition of African writing in European languages results in a hybrid literature, there is no question that for him such hybridity is undesirable, producing an elite literature that is of little relevance to the vast majority of African peasants and workers. His statement, made in *Decolonising the Mind: The Politics of Language in African Literature*, arguably the most passionate and eloquent literary manifesto to emerge from postcolonial Africa, is a challenge to fellow writers to refocus their energies on developing literatures in the indigenous languages of Africa. Having himself devoted considerable energy to writing novels in Gikuyu such as *Caitaani Mũtharaba-inĩ* and *Matigari Ma Njiruungi*, Ngũgĩ pledged that *Decolonising the Mind* would be his "farewell to English as a vehicle for any of [his] writings. From now on it is Gikuyu and Kiswahili all the way" (xiv). That he has not been able, as a professor now in the United States, to honor this pledge, at least in his critical writings, attests to the sad irony of the institutional demands placed on intellectuals in the Western academy and to the corollary irony that exile, for many African intellectuals in the second half of the twentieth century, has become a mandatory sentence for political consciousness-raising.

But Ngũgĩ's note also challenges the institution of literary studies to reexamine what gets taught as African literature and the manner in which it is taught. While this challenge has some implications for the study of African literatures in the Western academy, his immediate concern was with the relevance of literature for African students and their fellow citizens. Before he published *Decolonising the Mind*, Ngũgĩ, a professor at the University of Nairobi, had already engaged with a group of colleagues in a reorientation of the literary curriculum in the late 1960s. The new curriculum this group proposed would abolish the English department and substitute it with a department of African literatures and languages. "With Africa at the center of things," wrote Ngũgĩ and his colleagues, "not existing as an appendix or a satellite of other countries and literatures, things must be seen from the African perspective" (Ngũgĩ wa Thiong'o, Taban lo Liyong, and Owuor-Anyumba 150). In a number of essays written in the three decades following Kenyan independence, Ngũgĩ outlined what such an African perspective might be. Inspired by Frantz Fanon's emphasis on the "wretched of the earth," he argued for the primacy of the peasantry and to some extent the urban working class as the progenitors of a revolutionary national culture. At the same time, such grounding was informed by his desire to draw on a larger black diasporic imagination, particularly that to which writers from the Caribbean, such as George Lamming, contributed. Ngũgĩ's access to this diasporic tradition was inevitably through the medium of English, and his reading of this literature drew on the colonial education that he had received. As scholars like Carol Sicherman and Simon Gikandi ("Globalization") have argued, in the anglophone countries of colonial and postcolonial Africa the protocols of reading this literature—indeed, any literature—were derived from the Leavisite emphasis on moral codes and the great tradition (Leavis). Paradoxically, then, Ngũgĩ's turn to peasant culture, as Fanon would have predicted, already carried within it the traces of the colonial episteme from which he sought a radical break.

Chinua Achebe's plea on behalf of the African novel—"Don't fence me in"—provides a counterpoint to Ngũgĩ's aversion to African literatures written in European languages. By the time Achebe delivered the 1973 address "Thoughts on the African Novel" in Halifax, Canada, he had already staked his position in the debate on the desirability of writing in European languages. As he famously put it, he had been given the English language through the colonial education system, and he intended to use it. But he argues that, in using English, he also transformed it. In the classic essay "The African Writer and the English Language," Achebe demonstrates the ways in which African novelists draw on indigenous speech genres to create an aesthetic that is "in character" with the social languages and codes of the societies they depict. This transformation of European languages is, in his view, a microcosm for a larger transformation in African hands of the genre of the novel itself (62). Indeed, if, as he notes, novels such as *Things Fall Apart* and *Arrow of God* are to be read as an African response to the racism of colonialist fiction (in particular the fiction of Joyce Cary and Joseph Conrad), then the specific linguistic and stylistic innovations in African novels may well be seen as explicit attempts to appropriate the form of the novel for African ends.

The clearest of such ends in the first major phase in the literary history of the African novel was the cause of nationalism. As Benedict Anderson among others has argued, the rise of print culture and the creation of a literate public culture were intimately tied to the rise of creole nationalisms in Latin America. The rapid growth of the African novel in the era of African nationalism suggests that it, too, had a major role to play in shaping national consciousness on the continent. While recognizing the long history of fiction writing in Africa, a history that, with the recent republication of the Ghanaian novel *Marita; or, The Folly of Love*, by A. Native, traces itself back to at least 1888, Gikandi argues that it is Achebe who must be credited with the invention of a modern African literature. "Achebe," he writes, "was possibly the first of our writers to recognize the function of the novel not solely as a mode of representing reality, but one which had limitless possibilities of inventing new national community" (*Reading* 3).

Gikandi's claim is a compelling one, but it needs to be read against at least two paradoxes: first, that the European language production of much of this literature meant that it addressed only the colonially educated middle class; second, that relatively low rates of literacy, along with historical cultural traditions that were primarily oral, were at odds with the inherently private gestures of reading associated with the form of the novel. Here one might speculate on the sociology of consumption: What might it mean for a literary form historically associated with the rise of the European bourgeoisie to be made to carry the burden of an African nationalist (and, to Ngũgĩ, peasant) politics? Ngũgĩ's answer to this question, at least for the period of time that he was engaged with the peasantry in the highlands of Kamiriithu, was to jettison the genre of the novel and work in the medium of theater. Other writers, such as Ousmane Sembene, have turned to film as a more fitting medium to express the national ethos. Yet despite its alleged handicaps, the novel has remained a central genre in narratives of community and the creation of postcolonial identities in Africa.

Achebe's plea not to fence the African novel in was driven in part by a rejection of the (European) modes of criticism that were being brought to bear on the African novel under the guise of universalism. The novel as a genre, Achebe would remind us, has always been concerned with innovation and change, or as the Russian critic Mikhail Bakhtin would put it, the novel by its very nature invites heteroglossia, incorporating multiple social worlds and languages into it. Achebe argues that the kinds of questions one asks of African novels must be based not on allegedly universal criteria but on the very specific thematic, political, and aesthetic concerns of the authors who wrote those texts and the audiences and societies to which they were addressed. His plea was prompted also by a genuine desire to see the novel in Africa thrive and develop multiple legacies.

In retrospect, if it is difficult to define the African novel in a formal or even monothematic way, it is because it has indeed flourished in a variety of hybrid forms. For instance, some novels, like Camara Laye's *The Guardian of the Word* and Thomas Mofolo's *Chaka*, read like prose epics, while others, like Ousmane Sembene's *God's Bits of Wood* or Ngũgĩ wa Thiong'o's *Petals of Blood*, are best approached as novels written in the tradition of socialist realism. A high modernist style, emphasizing interior monologues, stream of consciousness, and a relative subordination of plot to character, is evident in novels like Yvonne Vera's *Under the Tongue* and Bessie Head's *A Question of Power*. Women writers in particular have been exemplary in their experimentation with form: the most celebrated epistolary novel from sub-Saharan Africa is undoubtedly Mariama Bâ's award-winning *So Long a Letter*, while critics have seen in the writing of Calixthe Beyala a self-conscious attempt at the style of writing popularized by French feminists as *écriture féminine*. Although magical realism is much debated as a formal category, some have argued for readings of novels such as Ben Okri's *The Famished Road* and Syl-Cheney Coker's *The Last Harmattan of Alusine Dunbar* as an explicit engagement with Latin American writers, even as detractors have argued for readings that tie these novels to local oratures and ontologies.

If the form and styles of African novels have shown great diversity, their thematic concerns too have been shaped by changing interests and priorities. If early novels like Mongo Beti's *Mission to Kala* or Ferdinand Oyono's *Houseboy* were primarily works that sought to expose the traumas of colonialism, other thematic developments have included—the list is partial—a focus on the city (Naguib Mahfouz's *The Cairo Trilogy*, Cyprian Ekwensi's *People of the City*), the celebration of rural life (Elechi Amadi's *The Concubine*, Flora Nwapa's *Efuru*), critique of the postcolonial condition (Ayi Kwei Armah's *The Beautyful Ones Are Not Yet Born*, Ngũgĩ wa Thiong'o's *Matigari*, Nuruddin Farah's *Maps*), civil war and strife (Ken Saro-Wiwa's *Sozaboy*, Boubacar Boris Diop's *Murambi: The Book of Bones*), women in modernity (Buchi Emecheta's *The Joys of Motherhood*, Ama Ata Aidoo's *Changes*), sexual violence (Lindsey Collen's *The Rape of Sita*, Achmat Dangor's *Bitter Fruit*, Chimamanda Adichie's *Purple Hibiscus*), migration to Europe and America (Emecheta's *Second-Class Citizen*, Leila Aboulela's *The Translator*), and the writing of ethnicities (Moyez Vassanji's *The Gunny Sack*, Abdulrazak Gurnah's *Paradise*).

Conventional literary histories of the African novel tend to organize its development into novels of the period of nationalism (late 1950s and 1960s); novels of disillusionment (1970s and early 1980s); novels that begin to make other identities—particularly gender—central to their perspective

(1980s and 1990s); and novels since the 1990s, which are often characterized by the exilic consciousness of their authors. Such a trajectory does indeed generally map the history of the novel in Africa, but it is important to remain alert to discontinuities as well. So, while women writers do enter the stage in larger numbers in the 1980s, writers such as Grace Ogot in Kenya, Nwapa and Emecheta in Nigeria, Aidoo in Ghana, and Nadine Gordimer in South Africa were writing well before their works received the kind of critical attention they deserved. Regional variations have also interrupted this smooth narrative of periodization; the delayed independence of apartheid South Africa is only the most visible of such variation. And if one were to add the element of popular consumption of novels and to focus on the sociology of reading, it may well be argued that for a certain segment of the market, literary taste has been quite consistent over time. The Kenyan writer David Maillu for a long time has had a following of readers much impressed by his handling of erotic matters. The surgeon-journalist-novelist Yusuf Dawood has had a following for his thrillers. Indeed, as Onookome Okome's essay in this volume, on Onitsha market literature, suggests, a serious study of the various popular fictions in Africa calls for a reconsideration of the academic locus of much of the discourse on the African novel.

Christopher Miller's belief that the critical study of African literature in the Euro-American academy impels us to reconsider the category of literature itself is based not only on the significance of the oral tradition to written literary forms but also on the oral genres of literary production that continue to flourish on the continent. Much of this cultural production is ignored by the Euro-American emphasis on the written text as the sole vehicle of a literary tradition. As Christopher Wise's essay does in this volume, Miller would have us recognize the different configurations of the interface of orality with literacy in various African contexts and their significance not only to written forms such as the novel but also to forms of orature that carry and create ethnic and national identities. An attention to matters of orality and the politics of (European-language) literacy in Africa foregrounds a crucial difference between Euro-American and African literary traditions. Such attention yields in students a more complex understanding of what Miller calls intercultural rather than multicultural literacy. If multicultural literacy is characterized by a model of cultural aggregation, intercultural literacy considers the dissonances and disjunctures that make cross-cultural conversations both more difficult and more rewarding.

Eileen Julien provides if not a counterpoint to Miller then at least a cautionary note. It is instructive to read her passage in the context in which it appears, the final chapter ("Toward New Readings of the Novel") in her book *African Novels and the Question of Orality*. Her project here is to critique the ideological uses to which orality is often put in Africanist literary criticism, the emphasis on continuities with oral traditions often rendering a text more "authentic." She writes:

> Against the familiarity and appeal of the traditional reading of "orality in the novel" I have argued that it is no longer viable and certainly not instructive to read "traces" (the forms) of oral traditions in the novel as signs of African authenticity. (154)

Julien finds the appeal to authenticity and its grounding in the oral tradition problematic not only because it is unreflectively essentialist—making orality an innate African characteristic and literacy an always alien form—but also because it verges on the prescriptive in the guise of the descriptive. While seemingly liberal in its attention to difference, such a paradigm also fences the African novel in. To say this, however, is not to disregard the relation of the novel in Africa to oral traditions but to insist on not presuming it. Hence we must "refuse the simple reflex that consists of seeing oral traditions as necessary and sufficient explanations—good or bad—of novels" (155). Rather, the task must be a critical one of studying oral and written texts together for their similarities and differences—to explore, for instance, if and how a particular novel appropriates, questions, and transforms oral forms and to what aesthetic and political effect.

I have often assigned these four passages on midterm exams in my African novel classes because by that point in the semester I hope to have stimulated student interest not only in the themes and concerns of the novels that they have read but also in the critical debates that have surrounded the novels. Presenting multiple perspectives on the question of the origins of the African novel, on the language and literacy question, on the historic role of the novel in nation formation, on the nature of formal and thematic adaptations, and on the circulation of African novels in the global marketplace—including the marketplace of the academy—allows me to "teach the conflicts" in the classroom (Graff) and to encourage a simultaneous self-awareness in the class on the ambivalent politics of academic consumption. If there is one lesson we learn through the exposure to the various novels and critical debates, it is that the most responsible approaches to reading African novels are those that tend to shy away from models of reading based either on absolute difference or on absolute similarity.

The circulation of African novels in the academy is a central concern for this volume. The African novel has steadily gained a standing in North American classrooms over the past four decades, with the culture wars of the 1980s and the emphasis on the values of multicultural curricula resulting in an exponential growth in the classroom demand for it. Continuing to appear in courses offered by programs and departments of African (and African diaspora) studies, African novels are now regularly taught as part of the course offerings of English, comparative literature, and foreign language departments. They are also often taught—sometimes to the dismay of literary critics who are wary of the documentary uses to which the novels might be put—in social science courses. The rise of a field of study designated postcolonial in literature departments has also meant that African novels are read and taught by those who may not identify themselves as Africanists.

Such a growth in readership and pedagogy is salutary, but it calls for a new dialogue between scholars who have had long-term training in African literary studies and those to whom the field is relatively new. Indeed, one of my personal points of satisfaction in putting this volume together is the mutual respect I have seen develop between contributors who come primarily from an Africanist training and those who come to African novels from a theoretical interest nurtured elsewhere. As the manuscripts circulated among a few of the contributors, it became clear that both groups gained: one group from their colleagues' long-term classroom experiences of teaching the African novel, the other from the radically innovative approaches that their (often younger) colleagues brought to the discussion.

Teaching the African Novel is intended as a teacher's companion that will be of interest to seasoned teachers as well as beginners in the field. It is not, it bears noting, a research companion to this rather large and often amorphous genre. There has been no attempt at comprehensive surveys of national, regional, or language-based literatures or even a comprehensive treatment of themes or major authors. What we offer instead are essays that keep in focus the conceptual, institutional, and practical matters of the teaching of the African novel. In doing so, individual authors have taken into account the available secondary literature on their subject and adjusted their discussions to a suitable and useful extension of this literature in their pedagogically oriented comments. Thus, given the extensive and readily available commentaries on both the anglophone and the francophone African novel in other venues, no need was felt to provide yet another commentary. By the same token, because instructors of Portuguese and Spanish have had fewer surveys of African novels available to them, the chapters that consider novels in these languages do attempt to survey some of this literature and make classroom recommendations on inclusions and exclusions.

But the focus of this volume on teaching rather than on research has also resulted in a rather painful irony. Because very few students in the North American contexts to which this volume is primarily geared have historically developed the level of fluency in an African language that would make the reading of African-language novels feasible in the classroom, the instances of such teaching are isolated. The interested reader of an article on, say, the strategies of teaching a Hausa novel may well be the same person who wrote the article! This statement is an exaggeration but not far from the truth. One instructor of Kiswahili who teaches at a prominent midwestern university (and who is himself a product of perhaps the most well-established African-languages program in the country, the University of Wisconsin, Madison) confessed to me that in over twenty years of teaching the language, he taught no more than three or four students who developed the kind of mastery of the language that could allow a meaningful literary study of a Kiswahili novel. It is useful to remember here that most students who study African languages in American classrooms are not aspiring literary critics but social scientists preparing themselves for fieldwork. Since training in African languages has never been central to the professional qualifications and identities of Africanist literary critics, the teaching and reading of African-language novels has primarily been an exercise in reading translations. So even as critics have sympathized with positions, like Ngũgĩ's, that argue for the importance of African-language literatures, there has been no corollary curricular change in prioritizing training in African languages. Thus, Bernth Lindfors's early admonition of the training of comparative literature graduates still resonates in a number of institutions of higher learning:

> I would like to know . . . whether any real progress has been made in recent years towards liberalizing language requirements so that Arabic may be substituted for German, Talalog for French, or Swahili for Spanish, when these or other non-European languages happen to be more relevant to a student's major research interests than any of the standard European tongues. (34)

There is indeed evidence that students in comparative literature are increasingly aware of the possibilities of learning an African language in their undergraduate and graduate years, and the increasing presence of African students and scholars who bring a knowledge of their own languages with them into the arenas of the academy has enriched the study of African literatures. For the purposes of this volume, though, since the actual teaching of African-language novels in the North American classroom has been so specialized and sporadic (even upper-level language courses often focus on reading newspaper articles instead of novels), it has not been feasible to include an essay on such teaching. The volume continues with the long-standing attention to the ways in which African-language speech genres permeate and transform traditionally European languages and to the challenges that the teaching of African-language novels in translation poses in North American classrooms.

Despite this conundrum of having to focus almost exclusively on African novels written in—or translated into—historically European languages, the volume has an admittedly large scope: it attempts to address the pedagogical options available to teachers of the African novel in a variety of institutional settings. The volume bears an unmistakable North American orientation, because one of the central concerns of the authors is to understand the discursive inventions of Africa and the nature of the circulation of knowledges between a continent that has seen more than its share of poverty, hunger, and political despair and metropolitan locations often oblivious to or uninterested in its plight. What are the political and ethical stakes in teaching African novels to students for many of whom the continent is no more than a space for the indulgence of an exotic fantasy? Or for students who have been told by the media and the culture that surrounds them that nothing good ever comes out of Africa? Such questions are always latent in the discussions that follow. Yet the North American orientation is by no means exclusivist: a case in point is the essay by the Nigerian critic Harry Garuba, who is now based in South Africa, which tells how Achebe's *Things Fall Apart* is read by students in three different geographic and institutional contexts in Africa.

The volume moves from essays that are largely conceptual and theoretical through those that engage with regional and thematic concerns to those that locate the teaching of African novels in specific institutional and classroom contexts. The tone varies from the primarily reflective to the primarily descriptive. The first section, "Theories and Methods," addresses the various methodological apparatuses and theoretical inclinations that have been brought to bear on the study of the African novel. What role does literary theory, often conceived of as a Western import, have in the study and teaching of the African novel? What are some of the critical debates that have risen in Africanist criticism in conjunction with its rise? What role has Marxism played in readings of the African novel historically, and what role might it continue to play in the contemporary classroom? How has the African novel framed history, and how might we see it as not just a register of historical change but also as key participant? How has the burden of political resistance shaped the aesthetic form of the African novel, and how does this shaping in turn inform our critical understanding of the origins of the African novel? What happens when gender and sexuality become the lenses through which African novels are read? What are the conceptual risks and rewards of engaging in and foregrounding the acts of linguistic and cultural translation?

The second section of the volume carries these larger theoretical and conceptual questions into thematic cartographies. Developing this volume has been an exercise of reimagining models of organizing African literature into coherent units that speak to specific and pressing thematic concerns. These units are meant not as boundary markers or discrete points of separation but as engagements with the questions and debates that have historically been raised in the study of African literature. To illustrate, consider the category of African. There has been no agreement over the years, although the initial definitional anxieties seem now to have settled, on what demarcates African literature from its other. I have touched on this debate in terms of the language question, but it is important to remember that different criteria, including race and region, have often been invoked in the debate. Thus, while for many the designation *Africa* generally invokes the region of sub-Saharan Africa, this volume encourages readers to map ways of meaningfully engaging the north-south divide instead of foreclosing the productive dialogues that have continued to take place in the literary traditions across the continent. Along similar lines, white writers of African origin or Asian writers from East Africa are also engaged in this volume, their work given neither special prominence nor special isolation. The point of the volume is to encourage a reading of Africa that is sensitive to its history of colonization but at the same time responsive to its present multiracial and multicultural condition.

The section "Regional Imperatives, Thematic Cartographies" attempts to present some of the thematic concerns that have evolved with particular prominence in specific regions of the continent. The essays here introduce readers to regional literatures that are still understudied, such as the Spanish-language novels from Equatorial Guinea or the lusophone fiction coming from the formerly Portuguese colonies. Readers will find essays that foreground some pressing regional concerns, such as the role of Islam in West Africa or the significance of the griot tradition and orality in the Sahel zone. Orienting thematic issues by region is not meant to suggest an exclusive purchase of a given theme by a particular area; rather, the discussions are meant to be starters for a comparative project of figuring those themes across the continent's literature. This gesture of articulating regional issues into continental perspectives is further expanded by essays on African migrant writers and on the influence of long-term global connections in East Africa. These essays invite us to rethink the idea of regional literatures in a global frame.

The last section of the volume, "Pedagogical and Institutional Contexts," brings together essays that offer concrete suggestions for course organization and describe, to adopt the current lingo, best practices. One essay presents the challenges and possibilities of placing an African novel in a broader survey course on the novel as genre. Another essay deals with teaching francophone fiction in a French-language classroom. Some of the essays, such as the one on teaching Gordimer's *Burger's Daughter* or the one on teaching Achebe's *Things Fall Apart*, take readers directly into the authors' classrooms. The essay on the Web-enhanced classroom and the essay on queer sexualities provide models for teachers and invite them to experiment with new teaching techniques and reading strategies. This section will appeal to those readers who want advice on the practical aspects of teaching African novels.

A common complaint made by seasoned North American teachers of African literatures is that, given the general lack of knowledge of matters African among most students, one always feels that one must begin at the beginning. Pull out a map of the continent, perhaps. Show a film or two by an African filmmaker to ensure that students have at least some cursory visual sense of African spaces and realities. It is a condition not unlike the one J. M. Coetzee's character Elizabeth Costello attributes to African novelists themselves. She says:

> The English novel is written in the first place by English people for English people. The Russian novel is written by Russians for Russians. But the African novel is not written by Africans for Africans. African novelists may write about Africa, about African experience, but they

> are glancing over their shoulder all the time as they write at the foreigners who will read them. Whether they like it or not, they have assumed the role of the interpreter, interpreting Africa to the world. Yet how can you explore a world in all its depth if at the same time you are having to explain it to outsiders? It is like a scientist trying to give his full creative attention to an investigation while at the same time explaining what he is doing to a class of ignorant students. It is too much for one person, it can't be achieved, not at the deepest level. That, it seems to me, is the root of your problem. Having to perform your Africanness at the same time as you write. (13)

Costello's remark begs all the questions about the novels being written, published, and consumed by popular audiences in Africa as opposed to those that receive international acclaim and recognition; it ignores the fact that many novels that do receive international acclaim are also read by Africans; and it overlooks the fact that the African author is as likely to serve as interpreter of a particular fictionalized African condition to a fellow African as to the world. Nevertheless her remark does register an anxiety shared by African writers as well as by the critics and teachers who engage with them. For the author the question is, How to invent a literary tradition and voice that is comprehensible but at the same time not pedagogical or anthropological? For the teacher the question is, How to engage in a pedagogy that is at once intercultural without being trapped into a simplistic exoticism? If the essays in this volume help in at least foregrounding some of these concerns, if not always in resolving them, they will have served a useful purpose.

Note

The page numbers for the four passages given in the epigraph to this introduction are Ngũgĩ wa Thiong'o, *Decolonising* 26–27; Achebe, "Thoughts" 99; Miller 158; Julien 155.

Works Cited

Aboulela, Leila. *The Translator.* Edinburgh: Polygon, 1999. Print.

Achebe, Chinua. "The African Writer and the English Language." *Morning Yet on Creation Day.* London: Heinemann, 1975. 55–62. Print.

———. *Arrow of God.* London: Heinemann, 1964. Print.

———. *Things Fall Apart.* London: Heinemann, 1958. Print.

———. "Thoughts on the African Novel." *Hopes and Impediments: Selected Essays.* New York: Doubleday, 1989. 91–99. Print.

Adichie, Chimamanda. *Purple Hibiscus.* Chapel Hill: Algonquin, 2003. Print.

Aidoo, Ama Ata. *Changes: A Love Story*. London: Women's, 1991. Print.
Amadi, Elechi. *The Concubine*. London: Heinemann, 1966. Print.
Anderson, Benedict. *Imagined Communities: Reflections on the Origin and Spread of Nationalism*. Rev. ed. New York: Verso, 1991. Print.
Armah, Ayi Kwei. *The Beautyful Ones Are Not Yet Born*. London: Heinemann, 1969. Print.
Bâ, Mariama. *So Long a Letter*. 1980. Trans. Modupe Bode-Thomas. Portsmouth: Heinemann, 1989. Print.
Bakhtin, Mikhail. *The Dialogic Imagination: Four Essays*. Ed. Michael Holquist. Trans. Caryl Emerson and Holquist. Austin: U of Texas P, 1981. Print.
Beti, Mongo. *Mission to Kala*. 1957. Trans. Peter Green. London: Heinemann, 1964. Print.
Coetzee, J. M. *The Novel in Africa*. Berkeley: Doreen B. Townsend Center for the Humanities, 1999. Print. Occasional Paper 17.
Coker, Syl-Cheney. *The Last Harmattan of Alusine Dunbar*. London: Heinemann, 1990. Print.
Collen, Lindsey. *The Rape of Sita*. London: Heinemann, 1993. Print.
Dangor, Achmat. *Bitter Fruit*. Cape Town: Kwela, 2001. Print.
Diop, Boubacar Boris. *Murambi: The Book of Bones*. 2000. Trans. Fiona McLaughlin. Bloomington: Indiana UP, 2006. Print.
Ekwensi, Cyprian. *People of the City*. London: Heinemann, 1963. Print.
Emecheta, Buchi. *The Joys of Motherhood*. New York: Braziller, 1979. Print.
———. *Second-Class Citizen*. London: Allison, 1974. Print.
Fanon, Frantz. *The Wretched of the Earth*. New York: Grove, 1963. Print.
Farah, Nuruddin. *Maps*. New York: Pantheon, 1986. Print.
Gikandi, Simon. "Globalization and the Claims of Postcoloniality." *South Atlantic Quarterly* 100.3 (2001): 627–58. Print.
———. *Reading Chinua Achebe: Language and Ideology in Fiction*. Portsmouth: Heinemann, 1991. Print.
Gordimer, Nadine. *Burger's Daughter*. New York: Viking, 1979. Print.
Graff, Gerald. *Beyond the Culture Wars: How Teaching the Conflicts Can Revitalize American Education*. New York: Norton, 1992. Print.
Gurnah, Abdulrazak. *Paradise*. London: Hamish Hamilton, 1994. Print.
Head, Bessie. *A Question of Power*. London: Heinemann, 1974. Print.
Julien, Eileen. *African Novels and the Question of Orality*. Bloomington: Indiana UP, 1992. Print.
Laye, Camara. *The Guardian of the Word*. Trans. James Kirkup. London: Fontana, 1980. Print.
Leavis, F. R. *The Great Tradition: George Eliot, Henry James, Joseph Conrad*. 1948. London: Chatto, 1973. Print.
Lindfors, Bernth. "Comparative Neglect." *Long Drums and Canons: Teaching and Researching African Literatures*. Trenton: Africa World, 1995. 33–36. Print.
Mahfouz, Naguib. *The Cairo Trilogy*. Trans. William Maynard Hutchins. New York: Knopf, 2001. Print.
Miller, Christopher. *Nationalists and Nomads: Essays on Francophone African Literature and Culture*. Chicago: U of Chicago P, 1998. Print.

Mofolo, Thomas. *Chaka*. 1931. Trans. Daniel Kunene. London: Heinemann, 1981. Print.

Native, A. *Marita; or, The Folly of Love*. Ed. and introd. Stephanie Newell. Leiden: Brill, 2002. Print.

Ngũgĩ wa Thiong'o. *Caitaani Mũtharaba-inĩ*. Nairobi: Heinemann, 1980. Print.

———. *Decolonising the Mind: The Politics of Language in African Literature*. London: Currey, 1986. Print.

———. *Homecoming: Essays on African and Caribbean Literature, Culture, and Politics*. Westport: Hill, 1983. Print.

———. *Matigari Ma Njiruungi*. Nairobi: Heinemann, 1987. Print.

———. *Petals of Blood*. London: Heinemann, 1977. Print.

Ngũgĩ wa Thiong'o, Taban lo Liyong, and Henry Owuor-Anyumba. "On the Abolition of the English Department." 24 Oct. 1968. Ngũgĩ wa Thiong'o, *Homecoming* 145–50.

Nwapa, Flora. *Efuru*. London: Heinemann, 1966. Print.

Okri, Ben. *The Famished Road*. New York: Vintage, 1991. Print.

Oyono, Ferdinand. *Houseboy*. 1956. Trans. John Reed. London: Heinemann, 1966. Print.

Saro-Wiwa, Ken. *Sozaboy: A Novel Written in Rotten English*. Port Hartcourt: Saros Intl., 1985. Print.

Sembene, Ousmane. *God's Bits of Wood*. 1962. Trans. Francis Price. London: Heinemann, 1976. Print.

Sicherman, Carol. "Ngugi's Colonial Education: 'The Subversion . . . of the African Mind.'" *African Studies Review* 38 (1995): 11–41. Print.

Vassanji, M. G. *The Gunny Sack*. London: Heinemann, 1989. Print.

Vera, Yvonne. *Under the Tongue*. Harare: Baobab, 1996. Print.

Part I

Theories and Methods

Olakunle George

African Novels and the Question of Theory

A good way to begin our discussion of the question of theory and how it might bear on the teaching of African novels is to foreground the term *theory* itself for some consideration. What is currently called theory in Anglo-American literary and cultural criticism refers to two related developments: first, a historical conjuncture that begins in the 1970s; second, a recognizable mode of conducting analyses of literary and cultural matters, one that became prominent since the 1970s. In this twofold sense, *theory* designates an intellectual moment and its manifestation in the range of conceptual and methodological perspectives that rose to prominence in Anglo-American academic criticism thereafter.

The opening paragraph of David H. Richter's preface to the second edition of his wide-ranging anthology of theory, *The Critical Tradition: Classic Texts and Contemporary Trends* (1998), offers a telling account of the explosion of theory:

> In the late 1960s, when I started teaching, literary criticism was primarily an arcane subspecialty of historical research, in which scholars quarreled about Philip Sidney's distinction between "poesy" and "poetry," or the relative influence of Horace and Longinus on Samuel Johnson. (v)

Yet by the mid-1970s "structuralism and semiotics, deconstruction, Lacanian psychology, Althusserian Marxism, Russian formalism, phenomenology, and reception theory rode successive waves into our awareness" (v). A good deal more has happened since the mid-1970s. Significant shifts and expansion have occurred in the directions theory is taking and in how these directions relate to the teaching of literary and other products of culture. The anthology *Redrawing the Boundaries: The Transformation of English and American Literary Studies* (1992), edited by Stephen Greenblatt and Giles Gunn, provides a useful guide to these shifts and expansion. In what follows, I explore the implications of theory, thus construed, for the teaching of African novels by revisiting some debates that have come up over the years regarding what African fiction should do in terms of form and philosophical vision.

It is not my intention to offer a survey of theories and perspectives regarding the African novel; the idea, rather, is to isolate a number of recurring issues at stake in the debates. I discuss these issues under four main rubrics meant to serve as umbrella categories: formalism, Afrocentrism, Marxism, and poststructuralism. I do not try to demonstrate that one set of critics or critical perspectives is right and another wrong, but neither do I reject the notion that some perspectives might be more intellectually exciting than others or that such evaluations have a place in discussions of African novels. My primary aim here is more modest: to offer a sketch of some major strands in African literary criticism; explain the claims each makes about African novels; and indicate how one might use them in different ways to enrich students' understanding of the forms, contents, and contexts of African novels.

Discussions of African literature have always tended to involve issues of relevance. The negritude movement of the first half of the twentieth century offers one illustration of this self-consciousness (see Irele, "Harlem Renaissance"). The thinkers and writers associated with negritude argued for a distinct universe of values shared by black peoples and based on a unique approach to nature that Africans are supposed to have. The critiques of negritude that came to be mounted by the writers and thinkers of the 1950s and 1960s have proved to be definitive.

But in a sense the critiques are themselves a tribute to the pioneering significance of negritude's impulse and passion. Thus, in the course of his influential criticism of negritude, Frantz Fanon found it necessary to reject Jean-Paul Sartre's patronizing interpretation in "Black Orpheus" (*Black*

Skin 109–40). Sartre, in "Orphée noir," his famous preface to Léopold Sédar Senghor's edited anthology *Anthologie de la nouvelle poésie nègre et malgache* (1948), had suggested that negritude's preoccupation with blackness and the poetry of origins was a negative phase in a dialectical progression. In this interpretation, negritude constitutes an antiracist racism that must be transcended in order for genuine racial emancipation to be realized. Only through this paradoxical twist, whereby blackness in particular and race in general become less important than class as a way of mobilizing people, can negritude realize its hopes. As Fanon saw it, the problem is that Sartre subsumes the full historical meaning of negritude under a Europe-centered vision that masquerades as neutral and transcendent: namely, the vision of a global proletariat unmarked by race and its effects. Negritude for Fanon, despite its essentialization of blackness and its mystification of Africa, speaks to a dimension of black peoples' specific positioning in the modern world (*Black Skin*). In Fanon's reading, it is this rigorous human specificity that Sartre's well-intentioned vision and similar universalist perspectives risk undervaluing.

Fanon's nuanced engagement of negritude is one example of a critical tendency that was strong in the first half of the twentieth century. Among African writers, one can also cite Ezekiel Mphahlele's assessment of writings derived from negritude's vision (*African Image*) or the quip from a young Wole Soyinka to the effect that tigers don't spend time proclaiming their "tigritude" (416). These landmark interventions are not restricted to university settings; they assume broader audiences and take for their purview vexed issues of black internationalism and self-definition. They are to be thought of, then, as cultural criticism of a sort that is relevant but not confined to the purposive boundaries of university liberal arts curricula.

With many African countries winning their independence in the 1960s, the consequent emergence of African literature as an academic venture led to related but newly inflected discussions. African writers were busy at work and gaining readership in Africa and beyond. Departments of literature were also being established, and so the need to systematize the study of the emerging field became necessary (see Gérard; Gikandi, "Globalization"; Izevbaye, "In His Own Image"; Mphahlele, "African Literature"). Formalism and protocols of close reading became important teaching tools in the service of this educational, institutional, and—it turns out—nation-building mission. From I. A. Richards and F. R. Leavis to American New Criticism and Northrop Frye's theory of archetypal myth patterning, formalism takes the literary text as an organic utterance and unit of meaning. In the interwar and post–World War II era, formalism in literary criticism sought to carve out a disciplinary space for the serious academic study of literature. As a method of interpretation, it is understood to have humanistic and social value, because it trains people to appreciate the objects of beauty that language invents. The ability properly to relate to literary structures is bestowed with particular relevance in an era of expanding industrialization and technologization. Formalist criticism thus gives the mission of equipping young minds to appreciate the arts as utilitarian value, even if this value cannot be quantified as that of vaccines or airplanes can.

In the light of the pedagogical dimension at the heart of formalism, and given its agenda of turning literature students into enlightened citizens, it is easy to see why formalism influenced major African critics. In "The State of Criticism in African Literature," published in 1975, D. S. Izevbaye writes of the importance of maintaining standards of academic rigor in the appreciation of African literature:

> Such a strict standard is necessary as a means of encouraging the right reading of literature and training the reader to uncover the stock attitudes behind cliché and other dead language forms. One of the functions of criticism is thus to encourage the right reading of literature as a weapon against indoctrination and the habituating of people to a certain mode of behavior through propaganda. ("State" 17)

Izevbaye suggests here that academic study of literature should equip students to recognize the many purposes that acts of language, in literature or other media he labels "propaganda," can serve. The purpose of criticism is to groom informed and discriminating citizens who, as a consequence, are able to see through propaganda in order to make informed decisions about life (see also Irele, *African Imagination*; Palmer, "Chinweizu" and *Growth*).

The formalist use of so-called universal and objective critical standards to interpret and evaluate African literature generated objections from more sociologically oriented critics. One early objection was Obiajunwa Wali's "The Dead-End of African Literature?," a riposte to the historic Makerere University conference of June 1962. Wali's polemic is part of an ongoing debate about the language African writers should use to be most effective stylistically and sociologically. His challenge that using indigenous languages is the best way to harness the full potential of African literature was one early formulation of a sociologically oriented vision. Ngũgĩ wa Thiong'o reopens the issue in *Decolonising the Mind*, where he discusses what he deems to be negative effects of European (colonial) languages on African cultures and recommends that greater attention be paid to indigenous languages and literary traditions.

In "The Nature of Things: Arrested Decolonization and Critical Theory," Biodun Jeyifo delineates two broad vectors in the sociological approaches that sought, in explications of African literature, to go beyond the formalists' preoccupation with intrinsic literary properties. One he calls a cultural-nationalist vision, the other the Marxist perspective. *Toward the Decolonization of African Literature*, coauthored by the Nigerian critics Chinweizu, Onwuchekwa Jemie, and Ihechukwu Madubuike, offers one example of the cultural-nationalist approach. This book set out to pull literary criticism away from what the authors saw as a Eurocentric vision, one enslaved to Western critical standards. As an alternative, they proposed an Afrocentric approach, one that paid due attention to the fact that African literary texts have their own traditions, which derive from the oral-expressive devices of African cultures. In the view of Chinweizu, Jemie, and Madubuike, critics who attempt to foster academic criticism of African literature in university settings impose the wrong standards on African literary texts:

> Eurocentric criticism of African fiction stems from colonialist attitudes whereby these critics see the African as an apprentice European whose literary production has no other canons to adhere to but those of whichever part of the Western tradition the critics happen to subscribe to. (8)

Formalist critics were central targets of their critique, but according to the authors of *Decolonization*, even a sociologically minded critic like Emmanuel Obiechina occasionally exhibits the Eurocentric malaise: "Although Obiechina's approach is generally sound, some trace elements from the muddled thinking in contemporary literary criticism still do creep into his presentation" (104). They attribute this lapse to the prevailing tendency to resort to Eurocentric perspectives in order to confer "respectability" on the study of African literature.

As many have remarked, the Afrocentrism of the authors of *Decolonization* is directly linked to the black aesthetic movement in the United States (Adéẹ̀kọ́; Appiah, *In My Father's House*). In the same way that black power is no longer as prominent as it was in the 1960s and 1970s, the polemical prose of Chinweizu, Jemie, and Madubuike seems dated today. But this is not to say that a commitment to black particularism and the integrity of indigenous orality (pre- or postcolonial) has disappeared in discussions of things African (see Julien). The critical question is how ideas of cultural particularism and Africa's vaunted oral backcloth are understood—the conceptual work they are called on to do. For instance, Abiola Irele, one of the most rewarding formalists to contemplate African literature, also speaks of "the African imagination" and insists on the centrality of dimensions of orality in any serious study of African novels. The difference is that, for an Irele and unlike a Chinweizu, writers draw on features of African oral expressive traditions precisely to transform them, through technical craft, into specific generic codes of written literature in modernity (*African Imagination* 23–38). Likewise, Izevbaye can reject crucial tenets of negritude as worldview or philosophy yet celebrate their elegant conversion to the register of a literary trope. In reference to *The Radiance of the King*, he speaks of Camara Laye's use of "the usual stereotypes about 'primitive' Africa to glorify her in a deliberately ironical manner." Nonetheless, Izevbaye's formalist leaning does not prevent him from endorsing the aesthetic possibilities of negritude as trope. "Laye succeeds," he writes, "because his literary use of these stereotypes converts them to metaphors" ("State" 4).

Conversely, Chinweizu, Jemie, and Madubuike do not reject the need for close attention to the way formal properties contribute to a novel's satisfactions:

> [A] work has to be evaluated not on issues of "pure craft" *alone*, but also on the values it urges upon its readers, implicitly as well as explicitly. Moreover, even issues of "pure craft" embody social values. The proper and inevitable question therefore ought to be, not whether there is ideology or not, but rather which ideology—European, African, Christian, Islamic, Buddhist, capitalist, socialist, communist, communalist, individualist, or what have you. We should therefore at all times be suspicious of claims of ideological virginity. (140; my emphasis)

What they reject, then, is the idea of ideology-free criticism and its consequent failure to recognize what they see as the unique formal properties and ideological investments of African writing. They reject the emphasis on Western formal criteria and what they see as an academicist illusion of objectivity. Looked at this way, formalism and Afrocentrism in African literary studies have at least one thing in common: a commitment to the shape and texture of novels, to the techniques and symbols storytellers necessarily deploy.

Beyond the polemical and overheated rhetoric of the authors of *Decolonization*, we can isolate a basic insight that can, at the present time, enrich the study of African literature. This is that the African novel is a product of a cluster of cultural, historical, and aesthetic determinations. These determinations serve to individuate the literature and simultaneously differentiate it from European literature. In terms of literary craft, African novels yield innovations that push beyond preexisting Western forms, yet the novels remain novels in the term's historical and formal definition. Chinweizu, Jemie, and Madubuike suggest this much when they write of the European modernist tradition:

> Developments since Joyce, Proust and Kafka, as for instance in the French *nouveau roman*, overwhelmingly demonstrate that the novel is an open form, and that there is no ideal form to which all novels must conform. In particular, we should not be misled by the connotations of the terms "well-made" or "pure" into idealizing or strenuously imitating the forms of the 19th-century European bourgeois novel. The forms of the novel are capable of change in every direction. In the making of the novel, it is "morning yet on creation day," to borrow a phrase from Chinua Achebe. (88)

In a similar vein, the colonial experience that informs many African novels suggests that what the latter might have to say would be substantively different from, often opposed to, what many canonical European novels are able to say. Thus, for instance, we might expect that, in authorial perspective and narrative impulse—the compulsion to bear witness—Joseph Conrad's rendering of Africa will be inflected differently from Sol Plaatje's in *Mhudi* or Ngũgĩ's in *The River Between*. Nonetheless, what connects all three is a historical trajectory and the pressures of form. At core, they share the impulse to capture reality in language, within the limits of their finite epistemological and technical resources. In the classroom, we might begin with this bottom line, in order more clearly to recognize how African novels make available fresh explorations and insights about human beings in history.

Our discussion so far has led up to the interplay of particularity and universality, about which critics of canonical European literatures have said much over the years. Both terms are often posed as a binary opposition, but some critics see their relation differently. In his essay entitled "Notes on

Hamlet," C. L. R. James invokes a commonplace tendency in European literary criticism to attribute the universality of a text to its ability to rise above its particular time and place. Of Shakespeare, he writes, "Ben Jonson thought that Shakespeare was not of an age but for all time. Not quite. Shakespeare was for all time precisely because he was so much of an age" (246). In this single, serene formulation, he displaces the particular-universal opposition altogether. In one sense, his claim can be understood as a version of the injunction generally taken to be the methodological prerequisite of Marxist-materialist criticism, to always historicize. But there is more. In claiming that Shakespeare is universal *because* he is produced by and bound to specific historical circumstances, James suggests that every creative act owes whatever universal meaning it has to the depth of its immersion in its local, particular determinations. In this way, he overcomes the conventional tendency to see universality as the antithesis of particularity. The universal becomes the profound ground and occasion for apprehending the particular in its pulsing immediacy.

The last point leads us to the question of Marxism in the criticism of African literature. The Afrocentric vision of Chinweizu and his coauthors cannot allow the kind of universality in particularity that James's Marxist account makes available. But if the surface of their rhetoric does not allow it, the inner logic of their intervention does. On one level, Chinweizu, Jemie, and Madubuike would seem to reject universalism and instead stress the particularity of African novels. However, on another level, they cannot afford to reject the notion of universality within particularity that I just outlined via James. To reject it is to reject the very raison d'être of their intervention, the very mission of Afrocentric criticism: the full recognition of blacks and Africans as universal human subjects. In the classroom, then, Chinweizu and his coauthors can serve to pose a question that our students should be encouraged to consider: What is gained from approaching African novels for their African particularities as well as the aesthetic possibilities they offer for exploring universal human passions? Following James, it is fair to say the gain is both substantive and political. Substantively, we broaden the meaning and relevance of African novels for students from diverse cultures and backgrounds. Politically, we go beyond old-style exoticization, where things African can be contemplated, when they are, only under the sign of difference.

Similarly, a Marxist perspective can enrich the study of African novels by moving beyond the limits of Afrocentrism. As we saw earlier, the authors of *Decolonization* reject the notion of objectivity in literary criticism and argue that every act of interpretation proceeds from an ideological assumption. By insisting that the relevant question to be asked of African criticism is "not whether there is ideology or not, but rather which ideology—European, African, Christian . . ." (140), Chinweizu, Jemie, and Madubuike intersect with one general premise of Marxist criticism. However, to ask what they have in mind by the term *African* is to face Marxist criticism's challenge for the study of African novels. Marxists identify the particularity of African novels as residing in the incorporation of African societies into a global capitalist system. They reject the idea that the central role of African writing is to rescue traditional African cultures from racist and colonialist discourses. Thus Chidi Amuta argues against the "appropriation" of Achebe's novels set in the precolonial past "into the metaphysical aesthetics of traditionalist scholarship." This appropriation has involved using the novels as "axiomatic reference points for diverse interests and opinions intent on rediscovering and commenting on 'traditional African society' and 'the culture conflict' . . . stock concepts which have since been adumbrated into a mini-catechism" (*Theory* 130).[1] To counter this tendency, Amuta argues that Marxism should

> provide analytical insight into and "explain" the social resonance and aesthetic integrity of literary works as art objects which contain (or do not contain) certain experiences, assume specific forms and articulate specific viewpoints of man and woman in society by virtue of their objective socio-historical determination. (60–61)

Like other Marxist critics of African literature, Amuta owes much to Western Marxism on the issue of literature's relation to history and society. For a Terry Eagleton or a Fredric Jameson, Marxist thinking is superior to bourgeois perspectives on history and society because Karl Marx succeeded in breaking away from the obfuscations of his predecessors and inaugurating instead a more comprehensive or totalized account. In the work of Jameson, for instance, one encounters an attempt to synthesize the contributions, not just of thinkers who see themselves as working in a Marxist conceptual frame but also those who distance themselves from Marxism. For Jameson, Marxism has the strongest accounts of (1) society construed in its most comprehensive sense (as a "totality"), and (2) humanity as at once makers and effects of history. Marxist literary theory is for him the "absolute horizon of all reading and all interpretation" (*Political Unconscious* 17). By this he means that Marxist theory understands the twists and turns of human doings so comprehensively that it can explain the work literature performs in society and also subsume other competing theories of literature. In other words, Marxism not only has the best explanation for the work literature does, it also explains where competing theories are coming from and why they are no more than inferior versions of Marxism's encompassing vision ("Metacommentary" and *Political Unconscious*).

The literary criticism that issues from this view is expansive. Literature is seen as a way of masking the inner content that literary texts hold for us, content that has to do with history, society, and the intersubjective interactions of individuals, who are invariably members of a social class. Literary form addresses the vicissitudes of social life by avoiding them or deflecting our gaze from them, except when the text is by a writer who consciously sets out to break this ritual of avoidance and deflection. If literature often uses formal techniques to mask the starkness of its inner content, the critic's task is to tease out this content by removing the mask. By attending to the techniques writers use to mask the full social meaning that cannot but express itself in literature, interpretation pays homage to literary form and, in that very gesture, makes visible the truth that form encodes (or hides, depending on the novelist's political investments). In the work of a writer who consciously sets out to convey a socialist message, the test of achievement is the success with which the ideological intent is artfully presented through the mediation of form. Therefore Amuta could write in reference to Ngũgĩ's *Petals of Blood*:

> Against the timid imputation of bourgeois critics, the decisive ideological thrust of *Petals of Blood* does not weaken its artistic integrity. On the contrary, the strength of the novel derives precisely from the sheer aesthetic force of its informing and objectified ideology. Here the dialectic of content and form is so intimate that there is no valid statement that can be made about any aspect of the formal realization of *Petals of Blood* that is not anchored to its express ideological mooring. (*Theory* 148)

Because orthodox Marxism developed in the context of European history, Africanist Marxists have argued that some conceptual and historical qualifications are necessary in order for it to be fully applicable to African history and literature (68–75). We need not enter into a consideration of what those qualifications entail or ask whether Amuta actually attempts anything like a thoroughgoing conceptual engagement with Marxism's pluses and minuses.[2] The relevant point here is simply that

Marxist Africanist critics take up crucial tenets of dialectical materialism while also drawing on thinkers, such as Fanon and Amilcar Cabral, who have been directly concerned with Third World societies and colonial exploitation. In this regard, Marxist critics drew inspiration from Fanon's critique of negritude and bourgeois nationalism (*Wretched*) as well as from Cabral's theorization of the motions of culture in the midst of revolution. They drew inspiration from Fanon's rejection of claims of an African metaphysics shared by all peoples of African heritage and from his assertion that the real agents of history in the decolonizing Third World countries were the rural peasantry and the lumpen proletariat of the urban shanties. They also took up his idea that the task of literature (and other idioms of artistic expression) was to give voice to the struggles of the oppressed for identity and social justice.

Neither Fanon nor Cabral set out to systematize their thoughts on how we might teach African novels,[3] still less to convince students why they should study literature when engineering or medicine are available as alternatives. In drawing on their work, Marxist critics were in effect putting together conceptual tools from heterogenous sources, in an attempt to fashion sociological and political interpretations of African novels. The use of insights from Third World as well as Western Marxist thinkers is therefore an instructive struggle, at the level of theory, by Marxist critics of African literature. Like what Jacques Derrida in dialogue with Claude Lévi-Strauss would call a handyman (*bricoleur*), they used the tools at hand to contribute to the study of African novels. I invoke Derrida here in part because, at about the same time that Africanist critics were struggling with the legacy of Marxism in an attempt to make it useful for the study of African novels, Derrida was developing what has come to be known as deconstruction. The theoretical enterprise, for Derrida, is an act of bricolage. By this he means that no one ever originates concepts in absolute purity: all theory necessarily adopts prior conceptual formations and traces. This critique of origin and celebration of bricolage are relevant to the issue of theory and the teaching of African novels.

Meanwhile, it is worth noting that, as sign of a historical conjuncture and intellectual ferment, theory in Anglo-American criticism is roughly concurrent with the decolonization era in Africa and struggles for recognition by American racial and ethnic minorities. Theory came on the scene in Anglo-American literary studies in the 1970s, when African novels were becoming more widely read and argued about. The study of African fiction in the United States grew urgent in part because of the struggles of African

Americans for recognition and because of the consequent establishment of black studies programs (Appiah, *In My Father's House*; Miller; Gates, "African American Criticism").

Perhaps the farthest-reaching contribution of poststructuralist thinking is its critique of signifying practices and the dynamic whereby language both conveys and fails to convey meaning. In this scenario of intertwined success and failure, language somehow manages to convince us of its handle on the substantiality of reality. Two main ideas subtend the poststructuralist moment in contemporary criticism. The first suggests that, although linguistic systems have an aura of naturalness and self-sufficiency, their effective functioning is based on processes that are taken for granted. Language conveys meaning not because of inherent, unmediated properties but because of conventions that turn out to be arbitrary. The second idea is that Western belief in objective knowledge, grounded in positivist science and the possibility of foundational certitudes, fed an ethnocentric understanding of self and other that (wittingly or not) rationalized Western denigration of other cultures. In an attempt to avoid this ethnocentric arrogance, current theory rejects the idea of a subject in complete knowledge of its desires and motivations. Similarly, notions of fixed individual and collective identity are interrogated and rejected. The claim is that what we know of ourselves—as individuals or as members of a social group—derives from multiple (and often disavowed) determinations, histories, and discourses (Arac; Culler).

These premises have been expanded in many directions and fields. In philosophy, one can cite Derrida's notion of the supplement, the rhetorical and conceptual logic by which a part, excluded in order for the whole to present the appearance of self-sufficiency, nonetheless exposes the illusion of wholeness precisely because of the fact of exclusion. Paul de Man takes the deconstructive logic in the direction of literary criticism, positing literary language as a slippery terrain where a text's deepest insights are to be found in its linguistic elisions and contradictions. As part and parcel of the development of various poststructuralist perspectives is the emergence of African American vernacular theory associated with Houston Baker and Henry Louis Gates, Jr., as well as of theories of postcoloniality associated with Edward Said and Gayatri Spivak (see Appiah, *In My Father's House*; Gates, *Signifying Monkey*; Said).

The criticism of African literature from at least the late 1980s has been influenced by these theories. One way in which poststructuralist ideas percolated into it is in the critique of notions of African authenticity as well as the view of literature as a transparent medium that can give us direct knowledge of past or present African realities. Poststructuralist perspectives suggest that African novels are, first and foremost, acts of language. Consequently, African novels are to be seen as specific uses of language that are subject to the conventions, slippages, and possibilities of meaning. Poststructuralist premises can inform the teaching of African novels in a number of ways. First, poststructuralism gives students the opportunity to acquire, through the labor of reading, some sense of the failures and possibilities of meaning inherent in all linguistic communication, including novels by storytellers who happen to be African. African novels thereby become robust products of the human faculty for language in all its promise and unpredictability. Second, it does away with the illusion of neutral, objective criticism that characterized formalism. And third, it makes possible a mode of reading that does not limit itself to pronouncing whether or not a novel is authentically African (as Afrocentric criticism sometimes does) or emancipatory in some untheorized sense (as Marxist criticism sometimes does).

At the least, poststructuralism enables us to question certain assumptions our students may take for granted. Such assumptions include the very idea of Africa, African tradition, or African identity, where Achebe's or Ngũgĩ's narratives constitute the more established window and norm (Amoko; Cobham, "Making" and "Misgendering"; Quayson). Other assumptions questioned are about literary realism, the representation of history, and the political claims of novels. Here, Mariama Bâ's *So Long a Letter* or Tsitsi Dangarembga's *Nervous Conditions* can usefully be compared with Nuruddin Farah's *Maps*, Dambudzo Marechera's *The House of Hunger*, or Yvonne Vera's *Butterfly Burning*. In this way, African novels are shown in their range and diversity, and our appreciation of the human and textual drama adumbrated in them is enriched.

By way of conclusion, I should like to address a debate that usually proves more befuddling than illuminating whenever it arises, about whether applying theory (by which poststructuralist or postmodernist theory is often meant) to African novels amounts to an imposition of a Western perspective. Now and again one encounters outright rejection of the applicability of theory to African literature. In some instances, arguments about theory give us good reasons why certain perspectives and reading protocols are flawed or inadequate (Appiah, "Tolerable Falsehoods"; Chrisman; Irele, *African Imagination*; Gikandi, "Poststructuralism").

In others, the arguments get couched as accusations of Eurocentrism or political quietism. As African literature becomes more and more institutionalized in humanities curricula in America and the rest of the English-speaking world, we may expect debates of various stripes to emerge now and again, some more consequential than others. A productive approach, then, would be constantly to reiterate to our students a basic truism regarding intellectual matters. It is that arguments about literary-critical methods are most illuminating when the point is to show why a competing perspective cannot get us where we wish to go, not when it is merely to proclaim that the perspective belongs to an irresponsible person.

The various critical approaches that have been sketched here exist contemporaneously with the African novels they were developed to address. This fact makes the relation of African novels to the critical theories that seek to explicate them quite different from the relation between theory and, say, modernism or the nineteenth-century novel. A sign of this unique inflection is that poststructuralism and postmodernism do not come after formalism, Afrocentric cultural nationalism, or Third World Marxism. Rather, all these formations and conceptual trajectories emerge at about the same time that the imaginative literature itself emerged, the era of decolonization and general questioning of imperial Europe's political and intellectual excesses. Against this background, merely "applying" theory to African literature shortchanges both the theory and the literature. By the same token, and quite paradoxically, contemporary arguments that simply reject theory (read: poststructuralism and postmodernism) in an a priori fashion overestimate (or undercomplicate) what they are arguing against. The limits as well as potentials of theory can be apprehended and articulated only when one enters into dialogue with it, not when one is either applying it or refusing to apply it. For this reason, arguments mounted in rejection of theory overlook the possibilities of productive interaction, and mutual interrogation, between theory and African novels.

In the foregoing pages, I have been suggesting that it is more promising to think of theory as itself a product of history and culture, very much like novels and poems. On these terms, we underplay what African novels can offer our students if we single-mindedly apply one theory or another to this or that novel. Rejecting theory outright won't do either. Rather, theoretical elaborations are to be understood not as neutral lenses that exist separately and aseptically apart from the literature they contemplate but as particular deployments of language, as instantiations of human desire just as much as imaginative literature is.[4] My purpose has been to draw out ways in which the rubrics I identified emphasize different, and sometimes intersecting, levels at which African novels may operate. From this perspective, Izevbaye is correct to suggest:

> The functions of criticism to literature, audience, and society are legion. In all cases some consideration to the text is essential; but no single critical orientation can be adequate. The best we can do is to discourage the complacency of simple attitudes and the tyranny of uniformity. ("State" 17)

To return to Derrida's idea, if theory is an instance of bricolage, our best course is to draw on as many theories as the novels we teach accommodate, anticipate, or dialogize. As literary texts generally tend to do, African novels often give us clues that we can use to understand and appreciate them. In this sense, many novels theorize themselves, initiating, in the grammar of narrative fiction, how we might go about reading them with profit. In a classroom setting, the most appropriate course for us, as teachers of the African novel, is to be discerning pluralists.

Notes

1. An excerpt from Amuta's *The Theory of African Literature* is reprinted in the anthology *Marxist Literary Theory: A Reader*, edited by Terry Eagleton and Drew Milne ("Materialism").

2. For a more detailed and philosophical consideration of this question, see George, esp. 73–104.

3. For a concise survey of Western Marxist literary and cultural theory, see Cohen. For a sampling of Marxist criticism of African literature, see Gugelberger, "Marxist Literary Debates"; Hunt; Nazareth; and Onoge. See also JanMohamed; Lazarus.

4. Jameson makes a similar point with regard to criticism in general: "The starting point for any genuinely profitable discussion of interpretation . . . must be not the nature of interpretation, but the need for it in the first place. What initially needs explanation is, in other words, not how we go about interpreting a text properly, but rather why we should even have to do so. All thinking about interpretation must sink itself in the strangeness, the unnaturalness of the hermeneutic situation; or to put it another way, every individual interpretation must include an interpretation of its own existence, must show its own credentials and justify itself: every commentary must be at the same time a metacommentary as well" ("Metacommentary" 5).

Works Cited

Adéẹ̀kọ́, Adélékè. *Proverbs, Textuality, and Nativism in African Literature.* Gainesville: UP of Florida, 1988. Print.

Amoko, Apollo O. "The Resemblance of Colonial Mimicry: A Revisionary Reading of Ngugi wa Thiong'o's *The River Between*." *Research in African Literatures* 36.1 (2005): 34–50. Print.

Amuta, Chidi. "The Materialism of Cultural Nationalism: Achebe's *Things Fall Apart* and *Arrow of God*." Eagleton and Milne 399–407.

———. *The Theory of African Literature: Implications for Practical Criticism.* London: Zed, 1989. Print.

Appiah, Kwame Anthony. *In My Father's House: Essays in the Philosophy of Culture.* Oxford: Oxford UP, 1992. Print.

———. "Tolerable Falsehoods: Agency and the Interests of Theory." *Consequences of Theory.* Ed. Jonathan Arac and Barbara Johnson. Baltimore: Johns Hopkins UP, 1991. 63–90. Print.

Arac, Jonathan. Introduction. *Postmodernism and Politics.* Ed. Arac. Minneapolis: U of Minnesota P, 1986. ix–xliii. Print.

Cabral, Amilcar. "National Liberation and Culture." *Unity and Struggle.* Trans. Michael Wolfers. New York: Monthly Rev., 1979. 138–54. Print.

Chinweizu et al. *Toward the Decolonization of African Literature.* Washington: Howard UP, 1983. Print.

Chrisman, Laura. *Postcolonial Contraventions: Cultural Readings of Race, Imperialism, and Transnationalism.* Manchester: Manchester UP, 2003. Print.

Cobham, Rhonda. "Making Men and History: Achebe and the Politics of Revisionism." *Approaches to Teaching Achebe's* Things Fall Apart. Ed. Bernth Lindfors. New York: MLA, 1991. 91–100. Print.

———. "Misgendering the Nation: African Nationalist Fictions and Nuruddin Farah's *Maps*." *Nationalisms and Sexualities.* Ed. Andrew Parker et al. New York: Routledge, 1992. 42–59. Print.

Cohen, Walter. "Marxist Criticism." Greenblatt and Gunn 320–48.

Culler, Jonathan. "Literary Theory." *Introduction to Scholarship in Modern Languages and Literatures.* 2nd ed. Ed. Joseph Gibaldi. New York: MLA, 1992. 201–35. Print.

Derrida, Jacques. "Structure, Sign, and Play in the Discourse of the Human Sciences." *Writing and Difference.* Trans. Alan Bass. Chicago: U of Chicago Press, 1982. 278–93. Print.

Eagleton, Terry, and Drew Milne, eds. *Marxist Literary Theory: A Reader.* Oxford: Blackwell, 1996. Print.

Fanon, Frantz. *Black Skin, White Masks.* Trans. Charles Lam Markmann. New York: Grove, 1967. Print.

———. *The Wretched of the Earth.* Trans. Constance Farrington. New York: Grove, 1963. Print.

Gates, Henry Louis, Jr. "African American Criticism." Greenblatt and Gunn 303–19.

———. *The Signifying Monkey: A Theory of African-American Literary Criticism.* New York: Oxford UP, 1988. Print.

George, Olakunle. *Relocating Agency: Modernity and African Letters.* Albany: State U of New York P, 2003. Print.

Gérard, Albert. "The Study of African Literature: Birth and Early Growth of a New Branch of Learning." *Canadian Review of Comparative Literature* 7.1 (1980): 67–92. Print.

Gikandi, Simon. "Globalization and the Claims of Postcoloniality." *South Atlantic Quarterly* 100.3 (2001): 627–58. Print.

———. "Poststructuralism and Postcolonial Discourse." *The Cambridge Companion to Postcolonial Literary Studies.* Ed. Neil Lazarus. Cambridge: Cambridge UP, 2004. 97–119. Print.

Greenblatt, Stephen, and Giles Gunn, eds. *Redrawing the Boundaries: The Transformation of English and American Literary Studies.* New York: MLA, 1992. Print.

Gugelberger, Georg M., ed. *Marxism and African Literature.* Trenton: Africa World, 1986. Print.

———. "Marxist Literary Debates and Their Continuity in African Literary Criticism." Gugelberger, *Marxism* 1–20.

Hunt, Geoffrey. "Two African Aesthetics: Wole Soyinka vs. Amilcar Cabral." Gugelberger, *Marxism* 64–93.

Irele, Abiola F. *The African Imagination: Literature in Africa and the Diaspora.* Oxford: Oxford UP, 2001. Print.

———. "The Harlem Renaissance and the Negritude Movement." *The Cambridge History of African and Caribbean Literature.* Vol. 2. Ed. Irele and Simon Gikandi. Cambridge: Cambridge UP, 2004. 759–84. Print.

Izevbaye, D. S. "In His Own Image: Literature and the Re-creation of Man." U of Ibadan. 10 Jan. 1985. Inaugural lecture.

———. "The State of Criticism in African Literature." *African Literature Today* 7 (1975): 1–19. Print.

James, C. L. R. "Notes on *Hamlet.*" *The C. L. R. James Reader.* Ed. Anna Grimshaw. Oxford: Blackwell, 1992. 243–46. Print.

Jameson, Fredric. "Metacommentary." *The Ideologies of Theory.* Vol. 1. Minneapolis: U of Minnesota P, 1988. 3–16. Print.

———. *The Political Unconscious: Narrative as a Socially Symbolic Act.* Ithaca: Cornell UP, 1981. Print.

JanMohamed, Abdul R. *Manichean Aesthetics: The Politics of Literature in Colonial Africa.* Amherst: U of Massachusetts P, 1983. Print.

Jeyifo, Biodun. "The Nature of Things: Arrested Decolonization and Critical Theory." *Research in African Literatures* 21.1 (1990): 33–48. Print.

Julien, Eileen. *African Novels and the Question of Orality.* Bloomington: Indiana UP, 1992. Print.

Lazarus, Neil. *Resistance in Postcolonial African Fiction.* New Haven: Yale UP, 1990. Print.

Miller, Christopher L. "African Literature and the Challenge of Intercultural Literacy." *Nationalists and Nomads.* Chicago: U of Chicago P, 1998. 152–70. Print.

Mphahlele, Ezekiel. *The African Image.* New York: Praeger, 1962. Print.

———. "African Literature and Universities: A Report on Two Conferences to Discuss African Literature and the University Curriculum." *Transition* 10 (1963): 16–18. Print.

Nazareth, Peter. "The Second Homecoming: Multiple Ngugis in *Petals of Blood.*" Gugelberger, *Marxism* 118–29.

Ngũgĩ wa Thiong'o. *Decolonising the Mind.* London: Currey, 1986. Print.

Obiechina, Emmanuel. *Culture, Tradition, and Society in the West African Novel.* Cambridge: Cambridge UP, 1975. Print.

Onoge, Omafume F. "Towards a Marxist Sociology of African Literature." Gugelberger, *Marxism* 50–63.

Palmer, Eustace. "Chinweizu et al. and the Evaluation of African Literature." *International Fiction Review* 15.1 (1988): 54–57. Print.

———. *The Growth of the African Novel.* London: Heinemann, 1979. Print.

Quayson, Ato. "Realism, Criticism, and the Disguises of Both: A Reading of Chinua Achebe's *Things Fall Apart* with an Evaluation of the Criticism Relating to It." *Research in African Literatures* 25.4 (1994): 117–36. Print.

Richter, David H., ed. *The Critical Tradition: Classic Texts and Contemporary Trends.* 2nd ed. Boston: Bedford, 1998. Print.

Said, Edward W. *Culture and Imperialism.* New York: Knopf, 1993. Print.

Sartre, Jean Paul. "Black Orpheus." Trans. John MacCombie. "*What Is Literature?" and Other Essays.* Cambridge: Harvard UP, 1988. 291–330. Print.

Soyinka, Wole. "On the Trail of *Transition.*" *Transition* 75–76 (1997): 414–19. Print.

Wali, Obiajunwa. "The Dead-End of African Literature?" *Transition* 10 (1963): 13–16. Print.

Nicholas Brown

Marxist Approaches to the African Novel

Marxism and Literature

Unlike other contemporary approaches to the narrative arts, Marxist analyses are interested primarily neither in what literature is nor, perhaps surprisingly, in what particular works mean. Rather, Marxist criticism subsumes both these questions under an investigation of what the literary work does. For this reason Marxist analyses of particular works of literature are inherently pedagogical; the question of what a work of art does clearly cannot be answered without reference to the immediate social situation in which the work intervenes. Further, since Marxism takes it as axiomatic that no social situation can be fully understood without reference to economic processes that have for some time been global in scale, the immediate social situation cannot remain the end point of interpretation. Marxism thus eschews exoticism and finds its pedagogical force in one stroke. The immediate situation of the novel is not to be considered as purely isolated, either by intervening space or intervening time, from the situation of the reader; rather, the two situations are linked, and it is the job of literary analysis to uncover the mediating links not only between the work of art and its intervention in a particular social situation but also between that situation and the quite different social situation of a variable us—in the current case, readers in North American classrooms.

To the extent that Marxist approaches to the novel will tend to read it against the background of the social conditions under which it was created, Marxism is a materialism. It holds that cultural phenomena cannot be understood without reference to the material conditions of the production and reproduction of human life. The classical version of this material basis or mode of production centers around a given society's system for meeting human needs and the relations among people that this system demands. "Subsistence agriculture," "feudal aristocracy," "industrial capitalism," and the "information economy" name modes of production in this sense. In its more sophisticated versions the mode of production must be considered to include, among other things, race and gender hierarchies, religious practices, and a society's system for understanding itself and for reproducing that self-understanding. As Amilcar Cabral, the leader of the Guinean independence movement, put it:

> Culture is the result, with more or less awakened consciousness, of economic and political activities, the more or less dynamic expression of the type of relations prevailing within that society, on the one hand between man . . . and nature, and, on the other hand, among individuals, groups of individuals, social strata or classes. (*Unity* 141)

If Marxism is a materialism, however, it must be distinguished from other, more familiar materialisms. One type would view the literary or cultural artifact as a mere expression of social realities. Society appears as a simple cause, the literary work as a simple effect. From this perspective, however, it is hard to see what the literary text tells us that could not have been learned more efficiently by looking at society itself. Another simple materialism would view social realities as the context of the literary work. In this case, the relationship between society and work is simply unspecified. Such a materialism, in the words of the Nigerian critic Chidi Amuta, "fails to establish confidently the relationship between [literary works] and their socio-political referents" (24). Without an idea of the relationship between text and context, this approach tells us little that could not have been discovered through careful attention to the text alone.

These tendencies, however, are rarely met in pure form, and indeed Marxist analysis does not oppose them but rather incorporates them. The conceptions of society as cause or context of the work of art are not wrong but merely incomplete. Unlike simple materialisms, Marxism will tend to see literature as what Ato Quayson has called a "politically symbolic act" ("Literature"; or what Cabral referred to as an "act of culture" [*Unity* 143]) whose potential effects reach back into a society's basic functioning.[1] The relation of the literary work to the society in which it was produced is specified as a complex feedback loop that many Marxists, using a term adopted from the German philosopher G. W. F. Hegel, refer to as dialectical.[2] Here, however, Marxism becomes not only a materialism but also an idealism: it presumes in the author a degree of agency—though this agency need not be fully aware of its own functioning—which cannot be entirely explained by social processes. It might even be more accurate to say that the objective functioning of society in fact entails this zone of subjective freedom. North American critical practice, evolving as it has from the New Critics and their practice of close reading, is often accused of being an idealism, of ignoring social, political, and historical realities in favor of basking in the unexplained and fetishized presence of the text itself (either as aesthetic object or as abstracted meaning). But Marxism need not reject the idealism of close reading; instead, idealism and materialism, close reading and sociologism, may be put into a dialectical relation to each other.

Another category central to many Marxist critics is ideology. Marxism contains several conflicting theories of ideology. It is not possible to give a succinct definition here that would be broad or complex enough to satisfy all Marxist critics; it can be said, however, that ideology in Marxist criticism does not refer merely to the explicit political program of an author or work. A work that clearly presents itself as a critique of postcolonial society may nonetheless silently support some of the basic presuppositions of that society. Similarly, a work that appears conservative may harbor subversive possibilities. (Emmanuel Ngara's assessment of Wole Soyinka, for example, focuses initially on the former possibility [*Ideology* 94–102 ("Myth, Pan-Africanism, and the Liberation Struggle")]; Biodun Jeyifo's develops the latter [11–22 ("The Hidden Class War in *The Road*)].) By one definition, *ideology* concerns the range of possible effects—rarely all positive, all negative, or all consciously intended—of that "politically symbolic act" that constitutes the literary work. *Ideology* is also used more casually to denote those aspects of a text that support, consciously or not, existing power structures and hierarchies. Aspects that tend instead to expose contradictions, fissures, and possibilities for change are often called utopian. For example, nostalgia, in African or other literature, is an ideological structure in the more technical sense. On the one hand, it registers a dissatisfaction with the present state of affairs and a desire to escape from some of the most baleful effects of contemporary life. In this respect it is utopian. On the other hand, it is often turned back into a defense of eroding privilege or a return to older hierarchies. In this respect it is ideological in the more casual sense.

Marxism and Africa

Marxism occupies a markedly different position in African letters than it does in North American discourse. In the United States in particular, cold-war tensions led not only to the marginalization of Marxist thought but also to a corresponding containment of Marxism into a discrete oppositional discourse. A similar process occurred in some African nations, but in others, particularly where Marxist ideas had played honorable or even central roles in anticolonial (or anti-minority-rule) liberation movements, the cold war produced the opposite effect. In southern Africa, for example, both the United States and the Soviet Union entered local conflicts for geopolitical advantage. But the Soviet bloc often took the more creditable role of supporting liberation movements, while the United States found itself providing aid to clients of apartheid South Africa. On achieving independence, states such as Angola and Mozambique joined a sizable club of African nations with a history of official socialism. In these countries Marxism became not so much a hegemonic ideology as an intellectual lingua franca—even if, in the post-cold-war era, this lingua franca came to be treated with a certain irony (see, e.g., the writings of the Angolan novelist Pepetela).

Even outside these areas, Marxism remained an intellectual resource for writers and thinkers who did not feel the need to form a defensive, self-described Marxist discourse. V. Y. Mudimbe reminds us that "the greatest influence on African thought from the 1930s to the 1950s was Marxism" (90). The subsequent decades in Africa saw not only writers and thinkers but also political leaders (often themselves respected writers and thinkers) both establishing a critical distance from the established Communist parties and actively engaging in the rethinking, adaptation, and revision of the Marxist legacy to address African realities. (The subject of Marxism *in* African novels as opposed to Marxist approaches *to* African novels can only be touched on occasionally here, but it is worth pointing out that many of the continent's greatest writers have explicitly endorsed Marxist principles. Ngara has explored the explicit appropriation of Marxism by Ngũgĩ wa Thiong'o, Ousmane Sembène, Alex La Guma, and Nadine Gordimer in his *Art and Ideology in the African Novel.*) In Mudimbe's analysis, Marxism remains less a separate tradition in Africa than one of the "principle sources" of African progressive thought (96).

Unlike the neoliberal orthodoxy of our own recent past, Marxism does not, then, "Westernize a virgin terrain" (Mudimbe 177). On the contrary, revisions, extensions, and adaptations of Marxism to realities of the global south—in political and economic theory and philosophy as well as in cultural theory—become a central strand of the Marxist tradition. In the field of cultural theory, Cabral is a key figure in the theorization of culture as a progressive social force that both supports and is molded by the struggle for national liberation (see his *Return* and *Unity*). The writings of Frantz Fanon, a Martinican Marxist and psychoanalyst who joined the Algerian liberation movement in 1954, have retained extraordinary force in their analyses not only of the role of race and culture in political domination and resistance to it but also of the corrosive cynicism that would attend the postcolonial moment. While Fanon is more concerned with culture in general than with the novel in particular, his works, particularly *The Wretched of the Earth* (1961), have been used to illuminate the central dynamics of whole genres of African literature from the period of national liberation and through the years following. To give one example, Neil Lazarus, in his *Resistance in Postcolonial African Fiction*, brings a Fanonian perspective to bear on Ayi Kwei Armah's searing novelistic indictments of postcolonial society.

Since the second half of the twentieth century, African Marxism can be roughly divided into three areas of concern. While these areas admit chronological presentation, they all remain live issues in contemporary debates and literary production. The first concerns the basic relation between colonized and colonizer, black and white, Third and First World, center and periphery. Here Fanon would be the towering figure. For Fanon, the peculiarity of the colonial system is that a regime of economic exploitation is mapped directly onto racial difference: "The cause is the consequence: you are rich because you are white, you are white because you are rich. This is why Marxist analysis should always be slightly stretched every time we have to do with the colonial problem" (40). The originality of Fanon's position lies in the notion that the signs "black" and "white," "native" and colonizer," do not refer to positive, given essences that meet each other in a hostile encounter; rather, it is the hostile encounter that creates the native and the colonizer. He expresses this idea dramatically: "For it is the settler who has brought the native into existence and who perpetuates his existence. The settler owes the fact of his existence, that is to say, his property, to the colonial system" (36). The native owes his status as a native to the presence of the colonizer, who owes his status as a colonizer to the relationship that brings them into contact.

The consequences of this insight to a generation of African writers cannot be overestimated and go far beyond self-identified Marxist writers: in fact, it might be said without too much exaggeration that an entire first generation of postcolonial African novels are concerned with exploring this dynamic. To cite the most illustrious example, Chinua Achebe has described his village novels as an attempt to counter the violence of the colonial "image of Africa" that creates a "native" to confront the civilizing European colonizer. This image, on which the colonial project depended for its ideological justification, was propagated not only in administrative texts like the fictional quasi-anthropological treatise that ends *Things Fall Apart* but also in such novels as Joyce Cary's *Mister Johnson* and, most famously, Joseph Conrad's *Heart of Darkness* (see Achebe 1–20 ["An Image of Africa"]). The classical response to this colonial racism is what Jean-Paul Sartre controversially called the "anti-racist racism" (xl) proposed by the negritude movement, whose most convincing theoretical exponents emerged from the Hegelian Marxist tradition.[3] The genius of Achebe's village novels (*Things Fall Apart* and the more nuanced and complex *Arrow of God*), however, is that they do not reverse racist image making from within the same dialectic, establishing a one-sided image of the colonizer. Rather, they narrate the colonial encounter from an imaginary perspective from which the antagonistic logic that sustained it appears effectively dead, and from which both this logic and the opposed entities it creates can be viewed dispassionately.

Despite the tremendous beauty and power of this perspective, it presents a problem. The colonial logic is not dead, and a second strand of African Marxism turns its attention to what some have called the neocolonial state, the independent nation that maintains a crippling economic dependence on the former colonizing power, other powerful economies, and multinational capital. This line of thought also owes a great deal to Fanon, in particular to the prescient chapter "The Pitfalls of National Consciousness" (*Wretched*), which accurately predicts many of the problems that would befall African states in the postcolonial period. In a

Marxist framework, the independence movements are seen not to resolve a crucial problem—namely, that the Manichaean colonizer/colonized dialectic masks a deeper system of economic exploitation. That the peripheral economy exports raw materials and cheap labor while importing finished products from the core economies leaves the peripheral economy at a permanent disadvantage, since the dominant countries maintain control over the most dynamic aspects of the world economy. Even countries with an enormous wealth of raw materials are at a permanent disadvantage if the technology and capital applied to extract it are centered elsewhere. This system of exploitation can be maintained—in some cases, more efficiently—without direct political control over the former colonies. What this new situation requires and produces is a very narrow class of local leaders whose interests are more closely aligned with their foreign partners than with the development of the national economy. A second generation of novels operates within the problematic of this neocolonial moment. Outstanding among these are *Petals of Blood* (Ngũgĩ wa Thiong'o), *The Beautyful Ones Are Not Yet Born* (Ayi Kwei Armah), and *Xala* (Ousmane Sembène).

A third strand of African Marxism concerns the analysis of the present moment, what some have called the era of globalization or multinational capitalism. Many Marxist thinkers have been reluctant to separate this historical period from the preceding one, and indeed there can be little question that not only neocolonial but also straightforwardly colonial problems persist. It might be best, then, to look at these issues not so much in terms of distinct historical moments as in terms of the increasing complexity of the African (and global) political and economic situation. Certainly contemporary history offers some novelties, like the end of the cold war and the accompanying opening up of the movement of goods and capital, the worldwide (and often forced) privatization of formerly government functions, or the increasing importance of both multinational corporations and international regulatory agencies. Some theorists have proposed that the most dynamic elements of the world economy are no longer industrial but cultural. On this view, the way knowledge and cultural forms circulate begins to assume the importance formerly held by the circulation of material goods.

The exploitation of African knowledge by First World interests has been called cultural imperialism: communal cultural property—from local ways of living and knowing to indigenous medical practices all the way to popular music, urban landscapes, and novels—is treated as raw material, which is then converted into copyrighted private property (from anthropology and pharmaceuticals to Paul Simon albums, Hollywood movies, and literary criticism) in non-African metropolitan centers, which then reexport these products, for profit, around the world. The philosopher Paulin Hountondji has offered the most detailed analysis of this phenomenon from an African perspective. Hountondji is concerned primarily with scientific and technical knowledge, but the basic argument can be generalized to include cultural forms like the novel. For him the central problem is that theoretical production, such as literary criticism, is in itself structurally oriented toward the interests of metropolitan centers—regardless of who is producing theoretical knowledge or where it is being produced. The industries that control the dominant channels of dissemination and communication (e.g., publishing houses with a global reach, universities with the resources to attract scholars from around the world) are centered in the core economies. The originality of Hountondji's argument lies in the explicit reference of the movement of knowledge to the larger "worldwide capitalist system" (248). It cannot be enough, that is, simply to try to alter the circulation of knowledge without first taking account of the system that determines that circulation. In economics there is a strategy called import substitution, which exploits weaknesses in the dominant economies in order to develop a regional industry that can then compete on the world market. This process has many positive effects, but it operates primarily in favor of the local ruling class; it does not fundamentally change the system in which it maneuvers. Intellectual import substitution—the elaboration of critical discourse at the regional level—is a necessary strategy, but it does not yet address the basic problem.

Marxism and African Literature: Two Debates

A fascinating debate around this last set of issues took place in Nigerian criticism in the 1980s. Achebe had already identified a species of "colonialist criticism" that attempted to assimilate African literature to European aesthetic standards and categories (68–90 ["Colonialist Criticism"]). Marxist criticism was by no means free of this tendency, which opened it up to the "ready charge" that Marxism was simply "alien to Africa" (Amuta 10). In the late 1970s, for example, Geoffrey Hunt, a lecturer in philosophy at the University of Ife, circulated a condescending and critically obtuse attack on Wole Soyinka that attempted for the purposes of critique to assimilate his work to European Romanticism.[4] (The argument—that Soyinka's recourse to mysticism is an expression of his class position as well as his genius and possibly not as progressive as it imagines itself—was, however, not without merit, and Soyinka's response, focusing more on Hunt's motives than his reasons, was distressingly shrill.) The most infamous example of Eurocentric criticism was immortalized by the Ghanaian novelist Ayi Kwei Armah in his funny but devastating response to Charles Larson's *The Emergence of African Fiction*, which tries to show Armah's formal debt to James Joyce. The "language of borrowing and influence," wrote Armah, "is usually a none too subtle way Western commentators have of saying Africa lacks original creativity" (38). After Armah's essay, the tendency to judge African works by European criteria—and of course there were African as well as North American and European critics who took this route—became known for a time as Larsony.

A group of self-described "bolekaja critics" (named after the "Come down, let's fight" attitude of passenger lorry drivers in western Nigeria) emerged to administer "a timely and healthy dose of much needed public ridicule" to a critical practice that was "smothering the sprouting vitality of Africa's literary landscape" (Chinweizu, Jemie, and Madubuike xii). Chinweizu, Onwuchekwa Jemie, and Ihechukwu Madubuike contended that "contemporary African culture is under foreign domination" (239) and that new modes of criticism had to be invented that would be adequate to the task of interpreting and evaluating African literature.

Although Soyinka and Chinweizu agreed that African novels should be discussed in terms of African aesthetic standards and practices, they did not agree what these standards and practices were or should be. Soyinka, himself labeled "obscurantist" by the bolekaja critics, preferred to call them "neo-Tarzanists." In the context of a debate on the decolonization of African literature, European influences could be ascribed as tokens of inauthenticity. Chinweizu diagnoses the "Euromodernist" Soyinka as having contracted "the Hopkins Disease"—a too-heavy reliance on the formal innovations of Gerard Manley Hopkins. The accusation here is that Soyinka's language is too obscure and allusive and that "traditional African poetry speaks a public language" (188). Soyinka gives better than he gets: the bolekaja critics' ideal of a literary language "simple and vivid, without surface complexity or clutter" (Chinweizu, Jemie, and Madubuike 187), is not particularly African but rather "Tennysonian" (Soyinka 90). On the one hand, this exchange is simply a kind of literary name-calling;

on the other, it points to a real problem with the rhetoric of literary decolonization. If any positive, empirical literary quality (density versus simplicity, allusiveness versus clarity, and so on) can be defended as genuinely African or derided as secretly European, then one has to wonder why Africanness is at stake at all rather than the specific merits of individual literary practices.

For the Marxist critic Amuta, the question of Africanness is essentially a red herring, a mistaken emphasis on what African literature is rather than on what it does:

> The quarrel gravitated around the vague question of whether to use "Western" or "African" aesthetic criteria. There are of course no such criteria, for aesthetic values and criteria are the products and instruments of specific groups and classes in specific societies. (3)

In other words, what determines aesthetic criteria, in both African contexts and elsewhere, is not so much ethnic and racial belonging as hierarchical power relations—which do, of course, in the postcolonial world as elsewhere, involve ethnic and racial belonging. As Amuta puts it, no doubt too brutally, the entire issue of African aesthetic criteria is "essentially an inter-class one, between bourgeois Western scholars and their African counterparts, over whose false consciousness should gain the upper hand" (3). For Ngara, writing around the same time on the other side of the continent, Soyinka's position is more or less that of cultural import substitution, of competing with the metropolitan vanguard: the "search for a myth was really a means of placing [Soyinka] in the tradition of such [mythopoetic modernist] poets as Yeats [and] Eliot" (*Ideology* 96).[5] The bolekaja critics represent a more progressive nationalist populism, which for Ngara nonetheless fails to address the real source of cultural and economic dependency.

Amuta's argument does not imply any skepticism about the issues of colonialist criticism or about real differences between African and Euro-American literature. On the contrary, the central problem with "traditionalist aesthetics"—and Amuta identifies several peripheral problems as well, many stemming from the naive and ahistorical conceptions of Africa and the West—is that "the pursuit of cultural (literary) decolonization rests on the false assumption that economic and political decolonization have been completed" (47). The insight here is twofold. First, economic and cultural domination are related; one cannot be resolved without addressing the other. Second, the difference between African and Euro-

American culture is precisely predicated on this relationship of domination. As with Fanon, the relationship of domination (a negative relation between two apparently positive entities) is the real positive entity; the qualities of the opposing sides are only epiphenomena of the antagonism itself. (In the neocolonial period, the antagonism that runs between these societies also runs through each; both African and Euro-American societies are riven with class and other antagonisms that act in the main to reinforce one another.) Amuta essentially endorses Hountondji's position: "Cultural imperialism is only an outward superstructural manifestation of economic imperialism. The crucial task before Africa is economic liberation which will in turn encourage a liberated literary culture" (47).

This position does not imply that culture is simply an appendage to economic and political struggles; it merely means that to attempt a purely cultural decolonization before economic decolonization has been completed is to put the cart before the horse. To place cultural production in the service of economic and political liberation is quite another thing, however, and is a matter of fostering new kinds of political subjectivity—a project that includes but extends beyond the stereotypes of agitprop and committed art.[6] In order to reach audiences where literacy cannot be assumed, African novelists such as Ngũgĩ wa Thiong'o have often turned to the theater. His Gikuyu-language theater experiments at Kamiriithu are meant to enable the Kenyan peasantry to discover the causes and effects of their own political, historical, and economic situation.[7]

Like literature, criticism is a social act: "all criticism is . . . politically predicated" (Amuta 199). In Nigeria, Amuta contributed to the debate by demonstrating that the conflict between African and Western aesthetics, and the conflict over what the former should look like, is in fact political: at stake is no less than control over the meaning of Nigerian literary culture and, by extension, Nigeria itself, which at that point was undergoing an intense period of economic and social crisis under military rule. Therefore the often hidden political valences of critical practices must be examined carefully. Amuta favors a pedagogy of the oppressed in line with the radical cultural theory of Cabral or the theater experiments of Ngũgĩ. That in our own immediate context—a volume on teaching the African novel intended for fairly orthodox classroom instruction in North America—such a program seems rather less practicable does not make the lesson of this Nigerian debate any less urgent. Books on African literature, like this one, intended primarily for a First World audience, must be particularly vigilant about whose interests are being attended to. To clarify this issue, one might turn briefly to another, North American debate about Marxism and African literature.

Around the same time as the Nigerian debate, the United States Marxist critic Fredric Jameson published a brief and controversial essay entitled "Third World Literature in the Era of Multinational Capitalism," which partly concerns the work of Ousmane Sembène and which famously suggests that "all third-world texts are necessarily . . . to be read as . . . *national allegories*" (69). Such a sweeping statement, coming from a First World literary critic, was taken by many to be yet another example of colonialist criticism, the imperial and restrictive imposition of meaning on African texts. And not without reason. The best and best-known response to Jameson's essay was written by another Marxist critic, Aijaz Ahmad, who took Jameson to task for asserting that "'national allegory' is the primary, even exclusive form of narrativity in the so-called Third World" (102). Jameson's article makes a number of rash suppositions about the "experience of colonized peoples" (76) and about Third World literature itself—much of which is not even available in European languages—that do not bear scrutiny. There is little point in defending Jameson's article, whose imperial sweep is plainly a grand rhetorical blunder, or in defending the principle thesis as Ahmad construes it.

But there is a slippage between Jameson's infamous statement and Ahmad's reading of it, and it hinges, this time, on the difference between what a work means and what it does. The key words of Jameson that are often elided in Ahmad's reply are "to be read as." Ahmad correctly finds it illegitimate to claim that all Third World texts are restricted to a certain kind of inherent meaning (in this case, an allegory of the national situation [104]); but "to be read as" such an allegory is something else altogether. "To be read as," in other words, is not a meaningless qualifier like "generally"; the phrase radically changes the meaning of Jameson's thesis, which is directed at the First World reader of African literature, not at African literature itself. The infamous sentence about national allegory is not a descriptive sentence about what Third World literature in itself means; rather, it is an imperative directed at First World readers: this is what Third World literature can do to us. Jameson in effect makes the same move as Amuta: the question of the meaning of a particular literature is at base a political one that takes its import from a particular context, and Jameson's recommendation is for the political effectivity (during the United States culture wars of the 1980s) of a mode of reading that forces the First World reader to "acknowledge an existence and a situation . . . that we do not know and prefer *not* to know" (66). In fact, Jameson's essay wavers between the version of this thesis that Ahmad considers indefensible and the more sympathetic version suggested here. The point is not to decide what Jameson is really saying but to recommend a particular version of it for contemporary First World teachers of African literature.

For both Jameson and Ahmad (as indeed for Amuta, Fanon, Cabral, Biodun Jeyifo, Grant Kamenju, Ngũgĩ wa Thiong'o, and many others), modern societies—perhaps all societies—are structured not by mere difference (gender, sexual, racial, ethnic, class, and so on) but by a fundamental antagonism. Ahmad speaks for most Marxists when he says that this antagonism has at its root the "ferocious struggle between capital and labour which is now strictly and fundamentally global in character" (104). What needs to be emphasized, however, is that in the late-twentieth and early-twenty-first centuries, this struggle can no longer be seen, if it ever could have been, as two positive entities confronting each other. The antagonism between capital and labor structures a host of other relations among differences whose particular configuration is inessential to the structuring antagonism. In Fanon, for example, a fairly straightforward relation of ultraexploitable African labor confronting the white man as the representative of European capital gives way, in the postcolonial moment, to a situation where members of an indigenous minority become the local representatives of capital, dominating a majority with some rights of citizenship. Even the contemporary problem of the propertyless masses (currently at the center of historical developments in Zimbabwe, South Africa, and elsewhere) is structured by this relation: the propertyless mark the outer limit of contemporary capital, since to remedy their situation would be to disturb the stability of property relations and drive away international investment.

Through all these changes there remains an antagonism between the wealthy countries and the economic periphery. This relation is complex, involving competition among the peripheral economies and among the wealthy nations in addition to, of course, class antagonisms within nations. Nonetheless, Jameson is surely right when, echoing Hountondji, he claims that Third World culture is

> in various ways locked in a life-and-death struggle with first-world cultural imperialism—a cultural struggle that is itself a reflexion of the economic situation of such areas in their penetration by various stages of capital. (68)

Unfortunately there is no easy way out of what is essentially a structural problem. Colonialist criticism is not simply a matter of questionable assumptions on the part of some Western critics; it is also a matter of the critic's location within social space and the economic relations that determine that location. What could be better evidence of this structural determination than lingering imperialist assumptions in an essay by a critic whose commitment to Third World liberation was, after all, never in question?

When specified as an intervention into the United States appropriation of African texts, the focus on national allegory has much to recommend it as a matter of practical criticism. The mode of political allegory recommended by Quayson has been tremendously productive for contemporary criticism—one thinks here of Jeyifo's reading of Soyinka's *The Road*, Quayson's own reading of Ben Okri's *The Famished Road*, Ngara's reading of Alex La Guma's *In the Fog of the Season's End*, and Amuta's reading of Achebe's *Arrow of God*.[8] But the specification of national allegory is useful in a First World pedagogical context, because, since the national situation is always related to other nations and in particular to the wealthy core economies, it demands self-reflexive questioning. Cheikh Hamidou Kane's *L'aventure ambiguë* is not just about an African experience of Being but also about the violence of European knowledge that it seeks to overleap; Pepetela's *A geração da utopia* narrates not just the decay of an African independence movement but also its origins in a new, United States–dominated regime of accumulation; and Achebe's *Arrow of God* is not just a rewriting of the precolonial past but also a forceful rewriting of European literature itself and a half-hidden allegory of the power of the dispossessed, who are so easily viewed in the First World as passive recipients of humanitarian aid, to restructure the social order. For First World students, African literature thus becomes not some other literature to be read alongside "our own" but a literature that engages, often antagonistically, with both our literature and, more profoundly, with ourselves.

Notes

1. Quayson's terminology deliberately echoes and revises that of the United States Marxist theorist Jameson.

2. For a productive recalibration of the Hegelian dialectic, see Quayson, "Introduction."

3. See, for example, Césaire; Senghor. Senghor's *Anthologie de la nouvelle poésie nègre et malgache de langue française* is prefaced by Jean-Paul Sartre's controversial defense.

4. A revised version of this essay is available in Gugelberger.

5. Ngara's *Art and Ideology in the African Novel* offers another important perspective.

6. Ngũgĩ wa Thiong'o's important *Decolonising the Mind*, which contains an account of his radical theater experiments at Kamiriithu, takes the rhetoric of cultural decolonization in an altogether more substantial direction than that of the bolekaja critics.

7. See his *I Will Marry When I Want* and, in *Decolonising the Mind*, "The Language of African Theater."

8. See "The Hidden Class War in *The Road*" in Jeyifo 11–22; Quayson, "Literature"; "The Price of Commitment: La Guma's *In the Fog of the Season's End*" in Ngara, *Art* 86–98; and Amuta 125–29.

Works Cited

Achebe, Chinua. *Hopes and Impediments: Selected Essays.* New York: Doubleday, 1989. Print.

Ahmad, Aijaz. "Jameson's Rhetoric of Otherness and the 'National Allegory.'" *In Theory: Classes, Nations, Literatures.* London: Verso, 1992. 95–122. Print.

Amuta, Chidi. *The Theory of African Literature.* London: Zed, 1989. Print.

Armah, Ayi Kwei. "Larsony; or, Fiction as Criticism of Fiction." *New Classic* 4 (1977): 33–45. Print.

Cabral, Amilcar. *Return to the Source: Selected Speeches.* New York: Monthly Rev., 1973. Print.

———. *Unity and Struggle.* London: Heinemann, 1980. Print.

Césaire, Aimé. *Discourse on Colonialism.* Trans. Joan Pinkham. New York: Monthly Rev., 1972. Print.

Chinweizu, Onwuchekwa Jemie, and Ihechukwu Madubuike. *Towards the Decolonization of African Literature.* Washington: Howard UP, 1983. Print.

Fanon, Frantz. *The Wretched of the Earth.* Trans. Constance Farrington. New York: Grove, 1963. Print.

Gugelberger, Georg M., ed. *Marxism and African Literature.* London: Currey, 1985. Print.

Hountondji, Paulin. "Recapturing." *The Surreptitious Speech:* Présence Africaine *and the Politics of Otherness, 1947–1987.* Ed. V. Y. Mudimbe. Chicago: U of Chicago P, 1992. 238–48. Print.

Hunt, Geoffrey. "Two African Aesthetics: Wole Soyinka vs. Amilcar Cabral." Gugelburger 64–93.

Jameson, Fredric. "Third World Literature in the Era of Multinational Capitalism." *Social Text* 15 (1986): 65–88. Print.

Jeyifo, Biodun. *The Truthful Lie: Essays in a Sociology of African Drama.* London: New Beacon, 1985. Print.

Larson, Charles. *The Emergence of African Fiction.* Bloomington: Indiana UP, 1972. Print.

Lazarus, Neil. *Resistance in Postcolonial African Fiction.* New Haven: Yale UP, 1990. Print.

Mudimbe, V. Y. *The Invention of Africa: Gnosis, Philosophy, and the Order of Knowledge*. Bloomington: Indiana UP, 1988. Print.

Ngara, Emmanuel. *Art and Ideology in the African Novel: A Study of the Influence of Marxism on African Writing*. London: Heinemann, 1985. Print.

———. *Ideology and Form in African Poetry*. London: Currey, 1990. Print.

Ngũgĩ wa Thiong'o. *Decolonising the Mind*. London: Currey, 1981. Print.

———. *I Will Marry When I Want*. London: Heinemann, 1981. Print.

Quayson, Ato. "Introduction: Mimesis, Dialectics, and the Bounding of Analytic Fields." *Calibrations: Reading for the Social*. Minneapolis: U of Minnesota P, 2003. xi–xl. Print.

———. "Literature as a Politically Symbolic Act." *Postcolonialism: Theory, Practice, or Process?* Cambridge: Polity, 2000. 76–102. Print.

Sartre, Jean-Paul. "Orphée noir." Senghor ix–xliv.

Senghor, Léopold Sédar, ed. *Anthologie de la nouvelle poésie nègre et malgache de langue française*. Paris: PUF, 1948. Print.

Soyinka, Wole. "Aesthetic Illusions: Prescriptions for the Suicide of Poetry." *Art, Dialogue and Outrage*. Ibadan: New Horn, 1988. 86–109. Print.

Eleni Coundouriotis

Why History Matters in the African Novel

For most students of African literature, historical context presents a staggering challenge. Where does one begin to explain Africa? And why should history be the preferred frame for reading the African novel? After all, any serious engagement with historical specificity would question the claim that there is a distinct genre called the African novel. In view of the immense diversity of the continent, what does *African* mean beyond a geographic designation of origin?[1] That today many African writers are émigrés raises all over again the problem of what African literature is. Lila Azam Zanganeh wonders how to define a literature "that takes root far from an emigrant's native land, where his work is barely read at all." She goes on to cite Kossi Efoui, a writer from Togo, who says provocatively, "For me, African literature is something that does not exist." Ultimately these essentializing debates are not of interest in themselves, but they illustrate the pressing need to engage historically the texts we read as African novels. A historical engagement means reading not only with an eye for the context that might explain but also with recognition of the agency of Africans as actors in the shaping of this context in both its material and discursive reality. The question of agency is critical and moves the problem of historical methodology from explanatory background to foreground—the lives lived, the stories told, the memories revisited and reexamined.

Because African novels are often used as texts for the study of African history, there is another context that needs to be considered: the influence of oral and written literature on the academic discipline of African history. Anthony King in his review of the memoirs of two prominent African historians, Jan Vansina and Roland Oliver, explains how African history challenged mainstream academic history, which was based on the model of imperial history, what Vansina has elsewhere described as "grand ideas and the panoramic canvass" constructed, of course, with Europe at the center ("Lessons" 397). Both methods and sources of African history, especially the use of orality, helped transform the discipline of academic history as a whole. The methods had to be thoroughly interdisciplinary, drawing on archaeology, anthropology, linguistics, and literature (King 130). Vansina, who pioneered the use of oral literature, described in an interview how orality changed the discipline of history:

> Historians are beginning to look upon [oral traditions] as the reflection today of historical consciousness and as a way in which we can learn how the descendants of people evolved in a historical sense, how they looked upon what is important in history, and what motivations there were. *In short, how they look at history itself or history as a cultural artifact.* ("Reflections" 4; emphasis added)[2]

This idea of "history as a cultural artifact" is key to illuminating the historicity of the African novel. The novel as cultural artifact is an obvious idea, but the novel as a depiction of the historical consciousness of Africans and hence of their agency needs foregrounding to a student readership. At the end of this essay, I turn to the work of another historian, Terence Ranger, who articulates the mutually reinforcing role of African academic history and the African novel in establishing African historiography.

Because African fiction emerged in the shadow of colonialism, it is important to situate the novel directly in relation to the political and cultural struggle for decolonization. But there is also a need to look beyond the legacy of colonialism, to a historical frame that both reaches into the precolonial past and begins to distinguish more recent developments as part of something different from anticolonial resistance. The canonical texts of the African novel, many published in the Heinemann African Writers Series, explore the transition from colonialism to independence.

As many of us teaching in the field know, our syllabi are often shaped by what is available in print. Beyond a certain core of texts, titles come into print and then become unavailable fairly quickly, making teaching a representative literary history of the African novel quite difficult.

On the positive side, new publishers are showing an interest in stepping into the vacuum left by the demise of the African Writers Series; they are making available a new range of literature that is reshaping the study of the novel. They also seem more willing than in the past to publish francophone novels in translation, so that we have available such important works as Ahmadou Kourouma's *En attendant le vote des bêtes sauvages* (*Waiting for the Vote of the Wild Animals*) and *Allah n'est pas obligé* (*Allah Is Not Obliged*) as well as Emmanuel Dongala's *Les petits garçons naissent aussi des étoiles* (*Little Boys Come from the Stars*) and *Johnny, chien mechant* (*Johnny Mad Dog*) for comparative courses on the novel. If one of the challenges of a historical approach to the African novel is to complicate the periodization of its development, now seems a good time therefore to undertake the challenge. Postapartheid South Africa, the civil wars of West Africa in the 1990s, the dissolution of the Somali state, the genocide of Rwanda all have a colonial dimension, yet they are not sufficiently explained by that dimension.

As this literature illustrates, the central problem of representation in the African novel has been violence. A historical approach to the novel must engage with the difficult moral and aesthetic issues raised by the representation of violence. African identity as constructed by outsiders is closely identified with violence, and much African fiction is an attempt to reclaim and recast that identity. Yet the reality in much of Africa has been one of persistent violent conflict that has prompted writers to give witness to this experience and to return to the past to historicize present national identities and their violent legacies. Women's fiction is particularly important here, as its trenchant critique of patriarchy connects forms of political violence to gender violence.

In his return visit to Makerere University on 8 August 2004, Ngũgĩ wa Thiong'o spoke about the urgent need for African universities to undertake projects of remembrance, of historical study, as a step toward imagining an African future ("Role"). The attack on him and his wife in their Nairobi hotel three days later demonstrates how incendiary such a project of historical memory continues to be. Ngũgĩ was promoting the publication of his first novel in twenty years, *Mũrogi wa Kagogo* (*The Wizard of the Crow*), a novel written in Kikuyu that satirizes Daniel arap

Moi's dictatorship in Kenya. In his lecture at Makerere, where he had been a student, he spoke of "re-membering" as a response to the "dismembering" of the native through colonialism. Remembrance, whether it is in the form of novels or history across a range of academic disciplines, he argues, is a crucial response to violence ("Role").

In *Manichean Aesthetics* (1983), the book that launched the historical study of the African novel in English, Abdul JanMohamed makes a strong argument for historical context, what he calls the "generative ambiance" of the novel (2). The African novel, he claims, cannot be understood unless properly contextualized in the politics of colonialism; any attempt to read literature as separate from politics erases the specificity of this body of work. He conceived the relevant context of the African novel as a space of cultural contact between Europeans and Africans. By contrast, critics before JanMohamed insisted on the importance of only an African context for the African novel. This essentializing tendency was in response to the novel's reception among European readers. As an imported genre affiliated with the culture of the colonizer, the novel was readily aestheticized and abstracted—an example is the reception of René Maran's *Batouala*.[3] In response, some critics argued for an African authenticity, or for the priority of an African literary context, that of oral literature, for the African novel. Emmanuel Obiechina's *Culture, Tradition, and Society in the West African Novel* takes this approach. As Ato Quayson concludes, Obiechina "sees the novel as reflective or mimetic of traditional beliefs and practices in an almost unmediated way" (*Strategic Transformations* 2). Obiechina's study, therefore, is less historical than anthropological. Quayson argues that in it "the novels become amenable to a positivist anthropological harvest in which details are read directly from cultural background to fictional world and back again" (2).[4] This unmediated reflexivity between text and context undermines historicism. As a method of study of the African novel, I would argue, historicism must posit the novel as one among several discursive practices taking place simultaneously, shaping and informing one another, rather than as reality and mirror.

Drawing from Frantz Fanon's cultural and psychoanalytic critique of colonialism, JanMohamed insists that the colonial encounter has created a "colonial pathology" (152) that not only pits the colonized and colonizer against each other but also places them in a self-contradictory and destructive trap. The colonizer wishes to civilize the native; if he succeeds, however, he will lose his social and political advantage, so he must perpetuate the impression of the colonized's inhumanity against the lie of his civilizing ideology. The colonized, on the other hand, is forced to adopt the "superior" culture of the colonizer and thus lose his own past as well as his "sense of historical direction"; if he refuses assimilation, he "remains, from the colonialist's viewpoint, a 'savage,' and the need to 'civilize' him perpetuates colonialism" (5). Colonizer and colonized, frustrated in their respective traps, each demonize the other and see their relation only in Manichaean terms (a phrase borrowed by JanMohamed from Fanon).

JanMohamed neatly creates an interpretive frame in which to place the colonial novel and examines its formal features in terms of Georg Lukács's theory of realism, which stresses the novel's ambition to intimate a social totality through the consciousness of individual subjects and readily lends itself to the historical. Moreover, instead of limiting himself to single works by individual authors, he examines the entire careers of the six authors in his study, thus demonstrating what biography, history, and the writing of fiction together can teach us about colonialism. JanMohamed's use of biography is especially interesting. It shows us one way in which context can come to the foreground: in the life stories of the authors, he examines who must negotiate through their fiction writing the Manichaean dynamic of colonialism and their self-fashioning in response to it. His examples are organized in pairs, each representing a geographic region of sub-Saharan Africa: Joyce Cary and Chinua Achebe on Nigeria, Isak Dinesen and Ngũgĩ wa Thiong'o on Kenya, Nadine Gordimer and Alex La Guma on South Africa. Thus West, East, and southern Africa are covered. JanMohamed uses the organization of his book to signal the deep structure of Manichaeanism, by placing a chapter on the European writer first, a chapter on the African writer second.

JanMohamed clearly set the agenda for the historical study of the novel around a very rigid periodization that places the colonial period at the center; everything before and after is subordinated to it. Although studies of the African novel have overwhelmingly focused on the colonial-postcolonial divide, his critical model of a Manichaean aesthetics (propelled as well by the wide influence of Fanon) continues to inform readings of the colonial situation and resistance to it. Yet to carry that aesthetics into the postcolonial period goes against the grain of what he is arguing for. His book captures an impasse that the novel can describe but not resolve. Manichaeanism may create the space of protest but does not show the way to active resistance. For readers of the African novel after JanMohamed, resistance becomes much more important. History as a subject of interest is not merely embedded in a realist aesthetics of representation but also transforms novel writing into actual interference in politics, for which authors are often persecuted.

Broadly speaking, there are three ways in which critics have argued for the novel's historical and political significance: they point to an African literary tradition that articulates coherently an answer to colonialism; they look at particular national contexts and claim a role for the novel's importance as a critique of nationalism and state power; and they locate the novel in an interdisciplinary context, especially in relation to ethnography, and see how it differentiates itself as a discourse.

Two exemplary studies that consider the African novel as a tradition are Simon Gikandi's *Reading the African Novel* (1987) and Kenneth Harrow's *Thresholds of Change in African Literature* (1994). Both works read comparatively across anglophone and francophone Africa. Gikandi offers a typology of narratives that map the body of the African novel. These are the parabolical, the biographical, the subjective, and the political. He concludes with a chapter that applies Roland Barthes's idea of rereading from *S/Z* to uncover a politics of language that stretches the function of the novel beyond representation. By using Barthes, Gikandi identifies the ways in which novelists (his examples are Chinua Achebe and Elechi Amadi, both Nigerians) use the language of the novel as a means of political agency that interrogates cultural practices based on myth and undermines the political uses of myth. History is less a matter of representation for Gikandi than it is of writerly agency.

His discussion of the political novel (Sembène's *God's Bits of Wood*, La Guma's *In the Fog of the Seasons' End*, and Ngũgĩ's *Petals of Blood*) looks more explicitly at the author's writing of a history and, as JanMohamed does, deploys a critical language informed by Lukács's *Theory of the Novel.* This ambition to depict the whole of African society and not merely the experience of the alienated intellectual (the goal of the subjective narrative) identifies the problem of history as a problem of politics: the hero must triumph over a crippling ideology of secondariness and alienation to conquer "the landscape of chaos" in which he is trapped (*Reading* 113). Agency again is highlighted by Gikandi as politics takes center stage.

The parabolical and subjective narratives also contain a historical dimension for Gikandi. The parabolical must convince us to cast aside "any external knowledge we may have about the historicism and social background of the world represented" in order to respond to the fiction and understand it as a "carrier of value and meaning" (2). This type of novel (examples are by Camara Laye and by Armah) engages indirectly with history as a set of preconceived notions that do not adequately reflect lived experience. Thus the exteriority of history in the parabolical narrative is in stark contrast to the realism of the political novel that takes on the task of writing history.

In his chapter on the biographical narrative, Gikandi discusses three francophone texts (Beti's *Mission to Kala*, Oyono's *Houseboy*, and Kane's *Ambiguous Adventure*). Education and the individual are the key themes here, but history is important again, because through education the protagonists of these novels develop an expanded sense of the social that also manifests itself as an awakening to history. African writers may engage history in various ways, but, as Gikandi shows, it is never far from their minds as a major topic.

Harrow's study foregrounds change as a thematic and structural problem for the African novel. As a theme, change highlights history: the African novel, born out of the colonial encounter, tells the stories of change in African life that results from that encounter. But for Harrow change is also the mechanism through which a literary tradition is established:

> For the poetics of African literature, [change] exists in the relationship between texts that have commented on each other, have grown on each other, have been formed on each other's words, and have collectively forged the processes of constituting a literary tradition. (3)

He argues that despite the immensity of the African experience, there is such a thing as an African literary tradition, and change in this tradition occurs because Africans are reading other Africans. Moreover, the changes reflected in literary traditions map the historical, political, and cultural changes of African peoples. What makes Harrow's book interesting as a historical approach is that its literary history parallels closely the political development of colonial and postcolonial Africa. He explains how a literature of witness (*témoignage*) turns into a literature of revolt as postcolonial disillusion settles in, and later it changes again into a literature of postrevolt.

Agency is important to Harrow; he follows closely how the lived experience of change and the choices made out of historical necessity shape the literature about African experience. In his chapter on Bessie Head's *Collector of Treasures*, he focuses on how "boundaries" between the new and the old shape women's identities. In Head's short stories, "the crossing of lines forms the quintessential action" (195). A historicist awareness emerges in the difference of perception between the narrator and the characters. Harrow repeatedly comes back to this point in the effort to take into account the gap in historical experience between a writer and the illiterate masses who are often his subject. He does not privilege one or the other; in fact, they are not even presented as alternatives. It is the way they reflect each other that yields the historical insight.

In his monograph on Ngũgĩ, Gikandi expands his ideas about the political narrative from his earlier *Reading the African Novel* and situates it in a fully elaborated national context of Kenya. Ngũgĩ's life, writings, and poetics afford Gikandi the opportunity to display the political relevance of writing about history. In his discussion of Ngũgĩ's essay "The Writer and His Past," Gikandi shows how the writer identifies the novel as a genre of history: "The novelist is haunted by a sense of the past . . . because of the generic imperative that he (or she) must come to terms with history" (*Ngugi* 255–56). The imperative of history posed many problems for Ngũgĩ. First was the realization in his early career that he had to confront the legacy of colonialism and the way it marked his identity through the silencing of his own history. As Gikandi notes, "history, even the history of events experienced first-hand, seems to be blocked by the narratives designed to represent it" (7–8). Thus the writer had to overcome two repressing historiographical paradigms: the colonial history, which repressed the violence of colonization, and the postindependence history mounted by the neocolonial state, which repressed the anticolonial struggle.

After Ngũgĩ mastered the form of the bourgeois novel in *A Grain of Wheat*, a novel that vividly portrays historical subjectivity, he confronted a second challenge in the realization that although he knew what he wanted to write, he was not sure he knew for whom he was writing (Gikandi, *Ngugi* 144). He thus changed his poetics and, in *Petals of Blood*, wrote a novel for and about a collective. He appropriated and transformed Lukács's notion of totality, using the collective instead of individual consciousness as an ironic reflection on totality. At its core, *Petals of Blood* had a utopian purpose: "to move [Kenyans] beyond the rhetoric of failure" (139). Gikandi demonstrates through his examination of Ngũgĩ's career that novelists in Africa have conceived their relation to history in two mutually reenforcing although at times also conflicting ways: as a reexamination of historical memory and as an attempt to set in motion political agency in the present by depicting Africans as agents of resistance and history.

Not all studies of the novel that have focused on particular national contexts take such an oppositional view of history. Quayson's *Strategic Transformations in Nigerian Writing* sees the novel's historical task as the cultural work of extending oral traditions. The novel imports and transforms orality to create a new discourse that emanates from an African cultural context but also contains the traces of European influence. Although Quayson, like JanMohamed, conceives of the novel as a space of cultural contact, he emphasizes the creation of an African (Nigerian) national ethos through the novel, a task that he sees as fundamentally historical.[5] By beginning his study with an examination of a colonial text, the Reverend Samuel Johnson's *History of the Yoruba* (1921), he suggests that the novels that come later are created at the interface of several discourses: oral traditions, the writing of an ethnic identity and its extrapolation as a model of national identity, and historiography. The transference of oral source into written, purportedly scientific text is transformative in a way that contributed to the "formation of Yoruba consciousness" (*Strategic Transformations* 35). Reading Ben Okri's postmodern *The Famished Road*, for example, Quayson highlights Okri's use of the mythopoeic (the story is narrated through the consciousness of an *abiku* child, a spirit child who exists between the living and dead) in order to show how Nigeria's incomplete grappling with its history may be one aspect of the historical but does not preclude the flourishing of other dimensions of nation making. Okri, according to Quayson, collapses the different moments of historical awareness into one synchronous jumble in which the mythopoeic then thrives (132–33).[6]

Quayson, speaking for one national context in particular (Nigeria), sees the novel as a space apart from politics but embedded in the social (as opposed to aesthetic) work of nation making. But he follows Okri in making the assumption that the novel can define itself by its subject; the disenfranchised, illiterate masses, who in their political disempowerment remain relatively immune to ideological control by the state, unlike their more educated urban compatriots.

Taking as his subject the Marxist-Leninist postindependence state of the Republic of the Congo (the former French Equatorial Africa), Dominic Thomas sees a different relation between literature and the state. In

Nation-Building, Propaganda, and Literature in Francophone Africa, he argues that both literature and the state aim at nation making, and they are not neatly opposed to each other. The state assumes an active role in ideologically "engineering" a literature of nationalism, to which a dissenting, second body of work responds (2). Thomas examines how history becomes part of the dissident project of nation making that criticizes the authoritarianism of the state and the state's propagandistic uses of national myths of origin. This dissident literature, of which Sony Labou Tansi is the preeminent exponent, is highly experimental in form and imports orality and popular culture to subvert the state's official culture. Using Achille Mbembe's theorization of the postcolony as a violent, grotesque dystopia, Thomas links Labou Tansi's preoccupation with the body to the nation so as to find, even at the moment of the body's most extreme duress, a defiance that mocks official culture (61). Labou Tansi is interested in history in a narrow sense, as an attempt to reappropriate historical agency away from the authoritarian state and reexamine contemporary circumstances.

Thomas finds in Emmanuel Dongala's work a broader investment in history that seeks to challenge the narratives of national origin promoted by the state. Dongala begins his *Le feu des origines* (*The Fire of Origins*) in precolonial times and develops a historical sequence that ends with the emergence of the one-party state. This attempt at historical explanation is strikingly different from Labou Tansi's allegorical narratives. But Dongala's histories are, as Thomas points out, "heterogeneous," setting in motion a multiplicity of points of view instead of insisting on a unitary narrative (147). This heterogeneity is most evident in *Les petits garçons naissent aussi des étoiles* (*Little Boys Come from the Stars*), which dramatizes a courtroom scene to allow the rehearsal of opposing views of history (Thomas 153).

Historical study of the African novel entails several interdependent approaches. One task is to develop a literary history, which is often interdisciplinary, locating novels in a larger frame of other narrative genres. Another task is to examine how authors see themselves as doing the work of history or, in other words, how they conceive of themselves as historians though their style is not always realistic. The scholar must also explain how the move from text to social and historical context is negotiated. Ideally one needs to get beyond the use of the literary text as documentary while maintaining that the text is embedded in a historical context.

All these components posit historical study as a method that articulates relations among different spheres of knowledge or discourses. The historical study of literature entails going beyond the representational or mimetic content of a work to grapple with the way it comments on stories embedded in texts of anthropology, history, sociology, journalism, and political science and to tease out how our understanding of the historical agency of African peoples is illuminated or obscured in these discussions. History is not always a project of remembrance. It can also be a means by which we lay claim to action, action that both shapes us individually in meaningful ways and places us as individuals in a transforming collective.

V. Y. Mudimbe's influential study about the discourses of representation of Africa, *The Invention of Africa*, set the stage for a rereading of the African novel in a more explicitly interdisciplinary context. If, as Mudimbe argues, the discourse of knowledge about Africa was a "discourse of competence" (175–76), then the novel had to establish its own authority. To do so, novelists had to gain an ethnographic authority that did not rely on authenticity, which would always be dubious (Coundouriotis). They attained authority instead by inflecting ethnography with history.

Christopher Miller in *Theories of Africans* describes anthropology's relation to the African novel in the colonial period "as a window and a mirror: as the means of gaining 'local knowledge' and as a reflection of European preoccupations projected onto Africa." Anthropology is the pathway through which "Europe wrote itself into the tradition of European-language literatures in Africa" (139). But the borrowed authority of African novelists, I argue in *Claiming History*, was more resistant than Miller accounts for. It sought to reappropriate the discourse of knowledge about Africa by recourse to historical explanation that on the one hand shattered the lie of the civilizing mission by depicting the colonizer's violence and on the other complicated depictions of Africans by showing them as agents of their own history.

The political implications of history have always been explosive, isolating novelists in their own national contexts. Ngũgĩ's pairing of remembrance and violence reminds us that remembering is not a simple stitching together; it also brings about a repetition of violence. How to tell, explain, and analyze a history of violence without provoking further violence is the most pressing problem in the historical narration of Africa. Recent attempts to take stock of the Rwanda genocide, for example, vividly dramatize this problem. In *L'ombre d'Imana* (*The Shadow of Imana*), Véronique Tadjo studiously avoids taking sides. Tadjo foregrounds individual stories and her own testimony to the suffering. Ambiguously positioned as both an outsider (she is not from Rwanda) and an insider (she is African), she creates a kind of protected space from which to contemplate genocide. What emerges again, as in the earlier historical fiction from Africa, is a crisis of authority, in this case brought on by the magnitude of the horror.

Authority persists as a problem of historical narration in other ways as well. The Zimbabwean writer Yvonne Vera insisted that academic history had nothing to offer her; instead she chose to intuit her people's history through imaginative understanding. Talking about her first novel, *Nehanda*, she claimed:

> I wrote it from remembrance, as a witness of my own spiritual history. By history, I simply mean a record. I felt I had an internal, intimate knowledge of our ancestors, and how they impact on our relationship with ourselves, to death, to life, to time, to sky, to rock . . . I had just become aware that I understood this, but somehow it wasn't anywhere in a book where I could read it, and I didn't know why, except maybe the knowledge had become discredited by other ways of seeing. (qtd. in Ranger, "History" 204)

Her intimate stories of women suffering the violence of history opens up silences that are convincing if not conventionally historical.

Vera's fiction is allusive and evocative, replete with graphic violence rendered in poetically beautiful language. The aestheticization of violence is a troubling feature of her work, but its intention is to claim and dignify the experience of the women who suffer. Speaking of her account of a woman's self-abortion in *Butterfly Burning*, Vera said, "I wanted to do it without crudity, with a certain elegance, so you feel you can still endure it and see beauty in it. And this beauty can only be in the language" (Interview 223). She makes big demands on her reader, both because of her subject matter and because of the difficulty of her prose. But her aim to help the reader endure being the witness is key to confronting African history, because so much seems unbearable. Her literary language is used to reveal and to screen at the same time.

Vera's ability to dissociate truthfulness from fact frees her fiction to describe Zimbabwe's troubled history in a new way. The historian Terence

Ranger, with whom Vera developed a warm friendship, remembers his first impression of her *Nehanda*, a novel that treated the same topic as his book *Revolt in Southern Rhodesia, 1896–97. Nehanda*, he said, was "an extraordinary feat of imagination," and he was intrigued by Vera's refusal to use any academic history or anthropology as a source. He concluded, "Vera's refusal to be bound by the facts struck me as sublime," yielding insights that were "more powerful and plausible than those recorded by anthropologists" ("History" 203). Important here is that the "discourse of competence" (to allude to Mudimbe's phrase again) cedes ground to the imaginative discourse of the novel. An African woman achieves an authority over historical narration not by imitating a professional discourse but by subverting it. The novelist intuits and evokes a truth about a historical memory through what she admits is deliberate distortion (Ranger, "History" 203).

Recent literature from South Africa is also challenging historiographical paradigms and methods. By employing a wider range of source materials, unconventional forms of narration, and a longer view of history, writers are breaking out of the Manichaean oppositions of apartheid. Zoe Wicomb's *David's Story* and its exploration of the history of colored identity shows how history as a collective project is marred by a series of lacunae that can be filled only through multiple individual perspectives and even then only incompletely. We may never be able to retrieve history as a totality, but for Wicomb the intimation of this totality and the examination of its shadows is the special task of the novelist.

Zakes Mda's *The Madonna of Excelsior* revisits a chapter of apartheid history—the immorality trials, which were a consequence of apartheid's prohibition of interracial relationships—but exhibits little of the constraint to follow the Manichaean aesthetics of the resistance literature from the apartheid era. Mda's depiction seems more in sync with the culture of accommodation and indirect forms of resistance that Mark Sanders describes in *Complicities: The Intellectual and Apartheid*. Mda also expands the novel's historiographical range by using his detailed references to Frans Claerhout's paintings as an imaginative source for the ethos of living under the Immorality Act and the kinds of creative resistance possible to it. Claerhout—a Belgian, a Catholic priest, and a self-taught expressionist painter—lived in South Africa after 1946. Mda finds in Claerhout's work the visual analogue to the celebration of African women's agency and sexuality that Mda's novel argues for. This borrowing from a European source reflects the trend in the field of the African novel to reexamine colonial culture.

Narrating the history of Africa will continue to pose major challenges. Despite the magnitude of atrocity that makes narration difficult, the extent of dislocation, and the likelihood of a largely expatriate intelligentsia, history continues to be at the core of the African novel's concerns, and it provides a rich focus for the study of the development of the genre. Wole Soyinka, seeking to inspire fellow Africans to a commitment to historical awareness as a deterrent to further violence, wrote:

> Our proposition is simply one of recollection, or . . . memory. The need for the preservation of the material and spiritual properties by which memory is invested. Acceptance of both its burdens and triumphs or—better still—its actuality, the simple fact of its anterior existence and its validity for its time. To accept that is to recognize the irrationality of mutual destructiveness on behalf of any values, any values whatsoever, however seductive—cultural, ideological, religious, or race-authenticated—that intervened and obscured or eroded those multiple anteriorities—of whatever kind—from which our being once took its definition. (62–63)

For Soyinka, history is a critical, analytic task. A truthful reckoning that can recognize both "burdens and triumphs" is important for the constitution of an African identity that has a sense of agency. This is a risky proposition, because Soyinka recognizes implicitly that history has been misused to distort and to prop up power in illegitimate ways. He also risks sounding as if he is promoting the retrieval of an anterior African authenticity that precedes colonialism. The key to his formulation of the historical task facing all students of Africa is on his double insistence that some sort of recuperation of African history from the distortions of colonial ideology is important but that this recuperation cannot take place in the framework of an authenticating essentialism. Indeed, a proper historical recuperation must undermine any tendency toward essentialism; it must historicize the circumstances under which a range of different essentialisms have brought on violent divisions.

I began with a reference to Ngũgĩ and end with a reference to Soyinka. The two writers have clashed over their different views on history since the 1960s. Ngũgĩ was especially impatient with what he considered Soyinka's aloofness from the historical struggles of the present (Gikandi, *Ngugi* 138–39). For teaching the African novel, however, both writers make eloquent defenses of history. A broader survey of the novel across the continent only confirms the centrality of history as theme and practice to this body of literature.

Notes

1. Even this definition of *African* has been problematized, when critics wondered whether African novels are African because they depict African content or because they were written by Africans. There was heated discussion of this question at the conference of African writers at Makerere University in Uganda in June 1962 (Ezenwa-Ohaeto 90–91).

2. Vansina gives an extensive overview of the historical study of Africa since the 1960s in *Living with Africa* (197–221).

3. The attempt to see *Batouala* in aesthetic terms was an attempt to dehistoricize the novel and obscure its anticolonial message. See Coundouriotis 24–36.

4. Extending his critique of the anthropological approach to African literature, Quayson sees Christopher Miller's more theoretically sophisticated *Theories of Africans* as an extension of Obiechina's method and faults Miller for being ahistorical (*Strategic Transformations* 2).

5. Lacking the neat focus on a particular national context, Quayson's more recent *Calibrations: Reading for the Social* abandons the critical concern for history. The social is the subject instead and allows for a reading of the novel as dynamic as that in *Strategic Transformations* but without a sense of the diachronic, what Quayson calls in his earlier work the historiographic.

6. I refer to the synchronicity of Okri's novel as a deliberate forgetfulness and use it to launch an antinationalist reading of the novel. History, I suggest, is opposed to the national as a form of dissent against the state (Coundouriotis 148–64). Quayson's concern with the mythopoeic shifts the emphasis to an ongoing project of creating a Yoruba identity, which takes place in a context of cultural and political struggle.

Works Cited

Coundouriotis, Eleni. *Claiming History: Colonialism, Ethnography, and the Novel.* New York: Columbia UP, 1999. Print.

Dongala, Emmanuel. *Johnny, chien mechant.* Paris: Le Serpent à Plumes, 2002. Print. Trans. as *Johnny Mad Dog.* Trans. Maria Louise Ascher. New York: Farrar, 2005.

———. *Les petits garçons naissent aussi des étoiles.* Paris: Le Serpent à Plumes, 1998. Print. Trans. as *Little Boys Come from the Stars.* Trans. Joë Réjouis and Val Vinakurov. New York: Farrar, 2001.

Ezenwa-Ohaeto. *Chinua Achebe: A Biography.* Bloomington: Indiana UP, 1997. Print.

Gikandi, Simon. *Ngugi Wa Thiong'o.* Cambridge: Cambridge UP, 2000. Print.

———. *Reading the African Novel.* Portsmouth: Heinemann, 1987. Print.

Harrow, Kenneth W. *Thresholds of Change in African Literature: The Emergence of a Tradition.* Portsmouth: Heinemann, 1994. Print.

JanMohamed, Abdul R. *Manichean Aesthetics: The Politics of Literature in Colonial Africa.* Amherst: U of Massachusetts P, 1983. Print.

King, Anthony. "Pioneering African Studies: Jan Vansina and Roland Oliver." *African Affairs* 99 (2000): 129–34. Print.

Kourouma, Ahmadou. *Allah n'est pas obligé.* Paris: Seuil, 2000. Print. Trans. as *Allah Is Not Obliged.* Trans. Frank Wynne. New York: Anchor, 2007.

———. *En attendant le vote des bêtes sauvages.* Paris: Seuil, 1998. Print. Trans. as *Waiting for the Wild Beasts to Vote.* Trans. Frank Wynne. London: Heinemann, 2003.

Lukács, Georg. *The Theory of the Novel.* Trans. Anna Bostok. Cambridge: MIT P, 1971. Print.

Maran, René. *Batouala.* Paris: Albin, 1921. Print.

Mda, Zakes. *The Madonna of Excelsior.* New York: Farrar, 2002. Print.

Miller, Christopher. *Theories of Africans: Francophone Literature and Anthropology in Africa.* Chicago: U of Chicago P, 1990. Print.

Mudimbe, V. Y. *The Invention of Africa.* Bloomington: Indiana UP, 1988. Print.

Muponde, Robert, and Mandi Taruvinga, eds. *Sign and Taboo: Perspectives on the Poetic Fiction of Yvonne Vera.* Oxford: Currey, 2003. Print.

Ngũgĩ wa Thiong'o. *A Grain of Wheat.* London: Heinemann, 1967. Print.

———. *Mũrogi wa Kagogo.* Nairobi: East African Educ., 2007. Print. Trans. as *The Wizard of the Crow.* Trans. Ngũgĩ wa Thiong'o. New York: Pantheon, 2006.

———. *Petals of Blood.* London: Heinemann, 1977. Print.

———. "The Role of the University in Africa Today." Makerere U. 8 Aug. 2004. Address.

Obiechina, Emmanuel. *Culture, Tradition, and Society in the West African Novel.* Cambridge: Cambridge UP, 1975. Print.

Quayson, Ato. *Calibrations: Reading for the Social.* Minneapolis: U of Minnesota P, 2003. Print.

———. *Strategic Transformations in Nigerian Writing.* Oxford: Currey, 1997. Print.

Ranger, Terence. "History Has Its Ceiling: The Pressures of the Past in *The Stone Virgins.* Muponde and Taruvinga 203–16.

———. *Revolt in Southern Rhodesia, 1896–97.* London: Heinemann, 1967. Print.

Sanders, Mark. *Complicities: The Intellectual and Apartheid.* Durham: Duke UP, 2002. Print.

Soyinka, Wole. *The Burden of Memory, the Muse of Forgiveness.* New York: Oxford UP, 1999. Print.

Tadjo, Véronique. *The Shadow of Imana.* Trans. Véronique Wakerley. Portsmouth: Heinemann, 2002. Print.

Thomas, Dominic. *Nation-Building, Propaganda, and Literature in Francophone Africa.* Bloomington: Indiana UP, 2002. Print.

Vansina, Jan. "Lessons of Forty Years of African History." *International Journal of African Historical Studies* 25.2 (1992): 391–98. Print.

———. *Living with Africa*. Madison: U of Wisconsin P, 1994. Print.

———. "Reflections on African History: Interview with Jan Vansina." By Ann McDougal. *Newsletter of the Canadian Association of African Studies* Fall 1993: 4–11. Print.

Vera, Yvonne. *Butterfly Burning*. New York: Farrar, 1998. Print.

———. Interview by Jane Bryce. Muponde and Taruvinga 217–26.

———. *Nehanda*. Harare: Baobab, 1993. Print.

Wicomb, Zoe. *David's Story*. New York: Feminist, 2001. Print.

Zanganeh, Lila Azam. "Out of Africa." *New York Times Book Review* 12 June 2005: 39. Print.

Tejumola Olaniyan

Political Critique and Resistance in African Fiction

This popular anecdote, as far as I can remember it, began life in the 1980s. At a sumptuous postspeech reception for a leading African novelist in one of America's major cities, a leading European American writer approached him and asked in all joviality and earnestness, "Why do you people talk so much about politics in your works?" Without skipping a beat and with an equally civilized mixture of friendliness and gravity, the African writer responded, "Why don't you people talk so much about politics in your works?" Exaggerated good-natured cheer by those around quickly doused the palpable tension.

Each time I hear the tale, I lament its missed opportunity for mutual education and fantasize about having both writers to a sumptuous dinner and then a serious postdinner conversation to more robustly address the subject. The two writers are provocative and thoughtful in the questions they asked, but they are simultaneously right and wrong in their manner of posing the questions and in the implications of the questions themselves. They are right to agree, even if only implicitly, on the presence of "so much politics" in African literature. They are wrong, however, to assume that, on the one hand, it is African writers only who write "so much politics" and that, on the other hand, American writers "don't talk so much about politics." African or American, there is no such thing as an apolitical novel or, more generally, apolitical literature.

Let me clarify the preceding statement. A novel presents us with ideas, characters, relationships, things, and worlds. Through carefully wrought language and alluring imagery, fiction makes us readers form opinions, ideas, and attitudes. To the extent that we are thus influenced one way or the other about something, the novel is being political in the only way it can be. A novel about the place of roses among flowers is surely not political in the conventional sense of dramatizing relations between governors and governed, but it is certainly political in the sense of subtly selling to us some opinion or attitude about roses or confirming and challenging the idea about them that we already have. Our actions are affected by our attitudes in deep and complex ways. It may turn out that the vocal city council member who persuaded her colleagues to vote our tax dollars to replace the beds of roses in the city park with chrysanthemums or vice versa had read decades ago some gripping novel about roses whose title she could not even remember.[1] What could be more political?

If then all fiction or literature is political one way or the other, how come so much is made of the political character of African fiction? There are two reasons. First, politics in African fiction is overwhelmingly of a specific, easily recognizable kind. Second, it is pervasive and very obvious in the texts. Let us think of politics at the macro and micro levels. The macro level is the realm of ruler-ruled relations and matters of the state, including the mobilization, distribution, and management of resources and ideas; it involves social relations between and among the state, groups, and individuals. The micro level is the realm of all formal and informal everyday transactions between and among individuals, groups, and nonstate institutions; it involves the production and circulation of ideas and attitudes in those domains and their subtle or unsubtle effects in forming and reforming the consciousness of individuals and orientation of institutions. Politics in African fiction is more perceptibly of the first kind.

Politics in African fiction is pervasively and obviously macropolitics, but it has a special orientation: a wide-ranging critical, oppositional attitude against powerful individuals and the formal institutions of state they run and the ideas and attitudes that sustain them. There is also opposition to all those individuals, informal institutions, and ideas and attitudes that are perceived as closely or remotely linked to the maintenance of the social condition under scrutiny. The composite catalyst of this orientation is the novelists' dissatisfaction with the condition of their societies: the social inequality, the widespread poverty and yawning gap between rich and poor, the nonexistent or collapsed infrastructure, the nepotism and corruption of those in power, and the deleterious effects of all these ills on human and social development. Resistance in African fiction is against the individuals and institutions that benefit from and perpetuate misery. There is no need to give examples; you could pick any novel by an African writer in the library or at the bookstore. Here are some examples nonetheless, in case you are preparing a course on the subject. They are randomly chosen: *Things Fall Apart* and *A Man of the People*, by Chinua Achebe; *So Long a Letter*, by Mariama Bâ; *Devil on the Cross* and *Petals of Blood*, by Ngũgĩ wa Thiong'o; *July's People*, by Nadine Gordimer; *God Dies by the Nile*, by Nawal El Saadawi; *Season of Anomy*, by Wole Soyinka; *Sweet and Sour Milk*, by Nuruddin Farah; *Bound to Violence*, by Yambo Ouologuem; *Autumn Quail*, by Naguib Mahfouz; *The Old Man and the Medal*, by Ferdinand Oyono; *The Beautyful Ones Are Not Yet Born*, by Ayi Kwei Armah; and *Fantasia: An Algerian Cavalcade*, by Assia Djebar.

The question we are immediately faced with now is, What explains this dominance of political critique and resistance in African fiction? I advance two theories. The first is what I call the colonial origin theory. It is common knowledge that modern African fiction, and indeed all modern African literature, is only as old as colonial rule in Africa. African fiction did not begin to flower until the emergence of resistance to European colonialism on the continent and the expansion of Western education among the colonized (Gikandi). Indeed, African literature gave decisive voice to African anticolonial nationalism. As African politicians battled the colonial regimes on the war front or constitution-drafting conferences in the political realm, African writers earnestly contributed to the decolonization effort in the realm of imaginative literature by rehabilitating the image of Africa smeared by decades of colonial racism and by satirizing the colonizers. Writers such as Mongo Beti, Camara Laye, Cheikh Hamidou Kane, William Conton, to add a few more names to those already mentioned, all gave voice to anticolonial dissent. In a few instances, the adroit politician and the accomplished writer found habitation in the same person. Léopold Sédar Senghor led Senegal to independence and was its president for twenty years, from 1960 to 1980; he was also one of the continent's finest poets.

The most quoted and perhaps most eloquent articulation of an anticolonial function for African literature is Achebe's, though it came well after independence. His goal, Achebe wrote in 1965, was to "help my society regain belief in itself and put away the complexes of the years of denigration and self-abasement" ("Novelist" 3). Whether the target in the anticolonial novel is a colonizer or a native, the attack implies a restorative act against a colonially induced inferiority complex. "The writer cannot expect to be excused from the task of re-education and regeneration that must be done. In fact he should march right in front," Achebe argued (4). Linking his goal directly with his novels such as *Things Fall Apart* and *Arrow of God* without naming the texts, he wrote:

> I would be quite satisfied if my novels (especially the ones I set in the past) did no more than teach my readers that their past—with all its imperfections—was not one long night of savagery from which the first Europeans acting on God's behalf delivered them. (4)

The argument of the colonial origin theory is that, given such a foundation of the African novel as a polemical counterdiscourse against European colonialism, it is to be expected that political critique and resistance would be and remain an essential part of its fabric even after independence was won. The victorious nationalist politicians expected the writers to sheath their swords after colonial rule—after all, "We have won!" But that did not happen, and many of the writerly weapons used against the colonizers proved quite valuable later on against the new black leaders who sat on the gilded thrones of the former white colonizers. Achebe's consummate satiric barbs at the colonial district officer in *Things Fall Apart* or Captain Winterbottom in *Arrow of God* became even more deadly, gleaming deconstructive spikes against the postcolonial politicians in *A Man of the People*.

The fought-for decolonization was only half successful: the colonizers were driven away, so there was deracialization of the state and bureaucracy, but there was no democratization, the needed other half. The nonresponsiveness of the government, its tyranny and lack of accountability, and the inadequate or absent infrastructure all remained or worsened after independence. Inevitably, the novelists could not but notice that eras may have changed, but the problems they fought against under colonial rule only metamorphosed or got more entrenched in the new postcolonial dispensation. The logic of the novel's origin in the flaming kiln of anticolonial struggles became normalized in the scholarly unconscious as the source of the novel's political character.

No theorist more forcefully helped establish that normalization, albeit indirectly, than the Martinican-born preeminent voice of the African anticolonial revolution, Frantz Fanon. In *The Wretched of the Earth* (1961), his widely read account of African decolonization, Fanon proposed three phases in the evolution of consciousness of the colonized intellectual elite about the decolonization struggle. In the first phase, the Westernized elite is preoccupied with demonstrating its assimilation of the culture of the colonizing power. The goal is to prove the civilizational capabilities of the educated native, as if evidence of the native's mastery of European culture would shame colonialism into folding up. But that evidence would not and did not make colonialism blink, so this phase soon runs its course and leads to frustrations of the native elite. A small bolt of lightning of self-consciousness hits the native elite and now begins to disturb its Europhilia. This second phase is described by Fanon as "just-before-the-battle" (222). The elite has not yet thrown its lot in with the other colonized masses and given voice and vision to their yearning, but it now remembers the native culture and history and begins to glorify them "in the light of a borrowed aestheticism and of a conception of the world which was discovered under other skies." Finally, in the third phase, "the fighting phase" (222), the native intellectual has made a close identification with the interests of the masses and becomes a catalyst of the people's revolutionary self-rebirth. The literature the elite produces in this phase is "a fighting literature, a revolutionary, and a national literature" (223)—in short, an anticolonial, anti-imperial, and antinationalist-bourgeoisie literature. In this elaborate scenario, political criticism and resistance in African literature originate and are inseparable from the colonial context of the birth of the literature.

The second contending explanation of the dominance of political criticism and resistance in African fiction is what I call the indigenous origin theory. The colonial origin theory, from the point of view of this second theory, is an overly truncated accounting of the phenomenon. In indigenous—the word often connotes "precolonial"—African societies, the theory argues, artists have always been critical monitors of the pulse of their societies. As a matter of accepted custom, they were never completely at ease with the throne, even when sponsored by the court. Therefore the political orientation of African literature, instead of being produced by the exigencies of the colonial context in which that literature emerged, was merely a new manifestation of an age-old function of the artist in African society. This theory subsumes the colonial origin theory by giving it the deep historical anchor it apparently lacks.

The indigenous origin theory also reclaims the autochthonous agency of African imaginative political art, an agency believed to be shortchanged by the location of the origin of political African fiction on the grounds that it was written rather than oral—in colonial rule (i.e., the colonizing Europeans were its catalyst). The most powerful, confident, and unassuming expression of this position is by Wole Soyinka in his important early essay "The Writer in a Modern African State" (1967). Soyinka writes, "The artist has always functioned in African society as the record of the mores and experience of his society *and* as the voice of vision in his own time. It is time for him to respond to this essence of himself" (20). African artists have always been the voices of vision in their times. The article was not on African political art; it was a searing critique of the European reception of early African literature and the racialist African literary-cultural nationalism known as negritude and its cult of self-worship. The nearly casual, nonargumentative way Soyinka made the statement at the time gave it an aura of unchallengeable truth. It became an ideological fact of the African artistic past: you knew it now if you had not known it before. One of the most important subsequent popularizers of the theory is the Ghanaian novelist Ayi Kwei Armah, in essays such as "Masks and Marx" and novels such as *Two Thousand Seasons.*

Without question, the colonial origin theory is the more frequently invoked today. The reason is the overwhelming evidence from the body of African fiction itself: the objects of attack of this fiction are the continuum of the colonial-postcolonial state, its bureaucracy, state apparatuses both ideological and coercive, and their managers and supporters, whether local or international. The time frame of most African novels is from the period of European colonial rule to the present. This temporal circumscription is simply a manifestation in fictional practice of a more widespread belief: that the greatest and continuing damage to African economies and social institutions has its origin squarely in colonialism and how it sutured Africa to the Euro-American world.

The classic formulation of this view was made by the radical historian and political economist Walter Rodney, in his book *How Europe Underdeveloped Africa*:

> The decisiveness of the short period of colonialism and its negative consequences for Africa spring mainly from the fact that Africa lost power. Power is the ultimate determinant in human society, being basic to the relations within any group and between groups. It implies the ability to defend one's interests and if necessary to impose one's will by any means available. . . . During the centuries of pre-colonial trade, some control over social, political, and economic life was retained in Africa, in spite of the disadvantageous commerce with Europeans. That

> little control over internal matters disappeared under colonialism. . . . Africans ceased to set indigenous cultural goals and standards, and lost full command of training young members of the society. Those were undoubtedly major steps back. (224)

Rodney's argument is that not even the centuries of the capture of and trade in Africans as slaves were as damaging as the eight or so decades of colonialism in most parts of the continent, because the slave trade, unjust and unequal as it was, was still a trade, in which African agency, albeit severely circumscribed, was exercised. Colonialism, on the other hand, was a fundamental crippling of indigenous initiative and agency, a condition that destroys society more deeply and makes meaningful recovery—social and psychological—an uncertain process at best.

It is for this reason that the colonial origin theory is so dominant, even in the rare instances when passing gestures are made to a much deeper indigenous provenance of politics in African art. Ngũgĩ wa Thiong'o, the distinguished Kenyan novelist, is our best example here. In novels such as *Petals of Blood* and *Devil on the Cross*; plays such as *I Will Marry When I Want* and *Mother, Sing for Me* (see Bjorkman); and books of essays such as *Writers in Politics*, *Barrel of a Pen*, and *Penpoints, Gunpoints, and Dreams*, to name a few, he has been a most eloquent scourge of the postcolonial African state, especially Kenya, and its misrule. In most of his works, the interrogative emphasis has been on the colonial period to the present. In *Penpoints*, subtitled *Towards a Critical Theory of the Arts and the State in Africa*, he ranges as far back as ancient Greece in his investigations, but merely to borrow metaphors to illuminate the postcolonial present. "I use Plato's allegory," he explains at the beginning, "to examine the relationship between intellectuals, the state, and the control of psychic space in a post-colonial society" (3). He does not forget to invoke the indigenous origin theory, but when he invokes it, it is offered as an aside that needs no argument: "Socrates, for instance, would have been very much at home in many of the pre-colonial African societies. In fact, he would not have been executed for asking awkward questions since this is what was often expected of artists and Athamaki (Philosopher-leaders)" (4), a claim that returns us to Soyinka's formulation of three decades before.

Next, we need to explore exactly how political criticism and resistance are manifested in the texts of African fiction. Writers are writers and not politicians. Writers and politicians both use words as instruments of their work but very differently, otherwise there would be no need to make any distinction between them. In a literary work writers may be closely engaged with the social and political realities of their society, but they cannot express that engagement as politicians would. Politicians assume a transparency of language in dealing with those realities and their constituency, while the operative language of writers in relation to society is of necessity veiled, ambiguous, elliptical—that is why their work is called fiction, a thing unreal, invented. Fictional language comments on the real world not directly but obliquely.

African writers who have made it their main task to write about immediate social and political relations must be masters of literary indirection to make their work aesthetically satisfying. Allegory, that figurative mode of representation that gives the widest latitude for literary indirection while still being clearly anchored to a reality outside the fiction, is therefore a favored mode of textualization of politics and resistance. Derived from the Greek *allēgoria* ("speaking otherwise"), allegory is a story with at least a double meaning: one surface or primary, the other subterranean or secondary. The relation between or among the levels of the story's meanings could be close or distant but is rarely one of complete correspondence. Part of the readerly pleasure of allegory is precisely in figuring linkages and associations among the several possible meanings intimated by the story. There are different kinds of allegory, depending on subject matter. The type common in African fiction is the political allegory, in which a story is seen as a creative riff on a social and political arrangement outside the text.

There are a great many examples of such allegory, but I give four: Armah's *The Beautyful Ones Are Not Yet Born*, Soyinka's *Season of Anomy*, Ousmane Sembène's *Xala*, and Ngũgĩ's *Devil on the Cross*. It is the apparent preponderance of political allegories in African and indeed many non-European literary traditions that made the American Marxist literary critic Fredric Jameson argue:

> All third-world texts are necessarily . . . allegorical, and in a very specific way: they are to be read as what I will call *national allegories*, even when, or perhaps I should say, particularly when their forms develop out of predominantly western machineries of representation, such as the novel. (69)

The oddness of the literature's obviously political character to a Westerner, explains Jameson, is "its tendency to remind us of outmoded stages of our own first-world cultural development and to cause us to conclude that 'they are still writing novels like Dreiser or Sherwood Anderson'" (65). Though Jameson argued in a clearly and robustly dialectical manner that "these reactions to third-world texts are at one and at the same time perfectly natural, perfectly comprehensible, *and* terribly parochial" (66), he was nonetheless roundly condemned for his overly broad, colonial mode of generalizing.[2] But Jameson is right in describing the Western reactions as parochial, for they ignore the irreducible situatedness of literature and the audience's responses to it.

One of the texts that has worked well for me in the undergraduate classroom is Sembène's *Xala*, also discussed by Jameson in his essay. The text is portable, and its endless turns of ironic humor also draw the students in. It helps that there is a film version, which I show from time to time. *Xala* is a grace-to-grass story of El Hadji, a member of the African elite that took over from French businessmen and leaders in a francophone African country after independence. El Hadji is stricken with *xala* ("impotence," in Wolof) on the night of his wedding to his third wife, so he cannot consummate the union. His anxious and eventful search for a cure laces this satirical tale with uncommon hilarity. What the novel does is put the African bourgeoisie and the political state it manages under a microscope and pronounces both as diseased, impotent. It juxtaposes the mindless ostentation and consumerism of this class with its unproductivity. El Hadji cannot really afford a third wife, but one of the wedding gifts he buys for her is a car. He is not a producer, as true bourgeois in other climes are, but a mere distributor, and, to his great shame, his store soon runs out of supplies when he cannot pay up. The would-be provider for the new wife and, alas, for the nation has no wherewithal to perform. In configuring the political, economic, social, and moral effeteness of the African bourgeoisie as (hetero)sexual impotence, Sembène pronounces the African state impotent. This idea runs through other texts: *Devil on the Cross*, by Ngũgĩ, and *The Beggars' Strike*, by Aminata Sow Fall, who is Sembène's fellow Senegalese.

Here is the broader context of *Xala*. Instead of the paradisiacal modernity that nationalist independence from colonial rule promised in the 1960s, what emerged was a neocolonial era marked by unproductivity: visionless leadership, collapsed or absent infrastructure, scarcity of basic necessities for the population, and a shameful incapacity to tap the enormous natural resources of the nations. The joke by radical elites from the so-called Third World about leading petroleum producers—from Iraq to

Nigeria and Venezuela—that they cannot manufacture a nut or bolt of an oil rig is more than forty years old but still apt. The justified merciless excoriation of the African elite by Fanon is now classic. The African bourgeoisie, he wrote in *The Wretched of the Earth*, is characterized by "intellectual laziness," "spiritual penury" (149), "absence of all ambition," and a gross "incapacity" to "fulfill its historic role of the bourgeoisie" (153). "The dynamic, pioneer aspect, the characteristics of the inventor and of the discoverer of new worlds," which are found in any bourgeoisie worth that name, are "lamentably absent." It is an unoriginal class with a signal lack of initiative; therefore its "mission has nothing to do with transforming the nation"; it is "content with the role of the Western bourgeoisie's business agent" (153). El Hadji is the embodiment of an unproductive local business agent of the Western bourgeoisie. The much larger geohistorical background of Fanon's critique is, of course, Karl Marx's lyrical articulation in *The Communist Manifesto* of that distinctive character of the European bourgeoisie: its productivity. The bourgeoisie has "accomplished wonders far surpassing Egyptian pyramids, Roman aqueducts, and Gothic cathedrals . . . created more massive and more colossal productive forces than have all preceding generations together." In a justified grandiose rhetorical flourish, Marx asked, "[W]hat earlier century had even a presentiment that such productive forces slumber in the lap of social labour?" (Marx and Engels 83, 85).

The nonproductivity of postcolonial African nationalism—and of the organ of its rule, the state—has become, for many of the continent's writers, simultaneously a sociopolitical issue and an epistemology. Impotence is a critique as well as a way of understanding the origin and nature of the postcolonial state. It is evoked to signify failure at the levels both of practical politics and of the conceptual configuration of social institutions. Perhaps because of the wild resonance of *productivity* in popular culture, this concept flaunts a racy sensationalism even as it retains great conceptual illumination.

While politics and resistance can be seen in much of African fiction, not all the novels are obviously political or take the macro realm of society as their focus. *Nervous Conditions*, by the accomplished Zimbabwean novelist and filmmaker Tsitsi Dangarembga, is set in the late 1960s on the eve of the anticolonial war against the Rhodesian regime, but, surprisingly, this political situation is hardly referred to in the text. On the contrary, the novel focuses on the coming of age of Tambudzai, the first-person narrator, and her many relationships: with her poor parents in the village; with her much richer, educated middle-class uncle, who lives in a big, well-appointed mission house some miles away; with her sibling, Nhamo, whom she replaces at the uncle's house when Nhamo dies; and with her cousin, Nyasha, who in rebelling against her Anglophile upbringing is afflicted by anorexia.

To all appearances then, Dangarembga is concerned only with the micro realm of interpersonal relationships in this novel. Tambudzai lends credence to this reading when right at the beginning she announces that her story is about "my escape and Lucia's; about my mother's and Maiguru's entrapment; about Nyasha's rebellion—Nyasha, far-minded and isolated, my uncle's daughter, whose rebellion may not in the end have been successful" (1). The main obvious issues are poverty and the extended family. Indeed, a common view of African women's writings one often hears at conferences is that the women are generally silent about and uninterested in the macro realm of nationalism and political criticism and resistance, which seem to be the obsession of the men. Examples are given of such well-known texts as *The Joys of Motherhood*, by Buchi Emecheta, about the unfulfilled expectations of Nnu Ego, who thinks she must sacrifice herself to heed her culture's dictate of having many children, especially boys; and *So Long a Letter*, by Bâ, about the different responses of two friends to big disappointments from their husbands.

This view is only superficially true. Yes, *Nervous Conditions* is silent on the macropolitical anticolonial resistance afoot at the time of its setting, but the silence is merely apparent. Early in the story, we are given that archetypal image of colonial encroachment that scholars of African literature are so familiar with: the appearance of the colonial administration building nearby as the ultimate sign of the village's loss of autonomy. "[T]o enable the administration of our area," the narrator tells us with the embarrassing honesty that is characteristic of children, "the Government built its District Council Houses less than a mile away from the places where we washed" (3). Henceforth, that location, literally on the periphery of the native homesteads nearby, becomes the controlling center of the lives of the people. There can be no better image of a world turned upside down, and a topsy-turvy world is another common image in African anticolonial fiction. The image is offered as one eloquent, ironic justification for the anticolonial war rumbling outside the text, if we read closely.

The poverty of Tambudzai's family is so harrowing and total that one could be forgiven for thinking it genetic. Following this thought, one would then have to thank the almighty colonizers for coming and educating Babamukuru and thus showing that only submission to the colonizers and their religion and ways can improve the lot of the natives. Except that we have the old and hardworking grandmother as a contrary, subversive example. It is she who gives us a cogent archaeology of the family's contemporary poverty, showing it as historical and little more than enforced pauperization. She talks of "bountiful harvests" and "many fat herd of cattle" in times gone by, before the colonizers, quaintly but understandably named wizards in her tale, came:

> Wizards well-versed in treachery and black magic came from the south and forced the people from the land. On donkey, on foot, on horse, on ox-cart, the people looked for a place to live. But the wizards were avaricious and grasping; there was less and less land for the people. (18)

The reference to forceful and racist colonial land acquisition is unobtrusive here, although that acquisition is the colonial-era issue that haunts Zimbabwe the most today. This passage is by no means the only reference to colonial racism in the text, though all the references are subtle. But subtlety hardly means silence or nonsignificance. Then there are many elliptical, furtive references to the anticolonial struggle. Tambudzai's ironic comment on why her conservative uncle loves her more than his own overly questioning daughter is the most telling: "I was not concerned that freedom fighters were referred to as terrorists, did not demand proof of God's existence nor did I think that the missionaries, along with all other Whites in Rhodesia, ought to have stayed at home" (155).

The character of the worthy patriarch, Babamukuru, is the finest example in the text of how the micro realm of personal relations is intricately interwoven with the macro sphere of national politics. He demonstrates the liberatory as well as the contradictory nature of anticolonial cultural nationalism. Not linked in any way with anticolonial rebellion and nationalism, he appears to us as no more than a compliant mission-educated native with a European college diploma, a big "white" house (63), a respectable family, and a secure position in the colonial mission service. He is a god and a leader to and deliverer of his people, to whom he condescends. But before we dismiss this figure as lost to the colonial system, he lets us know that he is also a committed cultural nationalist who does "not approve of European habits" (106). He is anxious that his daughter is overly Westernized and culturally deracinated and seeks to reverse that. He also keeps his wife, the equally educated Maiguru, firmly in her place as a woman. But what the nationalist often defends fiercely as "our" culture are either little more than superficial trappings of native tradition (e.g., proper greetings and respect for elders) or parts of its discriminatory ethos—the subordination of women, the sacralization of masculinity. For this reason Babamukuru is the target throughout the text of critical barbs by Nyasha or placid but sharply ironic observations by Tambudzai.

There is certainly a place in the coming postcolonial society for leaders like Babamukuru, but there is no reason to believe that even the anticolonial revolutionaries outside the text, who are about to start the armed struggle for independence, do not share his patriarchal views if obviously not his silence about or tacit support for the colonial status quo. So what sort of leaders are they? The shallowness of Babamukuru shows clearly when the fierce cultural nationalist reveals his colonial mentality by advising Jeremiah, his brother and Tambudzai's father, that a white Christian wedding is the solution to the poverty-induced crisis of Jeremiah's nineteen-year-old marriage (146–47). Babamukuru, whose family made much of his education and high status, is for them, in the colonial order, the all-knowing who resolves all. The text makes clear that he cannot fulfill those expectations.

This reading returns us to the more literal figuration of impotence in *Xala*. The obvious interpretation of the writers' use of impotence is as a social and political criticism of the state. But I suggest that impotence also points to a powerful feminist critique. After all, the African state, though not unique in this respect, is male-dominated and masculinist, and the group of people who suffer the most from its impotent, unproductive nature are the women. Mainini, Tambudzai's mother, is the most pitiful character, and all her problems are caused by the family's unrelieved poverty. But, as part of the novel's refusal to follow Babamukuru and condescend to the poor and illiterate, some of the most perceptive social analyses in the book come from Mainini. "This business of womanhood is a heavy burden," she proclaims. "And these days it is worse, with the poverty of blackness on one side and the weight of womanhood on the other. Aiwa!" (16). On the Anglophilia of the Western-educated people she sees around her, including her children, she makes what is perhaps the most quoted statement in the book, highly humorous if not for the unnerving tragic truth at its core: "'It's the Englishness,' she said. 'It'll kill all of them if they aren't careful,' and she snorted. . . . She went on like this for quite a while, going on about how you couldn't expect the ancestors to stomach so much Englishness" (202–03). It would have helped all of anglophone Africa to know precisely how much Englishness the ancestors could safely stomach!

African novelists, like all novelists, use myriad aesthetic devices and strategies to achieve their aims; they are limited only by their skill and imagination. But the mantle of political criticism and resistance that African writers willingly assumed appears to have imposed on them one particular device that could be said to be singularly pervasive in their work, whether political allegory or not: irony. Why irony, and why has it served the writers' agenda so well? Whether verbal or situational, irony is that oblique mode of expression or circumstance in which there is the perception of a clear disjunction or incongruity between words and their meanings, between appearance and reality, and between actions and their results. It presumes a desired and desirable fact or reality as yet unreached and being searched for in the wrong manner. It has conceptual and functional relations with words that serve as vehicles of attack or displeasure: *mock*, *scorn*, *jeer*, and the like. The ironist is concerned and sees much. The ironist stands on Mount Olympus and shows, with an unmistakable edge, discrepancies between our words and their meanings, between actions and results. J. A. Cuddon describes irony as "often the witting and unwitting instrument of truth. It chides, purifies, refines, deflates, scorns and 'sends up.' It is not surprising, therefore, that irony is the most precious and efficient weapon of the satirist" (430–31).

For writers committed to using their art for political criticism and resistance, as I have demonstrated African writers are, the allure of irony is irresistible. After all, what greater irony of modern African history can we have than the discrepancy between the expectations and reality of independence from colonization? Half a century after the first wave of independence, the irony remains raw and sore. Not only did the expectations of good governance, egalitarianism, and rapid modernization, in whose names the anticolonial struggles were fought, fail to materialize, conditions actually got worse in most countries and for decades after independence. The use of irony in African fiction is not just or so much at the level of device, in which you comb through pages for textual examples; it is at the systemic level, a ruling tone or temper. As historically conscious and sociologically attuned writers, Africans would have invented irony if it did not exist.

It is important to consider critically what the implications are of an overwhelming investment in political criticism and resistance by African writers. The historical and sociological justifications for such an investment are unimpeachable, but it is not impossible to imagine some young aspiring writers without that inclination being hushed—or, should we say, crushed—into quietude by the weighty, hallowed aura of the fighting tradition. The unabated emergence of new writers—even if the distribution is uneven among African countries and even if many of the new writers live outside the continent—who do not abandon the sanctified thematic of political critique but joyously and ingeniously bring fresh innovations to it makes the speculation of a crippling agenda no more than merely academic. I mean writers like Calixthe Beyala, Yvonne Vera, Chris Abani, Okey Ndibe, Helon Habila, Phaswane Mpe, Veronique Tadjo, Sefi Atta, Akin Adesokan, Chimamanda Adichie, K. Sello Duiker, Makuchi, and Uzodinma Iweala. In any case, that the political tradition still thrives is a reflection more of hardly improving sociological conditions than of the unconditioned choice of writers.

There is another matter that we may not be able to settle so easily. Over the years, the criticism of African literature has mostly mirrored the literature's preoccupation with political criticism and resistance. For a while, that mirroring, by its dominance, hampered investigations of issues in the text that were not considered political at all or not related to the macropolitical domain of the nation. It is partly for this reason that African literary criticism today is not richer, in both quantity and quality, in the exploration of issues about women, sexuality, age, disability, and environment—to name just a few of the many exciting strands that may be found in the literary texts. The striking irony is that even those literary texts that loudly announce their political pedigree also contain material for critical insights into these other issues worthy of study. Literary texts are by their nature more multivocal than criticism, and the lesson here is that for criticism to mirror too closely the apparent agenda of literary texts is to risk quick obsolescence.

Notes

1. Think of advertisements and how they work. Few of us confess to being influenced by them, and truly no one sees an ad on television and immediately runs to the store to purchase the advertised product. But if advertisements do not work, would manufacturers continue to waste their money on them?

2. For a brief, thoughtful introduction to the debate and a defense of Jameson along the lines I have hinted, see Lazarus.

Works Cited

Achebe, Chinua. *Arrow of God*. 1964. London: Heinemann, 1986. Print.
———. *A Man of the People*. London: Heinemann, 1966. Print.

———. "The Novelist as Teacher." 1965. *African Writers on African Writing.* Ed. G. D. Killam. London: Heinemann, 1973. 1–4. Print.

———. *Things Fall Apart.* London: Heinemann, 1985. Print.

Armah, Ayi Kwei. *The Beautyful Ones Are Not Yet Born.* London: Heinemann, 1969. Print.

———. "Masks and Marx." *Présence africaine* 131 (1985): 35–65. Print.

———. *Two Thousand Seasons.* London: Heinemann, 1979. Print.

Bâ, Mariama. *So Long a Letter.* Trans. M. Bode-Thomas. London: Heinemann, 1981. Print.

Bjorkman, Ingrid. *Mother, Sing for Me: People's Theatre in Kenya.* London: Zed, 1989. Print.

Cuddon, J. A. *The Penguin Dictionary of Literary Terms and Literary Theory.* Ed. C. E. Preston. London: Penguin, 1999. Print.

Dangarembga, Tsitsi. *Nervous Conditions.* Seattle: Seal, 1989. Print.

Djebar, Assia. *Fantasia: An Algerian Cavalcade.* Trans. D. S. Blair. Portsmouth: Heinemann, 1993. Print.

Emecheta, Buchi. *The Joys of Motherhood.* New York: Braziller, 1979. Print.

Fall, Aminata Sow. *The Beggars' Strike.* Harlow: Longman, 1981. Print.

Fanon, Frantz. *The Wretched of the Earth.* Trans. Constance Farrington. New York: Grove, 1963. Print.

Farah, Nuruddin. *Sweet and Sour Milk.* London: Heinemann, 1979. Print.

Gikandi, Simon. "African Literature and the Colonial Factor." *African and Caribbean Literature.* Vol. 1. Ed. F. Abiola Irele and Gikandi. Cambridge: Cambridge UP, 2004. 379–97. Print.

Gordimer, Nadine. *July's People.* New York: Viking, 1981. Print.

Jameson, Fredric. "Third World Literature in the Era of Multinational Capitalism." *Social Text* 15 (1986): 65–88. Print.

Lazarus, Neil. "Fredric Jameson and 'Third World Literature': A Qualified Defense." *Fredric Jameson: A Critical Reader.* Ed. Douglas Kellner and Sean Homer. New York: Palgrave-Macmillan, 2004. 42–61. Print.

Mahfouz, Naguib. *Autumn Quail.* Trans. Roger Allen. Ed. John Rodenbeck. Cairo: Amer. U in Cairo P, 1985. Print.

Marx, Karl, and Friedrich Engels. *The Communist Manifesto.* 1848. Trans. S. Moore. London: Penguin, 1985. Print.

Ngũgĩ wa Thiong'o. *Barrel of a Pen: Resistance to Repression in Neocolonial Kenya.* Trenton: Africa World, 1983. Print.

———. *Devil on the Cross.* London: Heinemann, 1981. Print.

———. *I Will Marry When I Want.* London: Heinemann, 1982. Print.

———. "Mother, Sing for Me." Ts.

———. *Penpoints, Gunpoints, and Dreams: Towards a Critical Theory of the Arts and the State in Africa.* Oxford: Clarendon, 1998. Print.

———. *Petals of Blood.* London: Heinemann, 1977. Print.

———. *Writers in Politics.* London: Heinemann, 1981. Print.

Ouologuem, Yambo. *Bound to Violence.* Trans. Ralph Manheim. London: Heinemann, 1968. Print.

Oyono, Ferdinand. *The Old Man and the Medal.* Trans. John Reed. London: Heinemann, 1967. Print.

Rodney, Walter. *How Europe Underdeveloped Africa*. 1972. Rev. ed. Washington: Howard UP, 1981. Print.
Saadawi, Nawal El. *God Dies by the Nile*. Trans. Sherif Hetata. London: Zed, 1985. Print.
Sembène, Ousmane. *Xala*. Trans. Clive Wake. Chicago: Hill, 1976. Print.
———, dir. *Xala*. Films Domireew, 1975. Film.
Soyinka, Wole. *Season of Anomy*. Surrey: Nelson, 1980. Print.
———. "The Writer in a Modern African State." 1967. *Art, Dialogue and Outrage: Essays on Literature and Culture*. Ibadan: New Horn, 1988. 15–20. Print.

Odile Cazenave

Women Writers and Gender in the Sub-Saharan Novel

In the last thirty years, African women writers have increasingly gone from a marginal position to center stage on the literary scene. Today they have managed to open a prominent space for discussion both in francophone and anglopone African literature. Several significant literary awards contributed to their recognition during these years: Mariama Bâ was awarded a Japanese literary award in 1981 for *Une si longue lettre* (1979; *So Long a Letter*), the Zimbabwean Tsitsi Dangarembga was awarded the Commonwealth Writers' Prize in 1989 for *Nervous Conditions* (1988), the South African Nadine Gordimer won the Nobel Prize in 1991 and the Booker prize in 1974, and the Algerian Assia Djebar received the prestigious Friedenspreis des Deutschen Buchhandels in 2000 and was elected to the Académie Française in June 2005. The media-covered success in the 1990s of writers such as the Cameroonian Calixthe Beyala and, more recently, of the Senegalese Fatou Diome, the South African Zoe Wicomb, the Ghanaian Amma Darko, and the Nigerian Chimamanda Ngozi Adichie has contributed to the increased visibility of women authors. Today, their undeniable presence on the literary scene raises the question of what happens when women and gender become a central parameter in African fiction, of how that presence has affected African literature.

This crucial question is not a new one. It has been raised, approached, visited, and revisited from different angles over the last twenty years, but no satisfying or definitive answer has resulted. Each approach to or way of framing the question is indicative of a new step or phase in the delimitation of the field of African literature.

More than twenty years ago, the 1987 African Literature Association at Cornell University organized a roundtable entitled "Male versus Female Narrative Theory." Its main objective was to identify the specific traits of sub-Saharan African women's writing:

> Critics argued that [African women's writing] is neither best defined by theme (e.g., polygamy, ritual sexual mutilations, infertility) nor by narrative structures such as autobiography or the epistolary form. Also rejected were aspects of the immediacy of communication—which may or may not be related to the epistolary or the autobiographical mode—and elements of the oral tradition, although these emerged as less circumscribed and more promising for analytical speculation. Only the question of the "sexualization of space"—or the different "spaces" inhabited by women and determined by culture—received serious consideration as a trait specific to African women's literature. . . . A healthy skepticism resulted from this discussion, with participants pointing out the limitations of theoretical approaches, and even questioning the necessity of defining a specificity of feminine African writing. (Makward and Cazenave 194)

Since then, the subject of women's writing has been addressed from many viewpoints. In this essay I revisit a number of them and reflect on the following points: (1) the importance and impact of gender as an analytic tool in our understanding of fiction, mainly of the novel, in sub-Saharan Africa; (2) the emergence of textual strategies and forms used more specifically by women writers—for instance, the epistolary novel; (3) the need to consider the relevance of Western feminist theories in the reading of African works—for instance, the influence of French feminists on African women writers' production; and, finally, (4) the implications of these points on our teaching African literature—that is, on how we design syllabi that acknowledge women writers' central presence in African literature today.

Gender as an Analytic Tool to Approach the African Novel

Until the early 1980s, sub-Saharan African women writers, especially francophones, were still largely relegated to the margins of the literary landscape.[1] Women were present mainly as characters, in books by men (as in Cyprian Ekwensi's *Jagua Nana* [1961], Ousmane Sembène's *Les bouts de bois de Dieu* [1962; *God's Bits of Wood*], Ahmadou Kourouma's *Les soleils des indépendances* [1968; *The Suns of Independence*], Mongo Beti's *Perpetue et l'habitude du malheur* [1973; *Perpetua and the Habit of Unhappiness*]). If the anglophone writers Flora Nwapa, Ama Ata Aidoo, Grace Ogot, and Buchi Emecheta paved the way as pioneers, the francophones were barely a handful until the end of the 1970s. The Cameroonians Thérèse Kuoh-Moukoury and Werewere Liking; the Malian Aoua Keita; and the Senegalese Aminata Sow Fall, Nafissatou Diallo, and Mariama Bâ constituted this core of women starting to write from within, "destroying the emptiness of silence," as Irène d'Almeida put it in the subtitle of her book. The 1980s brought a tremendous change in that regard.

African women's writing gradually moved from testimonial novels and novels of self-revelation to more overtly critical works.[2] The writers, in their depictions of the family and community, through strategies of systematic provocation (e.g., the use of marginal characters or the exploration of cultural phenomena that until recently were either taboo or dismissed as unimportant) and through an increasingly complex mode of representation, probed the hidden mechanisms that explain the increasing instability of modern Africa. Yet, whether writing on the African continent or from abroad, they went beyond a pessimistic, denunciatory stance. Instead, they searched for alternatives to a stagnant postcolonial Africa. Ultimately, the visionary quality of their writing has enabled them to break away from canonical masculine authority and to be recognized for their artistic contribution to literature.

Furthermore, the discrepancy of production between the anglophones and the francophones, which appears so markedly evident in Brenda Berrian and Art Broek's *Bibliography of African Women Writers and Journalists* (1985), no longer holds today. Since the late 1980s, francophone women's writing has exploded in terms of both quantity and visibility. This change called for a new critical assessment of women authors' writing as well as for the retooling of the critical apparatus. Gradually, critics started to acknowledge gender as a factor in the analysis of African literature.

In 1986, in their groundbreaking collection of essays *Ngambika*, Carole Boyce Davies and Anne Adams Graves pointed out a number of facts and features about African women's writing and about the reception of their work. Specifically, in her "Introduction to Feminist Consciousness and African Literary Criticism," Boyce Davies attempted to define or clarify a number of concepts, notably African feminism. The departing point of her analysis was that, put together, these two terms were and are almost an oxymoron, in the sense that many African women writers, from the early 1980s on, have rejected or at least resisted the designation *feminist* because of the highly Western connotations of the word.[3] Boyce Davies and Graves aimed at redefining feminism in a more specifically African context; beyond that, they set out guiding principles for a feminist criticism of African literature. Likewise, Filomena Steady reasserted the need for a theory of African feminism. To remedy the ambiguities of the term *feminism*, several attempts were made by women from Africa and the diaspora to conceptualize objectives that were closer to their needs and struggles. In particular, African American and Caribbean women writers and critics pushed for a womanist approach in lieu of feminism. In either case, the objective was to demonstrate the viability of a feminist criticism of African literature and its diaspora and the possibility for this criticism to exist without having to operate within the norms of what could be identified as traditional masculine Western literary criticism.[4]

Following the work of Boyce Davies and Graves, a number of critics contributed to mapping out the predicaments, characteristics, and challenges faced by African women writers. I review briefly some of these key contributions. In "Not Spinning on the Axis of Maleness" (1984) and "The Female Writer and Her Commitment" (1987), Molara Ogundipe-Leslie explores the interdependence between women's status and notions of race, gender, class, and family traditions, including those factors resulting from male behavior. In *Third World Women and the Politics of Feminism* (1991), Chandra Mohanty raises the question of a collective ground for resistance and finds commonalities in the themes and interests for feminist writing. Ten years later, in *Feminism without Borders: Decolonizing Theory, Practicing Solidarity* (2003), she reaffirms the necessity to think globally. Revisiting her "Under Western Eyes" (*Third World Women* 51–80), she tries both to rethink the staples of feminism and to argue for feminist solidarity through anticapitalist struggle. She also forces us to think of the bristling effects of the word *feminism* today and how it resonates with students.

With *Francophone African Women Writers* (1994), Irène d'Almeida focuses on francophone African women novelists in their appropriation of speech and of writing. Florence Stratton's *Contemporary African Literature and the Politics of Gender* (1994) considers gender as an analytic tool for African fiction. In her introduction, Stratton addresses the exclusionary practices of critics, mostly male, in ignoring gender and neglecting women's writings. To her, these practices resulted in the incompleteness of most criticism of African literature.

Stratton's work helped correct the neglect women authors had suffered and made us reassess the importance of gender in African literature. Kenneth Harrow's *Threshholds of Change in African Literature: The Emergence of a Tradition* (1994), through his analysis of Bessie Head's, Buchi Emecheta's, and Ama Ata Aidoo's narratives, was a genuine effort to put female writing on an equal footing with male writing. Following the path of both Harrow and Stratton, I brought forth the accomplishments of (francophone) African women novelists, how they renewed the genre to create a more political novel (see *Rebellious Women* 9). Since then, many critical works have revisited questions raised earlier about the importance of women in African literature today, about textual strategies and the tendency to associate women's writing with the epistolary, about the applicability of Western criticism to analyze African women's writing, and finally about gender and writing and the issue of essentializing.

The Epistolary Form

How the epistolary form has been considered by critics of African literature changed considerably in the last twenty years. In the early 1980s, the tendency was to associate it with women's writing (in combination with the choice of the autobiographical form) and to regard the genre simply as an initial step toward a more refined mastery of writing. The epistolary form in other words had no aesthetic quality; its sole purpose was to establish immediate contact with readers.

Three phases can be identified in the response to this kind of criticism. First, critics like Boyce Davies tried to understand why critics treated epistolary and autobiographical narratives differently, depending on the author's gender. She examines particular aspects of autobiography written by women as opposed to men. The crux of the matter is that men's and women's words are not considered the same: "whereas the man who speaks as 'representative of his people' . . . articulates both self and country, the woman's story is never seen as synonymous with the country's" ("Private Selves" 111).

Second is the response that analyzes these forms for their aesthetic quality. D'Almeida demonstrates how the choice of such forms has functioned not only as a mode of cognition but also as a "mode of recognition of the social and political constructs and ideologies in which not only the self, but the *gendered* self evolves." Through this "process of discovering/un-covering/recovering"(70), women authors have addressed the mechanisms of oppression that govern their status as women—as wives, mothers, and daughters. Inconspicuously but very effectively, the issue of a necessary interaction among oneself, one's family, and society was made very clear. The first semiautobiographical works allowed women writers to pass beyond the barrier of silence and the taboo against writing. Because their criticism of their society was indirect, they were able to forestall negative reactions from publishers and male critics. The epistolary novel further reinforced a feeling of immediacy, exchange, and intimacy, through a narrator with whom the reader could identify (Boyce Davies, "Private Selves").

Toward the end of the 1980s and throughout the 1990s, women writers moved away from the autobiographical and semiautobiographical to amplify and refine the epistolary form. Calixthe Beyala's *Le petit prince de Belleville* (1992; *Loukoum, the Little Prince of Belleville*) is particularly representative of that development. In what are usually called her Parisian novels, through the recurrent coupling of narrator and narratee, in a formal written exchange or more frequently as a conversation, a dialogue between two women, Beyala elaborated a complex system of antithetic and complementary female characters—for instance, in *Tu t'appelleras Tanga* (1987; *Your Name Shall Be Tanga*), *Assèze l'Africaine* (1994; "Assèze the African"), and *Les honneurs perdus* (1996; "Lost Honors"). Ken Bugul's *De l'autre côté du regard* (2003; "As Seen from the Other Side") and *Rue Félix Faure* (2005; "Félix Faure Street") make an abundant use of fragments of letters and of the narrator or narratee who finds a letter, diary, or manuscript, thereby creating echoes throughout the book. In their affinity for a plurality of voices and narrators as well as for placing the audience inside the narrative, women writers like Ken Bugul and Buchi Emecheta have moved from autobiographical writing and personal memory to fictional memory and biofiction.[5]

In the last fifteen years, African male writers too have increasingly returned to the epistolary form. From Ahmadou Kourouma (*Allah*) to Tierno Monénembo, from Henri Lopès to Alain Mabanckou, from J. M. Coetzee to Phaswane Mpe, they give the autobiographical and epistolary novel a renewed prominence, thus further contributing to the recognition of those genres' aesthetic qualities (see also Essomba). The epistolary combined with the autobiographical or semiautobiographical voice that emerged in the hands of a writer like Bâ can no longer be attributed to women writers alone.

Conversely, what was long considered the domain of male writers—politics and the national, or the use of a graphic, violent, vulgar, erotic, or pornographic language—can no longer be held as their prerogative. The Ghanaian Amma Darko explored in *Faceless* (2003) the postmodern fragmentation of language and images to depict, in a very vivid way, issues of utter family dislocation and urban violence. Writers like Beyala (*Sun*, *Your Name*, and *Honneurs*), Sandrine Bessora (*53 cm* and *Deux bébés*), and Fatou Diome (*Ventre* and *Ketala*) amply demonstrated creative ways of addressing political issues, especially with regard to immigration and displacement, through lenses colored in turn with humor, violence, and sexual imagery. Recasting postcolonial identities and writing between two worlds, to paraphrase Anne Donadey's book title *Recasting Postcolonialism: Women Writing between Worlds* (2001), they have been redefining the notions of home and family as well as the configurations of gender roles and gender in general.

This change in turn poses the question of specific textual forms and strategies in women's writing as well as the larger question of gendered writing.

Western Feminist Theories in the Reading of African Fiction

In the 1980s, African women writers and critics increasingly resisted the designation *feminist*, associating it with a discourse that felt quite remote from their preoccupations, interests, and objectives. Western feminist theoretical discourse, especially from French feminists, has therefore been unwelcome when it comes to the analysis of African women's writing. But recent works of criticism nevertheless attempt to address the issue of relevance and applicability of Western feminist theory to African literature.

In *Less than One and Double* (2003), Harrow demonstrates the possibility of using French feminist theory (Lacanian) to analyze African texts and films—for instance, works by Dangarembga and by Beyala—questioning the validity and limits of such research. I tried to highlight how his attempt goes beyond advocating the usefulness of a reading that applies Jacques Lacan or Julia Kristeva (Rev. of *Less*). In the process, he redefines certain critical parameters, especially with respect to the acts of enunciation and representation, the rapport of critic with text.

Interestingly, Beyala raises another issue, that of the influence of French feminists on her writing, notably Simone de Beauvoir. Beyala's essay *Lettre d'une Africaine à ses soeurs occidentales* (1995; "Letter of an African Woman to Her Sisters in the West") was received with ambivalence, especially on the part of African women, because of the portrayal she gave of Africa, of the African woman, and of Africans in general. The title itself is indicative of the author's choice of an intended Western audience and readership. Yet Beyala simultaneously positioned herself as a representative of her African sisters, as *the* African voice in France.[6] Her fictional writing has further cultivated her French readership, as increasingly her language and images call on French imagery and collective imagination (see Cazenave, "Calixthe Beyala's 'Parisian Novels'"). Nicki Hitchcott analyzes the ways in which Beyala cleverly manipulates and renegotiates stereotypical representations of both French and Africans to meet readers' expectations. Eventually, playing both on the erotic and the exotic, Beyala creates a performance of postcolonial identities for migrant characters. In her demonstration of Beyala's masquerade to challenge norms, including gender norms, Hitchcott makes an interesting use of Judith Butler's "Performative Acts and Gender Constitution" and points out that African criticism has much to gain from Butler's work.

In an almost reverse effort to move away from the critical apparatus in novel theory used to analyze African fiction, Donald Wehrs's *African Feminist Fiction and Indigenous Values* (2001) explores new ways of reading women's narratives in the context of indigenous values. The departing point of his analysis is that criticism of African feminist fiction generally conforms to Western literary theory and its main assumptions about feminism. Focusing on indigenous values, Wehrs refutes the assumption that African women writers generally reject indigenous values as a vehicle for patriarchal oppression. Ironic, though, is his choice of Emmanuel Levinas's and Paul Ricoeur's interpretations of ethics and morality to make his argument (see Cazenave, Rev. of *African Feminist Fiction*).

Harrow's and Wehr's approaches seem to go in opposite directions yet illustrate the critic's discomfort in having to face the dilemma of whether or not to use a theoretical apparatus that has been designed for and by the West. Another problem is that a number of non-Western critics, like Gayatri Spivak, Arundhathi Roy, and Edward Said, to mention three important names in postcolonial theory, have been trained in the

West. Abiola Irele discusses how relocation to the West has had long-term implications: for African literature, which was pushed into a back corner, and for the African critic. Our students are the first to ask how we can reconcile this paradox. How do we resolve our feelings of guilt when we apply a Western theoretical apparatus to a non-Western text?

As Harrow shows, we can start rethinking some of the existing terminology and critical parameters. For example, to speak simply of postcolonial literature today, when its production spans over fifty years, is no longer sufficient. For too long we have put in the same bag different generations of writers, different textual strategies, different perceptions of African literature (using the singular instead of the plural *literatures*), different issues of distribution and readerships. All need to be considered separately. To be writing when one is twenty at the time of independence, or twenty in the early 1980s, or twenty today makes a great difference. We need to introduce parameters that enable us to refine our understanding of African fiction. African women's writing can no longer be read simply against the grain of race, class, and gender. Other factors enter the picture—the age of the author and the location of writing, as examined by several critics: Boyce Davies in *Black Women, Writing, and Identity: Migrations of the Subject* (1994), Donadey, Cazenave, Hitchcott, and more recently Dominic Thomas in *Black France* (2006). This aspect brings me to my final point, that of an essentializing of writing.

Still an Essentializing of Writing?

This essay has discussed a number of points about how women's taking center stage in African literature has affected and shaped the field of criticism. Yet some things seem not to change. Despite francophone women writers' success and visibility, more space is still devoted in critical analyses to anglophone than to francophone writers. When there is a chapter on a francophone woman writer, it is most likely on Bâ and her first novel (Cazenave, "Vingt ans").[7] Sometimes the analysis will feature Aminata Sow Fall or Ken Bugul. But chances are it will be on Ken Bugul's first novel, *Le baobab fou* (1983; *The Abandoned Baobab*), athough she has written six more novels since then.[8] True, more recent essays may include discussion of Beyala or Véronique Tadjo, yet in general there is a vacuum of critical analysis about the newer voices, to the point that it creates a distorted view of the field.

The same imbalance is likely to be replicated in our classroom as we design our syllabi, especially for a course in translation, because translation is a main avenue of access to literature in a foreign language. An important issue in the field of francophone literature today (I am speaking here of sub-Saharan African literature, but the same can be said of other postcolonial francophone literatures) is the discrepancy between works produced in French and their publication in English.[9] So if we want to teach a course that reflects new developments in the field of African literature—that is, if we want to incorporate new African female voices—the francophones will be at a disadvantage. A writer whose work is unavailable in English is unlikely to be discussed in a critical analysis and unlikely to be taught in a class (in this case, unless it is a francophone literature class).

How do we reflect the visibility of African women writers in our syllabi? Does women's taking center stage in African literature mean that we should offer a new course on African women writers alone? Would cross-listing such a course with a women's studies or gender studies program be a plus or a minus? Does such a course give greater visibility to these works and writers, or does it reproduce a kind of ghettoization of them?[10] How do we respond when we receive an e-mail message like the following: "I am teaching an introductory course on African literature and can include only two women writers. Who would you suggest? Buchi Emecheta and Tsitsi Dangarembga? Mariama Bâ and Calixthe Beyala? What about Nadine Gordimer?"[11] Such a query may sound natural, given the structuring (or lack thereof) in the field.

The increasing visibility and success of women and gender in African literature in the last twenty years bring a number of short-term and long-term consequences both for criticism of African literature and for the curriculum. What was once only an introductory course has developed into a sequence of courses, raising issues of genre and canonicity. What do we teach, and at what level? On what basis do we select works and authors? Which women writers are selected and why? What explains the success of a writer like Beyala in American universities? These are questions we need to address when we design our syllabi. They are also symptomatic of the status and place of gender and women writers in sub-Saharan African literature.

A question that keeps recurring in the field of African literature is whether one can still think today in terms of gendered writing (women's writing). Conversely, we could ask how and why the question was posed in the early 1980s, in what context it made sense for women novelists breaking out of silence to an audience that encompassed society at large.

I would redirect the question and ask whether Bâ could have written then as she does today, twenty years later. Have women's conditions changed to such a degree that the need for a specifically female gaze collapsed on itself and is now obsolete? Or can it be that women writers are no longer focusing on the world of women?

African women writers now come to writing and publishing earlier, and the factors of age and location have been crucial in shaping their outlook on life. Furthermore, the reception of their narratives has evolved. The readership is no longer confined to women only, and the reductive equation of female writers = feminist writing = female readers no longer prevails. In other words, they have avoided the ghettoized situation of confinement to a readership divided along gender lines. African women writers, just like their male peers, have demonstrated in their writing the possibility of addressing pressing national and transnational issues, of bringing the political to the forefront of their narratives, of exploring and confronting history anew. Both women and men writers now pose questions about the becoming of Africa and its diaspora. They don't necessarily envision a promising future for African societies, as did the earlier generation of politically committed African writers. They don't provide answers, but they keep asking. In the process, they have redrawn a set of social configurations that include gender norms, and they have moved away from the gendering of writing.

In turn, in our critical analysis of African literature, we need to go beyond the usual gender divisions and, like Stratton, advocate for a redefinition of African literature based on an intertextual reading of both male and female writers.

Notes

1. Women writers from the Maghreb, or the Arab world, were not marginalized. Egyptian women writers started to publish already in the early twentieth century, not only in books but also in newspapers and magazines, some of them edited by women. Nawal El Saadawi started to publish in the mid-1950s. The Algerian Marguerite Taos Amrouche, writing in French, had her first novel, *Jacinthe noire* ("Black Hyacinth"), published in 1947. The sequel, *Rue des tambourins* ("Street of the Tabors"), came out in 1969. The Syrian Ulfat Udlibi's *Al Qarar Al Akheer* ("The Final Decision") was chosen the best storybook in the Arab world for 1947. Several Lebanese women writers, poets and novelists, were also publishing by the mid-1950s—for instance, Etel Adnan. By the 1970s, a number of them, such as Hanan al-Shaykh, had gained visibility.

2. See especially my introduction to *Rebellious Women,* which describes the different transformative steps in African women's writing.

3. See, for instance, Emecheta, "Feminism." Emecheta makes a point of distancing herself from Western feminist ways of seeing, especially with regard to sexuality.

4. In 1983, Alice Walker coined the term *womanist.* Her *In Search of Our Mothers' Gardens: Womanist Prose* was an attempt to define and delimit the philosophy and needs for African American women. Womanism enabled the women's movement to separate itself from feminism, which was clearly associated with white middle-class women; to go beyond the notion of black feminism; and to participate in the construction of identity politics along both gender and racial lines. See also Collins, "What's in a Name?"

5. See Emecheta's *The Family* (1990), *Kehinde* (1994), and *The New Tribe* (2000). For more on the use of the epistolary form in African women's writing, see Mortimer. Mortimer makes a compelling comparative analysis of the epistolary form in Bâ's *Une si longue lettre* and Assia Djebar's *Ombre sultane* (1987; *A Sister to Scheherazade*). See also Larrier. Larrier demonstrates African and Caribbean women writers' strengths as intergenerational transmitters of knowledge through an elaborate system of dialoguing.

6. Her subsequent essay, *Lettre d'une Afro-Parisienne à ses compatriotes* (2000; "Letter from an Afro-Parisian Woman to Her Compatriots"), makes her positioning even clearer, insofar as she anchors herself geographically and culturally. See Thomas 136, 137.

7. Comparatively little has been written on Bâ's second novel, *Un chant écarlate* (1981; *Scarlet Song*).

8. Note that Ken Bugul's later novels are at the opposite end of the spectrum from the first. Ignoring newer works by francophone African women writers, one runs the risk of presenting a very partial, scanty picture of them.

9. This discrepancy holds for both men and women writers; it is not a gender issue.

10. This question is not specific to women writers. We could ask it about French and francophone literature or about English and anglophone literature. It shows not only a different mapping of the field but also an acknowledgment that the field has expanded to the point of creating a need for new courses.

11. The same query might be made for a graduate-level course.

Works Cited

Bâ, Mariama. *Scarlet Song.* Trans. Dorothy Blair. London: Longman, 1986. Print. Trans. of *Un chant écarlate.* Dakar: Nouvelles Éditions Africaines, 1981.

———. *So Long a Letter.* Trans. Modupé Bodé-Thomas. Oxford: Heinemann, 1981. Print. Trans. of *Une si longue lettre.* Dakar: Nouvelles Éditions Africaines, 1980.

Berrian, Brenda, and Art Broek. *Bibliography of African Women Writers and Journalists, Ancient Egypt—1984.* Washington: Three Continents, 1985. Print.

Bessora, Sandrine. *53 cm.* Paris: Serpent à Plumes, 1999. Print.

———. *Deux bébés et l'addition.* Paris: Serpent à Plumes, 2002. Print.

Beti, Mongo. *Perpetua and the Habit of Unhappiness.* Trans. John Reed and Clive Wake. London: Heinemann Educ., 1978. Print. Trans. of *Perpetue et l'habitude du malheur.* Paris: Buchet, 1974.

Beyala, Calixthe. *Assèze l'Africaine.* Paris: Michel, 1994. Print.

———. *Les honneurs perdus.* Paris: Michel, 1996. Print.

———. *Lettre d'une Africaine à ses sœurs occidentales.* Paris: Spengler, 1995. Print.

———. *Lettre d'une Afro-Parisienne à ses compatriotes.* Paris: Mango, 2000. Print.

———. *Loukoum, the Little Prince of Belleville.* Trans. Marjolijn de Jager. Oxford: Heinemann, 1994. Print. Trans. of *Le petit prince de Belleville.* Paris: Michel, 1992.

———. *The Sun Hath Looked upon Me.* Trans. Marjolijn de Jager. Oxford: Heinemann, 1996. Print. Trans. of *C'est le soleil qui m'a brûlée.* Paris: Stock, 1987.

———. *Your Name Shall Be Tanga.* Trans. Marjolijn de Jager. Oxford: Heinemann, 1996. Print. Trans. of *Tu t'appelleras Tanga.* Paris: Stock, 1988.

Boyce Davies, Carole. *Black Women, Writing, and Identity: Migrations of the Subject.* London: Routledge, 1994. Print.

———. "Introduction to Feminist Consciousness and African Literary Criticism." Boyce Davies and Graves 1–23.

———. "Private Selves and Public Spaces: Autobiography and the African Woman Writer." *Crisscrossing Boundaries in African Literatures.* Ed. Kenneth Harrow, Jonathan Ngate, and Clarisse Zimra. Washington: Three Continents, 1991. 109–27. Print.

Boyce Davies, Carole, and Anne Adams Graves, eds. *Ngambika: Studies of Women in African Literature.* Trenton: Africa World, 1986. Print.

Butler, Judith. "Performative Acts and Gender Constitution: An Essay in Phenomenology and Feminist Theory." *Writing on the Body: Female Embodiment and Feminist Theory.* Ed. Katie Conboy, Nadia Medina, and Sarah Stanbury. New York: Columbia UP, 1997. 401–17. Print.

Cazenave, Odile. Rev. of *African Feminist Fiction and Indigenous Values,* by Donald Wehrs. *International Journal of African Historical Studies* 34.2 (2001): 490–91. Print.

———. "Calixthe Beyala's 'Parisian Novels': An Example of Globalization and Transculturation in French Society." *Women/Femmes.* Ed. Isabelle de Courtivron et al. Spec. issue of *Sites* 3.2 (2000): 119–27. Print.

———. Rev. of *Less than One and Double,* by Kenneth Harrow. *Research in African Literatures* 34.3 (2003): 187–88. Print.

———. *Rebellious Women: The New Generation of Female African Novelists.* Boulder: Rienner; Three Continents, 2000. Print. Trans. of *Femmes rebelles.*

———. "Vingt ans après Mariama Bâ: Nouvelles écritures au féminin." *Africultures* 1 Feb. 2001: 7–15. Web. 12 Aug. 2008.

Coetzee, J. M. *Disgrace.* London: Secker, 1999. Print.

Collins, Patricia Hill. "What's in a Name? Womanism, Black Feminism, and Beyond." *Black Scholar* 26.1 (1996): 9–17. Print.

d'Almeida, Irène Assiba. *Francophone African Women Writers: Destroying the Emptiness of Silence.* Gainesville: UP of Florida, 1994. Print.
Dangarembga, Tsitsi. *Nervous Conditions.* London: Women's, 1988. Print.
Darko, Amma. *Beyond the Horizon.* Oxford: Heinemann, 1995. Print.
———. *Faceless.* Accra: Sub-Saraharan, 2003. Print.
Diome, Fatou. *Ketala.* Paris: Flammarion, 2006. Print.
———. *Le ventre de l'Atlantique.* Paris: Carrière, 2003. Print.
Djebar, Assia. *A Sister to Scheherazade.* Trans. Dorothy Blair. Portsmouth: Heinemann, 1993. Print. Trans. of *Ombre sultane.* Paris: Lattès, 1987.
Donadey, Anne. *Recasting Postcolonialism: Women Writing between Worlds.* Portsmouth: Heinemann, 2001. Print.
Ekwensi, Cyprian. *Jagua Nana.* London: Hutchinson, 1963. Print.
Emecheta, Buchi. *The Family.* New York: Braziller, 1990. Print.
———. "Feminism with a Small 'f.'" *Criticism and Ideology.* Ed. Kirsten Holst Petersen. Stockholm: Nordiska Africainstitutet, 1988. 173–81. Print.
———. *Kehinde.* Oxford: Heinemann, 1994. Print.
———. *The New Tribe.* London: Heinemann, 2000. Print.
Essomba, J. R. *Le destin volé.* Paris: Présence Africaine, 2003. Print.
Harrow, Kenneth. *Less than One and Double.* Portsmouth: Heinemann, 2002. Print.
———. *Thresholds of Change in African Literature: The Emergence of a Tradition.* Portsmouth: Heinemann, 1994. Print.
Hitchcott, Nicki. *Calixthe Beyala: Performances of Migration.* Liverpool: Liverpool UP, 2006. Print.
Irele, Abiola. *The African Imagination: Literature in Africa and the Black Diaspora.* Oxford: Oxford UP, 2001. Print.
Ken Bugul. *The Abandoned Baobab: The Autobiography of a Senegalese Woman.* Trans. Marjolijn de Jager. New York: Hill, 1991. Print. Trans. of *Le baobab fou.* Dakar: Nouvelles Éditions Africaines, 1983.
———. *De l'autre côté du regard.* Paris: Serpent à Plumes, 2003. Print.
———. *Rue Félix Faure.* Paris: Hoëbeke, 2005. Print.
Kourouma, Ahmadou. *Allah n'est pas obligé.* Paris: Seuil, 2000. Print.
———. *Les soleils des indépendances.* Montréal: PU de Montréal, 1968; Paris: Seuil, 1970. Print.
Larrier, Renée. *Francophone Women Writers of Africa and the Caribbean.* Gainesville: UP of Florida, 2000. Print.
Lopès, Henri. *Dossier classé.* Paris: Seuil, 2000. Print.
Mabanckou, Alain. *Les petits-fils nègres de Vercingétorix.* Paris: Serpent à Plumes, 2002. Print.
Makward, Christiane, and Odile Cazenave. "The Others' Others: 'Francophone' Women." *Yale French Studies* 75 (1988): 190–207. Print.
Mohanty, Chandra Talpade. *Feminism without Borders: Decolonizing Theory, Practicing Solidarity.* Durham: Duke UP, 2003. Print.
———. *Third World Women and the Politics of Feminism.* Bloomington: Indiana UP, 1991. Print.
Monénembo, Tierno. *L'aîné des orphelins.* Paris: Seuil, 2000. Print.

Mortimer, Mildred P. "Women's Voice." *Journeys through the French African Novel.* Portsmouth: Heinemann, 1990. 133–64. Print.

Mpe, Phaswane. *Welcome to Our Hillbrow.* Pietermaritzburg: U of Natal P, 2001. Print.

Ogundipe-Leslie, Molara. "The Female Writer and Her Commitment." *Women in African Literature Today.* Ed. Eldred D. Jones, Eustace Palmer, and Marjorie Jones. London: Currey, 1987. 5–13. Print.

———. "Not Spinning on the Axis of Maleness." *Sisterhood Is Global: The International Women's Movement Anthology.* Ed. Robin Morgan. New York: Anchor, 1984. 498–504. Print.

Sembène, Ousmane. *God's Bits of Wood.* Trans. Francis Price. Garden City: Anchor, 1970. Print. Trans. of *Les bouts de bois de Dieu.* Paris: Livre Contemporain, 1960.

Steady, Filomena. "African Feminism: A Worldwide Perspective." *Women in Africa and the African Diaspora.* Ed. Rosalyn Terborg-Penn, Sharon Harley, and Andrea Benton. Washington: Howard UP, 1987. 3–24. Print.

Stratton, Florence. *Contemporary African Literature and the Politics of Gender.* New York: Routledge, 1994. Print.

Taos Amrouche, Marguerite. *Jacinthe noire.* 1947. Paris: Losfeld, 1996. Print.

———. *Rue des tambourins.* 1969. Paris: Losfeld, 1996. Print.

Thomas, Dominic. *Black France: Colonialism, Immigration, and Transnationalism.* Bloomington: Indiana UP, 2006. Print.

Walker, Alice. *In Search of Our Mothers' Gardens.* New York: Harcourt, 2004. Print.

Wehrs, Donald. *African Feminist Fiction and Indigenous Values.* Gainesville: UP of Florida, 2001. Print.

Lisa McNee

Translation and the African Novel: Reading as Re/Membering

We are lost without translation.

—Omotoso

The future of the African novel depends on the translator as well as on the writer, publisher, state, and reader, according to the Kenyan novelist Ngũgĩ wa Thiong'o (*Decolonising* 85). This is so not only because of the importance of the language of the novel but also because of the postcolonial politics underlined by titles such as *The Empire Writes Back* (Ashcroft, Griffiths, and Tiffin). As African writers like Ngũgĩ have turned to writing in African languages rather than in European languages associated with (neo)colonialism, the postcolonial translator has taken on a role of increasing significance. Although Ngũgĩ clearly states that the writer plays the most important role, in a recent interview he gives more importance to the translator than before, for "we interpret translation as conversation. And conversation assumes equality" ("Beyond Nativism" 162).

The conversation established by translations, whether on an individual basis or across cultures, is pedagogical in nature. Translations establish exchanges, conversations—bridges—between cultures and periods by reaching people who must learn to read and translate or recode when necessary in order to understand. In a metaphoric sense, these bridges allow the willing student or scholar to learn more about African literature. But careful attention to the language used to construct a bridge is a necessity. According to the Nigerian novelist Kole Omotoso, "A language carries with it its own culture and when you accept to use one language without any conscious attempt at translation into your own, you also accept the culture of that language" (53). In short, students facing postcolonial globalization must translate to re/member their own culture, recalling the familiar in another idiom.

In the comparative or world literature classroom, most of us see the benefits of this situation without taking the warning very seriously. Translations offer a window onto the world and allow students to travel without leaving the physical classroom. Meanwhile instructors in the foreign language classroom worry that many of their novice and intermediate students never truly stop translating texts, never achieve the goal of reading them without mental translation. They are less worried that students will not re/member their own culture. Yet Omotoso's warning for African students is pertinent for Western students as well. Translation is always about interpretation (Eco) as well as about the actual work of producing another text. Omotoso cautions that young African students who do not translate will forget their past; in contrast, young Western students unable to translate and interpret texts and contexts from other cultures will fail to understand the other worlds they wish to enter.

In Introduction to African Literature, which I teach on the third-year level, as well as in the world literature courses I have taught in the past, the emphasis has been on context for this reason. Because novels are longer texts and present certain difficulties for foreign language students, many of us in foreign languages assign translations as ancillary texts. But we do so too often without discussing the theoretical significance of a translation. In world literature courses, most of the texts are in English or English translation. In either case, the problems inherent in teaching translated texts without discussing translation as such appear again and again. The first and most obvious issue is related to context. Because students are constantly translating as they read the novels in the courses, the grounds for interpretation require attention. I give my students as much information as possible on the historical and cultural contexts of texts. In a general introduction to African literature or the African novel, this approach means some lecturing on the colonial period and the anticolonial movement before student read any novels. Because of the difficulty of the longer texts, we focus on shorter texts first, such as "Femme noire" or "Hoquet," famous poems by the negritude poets L. S. Senghor and L. G. Damas, respectively, or "Kiswahili," perhaps the most famous poem by Shaaban Robert.

Robert, a Swahili poet and a contemporary of the great negritude poets, presents students with a towering example of a writer using his native language during the colonial period, long before radical postindependence writers were able to take up their pens and choose an African language as the medium of expression. Comparing Robert's work with that of his contemporaries who wrote in French could allow a sharper definition in the presentation of the language issues at the heart of the identitarian politics of the time. By contrasting an African-language poem with francophone or anglophone texts, it is possible to emphasize that for most African writers the language question entails a choice not only among European languages but also between an African and European language. Moreover, the poem highlights the translation problems that face every student of African literatures.

Using Robert's poem requires some contextualization. In the French classroom, it is perhaps easiest to compare the text with those of negritude poets. The comparison may capitalize on students' previous knowledge of the negritude movement, or it may introduce the negritude poets to them. This movement of francophone Africa shared a strong emphasis on orature and the verbal arts of the precolonial cultures of Africa (Julien) with the anticolonial movements in East Africa, although the Swahili coast's particularly communalist approach to language and identity seems to have hindered a similar movement from emerging. Instead of experiencing assimilation as a hated policy imposed by colonizers seeking to make black Frenchmen, Waswahili benefit from their own communalist form of assimilation. A communalist society, according to Alamin Mazrui, is able to "absorb" newcomers who are linguistically assimilated; however, those newcomers are not required to give up their prior ethnic status (74–75).

This openness did not prevent oppression under colonial rule, though the people of the East African coast fought for African languages and African-language administration, instruction, and publications with greater success than francophone Africa's colonized peoples. The fruits were bittersweet: the British controlled language policy in East Africa as a result and promoted their variety of Kiswahili. *Kiswahili cha wastani* ("Standard Kiswahili") was an invention of the British colonial administration and the Inter-territorial Language Committee, which was established in 1930.

Later renamed the East African Swahili Committee, it preferred the southern dialects over the northern dialects, thus influencing contemporary Kiswahili literature in "irremediable ways" (Biersteker 77)

Colonial control led to continued bitterness, as Robert's 1947 poem "Kiswahili"—probably the best-known poem in Kiswahili, according to Ann Biersteker (39)—demonstrates. The poem also highlights the trickster nature of the translator:

> Lugha kama Kiarabu, Kirumi na Kiingereza,
> Kwa wingi zimeratibu, mambo ya kupendeza,
> Na mimi nimejaribu, kila hali kujifunza
> Lakini sawa na bubu, nikizisema nabezwa
> Titi la mama litamu, jingine halishi hamu.
>
> Mfano neno la jambo, mkato wa una jambo?
> Jibu lake si jambo, tafsiri sina jambo,
> Tazama hili pambo, lizidishavyo urembo,
> Wa kuulizana mambo, kwa usemi wenye umbo,
> Titi la mama litamu, jingine halishi hamu.
>
> Languages like Arabic, Latin and English,
> Have been significant, concerning much that is pleasing,
> And I have tried, in every way to study them,
> But like a mute, if I speak them I am despised,
> The mother's breast is sweetest, no other satisfies desire.
>
> For example the word *jambo,* is it a shortened form of *una jambo?*
> The answer is *si jambo*, translate it *sina jambo,*
> Examine this figure, the way it adds to the design,
> Of asking each other *mambo*, through structured speech,
> The mother's breast is sweetest, no other satisfies desire. (41)

Biersteker notes the bitterness of a man whose attempts to learn other languages in order to gain higher status have left him "like a mute" because of racism that denies his talents. In the relative Babel caused by attempts to learn Arabic as well as Latin, Islam as well as Christianity, the Swahili poet draws attention to loss of identity and to anomie rather than to the cultural wealth that should accrue from knowledge of other languages and cultures. Juxtaposing these languages with the native language presents the reader with a metonymic relation that suggests a particular interpretation or translation of the situation. The only solution to Babel is translation, but the language lesson is in vain unless Kiswahili, the poet's native language, prevails.

The poet seems to advocate action. As Biersteker notes, "this is an angry poem" (40). In the stanza in which the poet draws attention to translation, he says "translate it" in the imperative. A literal translation does not do justice to the irony of the situation, for one can easily imagine a Westerner who is a beginner in Kiswahili who asks this question about *si jambo*, the response to the greeting *hu jambo.* Many of the colonial settlers simply chose to learn a pidginized form of Kiswahili so as to order servants about instead of having conversations with people. They often shortened the greeting to *jambo* and dropped the pronoun markers. In short, the translator-cum–language teacher in the poem is a trickster of sorts, like the colonial translator Wangrin of *L'étrange destin de Wangrin* (Hampaté Bâ).

In the poem's stanzas on language learning, language is highlighted, as are the sociocultural patterns of interaction structured by language. Speech is structured, as Robert insists, but translation must go beyond the mere structures of speech; the translator must consider the speech act. Any attempt to translate a text must thus take into account the sociohistorical and cultural backgrounds that make this or any other interpretation possible. In other words, the fidelity of a translation depends on the text-external continuum as well as on the text-internal features. According to Umberto Eco, "translations do not concern a comparison between two languages but the interpretation of two texts in two different languages" (14). These languages might be different linguistic systems or different semiotic systems.

Although translation is a conversation or exchange predicated on equality, we cannot assume a conversation between equals in every case, as Ngũgĩ's fiction shows us quickly. Translation holds a possibility of resolving some of the inequalities of the postcolonial exchange, yet, like all exchanges, it is political. Indeed, translation has been an integral part of the imperial adventure, as Eric Cheyfitz describes it:

> We must be in translation between cultures and between groups within our own culture if we are to understand the dynamics of our imperialism. For our imperialism historically has functioned (and continues to function) by substituting for the difficult politics of translation another politics of translation that represses these difficulties. (xvi)

As Cheyfitz stresses, this repression leads to erasures of class culture, ideology, identity, and race (15). The politics of translation, then, are intimately linked to the repression that led to linguistic nationalism and a link between anticolonial struggles and language, particularly in East Africa, where the language question emerged early as a nationalist issue, and in francophone Africa, where the issue of authenticity took on special urgency in the light of the policy of assimilation.

Choosing a novel for a syllabus opens up this history of imperialism and colonialism, simply because choice implies selection and thus exclusion. This history is often hidden by other, practical concerns, such as the availability of the text or the availability of translations, ancillary translations, and texts designed for language courses. These concerns can lull the instructor into forgetting the inequalities in the postcolonial dialogue that both translations and original texts reveal. We cannot forget the poet's cry that for Kiswahili speakers of the colonial period, knowledge of other languages meant not empowerment but the reverse.

This conversation about language and inequality continues today among many African novelists and the Euro-American world that controls much of the publishing industry. I offer Ngũgĩ's novel *Matigari* as one possible work for a syllabus in a course on the African novel in which translation is highlighted. Ngũgĩ is one of the few major novelists to abandon English for an African language in order to enrich Gikuyu, his native language. The cost is high. He risked losing his readership because of his choice. Translation has been the solution for devoted readers of Kenya's most celebrated novelist, yet it also presents serious problems.

Ngũgĩ's first novel in Gikuyu opens as a conversation on peace that quickly fails because of inequalities that cannot be overcome. The English-language version of the novel opens with Matigari's return to his homeland after years in battle against the colonizer and his native flunky. Finally defeating the settler who stole his home, Matigari hides his weapons, girds himself with a belt of peace, and chooses to seek his family and his home. However, he finds that the children of his enemies continue the battle on another front; neocolonialism is the new adversary of those who fight for freedom and justice. His constant cries for liberty and justice for all soon mire him in trouble. He is jailed; he escapes under mysterious circumstances that are explained in the end (a beautiful prostitute sacrificed herself for him). Less understandable, perhaps, is the allegorical nature of this Everyman who changes appearance and age depending on who speaks of him.

The hero represents all the Mau Mau heroes who returned from war. The novel has a circular structure, for the hero must fight to return to the place where the narrative opens and find his weapons to fight the neocolonial adversaries that he encountered during his quest for a peaceful homeland. Although Matigari and Guthera, his female companion, disappear and are not found, his adoptive child, a waif who met him when Matigari wore the belt of peace, girds himself with Matigari's weapons and takes up his battle. Clearly, the dialogue that was meant to lead to peace cannot succeed unless there is equality.

Ngũgĩ states directly that a translation cannot succeed unless there is equality with the original. The question remains whether the English-language version of *Matigari* is successful. Although few Westerners have access to the Gikuyu original, *Matigari* remains a hotly debated novel that continues to stir attention (Gikandi, *Ngugi* 223). In the early 1990s, Simon Gikandi argued that the English translation appeared to face two directions at once, losing its identity in the process. The precursors of the novel are Gikuyu oral and prose traditions, while the translation "seems to affirm Europhonic generic conventions and linguistic practices found in [Ngũgĩ's] other texts" ("Epistemology" 163). The hero's name, repeated often throughout the novel, is translated each time, because it is a revolutionary and allegorical name (signifying the patriots who survived the bullets [Ngũgĩ, *Matigari* 20]) that carries much of the novel's core meaning. This convention takes on great significance for the reader of the English-language edition. According to Gikandi, the Gikuyu title refers to an event rather than to a person ("Epistemology" 165). The cover art of the original depicts the political struggle at the heart of the novel, but the modernist cover of the English version arouses no strong emotion (165–66).

As Gikandi's assessment of the translation's relation to the original shows, the dialogue that is translation for Ngũgĩ does not take place between the two "artifacts," as Gikandi calls the texts (165). Rather, it takes place between interpretations of the two versions of the novel, which seem so different that the original disappears into the translation. "Translation is hence a double-edged weapon: it allows Ngũgĩ's text to survive and to be read, but it is read and discussed as if it were a novel in English" (166). In this case, the secondary translation exerts unusual influence over the primary text, a reversal of the usual order. The English version of the novel exerts this influence because of the neocolonial power relations that continue to shape the reception of Ngũgĩ's writing. The ideal of translation as a conversation between equals assumes that power relations will be part of the discussion, but this discussion has been muted with regard to the work of most African novelists. Few have been able to put the language question directly on the table, as Ngũgĩ has done time and again.

Gikandi offers an elegant description of the double-edged sword that faces the reader of *Matigari* in English. The novel is flattened by the power politics of English as it is used in the postcolony; therefore the English reader receives a simplistic version, one that lacks the power of the original Gikuyu.

Under the weight of these arguments, one might decide to avoid the text altogether and teach one of Ngũgĩ's earlier texts written in English. I would argue that this is a misstep: it prevents students from engaging with the issues of language and translation that are essential in the comparative literature or foreign language classroom. These issues are at the heart of Ngũgĩ's work, which cannot truly be understood without some attempt to struggle with the problems inherent in this text. Because I cannot read Gikuyu, I have access only to this lesser version, the synecdoche that signals the complete version without offering it (Eco 67). In a sense, this difficulty applies to all culturally different books that we may teach, translate, or interpret in the classroom (Spivak).

Translation almost always presents this paradox: the impossibility of the attempt to be faithful to another text while being different from it (Mazrui 68). For some, this paradoxical state is natural to the African novel. According to Olabode Ibironke, African literatures in European languages exist

> primarily in the mode of translations without originals. This formulation registers the fact that African writers are necessarily translators, in that the distinctions between "source" and "target" are constantly interlocked and interchanging. (112)

At first the polemic does not seem to concern *Matigari*, written in Gikuyu and translated into English. Ibironke expressly addresses the issue as it relates to mental translation, not translation proper. But Gikandi and others have shown that the fictional language and conventions of the novel mean that this text too can be included in the larger discussion of the politics of translation (Gikandi, "Epistemology," *Ngugi*, and "Traveling").

The question of source and target languages takes on another dimension in the foreign language classroom. If students use a translation as an ancillary text, they may still translate as they read the primary text. Classroom discussion and lectures are designed primarily to give students contact hours with the target language. Since my language is French, I chose to enlarge the debate by including Werewere Liking's 1989 novel *L'amour-cent-vies*, translated as *Love-across-a-Hundred-Lives*. Examining this novel and comparing it with Ngũgĩ's *Matigari*, we find that the problem is more complex than the source language–target language model implies. Note that Marjolijn de Jager's translation, from French to English, remains in some ways as mysterious as the original text. The reader is inclined to ask the same questions when reading the translation as when reading the original. Perhaps one can give no higher praise to a translation.

But if we assess a translation only on the literal level, we do injustice to both text and translation. In a sense, we must constantly look at translation from a figurative as well as from a literal standpoint. Metaphor, as Cheyfitz writes, is almost a basic definition for translation, for the transference of meaning from one language to another, or the transference of sense in a language from one context to another (35–36). In contrast, metonymy depends on contiguity for effect. "Metonymy is the process whereby transference occurs between objects that are associated in an imaginary without being similar" (Granqvist 61). Metonymy, then, is likely to explain most cases of intralinguistic translation—that is, new versions of a text in the same language or artistic idiom. In both metaphor and metonymy, reading becomes a form of re/membering that is also a form of translation.

What can the figurative model of translation offer to the discussion? To what extent are these two novelists translators who work in the intersemiotic model of transmutation—that is, adaptation from one artistic form to another (Eco 67)? To what degree does intertextuality explain the translation taking place when the reader takes up either *Matigari* or *L'amour-cent-vies*?

Fictional language and the fictional forms chosen to create fictional worlds have been the subject of much debate in critical circles pressed to explicate the experimental fiction of Liking and the transformations in Ngũgĩ's constantly changing fictional practice. These worlds are embedded in other worlds, in ever-growing circles or dialogues, as the intertextual model seeks to explain. This embededness means that all literary works are translations without originals.

The intertextual mode is visible in Ngũgĩ's theories of translation and in his fiction. In the first phase of his work, a realist and historical strain dominated; in the second phase, this strain deepened into socialist realism (Gikandi, *Ngugi* 225); and in the third phase, it shifted toward African-language oral techniques (Ngũgĩ, *Penpoints* 123). Throughout it is clear that Ngũgĩ has been establishing dialogues with different sets of performances or texts in a classic intertextual mode. Students need to know about each of these phases in order to understand the conversations that are at play in the translation of *Matigari* as well as the intertextuality at play in the novel.

The same knowledge is needed to understand Liking's novel. While it is harder to establish such a chronology for her work, one can see that the dominant tendency is the attempt to ally ritual or initiatory language with experimental works of drama or fiction. In her multilayered, dialogic, and intertextual works, Liking tests generic boundaries as well as ideas about freedom, gender, and maturity (Wright 46). Students need to understand Liking's attempts to build bridges to other cultures in Africa as well as outside the continent in order to understand the liberation that her *chant-roman* or "song novel" represents for readers familiar with the use of French as a tool of assimilation. In this novel in particular, Liking creates a network of relations between medieval Mali and all periods of Cameroonian history. In order to understand the links to the past that the novelist builds, students need to know that anticolonialist movements are not and have not been exclusively nationalist in character. Especially in francophone Africa, they have been based on inter-African ties as well as on ties such as those built at the Bandung Conference. The dialogue with the past that Liking creates in *Love-across-a-Hundred-Lives* is presented in a lyrical fashion.

Intertextuality, or the dialogue between literary or cultural texts, is a kind of conversation or encounter that can be understood as a problem of translation for the African novel in particular, because of the need to transfer culturally unavailable information from one sociolinguistic context to another—what Kwaku Gyasi has named "creative translation" or "transposition" (85). Liking's experimental novel attempts to make this kind of conversation possible across hundreds of years and across many cultures, while Ngũgĩ's *Matigari* attempts to unite cultural and fictional worlds as well as various historical periods in an unnamed country at an unnamed period in time. By dedicating his novel to "all those who love a good story, and to all those who research and write on African orature, and to all those committed to the development of literature in the languages of all the African peoples" (v), Ngũgĩ opens the possibility of conversation with the readers of *Matigari*.

Liking makes a similar if more subtle dedication to her "grandmother-daughter, my double," her "grandfather-son-husband / This swatch of our entrails / This endless journey of twists and turns / Only to meet again always / Always Siamese and twins / Mirrors and reflections of Love . . ." (118). The dedication opens the novel by evoking the themes most important to the narrator and to the protagonist, Lem: reincarnation and past lives, the future, and love of the double. The double, Liking explains, was created by God so that all humans were hermaphrodites who "could always win at every game, at every turn, heads or tails" (120). But of course temptation leads to trouble: the man cheats, and

> God became angry and separated man from his double. "Since you like losing just so you can risk more, you'll play at least five times before finding your tail side up again, and for the rest of your life you'll regret having played the edges." (121)

In a real sense, Liking opens the intertextual dialogue with the dedication. Her tale about the hermaphrodites extends the dialogue to ancient Greece, to Plato's *Symposium*, which contains another tale of hermaphrodites split by gods. The question of authenticity, however, may lead us to ask whether or not this tale is a Bassa tale, an adaptation of Plato's tale, or simply an original reaction to the story of the double. If we look for the story's origin, as the source-target model would have us do on a figurative level, we must simply admit that the model does not help us understand translations without originals. We can point to possible intertextual dialogues without being absolutely sure of sources; indeed, "there are no virginal forms since all linguistic, cultural, and epistemological forms are always already shot through with their previous existence." The problem at the heart of evaluating a dialogue or translation-cum-dialogue is not a matter of derivativeness versus originality but the success of an adaptation (Ibironke 121).

A pedagogical problem with this viewpoint is that students in the foreign language classroom might lose interest in the original text, and students in the world literature classroom might lose interest in establishing connections between different cultural worlds. In my experience, however, students are delighted by the game of establishing cultural bridges between different fictional worlds. On the linguistic level, they are well aware of political imbalances among Standard English, French, or Kiswahili and dialectal variants, because I do discuss those. Since most Africans are bilingual or multilingual, the question of prestige in language use is likely to come up in any course on translation or language. A discussion of intertextuality and translation does not preclude frank debate on the problem of the politics of language; it requires such debate.

Discussing the problem of intertextuality is harder, however, because students do expect a focus on context, which is the most prominent feature in my third-year introduction to African literature course. The problem of memory recurs on both literal and interpretive levels. As Liking's text shows, some intertextual moorings are obvious. The story of Sunjata, for instance, is clearly anchored in Mali, as Roumben's is in Cameroon. The story of the hermaphrodites is harder to pin down. My graduate students find these puzzles fascinating and disturbing and are prepared to do research on the initiatory tales that Liking has published. In any case, having a translation without an original means that the memory of the original has been lost or erased. A discussion about the historical ruptures in Africa that led to erasure and loss of memory is a good starting point to address unclear intertextual moorings.

Those ruptures continue on many levels today. In fact, the chief problem in establishing dialogue, in Ngũgĩ's words, is that the use of Western languages leads to "mental translation going on all the time":

> A European memory is planted on our bodies, on our landscapes, on our intellect. We operate within that memory and, in the process, our memory will either disappear or will be remembered as a dream or mediated by that other, foreign, memory. ("Beyond Nativism" 163)

In other words, we encounter exactly the problem that most readers of Liking find: mysteries when we seek the answer to intertextual connections.

The conversation requires bridges across the years through memories. The question of memory thus remains similar for Liking ("Aesthetics" 55) and for Ngũgĩ. Liking's novel is an attempt to forestall or reverse loss of memory through an initiation that opens with a dialogue with Lem's grandmother, his ancestor and the woman Lem loves above all others. He does not want to remember his past lives; they are too frightening. He chooses to commit suicide—by hanging himself by a rope of knotted umbilical cords that he wishes to hang from a tree near a maternity clinic—rather than face his unusual future. He constantly runs from challenges, and these are many. A follower of Ziworé, a professor fighting dictatorship, he is under suspicion and flees. But he falls into what might be called a memory trap: he is bedeviled by memories from the court of Sunjata as well as from Roumben (Ruben um Nyobe), his own ethnic group's hero. He flees every time. His quest for courage involves ambivalence as well, as his name implies—"'Habit' or 'the Manner of Casting

Bridges'" (119). A creature of habit, Lem fails to respond adequately to new challenges. But as the caster of bridges, he is supposed to restore the memories of the past to the present and build connections through his art. In choosing to cast bridges and break with habit, he becomes a hero. His is the story of a successful initiation, but the psychological costs are high.

Although Lem is similar to the student in *Matigari*, in that he runs because of fear, has an inspirational professor who helps him demonstrate against dictatorship, and meets an initiatory figure, his story is very different. At the center of this complex, symbolic, initiatory novel (Wright 57), he is a psychologically complex figure. The student in *Matigari* is a secondary character with little depth: "while Ngugi may still desire realism as the highest form of representation, *Matigari* marks the limit of this desire and perhaps its impossibility" (Gikandi, *Ngugi* 236). The difference between Ngũgĩ's high realism in the first phase of his work and socialist realism in the second is slighter than the difference between either and Liking's experiments and psychological depth based on ritual and initiation, epic and legend.

According to Irène d'Almeida, "intertextuality serves as a tool in the process of making new meaning" (266) in Liking's fiction. Since intertextuality assumes reference to the past or to other works or words, some have assumed that it leads to derivativeness. And "translation without an original" often serves as a metonym for intertextuality. But it is the success of the adaptation that counts. Intertextuality of a novel functions as a translation from one sign system into another, according to Charles Peirce: it creates new meaning (Eco 69). The question remains whether intertextuality can be equated to the semiotician's discussion of different sign systems. The novelist's translation of Plato's tale of the hermaphrodites, for example, is a transfer of meaning from one system of writing to another. Moreover, the tale may have African antecedents, not only a Greek one, antecedents that might be based in oral performance, which would make such translation intersemiotic. D'Almeida and Ibironke do indicate that Liking's mode of translation might best be examined in the light of intertextuality as adaptation, a form of intersemiotic translation or transmutation (Eco 69).

The same observation applies to Ngũgĩ's very different fictional world. Both Liking and Ngũgĩ turned to the use of orality and tried to translate orature into writing in their works. Orality does not merely "authenticate" a work; the oral-aural provides an answer to the questions

Ngũgĩ poses concerning the inequalities of the postcolonial condition (Mazrui and Mphande 229). The answer is apparent in his choice to write in Gikuyu to reach the people and in his use of oral tales and forms in *Matigari*. Indeed, he claims that the novel is based on the tale his sister told her children about a man with an incurable wound who seeks a healer named Ndiiro. "The story depends on a repetition of the song that describes Ndiiro. I used the same structure in the construction of *Matigari*, the story of a wanderer in search of social justice in a post-colonial society" (*Penpoints* 124). We see an adaptation from a folktale to a form that Eco would call intersemiotic translation. This reading depends on our understanding orature as a dynamic performance art rather than as a static or purely verbal art form. Ngũgĩ's original text becomes a form of revision, or intralingual translation, if one sees the folktale as a purely verbal art form. But because it is a performance art, the folktale's translation into a novel must be seen as a form of intersemiotic translation.

This kind of adaptation is in fact common in African literatures, according to Gyasi, who focuses on "creative translation" (80). One of the hallmarks of this creative activity is the "transposition of African oral and traditional literary techniques of storytelling into the European written genre" (85). In the light of Liking's work, we might add the song, lullaby, epic, and initiation tale to the list of techniques successfully grafted onto the novel form. Ngũgĩ's novel includes proverbs and songs. The creative translations from oral performance genres clearly succeed in re/membering oral traditions in written narrative form.

Creative transposition of oral genres also turns translation into a form of memory. As we have seen, the cultural memory loss that Ngũgĩ and Liking see as a major problem in postcolonial Africa indicates a loss of bridges to the past, a loss of conversations with ancestors. Both novelists have different ways of translating that loss and creating texts that help re/member what was wounded, to heal and resolve the problem.

In this situation of anomie, Kwame Anthony Appiah advocates thick translation, a form similar to thick descriptions of cultures unfamiliar to the reader, a theory familiar to students of anthropology. Appiah links thick descriptions and translations to the context of literary production and pedagogy, for he sees translation as a pedagogical challenge and endeavor (818). Strikingly, he stresses the same point that Ngũgĩ does: translation does not occur except as a conversation between equals. And because translation is a pedagogical act, the use of translations in the classroom implies a particular pedagogy. Appiah's advice is as follows:

"First, stress that the continuities between pre-colonial forms of cultural production and contemporary ones are genuine . . . second, challenge directly the assumption of the cultural superiority of the West" (818).

I can think of no better advice for the teacher of the African novel concerned by the issues of translation raised here. If we follow this advice, Western students are more likely to understand the ruptures that have led to the pain that some see as a result of improper translation. Another mode of translation may lead to reading as a form of re/membering. This mode is that of Ngũgĩ wa Thiong'o and Werewere Liking—a conversation that makes equality a reality to our students.

Works Cited

Appiah, Kwame Anthony. "Thick Translation." *Callaloo* 16.4 (1993): 808–19. Print.

Ashcroft, Bill, Gareth Griffiths, and Helen Tiffin. *The Empire Writes Back: Theory and Practice in Post-colonial Literatures.* London: Routledge, 1989. Print.

Biersteker, Ann. *Kujibizana: Questions of Language and Power in Nineteenth- and Twentieth-Century Poetry in Kiswahili.* East Lansing: Michigan State UP, 1996. Print.

Cheyfitz, Eric. *The Poetics of Imperialism: Translation and Colonization from* The Tempest *to* Tarzan. Oxford: Oxford UP, 1991. Print.

d'Almeida, Irène Assiba. "The Intertext: Werewere Liking's Tool for Transformations and Renewal." *Postcolonial Subjects: Francophone Women Writers.* Ed. Mary Jean Green, Karen Gould, Micheline Rice-Maximin, Keith L. Walker, and Jack A. Yeager. Minneapolis: U of Minnesota P, 1996. 265–84. Print.

Eco, Umberto. *Experiences in Translation.* Trans. Alastair McEwen. Toronto: U of Toronto P, 2001. Print.

Gikandi, Simon. "The Epistemology of Translation: Ngugi, Matigari, and the Politics of Language." *Research in African Literatures* 22.4 (1991): 161–68. Print.

———. *Ngugi wa Thiong'o.* Cambridge: Cambridge UP, 2000. Print.

———. "Traveling Theory: Ngugi's Return to English." *Research in African Literatures* 31.2 (2000): 194–209. Print.

Granqvist, Raoul. "A Postcolonial Grammar of Translation: Chinua Achebe's *Things Fall Apart* as a Metonymic Text." Overvold, Priebe, and Tremaine 59–71.

Gyasi, Kwaku A. "Writing as Translation: African Literature and the Challenges of Translation." *Research in African Literatures* 30.2 (1999): 75–87. Print.

Hampaté Bâ, Amadou. *The Fortunes of Wangrin.* Trans. Aina Pavolini Taylor. Introd. Abiola Irele. Bloomington: Indiana UP, 1999. Print. Trans. of *L'étrange destin de Wangrin.*

Ibironke, Olabode. "The Horses of Knowledge: African Literature and the Canon of Translation." Overvold, Priebe, and Tremaine 112–30.

Julien, Eileen. *African Novels and the Question of Orality.* Bloomington: Indiana UP, 1992. Print.

Liking, Werewere. "The Aesthetics of Necessity: An Interview with Werewere Liking." By Michelle Mielly. *World Literature Today* 77.2 (2003): 52–56. Print.

———. *L'amour-cent-vies.* Paris: Publisud, 1989. Print.

———. It Shall Be Jasper and Coral *and* Love-across-a-Hundred-Lives: *Two Novels.* Trans. Marjolijn de Jager. Charlottesville: U of Virginia P, 2000. Print.

Mazrui, Alamin. "Shakespeare in Africa: Between English and Swahili Literature." *Research in African Literatures* 27.1 (1996): 64–79. Print.

Mazrui, Alamin, and Lupenga Mphande. "Orality and the Literature of Combat: The Legacy of Fanon." *Critical Essays on Ngugi wa Thiong'o.* Ed. Peter Nazareth. New York: Twayne, 2000. 228–48. Print.

Ngũgĩ wa Thiong'o. "Beyond Nativism: An Interview with Ngugi wa Thiong'o." By Ângela Lamas Rodrigues. *Research in African Literatures* 35.3 (2004): 161–67. Print.

———. *Decolonising the Mind: The Politics of Language in African Literature.* London: Currey, 1986. Print.

———. *Matigari.* Trans. Wangui wa Goro. Oxford: Heinemann, 1987. Print.

———. *Penpoints, Gunpoints, and Dreams: Towards a Critical Theory of the Arts and the State in Africa.* Oxford: Clarendon, 1998. Print.

Omotoso, Kole. "Africa Lost without Translation." *New African* 431 (2004): 52–53. Print.

Overvold, Angelina, Richard Priebe, and Louis Tremaine, eds. *The Creative Circle: Artist, Critic, and Translator in African Literature.* Trenton: Africa World, 2003. Print. Selected Papers of the African Lit. Assn. 27.

Spivak, Gayatri Chakravorty. "How to Read a Culturally Different Text." *Colonial Discourse / Postcolonial Theory.* Ed. Francis Barker, Peter Hulme, and Margaret Iversen. Manchester: Manchester UP, 1994. 126–50. Print.

Wright, Katheryn Lee. "Extending Generic Boundaries: Werewere Liking's *L'amour-cent-vies.*" *Research in African Literatures* 33.2 (2002): 46–60. Print.

Part II

Regional Imperatives, Thematic Cartographies

Zahr Said Stauffer

Rethinking the Arab African Novel: A Case for Thematization

Recently I was teaching a wonderful novel by the Britain-based Tanzanian writer Abdulrazak Gurnah, *By the Sea* (2001), about an elderly man struggling to make a life for himself as an asylee in a small seaside town in Great Britain. A student raised her hand an hour into the discussion to ask, "One thing I can't figure out is, where's this guy from?" "What do you mean by *from*?" I responded, though I had a good idea of the crisis of origins to which she was referring: the novel's characters, and indeed the novel itself, suffer from a sense of cosmopolitanism so pronounced, it becomes hard for both reader and teacher to know how to situate the text.

To begin with, Zanzibar, which Gurnah writes about, no longer exists as such, and its new geopolitical and nominal identity —Tanzania— never appears in the text. Characters in the novel speak Arabic, Swahili, Persian, and English; eat Indian and African food; practice Islam; read Sufi texts as well as British and American literature; and live and belong (or don't belong) all over the world. The culture of the novel is perhaps best summed up as a trading culture, a culture of monsoons, migration, exchange, and dislocation. Yet the novel allegorizes a larger problem, which invites further reflection on how to deal with texts that defy categorization.

This essay concerns itself with what I call the Arab African novel, a literary subgroup that may contain texts written in Arabic, French, English, and local languages, by writers from or in or writing about parts of Africa and the Middle East, including Mauritania, Morocco, Algeria, Tunisia, Libya, Egypt, Sudan, Ethopia, Somalia, Kenya, Uganda, and Tanzania. I argue that we as teachers should foreground a text's placelessness (or many placedness) as a thematic concern in the text, then raise questions about the text's origins and placement in the African literary canon. By discussing the thematic what, why, and where of the novel's world, we can broach the whence and whither questions raised in the larger contexts of curriculum and canon.

A number of criteria currently serve to organize the field of African literature into teachable units and to provide institutional homes for given texts and authors. In this essay, I suggest the ultimate ineffectiveness of any single one of the current categorical tactics (geography, language, historical context) in the light of the Arab African novel. Instead, I favor a metacritical approach that teaches about the formation of an African canon as it teaches the canon itself. That is, as we teach the Arab African novel, we must simultaneously do the work of teaching how to think about where the text might belong and what other African texts it speaks to. We must employ a more thematic approach, privileging the themes texts share despite differences in geography, language, and historical context instead of dividing the texts as Arab or African.

In what is perhaps the most famous Arabic-language novel of the twentieth century, the protagonist struggles to define himself in conversation with a white woman in London: " 'What race are you?' she asked me. 'Are you African or Asian?' 'I am like Othello—Arab-African,' I said to her" (Salih 38). The protagonist of the Sudanese novelist Tayeb Salih's *A Season of Migration to the North* has come up against the inability of essentializing taxonomies to capture individual subjectivity. Mustafa Saeed's perceived identity frustrates categorical divisions—Is he Arab? African? Asian?—yet the problem of his self-definition pertains also to the kind of categorical divisions that classify the very text from which he speaks. It is a problem particularly salient in the Arab African novel.

Geopolitical pressures might place such a novel either in Africa alone (for geographical reasons—as with a work by the Somali novelist Nuruddin Farah) or outside Africa, in the sphere of Middle Eastern studies (for linguistic reasons—as with a novel by the Egyptian writer Naguib Mahfouz). On the other hand, theories of globalization might throw all these authors into the same discourse, on the sole basis of their shared historical context, with insufficient theorization of their interrelation. Third World writers suffer from, and depict, similar circumstances and necessarily write national allegories (Jameson 69).[1] As writers of a "minor literature," they cannot help writing in a voice that "takes on a collective value" (Deleuze and Guattari 17). A globalizing syllabus often links diverse writers such as Chinua Achebe, Tsitsi Dangarembga, Salman Rushdie, and Salih to the theories of Frantz Fanon, Edward Said, and Homi Bhabha. There is room for such courses, and indeed students and teachers both enjoy them. But we should be aware of the limitations of this approach. In proposing any category that focuses on authors from all possible former colonies who write in many languages and display wide differences in terms of religion, class, and gender, we risk erasing historical and ethnic particularities and affirming the boundaries of a now long-critiqued orientalist field first described in the work of Said.

Of course, a field characterized by ethnic or nationalist Balkanization is not necessarily preferable, nor even potentially administrable. One can scarcely imagine a department (whether English, Middle Eastern, or African studies) able to field a course in Sudanese literature even if Sudanese were a stable category.[2] Part of the problem may lie in an institutional identity crisis that arises out of the (useful but problematic) interdisciplinary approach now widespread in the teaching of and thinking about literature. Are we historians who teach texts because they share dates and historical specificities? Are we anthropologists who teach texts because of their shared cultural rituals or insights? Or is there another possibility, based in a return to aspects of textual thematism our field has by and large rejected as ahistorical?

To make the argument for a thematizing approach, I first review the main categories currently used in differentiating and organizing African literature. I show why I think each of these criteria, when used independently, fails as an organizing principle, particularly with respect to the Arab African novel. Finally, I offer some curricular suggestions for pairing Arab African novels with other African texts.

Geography makes at once the most and least sense as an institutional category for organizing African literature: writers, writing from Africa, seem African even if they feel they are also or primarily something else (e.g., Muslim, Arab, Egyptian). Algeria's first president, Ahmed Ben Bella, proudly declared himself, "Muslim first, Arab second, and then Algerian.

I am also proud to be an African" (qtd. in Malak 3). Yet even if Arab African writers often do not self-identify primarily as African but view themselves as something additional or different, rooted in Islam and linked to a Levantine or Gulf Arab history in addition to or rather than a sub-Saharan African history, they nonetheless write from a shared worldview based on their geographic and political proximities.[3] Moreover, African writers writing from the African diaspora, whether about Africa or not, exemplify the problem inherent in basing our categorization on territory alone. Their existence supports a more inclusive definition of what it means to be an African writer. Geography offers a useful criterion, but it cannot be the only one.

Language seems at first a better model for organizing and conceptualizing African literature (works in languages such as Hausa, Swahili, Yoruba, or Gikuyu), since a literature so defined would be broad enough to be African, even when a work is not written from or about Africa. Administrative reasons support the use of language to make decisions for syllabi. But several problems inhere in such choices, foremost of which is the question of how to define which languages count as African. Even if we draw a tenuous line between the languages of European colonialism and all the indigenous languages, we are left with the heated debate over whether Arabic is an African language.[4] All too easily, the definition of Africa in such a perspective becomes exclusive rather than inclusive. The canon of Nigerian, Ghanaian, and Ugandan greats, for instance, occludes Sudanese and Egyptian writers of similar merit if we allow language alone to draw our curricular boundaries. While taking language into consideration makes a good deal of sense, it should not be the only criterion.

Nevertheless, for administrative reasons, language is at present the most significant factor in the institutional placement of courses on African literature. Francophone and lusophone African writers find homes on the syllabi of Romance language departments, and anglophone African writers are slowly joining other postcolonial anglophone writers on the curricula assigned by English departments. African- and Arabic-language texts may end up assigned in translation or not at all, as administrative factors frequently restrict offerings in the language and literature of less commonly taught languages. Many schools cannot offer even introductory courses in such languages. In consequence of these twin administrative issues (language barriers and a paucity of courses), Arabic-language literature has an especially difficult time finding its way out of isolation and into regular curricular placements. It is all the more important, therefore, that we learn to see Arab African literature in its African context (as well as in its Middle Eastern one).[5]

The tension between Arabic- and non-Arabic-language African literature has seemed to grow rather than abate as the model in the teaching of African literature has become more language-centered and less thematic. The language distinction may be sensible as a principle of organization, but divisions along the lines of language also raise thorny issues of political and ethnic hegemony that the benefits of administrability do not seem to justify. Witness the shift to a model borrowed from the organizational principle of La Francophonie, in which the mere fact of language becomes part of a postimperialist claim to cultural determinism. If the text is in French, whether it was written now or in the seventeenth century, from Quebec, Switzerland, Guadeloupe, Algeria, or Senegal, this model puts it in the same category. Surely this linguistic centrism represents its own latter-day orientalism, effacing all historical and geographic contingencies other than the designs and legacies of French imperial expansion.

The rising insistence on anglophone African literature as a field raises similar problems. Should the texts *Matigari* (by Ngũgĩ wa Thiong'o), *L'amour, la fantasia* (by Assia Djebar), *In the Eye of the Sun* (by Ahdaf Soueif), and *A Season of Migration to the North*, originally written in four different languages, not belong together in a course on African writers—although they all deal with the very questions of language choice and colonial education—simply because the term *anglophone* increasingly modifies African writers? These texts share a great number of thematic correspondences and offer points for rich discussion; they should not be artificially kept apart for reasons of linguistic difference.

I want to stress that for the purposes of the classroom, anglophonia and *francophonie* are exclusionary notions that raise more problems than they address.[6] Of course we should not cease to teach anglophone novels, but we should strive to define modes of inclusion that make more pedagogical, and perhaps more thematic, sense. Courses based on exclusive identity or language build into their syllabi a set of assumptions and exclusions that require examination and understanding rather than a priori adoption. The Arab African novel exemplifies the problem with using such exclusions to make our curricular decisions. Arab African authors frequently disappear from consideration for lack of an institutionally easy place to situate them.[7]

Thus geography and language may play some role in our organization of African literature, but the emphasis should shift to other organizing ideas. Recent studies point to the importance of Islam to African literature. Earlier classes in the literature of Islam centered on unified Arabic, Persian, Turkish, or Indian historical fields, but new syllabi might include such authors professing, rejecting, or otherwise foregrounding Islam as Cheikh Hamidou Kane, Ahdaf Soueif, Salman Rushdie, Ousmane Sembène, Yahya Haqqi, and Zadie Smith. This change demonstrates an institutional willingness to search for another rubric for teachers, and it should encourage us to propose the inclusion of African authors. Arab African novels frequently express Muslim belief systems, and Islam offers one way to group texts thematically and culturally without restricting one to a single territory, language, or historical context.

By contrast, world literature courses frequently do away with territory and language and link their texts mainly through historical context (colonialism, decolonization, national independence, etc.). Typically they stress the shared postcoloniality of texts hailing not from the whole world but from the so-called Third World.[8] Such courses make sense up to a point, and I ought to add that if these are to be a department's only courses teaching African texts, then ultimately I support them. But we ought to have courses that go beyond this transgeographic, transhistorical (if well-intended) form of orientalism. Just because a text hails from or features the developing world does not mean that it automatically displays all the traces and effects of colonialism. And to script the interconnection among texts as one beginning with disenfranchisement, lack of political hegemony, and passive responses to colonialism inscribes a history of power relations that everything about the postcolonial field and scholarly ethos seeks to rewrite. Even when analysis of texts focuses on elements that display the power inequities institutionalized by imperialism, we can avoid categorization according to those inequities by employing different strategies of selection and grouping.

Instead, we can organize our syllabi through textual similarities and connections that stress their individualities as texts rather than their mere adherence to institution-friendly teaching categories. Thematic clusters of inquiry that group novels offer one way to set up useful intertextual moments between African and Arab African novels. For example, a unit on London might begin with a comparison among anglophone texts by women: Soueif's *In the Eye of the Sun*, Buchi Emecheta's *Second Class Citizen*. One could expand the unit to include texts by men (Waguih Ghali's *Beer in the Snooker Club*) or texts focused on the idea of return to one's homeland after an experience in England (Achebe's *No Longer at*

Ease or Peter Abrahams's *A Wreath for Udomo*). Moving in a different direction, one could juxtapose treatments of London with narratives of the African city (Ayi Kwei Armah's *The Beautyful Ones Are Not Yet Born* or Naguib Mahfouz's *Palace Walk*). Still another possibility would be to turn explicitly to issues of colonialism and postcolonialism in relation to London as an imperial power (Jamal Mahjoub's *In the Hour of Signs* or Ngũgĩ's *Grain of Wheat*).[9]

This process should differ from building a syllabus as we have done in the past. Usually we proceeded by aiming at coverage of an area or genre or by beginning with a static category in mind that we then sought to fill with suitable texts. Instead, I advocate an approach that begins with a text and adds texts to it in a process of layering that speaks, with each addition, to questions of canonicity and intertextuality. Why do these texts belong together, and what ideas do they share or not share? Each pairing should raise the question of the canon as an explicit textual exploration in addition to the thematic and cultural problems the text presents and confronts.

It is only through consistent investigations into where the Arab African novel belongs that we will adequately address the institutional identity crisis presently before us.

Notes

1. "[Third World writers] necessarily project a political dimension in the form of national allegory" (Jameson 69).

2. Along with Salih, Christian anglophone minority writers from the Sudan, such as Taban lo Liyong, and Muslim anglophone British Sudanese writers, such as Jamal Mahjoub, give a sense of the category's diversity of perspective and origins.

3. Besides having some territorial features in common, such as the Nile or the desert, Arab writers share with many African writers the experiences of European colonialism and Islamic imperial expansion. Frequently, they also possess similar histories of technological advance, urbanization, and decolonization. The greater the physical proximity, linguistic overlap, and religious consensus between these authors, often, the tighter the nexus between them.

4. I follow Ngũgĩ wa Thiong'o, who distinguishes between "the linguistic encirclement of [the European] continent" and a group of African languages including Arabic, "Swahili, Zulu, Yoruba . . . and Amharic" (*Decolonising* 6).

5. This wider contextualization presents challenges for the scholar of Middle Eastern studies. Otherwise admirable accounts of the Arabic novel often fail to discuss —even mention— Africa, even when nationalism and place form a large part of the discussion (see Allen 79–83; Kilpatrick 8–17).

6. With authors writing in more than one language, such as Ngũgĩ, Sol Plaatje, Ahdaf Soueif, and Okot p'Bitek, a single-language requirement would have us overlook other important works in their oeuvre.

7. Privileging anglophone and francophone Arab authors over those who choose to write in Arabic plays out a kind of political disenfranchisement reminiscent of forms of colonial disempowerment. It may once have been the case that few Arab writers wrote in English (Said 406), but as the number of gifted Arab anglophone writers grows —Soueif, Fadia Faqir, Leila Aboulela, and Jamal Mahjoub are but a few of the emerging voices in that field— the inequity may continue unchecked unless we seek new ways to think about African and Arab African literature.

8. Such courses, relying on an undertheoretized categorization, often imply through their contents that the definition for *world literature* is "all the literature produced elsewhere." The alterity inscribed in this category of world thus reifies a divide between "our" Western world and "their" exotic non-Western one and demonstrates a rigid, binaristic spirit of thinking that we seek to avoid in our scholarship. We should take care to avoid it in our teaching as well.

9. These suggestions, along with the reading list in the appendix to this essay, downplay novels from a number of important African languages, including Amharic, Hausa, and Tswana. To my dismay, finding teachable texts in translation has often been difficult or impossible; I make my suggestions accordingly.

Works Cited

Abrahams, Peter. *A Wreath for Udomo.* New York: Collier, 1971. Print.

Achebe, Chinua. *No Longer at Ease.* 1960. New York: Anchor, 1994. Print.

———. *Things Fall Apart.* 1959. New York: Anchor, 1994. Print.

Allen, Roger. *The Arabic Novel: An Historical and Critical Introduction.* Syracuse: Syracuse UP, 1994. Print.

Armah, Ayi Kwei. *The Beautyful Ones Are Not Yet Born.* London: Heinemann, 1968. Print.

Bâ, Mariama. *So Long a Letter.* Trans. Modupé Bodé-Thomas. Portsmouth: Heinemann, 1989. Print.

Ben Jelloun, Tahar. *The Sand Child.* Trans. Alan Sheridan. San Diego: Harcourt, 1987. Print. Trans. of *L'enfant de sable.*

Dangarembga, Tsitsi. *Nervous Conditions.* London: Woman's, 1988. Print.

Deleuze, Gilles, and Félix Guattari. *Kafka: Toward a Minor Literature.* Trans. Dana Polan. Minneapolis: U of Minnesota P, 1986. Print.

Emecheta, Buchi. *Second Class Citizen.* New York: Braziller, 1975. Print.

Farah, Nuruddin. *Gifts.* London: Serif, 1993. Print.

Ghali, Waguih. *Beer in the Snooker Club.* 1964. London: Serpent's Tail, 1987. Print.

Gordimer, Nadine. *The House Gun.* New York: Penguin, 1988. Print.

al-Hakim, Tawfiq. *Maze of Justice: Diary of a Country Prosecutor.* Trans. Zeinab al-Hakim. Austin: U of Texas P, 1989. Print. Trans. of *Yawmiyat na'ib fi al-aryaf.* 1947.

Haqqi, Yahya. "*The Lamp of Umm Hashim" and Other Stories.* Cairo: AUC, 2004. Print.

Jameson, Fredric. "Third World Literature in the Era of Multinational Capitalism." *Social Text* 15 (1986): 65–88. Print.

Kilpatrick, Hilary. *The Modern Egyptian Novel: A Study in Social Criticism.* London: Ithaca, 1974. Print.

Mahfouz, Naguib. *Palace Walk.* Trans. William Maynard Hutchins and Olive E. Kenny. New York: Anchor, 1990. Print. Trans. of *Bayn al-Qasrayn.* 1956.

———. *The Thief and the Dogs.* Trans. Trevor Le Gassick and M. M. Badawi. New York: Anchor, 1984. Print. Trans. of *Al-Liss wal-Kilab.* 1961.

Mahjoub, Jamal. *In the Hour of Signs.* London: Heinemann, 1996. Print.

Malak, Amin. *Muslim Narratives and the Discourse of English.* Albany: State U of New York P, 2004. Print.

Mda, Zakes. *The Madonna of Excelsior.* New York: Farrar, 2004. Print.

Ngũgĩ wa Thiong'o. *Decolonising the Mind.* London: Heinemann, 1986. Print.

———. *Devil on the Cross.* Portsmouth: Heinemann, 1982. Print. Trans. of *Caitaani Mũtharaba-inĩ.* 1980.

———. *Grain of Wheat.* London: Heinemann, 1967. Print.

Said, Edward. "The Anglo-Arab Encounter." *"Reflections on Exile" and Other Essays.* Cambridge: Harvard UP, 2003. 405–10. Print.

Salih, Tayeb. *Season of Migration to the North.* Trans. Denys Johnson-Davies. New York: Penguin, 2003. Print.

Soueif, Ahdaf. *In the Eye of the Sun.* New York: Pantheon, 1992. Print.

———. *Map of Love.* London: Bloomsbury, 1999. Print.

Soyinka, Wole. *Ìsarà: A Voyage around Essay.* London: Methuen, 1990. Print.

al-Zayyat, Latifah. *The Open Door.* Trans. Marilyn Booth. Cairo: AUC, 2000. Print. Trans. of *Al-Bab al-Maftuh.*

Appendix: Additional Possibilities for Teaching the Arab African Novel in the Context of African Literature

Education and Identity

Mariama Bâ, *So Long a Letter* (*Une si longue lettre*)
Tsitsi Dangarembga, *Nervous Conditions*
Yahya Haqqi, *The Lamp of Umm Hashim* (*Qindil Umm Hashim*)
Tayeb Salih, *Season of Migration to the North* (*Mawsim al-Hiǧra ilā ash-Shamāl*)
Wole Soyinka, *Ìsarà: A Voyage around Essay*

Law and Literature

Chinua Achebe, *Things Fall Apart*
Nadine Gordimer, *The House Gun*
Tawfiq al-Hakim, *Maze of Justice: Diary of a Country Prosecutor* (*Yawmiyat na'ib fi al-aryaf*)

Naguib Mahfouz, *The Thief and the Dogs* (*Al-Liss wal-Kilab*)
Ngũgĩ wa Thiong'o, *Devil on the Cross* (*Caitaani Mutharaba-ini*)

Gender, Difference, and the Nation

Tahar Ben Jelloun, *The Sand Child (L'enfant de sable)*
Nuruddin Farah, *Gifts*
Ahdaf Soueif, *Map of Love*
Zakes Mda, *The Madonna of Excelsior*
Latifah al-Zayyat, *The Open Door (Al-Bab al-Maftuh)*

Jarrod Hayes

Approaches to Teaching the Maghrebian Novel: Allegory at the Crossroads

In both French studies and African studies, the Maghreb occupies a peculiar place. In French studies, it is—along with French Canada, the Caribbean, and sub-Saharan Africa—one of the four major regions into which francophone studies is frequently divided, which oddly implies that, even though Algeria, Morocco, and Tunisia are as much a part of the African continent as any sub-Saharan country, North Africa is as distinct from the rest of Africa as from, say, Quebec or the Caribbean. The Maghreb's relation with the field of African literary studies in general has also been somewhat tenuous. In the United States at least, African studies has often favored cultural production in English, and the lack of a significant body of Maghrebian literature in English has a double effect when it comes to setting the Maghreb apart: literatures in French and Arabic are simply less likely to be studied, and unlike West Africa, for example, the Maghreb has no former British colonies whose literary production might draw attention to the region and thereby compensate for this neglect.[1]

There are obvious reasons why it might sometimes be productive to study each region separately: early Islamicization (beginning in the seventh century BCE) and subsequent Arabization, resulting political and cultural ties with the Middle East, and a commonly perceived racial difference between North Africa and sub-Saharan Africa all set the Maghreb apart from the rest of the continent. Yet excluding the Maghreb from a general discussion of African literature runs the risk of reinforcing popular conceptions that sub-Saharan Africa is homogeneous and of naturalizing both the racialization that underlies the notion of a black Africa and the frequent slippage between Africa *tout court* and sub-Saharan Africa. Incorporating Maghrebian novels into African literature offers the potential of challenging these commonplace assumptions. Nevertheless, this essay argues that the Maghreb's peculiar place as both a part of and different from (the rest of) Africa should not be entirely effaced in any effort to integrate the Maghreb into a discussion of teaching the African novel. Rather, this peculiar place might be productively mined for its considerable pedagogical potential.

In June 1997 the Maghrebianist Hédi Abdel-Jaouad organized a conference in Hammamet, Tunisia, "Le Maghreb à la croisée des cultures" ("The Maghreb at the Crossroads of Cultures"), whose title offers a useful tool for conceptualizing the composite nature of Maghrebian cultures, a key factor in this potential. Despite the Maghreb's position of difference from and within (the rest of) Africa, the numerous approaches to teaching its novels provide multiple connections to the other approaches described in this volume. Indeed, there is probably at least one Maghrebian novel that could complement every chapter in this volume. I have taught Maghrebian novels in a number of different contexts, from a course in French on childhood narratives (designed to help bridge the traditional gap between French-language courses and upper-level courses for majors) to a variety of graduate seminars on panfrancophone topics. Between these two levels, I have taught an introduction to francophone literature in translation, a regionally focused course consisting entirely of Maghrebian novels, as well as non-region-specific courses in francophone studies, with specialized topics such as roots narratives or the relation between the French new novel and difficult postcolonial works in French.

Using the region-specific course as a starting point, this essay explores historical approaches to teaching Maghrebian novels, particularly in relation to the development of national identity after World War II. Though I organize the course by focusing on the participation of Maghrebian novels in the creation of national narratives, other approaches highlight the disruption of national narratives by representations of sexuality, gender, and ethnic specificity. The status of allegory in postcolonial studies is a beleaguered one, but allegory (that which obtains when a narrative at the literal level tells additional stories at other levels) offers a way to teach multiple and contradictory stories in a single text. As a pedogogical tool, therefore, the concept of allegory can help students keep track of a given text's sometimes contradictory meanings as well as understand how these meanings relate to one another.

History and the Maghrebian Novel

Perhaps the strongest factor in the Maghreb's character as a cultural crossroads is its complex history of being crisscrossed by many peoples: from time immemorial, when North Africa was inhabited by Berbers or Imazighen; to the Phoenician colonies such as Carthage (founded around 814 BCE); to the Punic Wars (263–146 BCE), which ended with the Roman conquest of Phoenician Africa and the simultaneous rise of the independent Berber state of Numidia; to the Vandal invasion, fall of Roman Africa (429 CE), and establishment of Byzantine control over formerly Roman Africa (533); to the Arab invasion, followed by about eight hundred years of various dynasties, the establishment of Ottoman domination over Algeria and Tunisia in the sixteenth century, and the French colonization of Algeria (after the conquest of Algiers in 1830) and Morocco and Tunisia (in the form of protectorates established in 1881 and 1912); to formal independence for Morocco and Tunisia in 1956 and, after eight years of bloody war, for Algeria in 1962.[2]

In addition to this cursory time line, the notion of a cultural crossroads evokes the changing shape of political borders of the region, reaching at times as far north as the Iberian Peninsula during dynasties such as the Almoravids (1062–147) and the Almohads (1147–269) and, under the Almoravids, as far south as Timbuktu and the ancient empire of Ghana. It is by thus bridging Europe and sub-Saharan Africa that the Maghreb offers the pedagogical opportunity to help students question the European "invention of Africa" (see Mudimbe), which asserts the fiction of Africa as a cultural whole that sets itself apart as Europe's complete other. Finally, whereas the Maghreb is considered to be a part of the Orient by the French, in Arabic it is named as the place where the sun sets (i.e., the West); in its very name, therefore, it challenges the many *idées reçues* that constitute the Orient as still another European invention.

The Maghreb's long history of violence, conquest, and oppression has left many wounds; yet it is precisely by keeping these wounds open that many Maghrebian writers have been able to exploit this history as a source of cultural diversity. One finds an eloquent example of such exploitation in Yacine Kateb's *Nedjma* (1956), whose treatment of diversity can also serve as an introduction to other writers. Kateb reveals the importance of Maghrebian history as a cultural crossroads by describing the personal trajectory of one of his protagonists, a to-and-fro that reveals an affective relation with this history's many layers:

> I have lived in both places, the rock, then the plain where Cirta and Hippone knew greatness [la grossesse] and then decline. . . . [G]lory and fall will have founded the eternity of ruins upon the rise of the new cities, more alive yet severed from their history, deprived of the charm of childhood to the benefit of their ennobled specters. . . . Constantine and Bône, the two cities that dominated ancient Numidia, today reduced to a French department. . . . Two souls struggling for the power abdicated by the Numidians. Constantine struggling for Cirta, and Bône for Hippone, as if what is at stake with the past [l'enjeu du passé], congealed in a fatherland apparently lost, constituted the only ordeal for the future champions. . . .
> (232–33 [trans. modified]; 174–75)[3]

As the novel's setting shifts back and forth between the then-contemporary cities of Constantine and Bône (they would become Qacentina and Annaba after independence), the characters are also obliged to pass through the ruins, literal and imaginary, of the Numidian cities of Cirta and Hippone that lie beneath them. This itinerary thus becomes a metaphor for reconnecting with moments from Algeria's living past, which the characters carry within themselves:

> Not the remains of the Romans. Not that kind of ruins, where the soul of the multitudes has only had time to languish, while engraving their farewell in the rock, but the ruins left as traces [en filigraine] from all times, the ruins steeped in the blood of our veins. . . .
> (232 [trans. modified]; 174)

The narrative, structured by a geographic movement that is also historical, thereby posits the characters' stories as an allegory of Algeria's history, which is one reason *Nedjma* is often considered *the* novel of Algerian identity. This link between the present and a shared past—also a link between individuals and the collective—represents "what is at stake in the past": the role of history in a nationalist revolutionary project. The ghosts Kateb conjures up from the past ("ennobled specters") provide a source of inspiration for the national consciousness ("a fatherland" only "apparently lost") that will lead to resistance to French colonialism (the resisters as "future champions").

The Politics of History

The Arabs were certainly the conquerors who established the most permanent as well as the most discernible presence in the Maghreb, but Kateb digs deeper into the past to characterize the Arab conquest as one among many carried out by outsiders arriving in the Maghreb with the desire to possess it. In so doing, he disrupts more official expressions of national identity, such as the one articulated by the famous slogan "Islam is my religion, Arabic is my language, Algeria is my fatherland." Uttered in the 1930s by Sheikh Abd-el-Hamid Ben Badis, leader of the Association of Ulema, this formula defines Algerian identity in part by excluding Algerians who are not Muslim or Arabic-speaking—that is, most notably, Berbers and Jews.

While official policies of postindependence Arabicization have attempted to assert one origin of Maghrebian culture (the Arab origin) at the expense of all others, Kateb as well as many other Maghrebian writers might be characterized by the resistance they offer to such attempts at homogenization:

> Wadis dried out in favor of lesser brooks leading up to the confluence, the sea where no springs recognize their own sound: horror, *mêlée*, void—the ocean—haven't we all seen our origins blurred like a stream in the sand. . . . (*Nedjma* 128 [trans. modified]; 97)

By blurring the multiple origins of Algerian identity, Kateb insists on the impossibility of teasing out one origin above all others and instead valorizes the *métissage* that characterizes Maghrebian history. In opposition to the Arab roots stressed by dominant versions of nationalism, he celebrates the rhizomatic aspect of Maghrebian cultures.

Denial of the Berber elements of Maghrebian culture on the part of postindependence regimes (especially in Algeria, but also to a certain extent in Morocco) continues the tendency of a certain brand of preindependence nationalism, which insisted on unity at the expense of cultural diversity.[4] Kateb's representation of an organic connection to all aspects of Maghrebian history thereby dislodges Arabic languages and Arab culture from their dominant position by insisting that the Arabization of the Maghreb has been far from complete. In finding revolutionary inspiration in a Berber past, he fulfills his stated desire to be "au sein de la perturbation, l'éternel perturbateur" (qtd. in Bonn, *Roman* 67 [from a 1958 interview]; "the eternal disruptor in the midst of disruption"). In other words, although the Algerian revolution was challenging colonialism and would ultimately put an end to French rule in Algeria, Kateb also felt that the revolution itself needed to be challenged from within to prevent it from solidifying into a new form of oppression—and history has proved him right.

Kateb might be one of the most eloquent poets of the heterogeneity of Maghrebian culture, history, and identity, among writers at least, but he is not alone. The title of an essay I often teach by the Moroccan writer Tahar Ben Jelloun—"Défendre la diversité culturelle au Maghreb" (1991; "Defend Cultural Diversity in the Maghreb")—might therefore be read not only as a major project of many Maghrebian writers but also as the potential of Maghrebian literature to enhance an appreciation of diversity in Africa as a whole. Interventions such as Kateb's—which conjure up a rich past to challenge official versions of national identity—thus have a political urgency for Maghrebian writers. At the same time, in classrooms far removed from North Africa, Maghrebian novels offer the pedagogical benefit of complicating our understandings of identity through these very rereadings of history.[5]

My region-based course on the Maghreb has attempted to realize this potential by enriching students' understanding of how individuals inhabit their national identities. The most recent version of this course is entitled Our Nations, Our Selves: Writing Maghrebian Identity, and its description begins with the following questions:

> Why do we believe in our country?
> Why do we take affronts to our nation so personally?
> What role does national belonging play in our sense of who we are?
> How important is our nation's history to our identity?
> To what extent does that history become myth- or legend-like?
> What happens to our sense of self when we are marginalized in our nation's public sphere?
> What would happen to our sense of self if we lost our nationality?
> Can nations, identity, and national identity be compared to fiction?

These questions could be asked of Americans and receive answers, passionate in some cases, quite relevant to current events. Through them, I drew on students' possible connections to key questions explored in

Maghrebian novels to discourage students from reading these novels as totally foreign. Although it is important, from the standpoint of a pedagogy that values multicultural knowledge, to encourage the skill of recognizing, appreciating, and understanding difference and to discourage a projection of ourselves onto other cultures, the current political climate in the United States makes such an erasure of difference unlikely. Recent United States military interventions in the Middle East have given rise to a proliferation of anti-Muslim stereotypes in the media that portray Arab and Muslim countries as fundamentally at odds with the United States. Making familiar what students might otherwise find foreign and inaccessible allows them to negotiate between their own cultures and the ones they are studying and to challenge this alterity by complicating the opposition between sameness and difference, between self and other. These questions also challenge the imagining by American students of an Africa qua total difference.

The National Politics of Literary History

The syllabus for my course on the Maghreb includes the following novels:

Mouloud Feraoun's *Le fils du pauvre* ("The Poor Man's Son") (Algeria, 1950)
Albert Memmi's *La statue de sel* (*The Pillar of Salt*) (Tunisia, 1953)
Rachid Boudjedra's *La répudiation* (*The Repudiation*) (Algeria, 1969)
Tahar Ben Jelloun's *L'enfant de sable* (*The Sand Child*) (Morocco, 1985)
Assia Djebar's *Ombre sultane* (*A Sister to Scheherazade*) (Algeria, 1987).

This reading list is organized along chronological lines so that students can more easily keep track of evolving approaches to literary intervention in the development of national identities. The course thus relies on a version of literary history that, implicitly or explicitly, informs many studies of Maghrebian literature,[6] a version that is heavily indebted to Frantz Fanon's outline of national literary history in *Wretched of the Earth*:

> First, the colonized intellectual proves he has assimilated the colonizer's culture. . . . This is the phase of full assimilation where we find Parnassians, Symbolists, and Surrealists among the colonized writers.

> In a second stage, the colonized writer has his convictions shaken and decides to remember. . . . Old childhood episodes will be brought back from the depths of memory, old legends will be reinterpreted on the basis of a borrowed aesthetic . . . and of a concept of the world discovered under other skies. Sometimes this precombat literature is steeped in humor and allegory. . . .
>
> Finally a third stage, a combat stage where the colonized writer, after having tried to lose himself among the people, with the people, will rouse the people. Combat literature, revolutionary literature, national literature emerges. (158–59 [trans. modified]; 162 in French)

Though supposedly a generic outline of literatures of the colonized African nation, this sketch is heavily influenced by Fanon's participation in the Algerian revolution. In fact, his importance in the articulation of pan-Africanism and his insistence that the Algerian revolution be closely tied to the national movements of other African countries underscore the importance of including the Algerian case in approaches to teaching the African novel that focus on the question of nationalism. Conversely, a study of Maghrebian novels that highlights the Maghreb's cultural diversity can, while productively using the Fanonian schema as a general organizing principle, explore ways in which Maghrebian literary history will always spill out of the confines of this schema.

My course begins with Fanon's second phase, during which writers schooled in the French tradition began to write as nationalist movements were gaining strength after World War II. By asserting a national identity consisting partially of a precolonial culture that survived colonialism and partially of a new project for what would emerge after independence, these writers produced texts that began to distinguish themselves from the literature of metropolitan France. In these works, childhood narrative was the privileged genre for asserting selfhood in the context of developing national consciousness.

The first example I teach from this period, Feraoun's *Le fils du pauvre*, tells the story of Fouroulou Menrad (an anagram of the author's name) as he grows up in a Kabyle village. After an attempted apprenticeship of Kabyle codes of masculinity (which mostly fails), Fouroulou embarks on a French colonial education. But if *Le fils du pauvre* might be characterized as a kind of success story, Memmi's *La statue de sel* refuses to associate French education with a form of progress or civilization and offers a detailed analysis of the resulting alienation. After internalizing a colonial rejection of his culture, the Jewish narrator, Alexandre Mordekhaï

Benillouche, is in turn rejected by the very civilization he has been taught to strive for.

Fanon's third phase includes Maghrebian novels that became more explicit in their representation of resistance to French colonialism, which was now more overt, direct, and even violent. Some critics thought that this combat literature should be written in a social realist mode.[7] The best writers of the period, however, resisted such prescriptions. For example, Abdelkebir Khatibi characterizes *Nedjma* through a description of Kateb's "terrorist technique that shatters the structure inherent in the novel and creates a dazzling language that fires off rockets in all directions" (103). Here Khatibi articulates a notion of combat literature that does not limit itself to representing political struggle; rather, it also allows itself to be transformed through that struggle. His description could apply equally well to Mohammed Dib's *Qui se souvient de la mer* (*Who Remembers the Sea*) (Algeria, 1962), whose narrator remembers his childhood as the bombs set off by his wife against the colonizer also destroy their marriage and his masculinity. Unfortunately, both novels often prove too difficult for undergraduates, especially when taught in French. For my Mahgreb course, I therefore introduce the Algerian revolution through Fanon's essay "Algeria Unveiled" (1959) and Gillo Pontecorvo's film *The Battle of Algiers* (1966). In other contexts, however, I have had some success in teaching *Nedjma* in both French and English by guiding students through the novel's complex narrative structure.[8]

Teachers who are able to develop successful strategies for teaching Kateb and Dib can reap great benefits, since both novelists show how Fanon's model of literary history can mislead in suggesting that the characteristics of each period are superseded by those of the next. By narrative intercutting between childhood and the national struggle, both novelists serve as vivid examples of how, in an alternative reading of Fanon, one can see each subsequent phase as preserving the characteristics of previous phases while superposing another layer of complexity, a complexity that is in part historical. By establishing a parallel between a childhood narrative and the story of the birth of a nation, novels such as Kateb's and Dib's make the former an allegory of the latter. They might therefore be said to constitute rereadings of the childhood narratives of earlier periods that reveal them to be more politically sophisticated than some critics inspired by Fanon have thought.

I also make up for the gap left by leaving out Kateb and Dib by teaching the combat literature genre through subsequent periods, which continue this process of layering. This approach works well, because after independence, the story of growing up, though transformed, remains an important allegory for the birth of the Maghrebian nation. For younger writers growing up during the independence movements, combat narratives were a part of the stories of their childhood. And once the disappointment with postindependence reality sets in, criticism of the national government parallels the criticism once made against colonialism.[9] Boudjedra's *La répudiation*, for example, tells the story of Rachid's childhood and of his mother's repudiation by his father. Rachid narrates his past to his nurse-lover as a patient-prisoner in what is either a psychiatric hospital or a prison (or possibly both). His incarceration is described as the result of his political activities, though he is likely mentally ill as well. His revolt has continued after the revolution but is also allegorized before it in his revolt against his bourgeois father, who was first a collaborator with the colonizers, then an ardent though hypocritical nationalist, and finally a fundamentalist (in what is an uncanny prediction of the turn Algerian politics would take in the 1990s).

The last two texts in my course also represent these trends. Ben Jelloun's *L'enfant de sable* tells the story of Ahmed, who is born a girl into a family that already has seven daughters, is raised as a boy by his/her father, and is married to a woman. Ahmed relinquishes his acquired masculinity after his/her father's death. In this allegory of becoming a woman—which Ahmed quite literally does by renaming himself/herself Zahra—gender becomes a performance fit only for a freak show, in which the bearded Zahra subsequently gains employment. That Ahmed's story coincides with Morocco's independence makes this tale of gender a national allegory as well. Djebar's *Ombre sultane* tells of two women, Isma and Hajila, who have shared a husband. In fact, Isma, who narrates the life stories of both women, arranged the second marriage as a means of gaining her own freedom. While her relationship with her husband, whom the novel simply calls "the man," might be characterized as a love story, Hajila's relationship is one of rape and abuse. Hajila finds her freedom by first donning a veil, then by going out either to relish the homosocial promiscuity of the women's *hammam* ("bath") or to remove her veil in public.

The Sexual Politics of National Literature

As the examples of Boudjedra, Ben Jelloun, and Djebar suggest, gender and sexuality can play an important role in Maghrebian narratives of national identity. In "Défendre la diversité culturelle au Mahgreb," Ben Jelloun clarifies this role by suggesting its political nature:

> In general, the novel of French expression is where one finds the most audacity in contesting the social order and transgressing taboos, especially sexual ones. The fact that these authors write in French pushes them further in their critiques. . . . This attempt to unveil, this door opening onto a secret, onto a hidden wealth, is severely and often brutally criticized by Maghrebian intellectuals who write in Arabic. This openness toward the West, this hand extended in the spirit of exchange, this use of the other's language are considered by some to be treason. (272)

Here Ben Jelloun associates betrayal of nationality (writing in the language of the colonizer, revealing the nation's dirty secrets to outsiders) with sexual transgression. Furthermore, in the first sentence, he sets up a parallel between violating sexual taboos and political contestation. In a sense, then, for Ben Jelloun novelistic representations of nonnormative sexualities offer Maghrebian novelists another way to carry out, in Kateb's famous words, disruption in the midst of disruption.

One finds a personification of such sexual disruption in Boudjedra's *La répudiation*. The character Zahir is not only the narrator's homosexual brother, he is also his political mentor. Zahir is the one who points out that their father, Si Zoubir, collaborates with French colonial rule. Patriarchal authority is thereby associated with colonialism, and the father is considered so much a threat to the Secret Members of the Clan (a barely veiled reference to the FLN [Front de Libération Nationale]) that the members kill him, perhaps with the complicity of Si Zoubir. The novel, however, does the opposite of what the father and the new national elite try to do; it foils their attempt to eliminate queerness by describing in full detail what they seek to remove from view. The scene in which Zahir has sex with a buddy on a rooftop terrace as Zahir's mother and siblings look on is one of the longest and most beautiful descriptions of same-sex eroticism in all of African literature. It is perhaps not even surpassed by the more recent works of such openly gay writers as Rachid O. (Morocco) and Eyet-Chékib Djaziri (Tunisia) or by Nina Bouraoui's novel of lesbian love *La vie heureuse* (2002; "The Happy Life").[10] Boudjedra's revelations, then, carry out just the sort of unveiling described by Ben Jelloun.

Sexual revelations serve similar political purposes in Driss Chraïbi's first novel, *Le passé simple* (*The Simple Past*) (Morocco, 1954), which begins as Driss, the protagonist-narrator, defies his father by refusing to keep fast after sunset one evening during Ramadan. (The father is punishing the entire family by forcing them to remain hungry, because another son is out getting drunk instead of returning home to break the fast with the family.) This filial revolt ends with Driss's revelation of his father's dirty secrets (his father smokes pot, drinks alcohol, and has a mistress and illegitimate children on the side), but not before his father kicks him out onto the streets. These revelations parallel the novel's political ones, which are unveiled as a homeless Driss quickly discovers that all his friends have been bought off by his father. (Like Si Zoubir, his father collaborates with colonial authority despite his supposedly nationalist leanings.) When the father finally buys off Driss as well, by sending him to finish his studies in France, the revolt against paternal authority is ultimately co-opted. Furthermore, this recuperation of resistance is accompanied by the normalization of Driss's sexuality, which involves not becoming exclusively heterosexual, as Western readers might expect, but rather refusing to play the passive role any longer in sexual intercourse with other men (although he is still willing to penetrate them).

Both Boudjedra and Chraïbi bridge the split that, according to Fredric Jameson, defines the modern, capitalist West:

> [the] radical split between the private and the public, between the poetic and the political, between what we have come to think of as the domain of sexuality and the unconscious and that of the public world of classes, of the economic, and of secular political power. (69)

Bridging it is precisely the work of national allegory, the concept with which Jameson characterizes Third World literature: "Third-world texts, even those which are seemingly private and invested with a properly libidinal dynamic—necessarily project a political dimension in the form of national allegory" (69). While *Le passé simple* does not necessarily confirm Jameson's generalization (one subsequently criticized by a number of people),[11] it does have an allegorical level that is quite accessible. (Though I do not teach the novel in my course on the Maghreb, I have taught it in several others, most frequently in English translation.) Driss's revolt against a tyrannical father clearly allegorizes a revolt against colonial rule, also represented by the father in his complicity with colonialism. When this revolt turns out to be a reconciliation (literally with the same tyrannical father, allegorically with the tyrannical monarch-to-be), Chraïbi suggests that the anticolonial revolt particular to Morocco is being co-opted into another form of oppressive rule by its leader—or at least its figurehead, the future Mohammed V, who appears quite literally in the novel to give his blessing for Driss's journey to France.

In Jameson's conceptualization, it is precisely sexuality at the literal level that projects political meaning at the allegorical level. In *L'enfant de sable* as well, Ben Jelloun offers a fairly explicit clue as to the allegorical function of sexuality through a birth announcement published by Ahmed's father. At the end of the announcement, the father proclaims, "This birth will bring fertility to the land, peace and prosperity to the country. Long live Ahmed! Long live Morocco!" (19). If there is any doubt as to the political implications here, the novel clarifies, "The last sentence also caused a stir. The French police did not at all care for the 'Long live Morocco!' The nationalist militants did not know that this rich craftsman was also a patriot" (20). Yet such a strong connection made between the birth of a future male citizen and the birth of the independent nation suggests that national becoming requires the heterosexual reproduction of male citizens and that nationalism depends on sexual normativity. But what happens to this relation when Ahmed's birth is rejected as a hoax, when maleness itself is revealed to be a fiction, when Ahmed's heterosexuality is questioned not only through marriage with a woman but also through several homoerotic scenes that are a part of his becoming a woman?

One answer to these questions can be found by reading Jameson through Paul de Man's notion that "any narrative is primarily the allegory of its own reading" and "the narrative of its own deconstruction" (76–77). If national allegories can also be read as allegories of reading, whenever the sexuality that signifies allegorically at the level of national politics is one that violates a nation's family values, the de Manian deconstruction carried out by the allegory of reading can also be understood as a queering that deconstructs national narratives, indeed even national identity itself.

Engendering Nations

That this queering was not welcomed by some nationalists is evidenced by the scandals caused by Chraïbi's and Boudjedra's novels. *Le passé simple* was harshly criticized not only for titillating readers with representations of sexuality but also for spitting on Islam in the institution of paternity. (The spit is literal; in one scene the father forces the entire family to line up and spit in his face.)[12] The scandals caused by novels that gave a prominent place to queerness were not isolated, as Abdelkebir Khatibi points out in describing reactions to Djebar's first novel (published in 1957):

> Algerian revolutionaries found it indecent that, in this novel, Djebar would only be preoccupied with the sexual problem while Algeria was in the grasp of a horrible war. Hadn't they understood that the protagonist's discovery of her body in *La soif* ["Thirst"] was also an important revolution? (62)

These reactions reveal just how threatened some male nationalists felt by open discussions of women's sexuality. Yet, although Ben Jelloun in *L'enfant de sable* reveals the gendered nature of nationalism by associating masculinity with nation building, his metaphoric use of the term *unveil* in his essay discussed above ("Défendre" 272) is disconnected from the physical veil some Maghrebian women choose or are constrained to wear. The implicit parallel between feminist and queer menaces he makes in the novel thus remains elusive in the essay. In contrast, Djebar's work has consistently incorporated detailed stories of women's lives and the many forms their resistance to male domination can take, thereby granting a female specificity to forms of gendered resistance to dominant nationalist discourses. She has shown, in other words, that gender insubordination can provide a means of queering the nation that is just as important as the so-called unveiling of nonnormative sexualities.

Teaching a novel such as *Ombre sultane*, however, comes with its own dangers. American students, familiar with images of burka-clad women, can be too quick to associate all forms of veiling with the oppression of women. (The forms are often lumped into a single practice, with total disregard for the multiplicity of garments the term *veil* can mean as well as reasons for and ways of wearing them.) Arab or Muslim societies, in this view, are considered misogynistic in essence. But teaching Djebar with Fanon's essay "Algeria Unveiled" can draw attention to the colonial (and often masculinist) history of Western desires to unveil Muslim women. Other essays by feminists can further encourage students to interrogate Western tendencies to project misogyny onto Arab or Muslim societies while ignoring and underestimating specifically American forms of misogyny: Francesca Canadé Sautman's "Hassiba Boulmerka's Raised Fist: The Body of Evidence and Muslim Herstory," Homa Hoodfar's "Return to the Veil: Personal Strategy and Public Participation in Egypt," Chandra

Talpade Mohanty's "Under Western Eyes: Feminist Scholarship and Colonial Discourses," and Marnia Lazreg's "Feminism and Difference: The Perils of Writing as a Woman on Women in Algeria." Such secondary texts foster readings of *Ombre sultane* that highlight Hajila's complex relation to the veil she puts on and then removes. For in fact this veil comes to symbolize not her oppression but her freedom, in that it allows her to escape from an oppressive household and circulate in public. These essays also foster interpretations of the novel that resist the urge to dismiss Hajila's experience of marriage as violent and abusive by restricting the implications of Djebar's representation of it to polygamy. Polygamous marriage, after all, has no monopoly on domestic violence and marital rape.

By bringing Hajila out of the private space of the home and into the public sphere of nationalist discourse, Djebar makes it clear that the personal is indeed political and thereby demonstrates the feminist potential of Jameson's notion of national allegory. Djebar's work also serves as a fine example of how teaching novels by Maghrebian women writers can strengthen approaches to the African novel that stress the importance of African feminisms, particularly Arab feminisms in Africa, whose tradition, especially in Egypt, is over a century old.[13]

The Challenge of Ethnography

Reading *Ombre sultane* for its gendered disruption of masculinist articulations of national identity can also provide a starting point from which one may go back and reread earlier childhood narratives by Maghrebian men as novels of masculinity. Like Djebar's first novel, early childhood narratives were frequently criticized by nationalist critics. Writers of the colonial period who dealt with Kabyle culture were branded as *berbéristes* by some, who considered such a focus as distracting attention from the anticolonial cause, not to mention as pandering to the exoticizing gaze of Western readers. Representations of ethnic specificity like those of Feraoun and Mouloud Mammeri (whose *La colline oubliée* ["The Forgotten Hill"] would make an excellent teaching text, were it not for the fact that it is out of print and difficult to find) thus pose challenges to the homogenizing tendencies of official nationalism that parallel the ones carried out by Boudjedra, Ben Jelloun, and Djebar in their treatment of gender and sexuality.

The earlier childhood narratives provide further evidence of the political implications of Kateb's treatment of history. In my course on the

Maghreb, Feraoun's and Memmi's novels show that the Maghreb's ethnic diversity (whose richness Kateb explores) not only existed in the past but was also still flourishing as the independence movements were gaining strength in the wake of World War II. They also confront students with a Jewish and a Berber Maghreb early on in the semester. Feraoun even presents students with indigenous African characters, Kabyle characters, with blond hair, thereby confounding assumptions that Africa necessarily equals racial difference.

These childhood narratives also bring a pedagogical advantage to the classroom; they tend to be popular with students, who find in the protagonists' pursuit of an education a parallel with their own. And as these novels were written before experimentation with novelistic form and narrative structure became widespread under the influence of the French new novel, they are often easier to read. Because *Le fils du pauvre* is also relatively short, I have taught it to students who had as few as four semesters of college French. (Unfortunately, the book has not been translated into English.) In the course on childhood narratives designed to bridge language learning and upper-level courses in French cultural and literary studies, I taught Feraoun along with Camara Laye's *L'enfant noir* in a very successful pairing of Maghrebian and sub-Saharan literature that could easily be replicated in a number of different courses, whether focused on period or theme.

Despite accusations that some of these novels were not political enough, they too can be read in allegorical ways. I teach Feraoun along with two readings that facilitate allegorical interpretations of his novel's politics: Pierre Bourdieu's "The Sentiment of Honour in Kabyle Society" and selections from Lazreg's *The Emergence of Classes in Algeria*. I can assure those wary of giving work as theoretical as Bourdieu's to undergraduates that, when students have read it after Feraoun's fifth chapter, they are armed with concrete examples to illustrate Bourdieu's theorization of honor. When Fouroulou is accidentally wounded by a member of the rival moiety, the entire village engages in a fierce battle between its two halves until traditional authorities (i.e., not French) step in to stop the fighting by declaring the two moieties to be official enemies. For American readers, this fight scene will likely represent a total breakdown in social order. Bourdieu, however, describes such battles as part of the normal functioning of a legal system based on honor, a system that is not limited to Kabylia or even North Africa but that characterizes or has characterized much of the Mediterranean.

Both Feraoun and Bourdieu offer examples of the gendered nature of the "sentiment of honor," since men's honor depends on the virtue of the women in their family. Both writers describe the *éducation virile* by which a man is brought up to defend that honor. However, pairing Feraoun and Bourdieu does much more than bring in a secondary text to elucidate and clarify a primary (literary) one, which is the way interdisciplinary approaches to literary studies often work. Discrepancies between the two allow the experience of reading them together to challenge both the sociological and the literary sides of this textual encounter. Fouroulou, for example, is more defined by how he fails at his male education. Whereas Bourdieu describes fighting with weaker parties to be dishonoring, Fouroulou is tacitly allowed to beat up smaller boys and his sisters because he is too much of a weakling to win in fights with his equals. In Feraoun's representation, therefore, the system of honor can be reproduced only by breaking its rules; in an interesting internal contradiction, becoming a man first involves unmanly behavior.

The gendered aspect of this traditional education is paralleled in the novel's use of family history as an allegory of colonization. Lazreg describes in detail the changes French colonialism brought to Algeria's property structures as well as the means by which these transformations were enacted: the outright expropriation of uncultivated lands, the requirement of property titles that led to land seizures for those who did not submit, and heavy taxes and legal fees that often obliged landowners to put up their property as collateral for loans with exorbitant interest rates. The resulting indebtedness often forced the heads of families to migrate to France for work. In Feraoun's novel as well, not only must Fouroulou's father go into debt to pay for his son's education but he also emigrates to France for work. This whole process of impoverishment (which, through Lazreg, one can understand as being institutionalized) begins when, after the grandmother's death, the two sons divide up the family property in a decision that, before colonization, would have been considered dishonoring. (Historically, then, French attacks on precolonial property structures were intertwined with the imposition of French law, itself an attack on the honor system.) In other words, Feraoun's family allegory of colonial land expropriation is gendered in that it coincides with the breakup of an extended family headed by a woman into two nuclear families headed by men in the image of French patriarchy.

It is through this gendered aspect of the national allegory that *Le fils du pauvre* also becomes an allegory of reading that involves a complex layering of levels of meaning. To begin with, Feraoun associates childhood with a precolonial society, whose kinship, property, and legal structures would face a violent onslaught carried out by colonial transformations that are also an attack on male honor. Yet since the childhood that might offer a refuge for male honor in precolonial traditions is feminized in that it precedes Fouroulou's masculinity, a return to it offers no alternative for a nationalist vision predicated on reasserting such honor. Further, coming to male honor requires carrying out a gendered violence that might be said to allegorize colonization, not resistance to it. The emasculation that involves returning to a man's premanly childhood might therefore be seen as the most appropriate allegory for resistance to colonialism in all its patriarchal splendor. In other words, the national identity recovered in Feraoun's return to precolonial roots cannot belong to a male-centered nationalist discourse, which is challenged in a way that constitutes yet another parallel to Kateb's "disruption in the midst of disruption."

In conclusion, while I have used one particular course on the Maghreb as the starting point for these reflections on teaching the Maghrebian novel, my purpose has been not to promote a single pedagogical approach at the expense of others but rather to assert the value of multiple approaches, much as this volume does as a whole. Since my course focuses on histories of nation building and the construction of national identity, questions of sexuality, gender, and ethnic difference might seem secondary. Yet these secondary questions can disrupt and challenge dominant versions of national history; they can become central in any consideration of the Maghrebian novel. In fact, they can just as easily become the organizing principle for different, though equally productive, courses.

The multiple approaches to teaching the Maghrebian novel both highlight and are strengthened by the diversity in the Maghreb that *is* emphasized by many of the novels discussed in this essay. And this diversity further nuances approaches to teaching the African novel that draw on cultural differences in Africa to challenge its reification as a homogenous whole in colonial discourse.

Notes

1. My training and departmental affiliation have led to an almost exclusive focus on Maghrebian literature in French, but whenever possible here, I point to teachable texts originally written in Arabic. The special issue of *Research in African Literatures* entitled *Arabic Writing in Africa* and edited by Farida

Abu-Haidar contains a number of essays on Maghrebian novels in Arabic that would be helpful for anyone considering teaching them. After all, the Maghrebian novel offers an obvious resource for a teacher looking for an approach to the African novel that highlights the specificities of sub-Saharan African Islam as well as draws attention to Arabic as an African language. A good place to start in this regard would be the novels of the Algerian writer Tahir Wattar (usually transliterated into French as Tahar Ouettar), some of which are available in French or English translation. These novels constitute an important part of not only African novels in Arabic but also contemporary Arabic literature as a whole. The best known are *Al-Laz* ("The Ace"), *Al-Zilzal* (*The Earthquake*), and *'Urs baghl* ("A Mule's Wedding"). For a study of his work, see Cox. Wattar has also been one of the most vocal opponents of the use of French as a literary language in the Maghreb.

2. For a detailed introduction to Maghrebian history and culture, readers of French may consult the excellent *L'état du Maghreb* (Lacoste and Lacoste). Such a general introduction is hard to find in English, but together, *The Historical Dictionary of Algeria* (Naylor and Heegoy), *The Historical Dictionary of Tunisia* (Perkins), and *The Historical Dictionary of Morocco* (Park) provide a thorough historical introduction as well as a good substitute for a cultural introduction.

3. For works with published translations listed among the works cited, page numbers refer to these translations. When translations are my own, page references are to the French original. When I have modified a published translation or included words from the French original, modification is indicated and page references to the original follow those to the translation.

4. The most notable resistance to both Arabization and Arabicization (though it has not tended to take the form of resistance to Islamicization) has occurred in predominantly Berber areas, especially in Kabylia in Algeria, the site of riots in 1980 and 2001 against the hegemony of Arabic and in support of official recognition of Tamazight (the Berber language). Note that Tunisia stands apart in its moderation in this regard, in part because Arabic instruction suffered much less there during the colonial period. However, Tunisia's quasi-official self-designation as *le pays de la tolérance* ("the country of tolerance") has done an efficient job of drawing attention away from specifically Tunisian modes of political repression. It is also much easier for the Tunisian state to promote diversity given the relative lack of survival of Berber culture there in comparison with Morocco and Algeria and given the departure of most of its remaining Jewish population after the Six-Day War.

5. Teachers wishing to focus on literary rewritings of Maghrebian history have a number of choices. Assia Djebar's *Loin de Médine* (*Far from Medina*) (Algeria, 1991) retells the history of the founding of Islam from the point of view of both the women who participated in it and the women who opposed it. Tahar Djaout's *L'invention du désert* ("Invention of the Desert") (Algeria, 1987) rewrites the history of the Almoravid dynasty by narrating its overthrow by the Almohad founder Ibn Tumart (who also, in this version, repressed manifestations of male same-sex desire). Djaout's *Les chercheurs d'os* ("The Bone Searchers") (Algeria, 1984) digs up the bones of freedom fighters from the revolution as a

way of bringing skeletons out of the closet of its legacy. Driss Chraïbi's *La mère du printemps* (*Mother Spring*) (Morocco, 1982) recounts the Islamicization of Morocco as lived by its original Berber inhabitants, whose reactions ranged from total acceptance to resistance.

6. The classic literary histories of the Maghreb are all in French: see Arnaud; Bonn, *Littérature* and *Roman*; Déjeux; and Khatibi. General studies in English of Maghrebian literature in French, having come a bit later, tend to be less concerned with constructing a literary history (see Kaye and Zoubir; Woodhull; Hayes; and Bensmaïa). Though more specific in topic or choice of writers, both Donadey and Vogl should also be consulted in a general survey of literary criticism on the Maghreb.

7. In postindependence Algeria, the nationally owned press—the SNED (Société Nationale d'Édition et de Diffusion)—canonized this aesthetic, which subsequently fell out of favor, in part because of the SNED's formulaic adherence to the combat novel genre.

8. Gontard provides a summary of the novel's plot in a graph, which I have given students to help them keep track of where they are in a chronological sequence of the novel's events (38). Some aspects of Gontard's summary, however, have been challenged by other critics (see, e.g., Arnaud 2: 320–26). Yet pointing out such discrepancies can also provide an opportunity to discuss how summarizing a plot can be an interpretative endeavor.

9. There is a rich sub-Saharan corpus in French that shares this feature (see Kourouma; Labou Tansi).

10. See Rachid O.'s *L'enfant ébloui* (1995; "The Dazzled Child"), *Plusieurs vies* (1996; "Several Lives"), *Chocolat chaud* (1998; "Hot Chocolate"), and *Ce qui reste* (2003; "What's Left"); Djaziri, *Un "poisson" sur la balançoire* (1997; "'Fish' on a Swing") and *Une promesse de douleur et de sang* (1997; "A Promise of Suffering and Blood"). See also Bouraoui, *Garçon manqué* (2000; "Tomboy").

11. For the strongest of these criticisms, see Aijaz Ahmad's response to Jameson in "Jameson's Rhetoric of Otherness and the National Allegory" (95–122).

12. Despite Ben Jelloun's suggestion that in Mahgrebian novels "Arabic—the language of the Qur'an—lends itself less easily to the game of denunciation" ("Défendre" 272), that French-language novels have a monopoly on such political uses of sexual transgression, Boudjedra's more recent novels in Arabic continue to give a prominent place to sexuality. In addition, Mohamed Choukri's *Le pain nu* (*For Bread Alone*) originally composed in dialectal Arabic, has caused and continues to cause reactions similar to those against Chraïbi and Boudjedra. For example, it was banned from classrooms at the American University of Cairo.

13. For a sampling of the Arab feminist tradition, see Margot Badran and Miriam Cooke's *Opening the Gates: A Century of Arab Feminist Writing*.

Works Cited

Abu-Haidar, Farida, ed. *Arabic Writing in Africa*. Spec. issue of *Research in African Literatures* 28.3 (1997): 1–236. Print.

Ahmad, Aijaz. *In Theory: Classes, Nations, Literatures*. London: Verso, 1992. Print.

Arnaud, Jacqueline. *La littérature maghrébine de langue française*. 2 vols. Paris: Publisud, 1986. Print.

Badran, Margot, and Miriam Cooke, eds. *Opening the Gates: A Century of Arab Feminist Writing*. Bloomington: Indiana UP, 1990. Print.

Ben Jelloun, Tahar. "Défendre la diversité culturelle au Maghreb." Lacoste and Lacoste 271–72.

———. *L'enfant de sable*. Paris: Seuil, 1985. Print.

———. *The Sand Child*. Trans. Alan Sheridan. New York: Ballantine, 1987. Print.

Bensmaïa, Réda. *Experimental Nations; or, The Invention of the Maghreb*. Trans. Alyson Waters. Princeton: Princeton UP, 2003. Print.

Bonn, Charles. *La littérature algérienne de langue française et ses lectures: Imaginaire et discours d'idées*. Sherbrooke: Naaman, 1974. Print.

———. *Le roman algérien de langue française: Vers un espace de communication littéraire décolonisé?* Paris: Harmattan, 1985. Print.

Boudjedra, Rachid. *La répudiation*. Paris: Denoël, 1969. Print.

———. *The Repudiation*. Trans. Golda Lambrova. Colorado Springs: Three Continents, 1995. Print.

Bouraoui, Nina. *Garçon manqué*. Paris: Stock, 2000. Print.

———. *La vie heureuse*. Paris: Stock, 2002. Print.

Bourdieu, Pierre. "The Sentiment of Honour in Kabyle Society." *Honour and Shame: The Values of Mediterranean Society*. Ed. J. G. Peristiany. Chicago: U of Chicago P, 1974. 191–241. Print.

Camara Laye. *L'enfant noir*. Paris: Plon, 1953. Print.

Choukri, Mohamed. *For Bread Alone*. Trans. Paul Bowles. San Francisco: City Lights, 1987. Print.

———. *Le pain nu*. Trans. Tahar Ben Jelloun. Paris: Maspero, 1980. Print.

Chraïbi, Driss. *La mère du printemps (L'Oum-er-Bia)*. Paris: Seuil, 1982. Print.

———. *Le passé simple*. Paris: Denoël, 1954. Print.

———. *The Simple Past*. Trans. Hugh A. Harter. Washington: Three Continents, 1990. Print.

Cox, Debbie. "The Novels of Tahar Wattar: Command or Critique?" Abu-Haidar 94–109.

Déjeux, Jean. *Littérature maghrébine de langue française: Introduction générale et auteurs*. Sherbrooke: Naaman, 1973. Print.

de Man, Paul. *Allegories of Reading: Figural Language in Rousseau, Nietzsche, Rilke, and Proust*. New Haven: Yale UP, 1979. Print.

Dib, Mohammed. *Qui se souvient de la mer*. Paris: Seuil, 1962. Print.

———. *Who Remembers the Sea*. Trans. Louis Tremaine. Washington: Three Continents, 1985. Print.

Djaout, Tahar. *Les chercheurs d'os*. Paris: Seuil, 1984. Print.

———. *L'invention du désert*. Paris: Seuil, 1987. Print.

Djaziri, Eyet-Chékib. *Un "poisson" sur la balançoire*. Lille: Gai-Kitsch-Camp, 1997. Print.

———. *Une promesse de douleur et de sang*. Lille: Gai-Kitsch-Camp, 1998. Print.

Djebar, Assia. *Loin de Médine: Filles d'Ismaël*. Paris: Michel, 1991. Print.

———. *Ombre sultane*. Paris: Lattès, 1987. Print.

———. *A Sister to Scheherazade.* Trans. Dorothy S. Blair. Portsmouth: Heinemann, 1993. Print.

Donadey, Anne. *Recasting Postcolonialism: Women Writing between Worlds.* Portsmouth: Heinemann, 2001. Print.

Fanon, Frantz. "Algeria Unveiled." *A Dying Colonialism.* 1959. Trans. Haakon Chevalier. New York: Grove, 1965. 35–67. Print.

———. *The Wretched of the Earth.* Trans. Richard Philcox. New York: Grove, 2004. Print. Trans. of *Les damnés de la terre.* 1961. Paris: Découverte, 1987.

Feraoun, Mouloud. *Le fils du pauvre.* 1950. Paris: Seuil, 1954. Print.

Gontard, Marc. Nedjma *de Kateb Yacine: Essai sur la structure formelle du roman.* Paris: Harmattan, 1985. Print.

Hayes, Jarrod. *Queer Nations: Marginal Sexualities in the Maghreb.* Chicago: U of Chicago P, 2000. Print.

Hoodfar, Homa. "Return to the Veil: Personal Strategy and Public Participation in Egypt." *Working Women: International Perspectives on Labour and Gender Ideology.* Ed. Nanneke Redclift and M. Thea Sinclair. London: Routledge, 1991. 104–24. Print.

Jameson, Fredric. "Third World Literature in the Era of Multinational Capitalism." *Social Text* 15 (1986): 65–88. Print.

Kateb, Yacine. *Nedjma.* Paris: Seuil, 1956. Print.

———. *Nedjma.* Trans. Richard Howard. Charlottesville: UP of Virginia, 1991. Print.

Kaye, Jacqueline, and Abdelhamid Zoubir. *The Ambiguous Compromise: Language, Literature and National Identity in Algeria and Morocco.* London: Routledge, 1990. Print.

Khatibi, Abdelkebir. *Le roman maghrébin.* 1968. Rabat: SMER, 1979. Print.

Kourouma, Ahmadou. *Les soleils des indépendences.* Paris: Seuil, 1970. Print.

Labou Tansi, Sony. *La vie et demie.* Paris: Seuil, 1979. Print.

Lacoste, Camille, and Yves Lacoste, eds. *L'état du Maghreb.* Paris: Découverte, 1991. Print.

Lazreg, Marnia. *The Emergence of Classes in Algeria: A Study of Colonialism and Socio-political Change.* Boulder: Westview, 1976. Print.

———. "Feminism and Difference: The Perils of Writing as a Woman on Women in Algeria." *Feminist Studies* 14.1 (1988): 81–107. Print.

Mammeri, Mouloud. *La colline oubliée.* Paris: Gallimard, 1992. Print.

Memmi, Albert. *The Pillar of Salt.* Trans. Edouard Roditi. Boston: Beacon, 1992. Print.

———. *La statue de sel.* 1953. Paris: Gallimard, 1966. Print.

Mohanty, Chandra Talpade. "Under Western Eyes: Feminist Scholarship and Colonial Discourses." *Third World Women and the Politics of Feminism.* Ed. Mohanty, Ann Russo, and Lourdes Torres. Bloomington: Indiana UP, 1991. 51–80. Print.

Mudimbe, V. Y. *The Invention of Africa: Gnosis, Philosophy, and the Order of Knowledge.* Bloomington: Indiana UP, 1988. Print.

Naylor, Phillip Chivages, and Alf Andrew Heegoy. *The Historical Dictionary of Algeria.* Metuchen: Scarecrow, 1994. Print.

O., Rachid. *Ce qui reste.* Paris: Gallimard, 2003. Print.
———. *Chocolat chaud.* Paris: Gallimard, 1998. Print.
———. *L'enfant ébloui.* Paris: Gallimard, 1995. Print.
———. *Plusieurs vies.* Paris: Gallimard, 1996. Print.
Park, Thomas Kerlin. *The Historical Dictionary of Morocco.* Lanham: Scarecrow, 1996. Print.
Perkins, Kenneth J. *The Historical Dictionary of Tunisia.* Lanham: Scarecrow, 1997. Print.
Pontecorvo, Gillo. *La battaglia di Algeri.* Casbah Film, 1966. Film.
Sautman, Francesca Canadé. "Hassiba Boulmerka's Raised Fist: The Body of Evidence and Muslim Herstory." *Found Object* 7 (1998): 9–32. Print.
Vogl, Mary B. *Picturing the Maghreb: Literature, Photography, (Re)Presentation.* Lanham: Rowman, 2003. Print.
Wattar, Tahir. *The Earthquake.* Trans. William Granara. London: Saqi, 2000. Print.
———. *Al-Laz.* Algiers: SNED, 1974. Print.
———. *'Urs baghl.* 1978. Algiers: SNED, 1980. Print.
———. *Al-Zilzal.* Algiers: SNED, 1974. Print.
Woodhull, Winifred. *Transfigurations of the Maghreb: Feminism, Decolonization, and Literatures.* Minneapolis: U of Minnesota P, 1993. Print.

Christopher Wise

The Novel, Historiography, and the Griot Epic in the Sahel

This essay is intended to serve as a guide for educators of students who are already familiar with the novel of realism but who bring with them predictable assumptions about its general worth and universality. The belief that the novel is a compelling genre for all people everywhere tends to be based on a universal concept of humankind or the comforting platitude that, despite arbitrary cultural differences, all people everywhere are the same because they partake of the same human essence. My argument here is that the African novel cannot be adequately appreciated without reference to local belief systems, many of which developed independently of Western influence. Moreover, cultural traditions across the African continent have generally been transmitted in oral forms, so educators need to understand how oral-based societies differ from societies of the West. I suggest that instead of approaching the African novel as a national allegory or as a cultural technology imported from Europe in the 1950s, we should teach it in comparison with indigenous African traditions, provided that the effort is made to carefully study them.

The impossibly broad rubric of African orature or the African novel necessitates a reduction in the scope of any relevant discussion, to make it manageable, although one may certainly speak of oral traditions across broad regional zones, especially those united by geopolitical crises that draw together diverse ethnic groups—for example, drought, famine, disease, and deforestation. The Burkinabè scholar Joseph Paré has argued that regional approaches to African literary study offer more coherent alternatives to literary paradigms that are focused on the concept of a single nation-state, especially in regions that face similar struggles because of a harsh environment (Paré and Wise 2–3). In this essay, I follow Paré's lead by addressing the topic of orature in the Sahel zone, a region now encompassing Mali, Niger, Burkina Faso, Mauritania, Senegal. It goes without saying that one might also discuss the topic of orature in relation to the rich cultural traditions of southern Africa, eastern Africa, and many other places across the continent. Because the Sahel has preserved a rich literary tradition long predating the colonial era, it offers a particularly fascinating example of the depth and complexity of indigenous African traditions.

Timbuktu, Djenné, Ouadane, and Kano have enormous libraries of chirographic manuscripts, some dating back hundreds of years, but these texts remain unknown in the West. Like the transcribed griot epics of Sundiata Keita, Askia Muhammad, El Hajj Umar Tall, Samory Touré, and others, such literary texts pose a challenge for non-African readers who seek to appreciate genres emanating from the continent. It is certainly more difficult to read a careful transcription of an oral epic like John William Johnson's *The Epic of Son-Jara* (Johnson and Sisòkò) or a medieval manuscript from the Songhay Dynasty than an elegantly written novel like Chinua Achebe's *Things Fall Apart* or Yambo Ouologuem's *Le devoir de violence* (*The Duty of Violence*). Students are nonetheless robbed of the opportunity to learn when their reading biases are not challenged.

The Mande concept of *nyama* ("vital power"), not the post-Socratic Logos, is the key to understanding the cultural documents of the Sahel; but if so, it follows that the African novel should not be taught as a compelling variation on an essentially European genre. Western perspectives about authority and textual ownership spring from a Kantian (and ultimately Platonic) orientation to objective reality, an orientation that tends to leave most Sahelian readers indifferent. It is difficult to convey the dynamic orality-aurality of African literature unless the teacher is willing to draw attention to Platonic ideals of the soul (or psyche) and the word (or Logos), so that students may begin to understand how their own orientations to language are by no means natural but matters of cultural construction. They must come to see that their most basic assumptions about language may seem alien or naive to many African peoples. Unlike the word that is "colorless, shapeless, and untouchable" (Plato, *Plato's* Phaedrus 28), the word in the Sahel is commonly believed to be a powerful means to a highly pragmatic end, a dangerous substance that may even disable the body of the other. In such a context, the bottom may be said to drop out of the invisible ground of truth, which is the source of so much serenity in the West.

Hegel once described the European novel of realism as a "bourgeois epic" (592), and subsequent generations of critics have followed his lead in theorizing the novel's historic rise in relation to the emergence of a new middle class in Europe—but also in relation to the invention of movable type, the upheavals of the Protestant Reformation, and other important developments at the beginning of the modern period. According to the work of influential theorists of the novel such as Georg Lukács, Theodor W. Adorno, Ian Watt, and Fredric Jameson, the novel of realism comes into being precisely at the moment that an older, agrarian, and feudally based economy is displaced by a more viable strategy for meeting the problems of economic scarcity: the capitalist mode of production. The novel as a form documents the shock of the new or modern, which is experienced as a trauma by the alienated individual who must navigate a way through a disorienting cultural landscape. In this Hegelian-Marxist reading, the novel is a kind of cognitive map or literary form that turns on the problems of subject formation. It is a "machine for constructing subjectivity," as Jameson has put it, and is deeply bound up with questions of individual rights, hence its connection to secular humanist ideology (*Postmodernism* 52).

In making any inquiry into the usefulness of the novel of realism as a West African genre, especially in largely rural nations like Mauritania, Mali, Niger, and Chad, one can safely hypothesize that the novel has not enjoyed much success, because the modern itself has not disrupted the Sahel as profoundly as it has the European continent. Cheikh Hamidou Kane's *Ambiguous Adventure* (1961) and Achebe's *No Longer at Ease* (1960), highlighting the struggles of the individual alienated from traditional society, may offer compelling and accurate representations of the experiences of the new comprador subject, but the situation that those novels describe remains relatively peripheral, if not anomalous.

Thomas Sankara, the Burkinabè president who was assassinated in 1987, once remarked:

> I don't like African novels any more than I like African films. Those I've read have really disappointed me. It's always the same story: young man from Africa leaves for Paris, suffers, and returns home, at odds with tradition. . . . I don't like this way of depicting people. . . . The African writers I like best are those who deal with concrete problems, even if I don't agree with their position. (159)

Sankara's rejection of the novel of realism, which Sankara claims does not even address a viable problem, certainly resonates with the views of many Africanist scholars, who tend to underscore the relatively small impact of European culture on the region. The Burkinabè cultural figure Titinga Frédéric Pacéré cites the drum *zabyouré* ("performed phrase," in Mossi drum language), that "[t]he tamarind tree may fall upon the earth, but its good taste will remain forever." About this *zabyouré*, he observes, "In contemporary culture, this phrase refers to African culture in the aftermath of colonization. Despite subjugation and 'defeat,' its profundity and integrity remain unaffected" (47). This view sharply contrasts with the theses of figures like Jameson, Frantz Fanon, and V. S. Naipaul, who have preferred to emphasize the devastating aspects of the modern on indigenous cultural traditions.

To put this rejection in slightly different terms, Adorno's suggestion that alienation is how the collective tends to be experienced in modern Europe (33) is a thesis that falls flat in the Sahelian context.[1] Instead, widely divergent scholars like Joseph Paré, Thomas Hale, and Paul Stoller speak of the integrity and resilience of traditional cultural systems in the Sahel, which Paré and RÉLIS scholars (Réseau d'Études Littéraires Sahéliennes ["Network for Research in Sahelian Literatures"]) have described in terms of their "sahelity" (*sahelité*) (Paré and Wise 2) and which Hale and Stoller, following the lead of the archaeologists Roderick MacIntosh and Susan MacIntosh, have termed "deep Sahelian culture" (164). All these scholars maintain that the cultural traditions and institutions of the Sahel, many dating back hundreds of years, enjoy relatively good health and have by no means been devastated by the innovations of the new.

With the increased use of Internet technologies, there will no doubt be further challenges to traditional belief systems, but, as Walter J. Ong has pointed out, West Africa enters into the era of electronic media as a "verbomotor" society, or as a culture that has known writing for many centuries but whose outlook has remained oral-aural ("African Talking

Drums" 118). It is therefore likely that the novel will continue to be a marginally significant form of cultural technology in this context or that the form it takes will be mediated by more sophisticated technologies of electronic media.[2]

While the theses of theorists of orality-literacy contrasts like Ong, Jack Goody, and Eric Havelock may be useful in conceptualizing important differences between primary oral and secondary oral cultures, the concept of textuality evoked here does not necessarily refer to a visual object or "standard to follow" with the eyes, as suggested by Ong (*Orality* 76). Rather, textuality may be a trace or material residue that is available to any of the five senses. Ong tends to exaggerate the invisible character of the spoken word, which he insists successfully evades reification in any spatial sense. But that the aspirated word cannot be seen by the human eye does not mean that it lacks in materiality. Though the oral-aural word cannot be seen, it can nonetheless be experienced as an audible force that penetrates the body from the outside. No matter how skillfully crafted a novelized treatment of the griot epic may be,[3] the oral-aural epic is irrevocably transformed when rendered in written form, as in Camara Laye's novelized version of the epic of Sundiata Keita, translated into English as *The Guardian of the Word*, or Johnson's transcription of *The Epic of Son-Jara* (Johnson and Sisòkò). Even written Sahelian texts are not imagined in this context to be mere representations of the real, nor are they believed to be prosthetic copies of a word that stands in for an absent ideal: they are instead construed as powerful and even deadly actions that inevitably transform the real.

In other words, the goal of the Sahelian writer and bard is to intervene in history as a violent agent of social change. The griot and the writer alike are often feared as sorcerers whose words have the power to cure or cause great harm. The West African belief that a word is first and foremost an occult power, *nyama*, rather than a mimetic and lifeless copy of an unreal referent inevitably affects the writing of a novelist. But it is nearly impossible to come to terms with this aspect, if the work of such a novelist is compared only with the great bourgeois epics written by European and American authors or even fellow African or postcolonial novelists. Whereas a novel is a printed book with a spatial and reified character, griot accounts of the life of Sundiata Keita, Askia Muhammad, El Hajj Umar Tall, and others do not circulate in Sahelian society as inert objects that may be typographically reproduced and sold at a profit. The scribal text, which has existed in West Africa for hundreds of years, bears obvious similarities to the typographic text, insofar as both involve the inscription of visual characters on a flattened surface; however, these similarities can be misleading.

In the first place, the chirographic text more obviously displays the writer's labor: it is an object marked by the hand of the scribe. Yet it may be more akin to the oral-aural text of the griot than to the typographic text, at least according to local definitions of the word as a toxic or liquid substance or a thing that is neither living nor dead but a real though nonmetaphysical source of power in the world. That the word is written on a sheet of paper does not mean that it is dead or that it has been crucified and must now undergo its Christian resurrection, in Father Ong's sense. Dead words are not really dead in the Sahel to begin with, and the fact of the reader's literacy is largely insignificant: the word may go into the body through the ears, the eyes, the mouth, and so on—so long as it goes in. Greco-Christian beliefs about the hollowed-out subject or eternal soul imagined as an indwelling though absent receptacle on which an ideal word is inscribed do not always seem relevant to Sahelian peoples.

The scribal chronicles from Timbuktu offer compelling evidence of West African beliefs about the purpose and utility of writing that often contradict the metaphysical assumptions of the West. Even ostensibly representational texts, such as narratives of historical events in the region, do not seek to faithfully mirror the real, as in the construction of a textual universe wherein signs are imagined to enjoy an Adamic relation with the things they name; instead they are a deliberate means of benefiting one's political allies and enacting lethal violence against one's enemies. Traditional or academic beliefs about historiography, often construed as a quasi-objective rendering of actual historical events, would seem guileless and naive to the Sahelian chronicler, whose writing is an act that can achieve a highly pragmatic if not immoral end. As Barbara Hoffman has shown in her field work conducted in Mali, words in this context are intended "to stir, to move, to arouse strong emotions, to evoke that which is possible, not to describe that which is verifiable" (80).

For the Sahelian chronicler and bard alike, the liquid character of the text, not any absent metaphysical ground, is essential. Both believe this autonomous fluid can be found in the written ink of the scribe and the aspirated breath of the griot. Both imagine their respective texts to be an occult substance that invades the body—despite the long-standing influence of Islam on the region and despite obvious differences in the fluids employed by scribe and griot. The real circulates in discourse that is already present in the world of senses without the need for an extrasensory double. Amulet writing in the Sahel often involves the transcription of a Qur'anic sura, which is written on a sheet of paper or parchment but then washed into a vial that is drunk like a medicine. The liquid words enter the body as a powerful force, and it is irrelevant if those who drink these words are alphabetically literate. Practices of this nature echo those of the ancient Egyptians, who buried their illiterate dead with scrolls containing spells that would aid them on their journey to Duat, the underworld, in their quest to become transfigured in the afterlife. In Egypt, the illiterate dead also consumed their personalized books (or scrolls) of the dead as elixirs, which implies that the capacity to read the papyrus manuscript with one's eyes was a kind of scholarly luxury (in fact, only a small portion of the ancient Egyptians could read) (Goelet 147).

For medieval Songhay-Soninké scribes like El Hajj Mahmoûd Kâti and Ibn al-Mukahtar, who are the main authors of the *Tarîkh el-Fettâch*,[4] as well as for contemporary Sahelian griots who also happen to be Muslim, the observation of Islamic religious practices does not necessitate the rejection of beliefs that predate by many centuries the arrival of Muslim traders in the region. Quoting I. M. Lewis, Thomas Hale argues that "metaphysical interventions [of the scribes of the *Tarîkh el-Fettâch*] depend for their validity on Muslim sources and goals" (*Scribe* 34). However, the use of the term "metaphysical" in this case—that is, in reference to the well-documented participation of Kâti and other Songhay-Soninké scribes in occult practices such as sorcery, witchcraft, and spellbinding—may be misleading, since their acts are not underwritten by any extrasensory ideal. If they were, the practices would in no way be inconsistent with Muslim beliefs and goals: their spoken words would be imagined as living copies of the heavenly book ("the spoken word" is the meaning of the word *Qur'an*), whereas their written words would be imagined as prosthetic copies of a copy (or mere *mus'haf*). The authors of the *Tarîkh el-Fettâch*, however, show little awareness of Islamic metaphysics.[5] In fact, nearly all their references to language contradict orthodox doctrines of the Book, at least those that prevail in the Arab world some three hundred years after the death of the Prophet.

El Hajj Mahmoûd Kâti was born in 1468 CE and was a contemporary of Christopher Columbus, Johannes Gutenberg, Rabelais, and Michel de Montaigne. Although he wrote the chronicle (or at least portions of the chronicle) in the Arabic language, his mother tongue was Songhay, and he was of Soninké and Songhay origin. The Soninké term for the occult word is *ñaxamala*, which is better known in the Mande form as *nyama*.[6] The Mande griot belongs to an artisan caste called the *nyamakala*, who are possessors of occult power, whereas the griot in the Songhay language is referred to as *jesere*, a term identical in meaning to the Mande version.[7]

The text of the *Tarîkh el-Fettâch* offers ample evidence of the authors' unorthodox orientation to speaking and writing. In one humorous instance, which was parodied by Ouologuem in his novel *Le devoir de violence*, Askia Mohammed curses the son who deposed him, stating, "Oh my God, put him to shame by exposing his private parts to all!" (Kâti 83 [in Arabic], 155 [in French]; my trans. in English).[8] The author informs his reader that "God heard his curse," as the Askia Moûssa fell from his horse the next day, exposing himself to his entire army. In some cases, pagan magic is relied on to attack heathen belief systems in the name of Islam: for instance, a spoken utterance of the Askia Mohammed causes a tree to magically uproot itself and smash a Mossi fetish (70; 135). In another instance, a Muslim holy man utters an imprecation that causes the sudden death of the Chi Ali, who is the principal villain of the *Tarîkh el-Fettâch* (51; 98). Kâti similarly applauds the treachery of the Askia Mohammed in dishonestly procuring a hair from the head of the Prophet, which he greedily swallows and thereby increases his own spiritual power. "Ah! What a clever trick," he exclaims, "and how very profitable! What a celestial favor! How abundant [his blessings]!" (69; 132). The author of the *Tarîkh el-Fettâch* also has no scruples about using his skills as a writer to exact vengeance on his enemies. A particularly revealing instance occurs when he seeks vengeance against the Kabara-farma Alou, a Songhay eunuch whom he describes as "evil, obese, dishonest, ignorant, arrogant, and mule-headed" (126; 231). When the Kabara-farma appropriates a piece of land that rightfully belongs to Kâti, also hitting him in the face and knocking him to the ground, the author responds by encouraging one of his disciples to write a magical spell on a sheet of paper, attaching the amulet to a goat, and then ritually piercing it with a spear. "A year later," the author writes, "on the very day that [his disciple] killed the goat with his lance, God caused the Kabara-farma to die in the same manner" (131; 238).

Although Kâti was a devout believer interested in securing Islamic hegemony throughout the region, his orientation to language was closely akin to that of the Songhay griots, who explicitly affiliated themselves with pre-Islamic religious influences like Sonni Ali Ber, Kassaye, and the underwater kingdom of the *zinn* (river spirits). In fact, Kâti never questions the existence of a whole host of magical creatures, including the kingfish (water sprite) from the Niger who is said to have ruled Gâo before the coming of the Arabs (30–31; 49–51).

That Songhay-Soninké scribes are influenced by local and non-Islamic conceptions of the word does not mean that they do not wish to tell the truth in their historical narratives. Hoffman, Patrick McNaughton, Joseph Henry, and other researchers have tended to emphasize the indifference of Sahelian peoples to Western morality. "[I]ssues of good and evil seem rarely to drive the Mande," McNaughton asserts (51). His point is valid; but this dimension of local beliefs about the power of the spoken and written word can confuse and even alarm outside observers. Father Joseph Henry, who was a Catholic priest among the Bambara in southern Mali, once underscored this aspect of Mande culture, conflating indigenous religious beliefs with European satanism cults.

The scribes especially place a high value on truth telling, although they do not necessarily affirm any ideal ethics or moral categories, especially Greco-Roman ones. The author of the *Tarîkh el-Fettâch* emphasizes the importance of remaining faithful to one's vows or religious utterances. In fact, he repeatedly asserts that the empire of the Askias goes into decline because the vows of Askia Mohammed, as well as of the Askia Daoûd, are not reenunciated by the descendants who inherit the throne. Speaking the truth means that one will perpetually honor one's vows; it does not imply that the one who makes the vow is uniquely in possession of the truth or Logos. When Kâti states that it was adultery (*zena*) that brought about the fall of the dynasty of the Askias, he points to the failure of the Songhay elite to honor the inaugural oaths that enabled the establishment of the dynasty. Note that *zena*, as it is used in the original Arabic text, is close in meaning to the French term *avouer* for "adultery," as in the breaking of a religious promise.

During his hajj, the Askia Mohammed makes three vows on the grave of the Prophet to accord certain privileges to the descendants of his traveling companion, the Mori Haougaro. One of these oaths is that the Mori Haougaro's children will never be sold into slavery. The Askia Mohammed's oaths to the Mori Haougaro are later sealed with a curse that is pronounced on any of his heirs who fail to honor his word. The author of the *Tarîkh el-Fettâch* bears testimony that he witnessed a slave auction during which the Mori Haougaro's descendants were sold and their pleas for clemency were ignored. Kâti speculates that "it was the curse of the

Askia Mohammed that brought about [the ruin of the Songhay], either entirely or in part, due to the fall of his descendants into baseness and depravity" (75; 143).

The Songhay griot epic of Mamar Kassaye, recently transcribed by Hale from the words of the *jesere* Nouhou Malio and published as *The Epic of Askia Mohammed* (Hale and Malio), retells much of the same history as the *Tarîkh el-Fettâch* and the *Tarîkh es-Soudan* though emphasizing the involvement of historical figures who play a smaller part in the chronicles. In particular, *The Epic of Askia Mohammed* highlights the role of those who are linked to pre-Islamic belief systems, affiliating the heritage of the griot with powerful occult figures in the text like the Chi Ali (Sonni Ali Ber or Si) and Kassaye. Askia Mohammed is referred to only by his Songhay name as Mamar Kassaye and is said to have been fathered by a *zinn* who rules a kingdom at the bottom of the Niger River. An important link between the scribal chronicles and the *Epic of Askia Mohammed* is their common reference to legends of pre-Islamic Gâo, which is ruled by a giant fish. This great underwater *zinn*, who fears only Solomon, the son of David, is killed by two brothers who journey to the region from Medina, the home of the Prophet.

The Mande word for griot is *djeli*, whereas the local name for the Niger is the Djoliba or the "River of the Griots." As an artisan of the word, the *djeli* is a kind of smith who works with a highly dangerous substance: his own bodily fluids, which he coaxes up from his lungs with the aid of musical accompaniment. The griot's first loyalty is always to the *zinn* of the Djoliba, because the spoken word is precisely that, a water spirit. The etymology of the English word *spirit*, from the Latin *spiritus*, also underscores aspiration or breathing: the spirit is the wet word that is expectorated into the ear of the other. This is the great *zinn* that is challenged but not destroyed by the arrival of the Islamic religion. Flatly contradicting the Timbuktu chronicles, Nouhou Malio claims that this water sprite is the secret father of Mamar Kassaye (or Askia Mohammed), thereby increasing Mamar Kassaye's prestige as a man of power (or *nyama*).

In the text of the *Epic of Askia Mohammed*, Malio depicts Mamar Kassaye as the model of the hard man but also a man who respects the word of the mother. Only once does he forget the true source of his power, when he dares attack a local tribe called the Bargantché. He cannot defeat these people, Malio tells us, "for he has in his stomach the milk of a Bargantché [woman]" (30). The *nyama* or word of the mother is also the blood and milk of the mother: it is the spiritual reservoir from which Mamar Kassaye draws his occult power, but it is also the actual substance of his body, the presymbolic matter of the mother. One avoids eating the bodily fluids of the other in order to preserve one's spiritual integrity, for when such fluids are mixed with one's own, the composition of the body is altered. Not surprisingly, in nearly every recorded legend of the griot's origin, the griot is described as having become one by violating the taboo against consuming the fluids of the other when he eats the flesh of his brother. This abhorrent act is what causes him to lose his noble status, unlike the brother who offers up his flesh to be consumed, to whom the griot must now sing praises. The Songhay-Soninké nobleman then is literally the pure man, the one who, unlike the griot, has not ingested the *nyama* (sometimes translated as "filth" or "shit") of the body.

In the last third of the epic, Malio recounts the tragic tale of Soumayla Kassa, the heir to the throne of Mamar Kassaye, who sets off a catastrophic chain of events leading to the fall of the Songhay Dynasty. Like Mamar Kassaye, Soumayla Kassa is an extremely hard and powerful man who is widely feared throughout the Songhay kingdom and in regions beyond its borders. However, he violates a number of taboos that estrange him from the Songhay-Soninké ruling elite and that make him unable to control the chaos that his actions unleash.

First, Soumayla Kassa marries a slave woman of ignoble origin, whom he does not free but keeps in a condition of servitude. In a tone of rebuke, the griot Malio states, "He married her just like that, since he was their chief" (42). As *askia* ("king"), Soumayla Kassa may have had the power to act in this way, but his actions alienate the nobles, particularly the women. Later, he marries a Songhay-Soninké noblewoman named Sagouma. But now he has placed Sagouma in the humiliating position of being second wife to a woman of ignoble origin, the slave he married but did not set free. To complicate matters, his first wife is the legal property also of the family of Sagouma, his second wife. Later, his first wife gives birth to a son named Amar Zoumbani. It is apparent through his many actions that Soumayla Kassa greatly favors his son of mixed origin, but this preference places the Songhay-Soninké elite in an awkward position, as they are now compelled to overlook Amar Zoumbani's ambiguous social status. Meanwhile, Sagouma gives birth to twin sons whose noble blood is pure.

The stage is now set for catastrophe: when Amar Zoumbani becomes a man, he vies for the hand of a rich and beautiful woman of Gâo, but the brother of Sagouma, a nobleman, is also a suitor. Amar Zoumbani seems likely to win the contest for the woman's hand, because of the wealth of his father. The son of Soumayla Kassa gives to the griots ten horses, for them to sing his praises. Sagouma then reminds her noble brother that the first wife of Soumayla Kassa is the legal property of their family, which means that Amar Zoumbani—the beloved son of the *askia*—is also their property. The next day, the brother of Sagouma commits the bold act of taking his slave Amar Zoumbani by the wrist and presenting him as a gift to the griots, hence showing the superiority of his generosity. Amar Zoumbani now learns the truth of his origins, and his father later admits that he did not even bother to free Amar Zoumbani's mother. "If at least I had freed your mother," Soumayla Kassa tells him, "but to tell the truth, I didn't free her" (44).

Soumayla Kassa retaliates against the brother of Sagouma by brutally murdering him, and Sagouma responds by killing their twin sons, the noble children whom Soumayla Kassa fathered. But Sagouma's thirst for vengeance against her husband is not satisfied. For seven years, she wanders in the land of the Arma (the Spanish and Arab Moroccans), seeking a man who will kill both him and Amar Zoumbani. "If you wish to marry me," she tells her suitors, "my dowry is Soumayla Kassa. / The bull sacrificed at my wedding is Amar Zoumbani. / Any man who has not killed these two will not marry me" (50). At last, Sagouma finds an Arma man, named Bayero, who is willing to commit these deeds. It is significant that Bayero plans his attack on Gâo with the full cooperation and support of the Songhay-Soninké elite. Malio implies that the Songhay Dynasty falls because it fragments from within as a result of the unwise actions of Soumayla Kassa. Never does he depict the Spanish Moroccan Arma as inherently more powerful than the Songhay: in fact, Soumayla Kassa succeeds in killing the Arma leader by the end of the epic, ostensibly with Sagouma's support.

More significant for the griot is that Soumayla Kassa finally comes to understand that he cannot circumvent the matter of the mother. In other words, the father-son relationship is always already subordinate to the mother-child relationship, because of the maternal blood debt that the son owes the mother. For the griot, the fall of the Songhay is therefore directly linked to Soumayala Kassa's failure to respect the mother. This revelation occurs when, in the course of battle, he and his son are suffering from thirst and seek water. Amar Zoumbani finds a clay pot that is filled with putrid water; he is so thirsty, he drinks from the pot and even leads his father to it, encouraging him to drink as well. At first, Soumayla Kassa cannot believe his eyes. "That's the water?" he asks his son four times, each time receiving an affirmative response. He can no longer deny the evidence of his senses. Malio puts it this way: "Even if one buys a house cat for 50,000 francs, it will only catch mice" (60). Amar Zoumbani has revealed himself to be a man of ignoble blood, a man willing to sell his birthright for a bowl of dirty water. "You have returned home," Soumayla Kassa tells his son. Now the father insults the son. "The fact of drinking his own mother's breast milk," Malio states, "that is the insult which he gave to him" (60).

At stake here is not merely an issue of social class but the matter of Amar Zoumbani's blood, which is also the matter of the mother and the word.[9] Unlike the ideal receptacle on which the Logos is written, the soul or psyche of the individual in the Songhay epic remains a matter of aspirated breath that ushers from the cavern of the lungs: the self is born from spirit, or from the cavernous container that is made of the blood of the mother. It is a matter of wind blowing into the ear of the other, whereas the word of the scribe enters the body on the wet lens of the eyes as an autonomous *ja*, a liquid double that is soundless but still construed in terms of its power rather than in terms of any ideal truth. In a note to the *Epic of Son-Jara*, Johnson describes the *ja* as "a spiritual wraith" that may wander out of one's body while sleeping. The *ja* is "visible as one's shadow in the sunlight," which can be seen in mirrors; it is also the image that appears in photographs (Johnson and Sisòkò 132). In some instances, the power of the voice is such that it may even evoke an apparition or visual double that is seen by the eyes.[10]

Beliefs of this order, which may seem archaic or simply too fantastic for Western readers to take seriously, do not imply that African writers are primitive in their thinking about language. Nor do they imply that such writers are oblivious to their unique orientation to language. In fact, the exact opposite is true. As Derrida has shown, Romantic ethnography depends on the logocentric view that peoples without writing are naturally innocent. In this racist, anthropological model, the spoken word reflects the truth or Logos more accurately than the written word (see Derrida, *Of Grammatology* 109–19).

African writers generally find such notions of truth to be naive. Although not identical to Derrida's views about language, the views of many West African writers are consonant with the deconstructive notion that "liquid is the element of the *pharmakon*" (Derrida, *Dissemination* 152) or that "saliva is the element which sticks the unities [of speaking and writing] together" (Derrida, *Of Grammatology* 161). Hence, when one asserts that both the oral and written texts for African novelists should be conceived as liquid, the point is not that such writers are Romantic primitives but that their complex views about writing cannot be reduced to realist epistemologies promoting a strictly reflectionist aesthetics. Jameson's argument that the novel is a form of "neutral technology" is simply false in this context, for it implies a subject-object dialectic wherein one of the main values of novel writing becomes what Lukács called "typicality," by which he meant an essentialist adequation between what is inside and outside the container of the human head (33). Hegelian-Marxian notions of knowledge parallel more conservative ones, such as the Aristotelean notion of adequation, the Thomist (or realist) notion of integrity, as well as the Cartesian notion of *ratio*, which finally laid the foundations for the Kantian concept of the human subject. For this reason, even an exemplary critic like Jameson will insist that, "the problem [for novel writers] is still about representation" (127).

For African novelists, representation is not necessarily the problem. They are often more interested in exploring what can be said to precede the subjective perception of objective form. In Plato's *Timeaus*, objective knowledge results from the meeting of the internal fire of the Logos burning in the armillary sphere of the human brain with the external fire that constellates the radiant object on the horizon. Both these fires collide in an explosion of brilliant colors on the lens of the human eye. While writers who are heirs to the Greek philosophical tradition tend to privilege the visually apprehended form, African writers tend to be far more attuned to the word that blows into the receptacle of the ears, a word that can alternately become a good or evil spirit, rather than the absolutely good or ideal word (in Aristotle, the word emptied of matter).

In the Sahel, this occult word for *spirit* goes by many names: the Mande *nyama*, Soninké *ñaxamala*, Wolof *ñeeño*, Fulfulde *nyeenyo*, Toucouleur-Fulfulde *nyaama*, to name only a few. But like the ancient Egyptian belief that *heka* can manifest itself as both good and evil (Te Velde 185) or the Jewish notion that *ruah* is not absolute good but volcanic (or good-evil spirit),[11] West African notions of spirit imply a transcending of the good-evil binaries of Western logocentrism or the Platonic theory of the Logos as absolute good.

In the *Tarîkh el-Fettâch*, the word that blows into the ears of the other is the vow, pledge, oath, covenant, or promise. Kâti insists that the Songhay Empire fell precisely because the descendants of the Askia Muhammad failed to honor his vows. The point that Kâti emphasizes, however, is not merely that the *askia*'s sons failed to honor their father's prior political commitments but also that they failed to feel any compassion for those whom they ruled—for instance, the descendants of the Mori Haougaro who were sold into slavery. Unlike their more pious father, the *askia*'s sons grew to be callous, power-hungry, and heartless. The vow in this context is uttered as an expression of great compassion for the other. As Hagar pities her son, Ishmael, who is dying of thirst, only eyes that are filled with water or flooded with tears of compassion for the other can finally see the true source of water—in this case, the well of Zam-Zam enabling the founding of Mecca. The vow is not about rational knowledge of what is seen but about a blurry-eyed compassion for the suffering of others.

This understanding of the word implies an indifference to truth as an objective form on the horizon, as one becomes preoccupied with an issue of far greater urgency. We might speak comparatively of the deconstructive notion of the yes that is said to precede philosophy's question of being. In the end, Mahmoûd Kâti's notion of the vow is not terribly different from that of Derrida or even that of Martin Heidegger. Heidegger affirmed the *Zusage* ("accord, acquiescing, trust, or confidence" [76])[12] or, in Derrida's formulation of this Heideggerian notion, "that which is most irreducible, indeed most originary in thought" (*Acts* 95). Kâti's pious vow and Heidegger's *Zusage* may be described as interlingual translations of each other, despite the cultural differences between the two, which are tremendous and must not be elided.

One of the griot's chief functions as a member of the *nyamakala* is to perform at name-giving or circumcision ceremonies. In other words, the griot is not simply a singer of epic tales but also a kind of mohel who delivers the knife cut with his or her hand, the one who gives the name (or law) by performing a violent act of cutting. Circumcision here is comparable with what Jews call *milah*, a writing that is simultaneously a naming and a cutting. Tribal scarring in West Africa is also a way of marking the body or of leaving a trace on the body of the other. One is violently given a name by the other, which is a cut or wound but also a sign of one's indisputable rights in the tribe: the incision is a mark of a sacred pledge.[13] One may think of Derrida's "Circumfession," which tells the story of his own circumcision in El Biar, Algeria, as a distinctly African narrative. Note that the *nyama* writing that is circumcision is an Egypto-African rite that long predates its Jewish counterpart.

One of the best-known and most debated novels highlighting African notions of writing is Ouologuem's *Le devoir de violence*. This novel has provoked much helpful commentary, but it also retells the history of the *askias* and can instructively be compared with the *Tarîkh el-Fettâch*, the *Tarîkh es-Sudan*, and the *Epic of Askia Muhammad*. But many African novels invite such comparison, far more than can be listed here.[14] I draw attention to two lesser known novels, Mohammed Mrabet's *The Lemon* and Norbert Zongo's *The Parachute Drop*.

Mrabet's underappreciated novel was first an oral text: Mbrabet composed it by speaking into a tape recorder instead of holding a pen in his hand. Later, his novel was translated and transcribed with the help of his friend, the American writer Paul Bowles. It tells the story of a young boy, a Maghrebian Berber like Mrabet himself, who is cast on his own resources when he is expelled from school. Abdelslam gains the nickname of the Lemon because of an incident that occurs after he is threatened with sexual assault by a man who initially befriends him. To fend off the older man, Abdelslam hides razor blades inside a lemon, which he then employs as a weapon, scarring his adversary by writing on his face with the sharp blades. Mrabet's novel meditates on orality and writing and on a God who is said to violently write in blood. *The Lemon* is both a labyrinthine puzzle and a simple tale of a boy's initiation. Through a Lukácsian lens, it may seem little more than a quirky bildungsroman, an off-beat novel of social formation. One gradually realizes, however, that Mrabet does not orally recount his tale simply because he lacks Bowles's writing skills. That he speaks rather than writes is significant, for this act affirms the phonocentrism of orthodox Islam—a phonocentrism that is also inextricable from an African thinking of narrative composition as a writing in blood. While the Judeo-Maghrebian Derrida dreams of a pen that is also a blood-filled syringe ("Circumfession" 10), the Islamo-Maghrebian Mrabet declines to lift the bloody pen at all, for he asserts that no merely human writing can alter a destiny that has already been inscribed in the Book (67).

The Parachute Drop tells the story of a corrupt African dictator in the fictional nation of Watinbow. Zongo's novel functions as a kind of national allegory, but it does more. The Hegelian-Marxist aesthetics of typicality, or the idealist-materialist dialectic between what Wilhelm von Humboldt once called inner and outer form (113), is of limited applicability here. Zongo's dictator Gouama is loosely modeled on the former Zaire's Mobutu Sese Seko. Like Mobutu, Gouama manipulates traditional African culture to serve his own interests, but he also—like Mobutu—is involved in occult sorcery. Any critique that neglects to account for the vital role of indigenous beliefs in African politics today will miss what is truly happening in the novel and in West African society at large.

Zongo does not reject such beliefs as primitive superstition; he merely shows us what happens when they are cynically manipulated for political gain. He also shows how lethal the admixture of politics and sorcery can be, especially when Africa's leaders rely on sorcerers as political advisers. During the coup in which he is overthrown, for instance, Gouama takes off his clothes and wrestles in the mud with a black donkey, following the political remedy of his marabout adviser. This is high comedy, but Zongo also seeks to dramatize the terrible degradation of politics in Africa today, especially in the realm of political discourse. In Watinbow, the spoken word is reduced to little more than an instrument of brutality, a matter of pure force or evil spirit. Zongo advocates truth telling at all costs, even the cost of one's own life.[15]

Speaking the truth for Zongo is not a matter of assuming a transcendental ethical standpoint but of holding firm to the promises one makes to the other. Like the sons of the Askia Muhammad, Gouama fails to honor his sacred promises to the people of Watinbow: he does not uphold his vows. If Africa's politicians are liars, Zongo suggests, their lying results from their being adulterers—that is, vow breakers. In his journalism, he often remarked that "the fact is sacred," but "the fact" in this case did not simply mean Cartesian *ratio* (Wise, "Chronicle" 19). As Derrida put it in another context, "This *Faktum* is not empirical fact" (*Acts* 96). Instead, Zongo means the sacred pledge or promise that is always prior to objective knowledge. "What example did you set for the people when you were in power?" a young man asks Gouama. "If you presume to guide the destiny of others, you must be willing to sacrifice your own destiny, your own personal desires" (112).

The dizzying intersection of cultural influences in Africa can overwhelm those teachers of literature who simply want to enrich their syllabuses with an occasional novel by a postcolonial writer. One wonders if educators do their students any great service by assuring them that the aims of African writers are the same as those of the great European realists, the early architects of the novel form. The African novel will nearly always seem mediocre in comparison with the European novel if students are not challenged to examine their unarticulated assumptions about language.

While no theory of language can escape some variety of magical thinking, not all theories of language are reducible to the Platonic parataxis of truth. One must seek to transform hegemonic beliefs about language, so that reflexively logocentric biases are no longer assumed to be natural or inevitable. The true task for teachers of the African novel is to dislodge student assumptions about the printed book's ultimate worth—indeed, about the value of any mechanically reproduced text—and thereby enable them to gain access to a far wider range of African cultural documents.

Notes

1. In *Late Marxism*, Jameson observes that "the monad" in Adorno's *Aesthetic Theory* is "at one and the same time a reflection and not a reflection, just as the work of art itself is social and non-social all at once—or, better still, social through and through by virtue of its very antisociality. This is of course the classical form of the Hegelian dialectic, the identity of identity and non-identity" (177).

2. Film can also be a powerful tool in helping students better understand the West African setting. Among studies of Sahelian films are Ilboudo; Sembène; and Thackway. Relevant films are Dani Kouyaté's *Keita! Heritage of the Griot*, Cheikh Oumar Sisòkò's *Guimba*, and Adama Drabo's *Taafé Fanga*.

3. The griot is a West African bard who sings the epics (literally, "voicings") about important cultural heroes like Sundiata Keita, Askia Muhammad, and El Hajj Umar Tall. The griot's songs are generally performed on a molo or kora, stringed instruments made from animal skins and gourds. The most comprehensive study of the griot is Hale's *Griots and Griottes.*

4. Although Mahmoûd Kâti is credited by the French translators Maurice Delafosse and Octave Houdas as the main author of the *Tarîkh el-Fettâch*, Nehemia Levtzion suggests that the manuscript attributing authorship to Kâti was a forgery, written under the direction of the nineteenth-century Macina-Peulh jihadist Sékou Ahmadou. The true author, according to Levtzion, was Ibn Al-Mukhtar, a grandson of Mahmoûd Kâti. My view is closer to Hale's, who suggests that the *Tarikh el-Fettâch* is "a product of many people over the centuries" (*Scribe* 52). In this essay, I refer to the author simply as Kâti.

5. One notable exception in the *Tarîkh el-Fettâch* occurs when the author notes the consternation of local Islamic notables at the Askia Daoûd's custom of spitting into the sleeves of his eunuch attendants (Kâti 114 [in Arabic], 208–09 [in French]).

6. The Soninké, related to the Mande, are the ancient rulers of Wagadugu from the Ghana Dynasty, preceding the Mande Dynasty, which was founded by Sundiata Keita.

7. Hale states that in numerous interviews conducted with Songhay griots in Niger, he could find none who differentiated between the terms *jesere* and *nyamakala* (*Scribe* 36).

8. I cite from both the Arabic original and French translation of the *Tarikh el-Fettâch.* Currently, Hala Abu Taleb and I are preparing an English-language translation. John Hunwick has published an English-language translation of the *Tarîkh es-Soudan*, entitled *Timbuktu and the Songhay Empire.*

9. For an alternative view, see Hale, *Scribe* 130–31. See also Kilpatrick.

10. One striking example of a conjuration rite is recorded in the *Tarîkh es-Soudan*: "So Dawud took the matter [of one of his enemies] to a man well-versed in witchcraft, and he performed sorcery for him against the Aribanda-farma. At his request, Dawud brought a large jar with water in it. The sorcerer uttered some incantations into it and called the Aribanda-farma by name, and the latter replied. The sorcerer said, 'Come forth to me,' and there emerged from the water, by the power of God the Most High, a man resembling the Aribanda-farma in shape and appearance. Then the sorcerer put manacles on his legs and plunged a spear into him, saying, 'Go!,' and the man immersed himself in the water. Dawud then went to Gao, and had scarcely reached there when the aforementioned Aribanda-farma died" (Hunwick 141).

11. It is important to distinguish between this concept of spirit or *ruah* in Judaism and the one that emerges after the great medieval philosopher Maimonides, who introduces Aristotle into Jewish theology. See Derrida's *Of Spirit* for an interesting discussion of *ruah* as compared with the German *Geist*, Greek *pneuma*, and Latin *spiritus* (100–01).

12. For further discussion of Heidegger and the *Zusage*, see Derrida, *Of Spirit* 129–33.

13. El Hajj Sékou Tall states: "Circumcision and excision (*taadordy* in Fulfulde; *ban'ngo* in Moré; *soly* in Bambara, etc.) warrant promotions for the young (girls and boys). Besides these two practices, there is teeth-sharpening, tattooing and scarification of the skin at precise places on the body (the stomach, shoulders, temples, lips, forehead, cheeks), all of which function as symbols and remain the only true means to concretely and solemnly consecrate the promotion of those individuals selected; that is, they guarantee the appurtenance of the group as a collective body, or as a socially ratified entity. Ritual promotion is thus at one with the question of Human rights. Such rights are concretized within these contexts to the child's advantage, especially the Right to Education. In these ways, the young and old partake of intimate communion with the patrons of the collective body or the socially ratified group. These practices constitute for the young their supreme right to receive an education and instruction in the ways of their people" (58). To Tall's remarks, I would add that whatever one's personal views regarding such practices, one would do well not to articulate a political criticism of them without first seeking to understand them.

14. Achebe's often taught *Things Fall Apart* reveals a great deal about the role of folk aphorisms in the contemporary novel, especially with respect to indigenous views about language's autonomy. Other exemplary texts are Ngũgĩ wa Thiong'o's *The River Between*, a novel on the theme of circumcision, and his oral-aural novels *Devil on the Cross* and *Matigari*. Also strongly recommended is Amadou Hampaté Bâ's *The Fortunes of Wangrin* and his transcription of the Fulani initiation epic *Kaidara* (1988). But the point of this essay is not to locate African novels that may neatly fit a theory of orality-aurality; it is to encourage educators to read the African novel for what it is, not approach it as a new variant of a largely Western genre.

15. Zongo was assassinated in 1998 for his editorials criticizing the regime of President Blaise Compaoré of Burkina Faso. His assassination led to a period of extreme political unrest for the Burkinabè, especially in Ouagadougou.

Works Cited

Achebe, Chinua. *No Longer at Ease*. Portsmouth: Heinemann, 1960. Print.

———. *Things Fall Apart*. Portsmouth: Heinemann, 1958. Print.

Adorno, Theodor W. *Aesthetic Theory*. Trans. C. Lenhardt. London: Routledge, 1984. Print.

Camara Laye. *The Guardian of the Word*. Trans. James Kirkup. New York: Vintage, 1980. Print.

Derrida, Jacques. *Acts of Religion*. Ed. and trans. Gil Anidjar. New York: Routledge, 2002. Print.

———. "Circumfession." *Jacques Derrida*. By Derrida and Geoffrey Bennington. Trans. Bennington. Chicago: U of Chicago P, 1993. 3–315. Print.

———. *Dissemination*. Trans. Barbara Johnson. Chicago: U of Chicago P, 1981. Print.

———. *Of Grammatology*. Trans. Gayatri Chakravorty Spivak. Baltimore: Johns Hopkins UP, 1976. Print.

———. *Of Spirit: Heidegger and the Question*. Trans. Geoffrey Bennington and Rachel Bowlby. Chicago: U of Chicago P, 1991. Print.

Drabo, Adama. *Taafé Fanga*. Taare Film, 1997. Film.

Goelet, Ogden. "A Commentary." *The Egyptian Book of the Dead: The Book of Going Forth by Day*. Trans. Raymond Faulkner. San Francisco: Chronicle, 1998. 137–69. Print.

Hale, Thomas. *Griots and Griottes: Masters of Words and Music*. Bloomington: Indiana UP, 1998. Print.

———. *Scribe, Griot, and Novelist: Narrative Interpreters of the Sonhay Empire*. Gainesville: UP of Florida, 1990. Print.

Hale, Thomas, and Nouhou Malio. *The Epic of Askia Mohammed*. Bloomington: Indiana UP, 1996. Print.

Hale, Thomas, and Paul Stoller. "Oral Art, Society, and Survival in the Sahel Zone." *African Literatures Studies: The Present State*. Ed. Stephen Arnold. Washington: Three Continents, 1985. 163–69. Print.

Hampaté Bâ, Amadou. *The Fortunes of Wangrin*. Trans. Aina Pavolini Taylor. Bloomington: Indiana UP, 1999. Print.

———. *Kaidara*. Trans. Daniel Whitman. Boulder: Rienner, 1988. Print.

Hegel, Georg W. F. *Hegel's Aesthetics: Lectures on Fine Art*. Trans. T. M. Knox. Vol. 1. Oxford: Oxford UP, 1975. Print.

Heidegger, Martin. *On the Way to Language*. San Francisco: Harper, 1982. Print.

Hoffman, Barbara G. *Griots at War: Conflict, Conciliation, and Caste in Mande*. Bloomington: Indiana UP, 2001. Print.

Humboldt, Wilhelm von. "On the Task of the Historian." Trans. Linda De-Michiel. *The Hermeneutics Reader*. Ed. Kurt Mueller-Vollmer. New York: Continuum, 1985. 105–19. Print.

Hunwick, John. *Timbuktu and the Songhay Empire: Al-Sa'di's* Ta'rikh al-Sudan *down to 1613, and Other Contemporary Documents*. Leiden: Brill, 1999. Print.

Ilboudo, Patrick G. *Le FESPACO: Les cineaestes africains et leur œuvres*. Ouagadougou: Mante, 1988. Print.

Jameson, Fredric. *Late Marxism: Adorno; or, The Persistence of the Dialectic*. London: Verso, 1990. Print.

———. *Postmodernism; or, The Cultural Logic of Late Capitalism.* Durham: Duke UP, 1991. Print.

Johnson, John William, and Fa-Digi Sisòkò, eds. *The Epic of Son-Jara: A West African Tradition.* Bloomington: Indiana UP, 1992. Print.

Kane, Cheikh Hamidou. *Ambiguous Adventure.* Trans. Katherine Woods. Portsmouth: Heinemann, 1961. Print.

Kâti, Mahmoûd. *The Tarîkh el-Fettâch.* Bilingual ed. Trans. Octave Houdas and Maurice Delafosse. Paris: Librairie D'Amérique et D'Orient, 1981. Print.

Kilpatrick, Sean. "Animism, Syncretism, and Hardness: The Epic of Askia Mohammed." Wise, *Desert Shore* 87–97.

Kouyaté, Dani. *Keita! Heritage of the Griot.* Afix Productions, 1994. Film.

Levtzion, Nehemia. "A Seventeenth-Century Chronicle by Ibn Al-Mukhtar: A Critical Study of *Ta'rikh Al-Fattash.*" *Bulletin of the School of Oriental and African Studies* 34 (1971): 571–93. Print.

Lukács, Georg. "Realism in the Balance." *Aesthetics and Politics.* Ed. and trans. Ronald Taylor. London: Verso, 1977. 28–59. Print.

McNaughton, Patrick R. "The Semantics of *Jugu*: Blacksmiths, Lore, and 'Who's Bad' in Mande." *Status and Identity in West Africa: Nyamakalaw of Mande.* Ed. David C. Conrad and Barbara E. Frank. Bloomington: Indiana UP, 1995. 46–57. Print.

Mrabet, Mohammed. *The Lemon.* Trans. Paul Bowles. San Francisco: City Lights, 1969. Print.

Ngũgĩ wa Thiong'o. *Devil on the Cross.* Portsmouth: Heinemann, 1987. Print.

———. *Matigari.* Portsmouth: Heinemann, 1998. Print.

———. *The River Between.* Portsmouth: Heinemann, 1990. Print.

Ong, Walter J. "African Talking Drums and Oral Noetics." *Interfaces of the Word: Studies in the Evolution of Consciousness and Culture.* Ithaca: Cornell UP, 1977. 92–120. Print.

———. *Orality and Literacy: The Technologizing of the Word.* New York: Routledge, 1992. Print.

Ouologuem, Yambo. *The Duty of Violence. The Yambo Ouologuem Reader:* The Duty of Violence, A Black Ghostwriter's Letter to France, *and* A Thousand and One Bibles of Sex. Trans. and ed. Christopher Wise. Trenton: Africa World, 2008. 1–208. Print. Trans. of *Le devoir de violence.* 1968.

Pacéré, Titinga Frédéric. "Saglego; or, Drum Poem (for the Sahel)." Wise, *Desert Shore* 45–72.

Paré, Joseph, and Christopher Wise. "Introduction: The Land of the Blood Boiling Sun." Wise, *Desert Shore* 1–18.

Plato. *Plato's* Phaedrus. Trans. Stephen Scully. Newburyport: Focus Philosophical Lib., 2003. Print.

———. *Timaeus.* Timaeus *and* Critias. Ed. and trans. Henry Desmond Pritchard Lee. New York: Penguin, 1971. 27–124. Print. Penguin Classics.

Sankara, Thomas. *Thomas Sankara Speaks.* Trans. Samatha Anderson. New York: Pathfinder, 1988. Print.

Sembène, Ousmane. *Africa and the Centenary of Cinema.* Paris: Présence Africaine, 1995. Print.

Sisòkò, Cheikh Oumar. *Guimba.* Direction de la Cinématographie Nationale, 1995. Film.

Tall, El Hajj Sékou. "Key Concepts and Traditional African Society: Liberty, Equality, Human Rights, Duties, Prohibitions, Solidarity, Coexistence, Peace." Trans. Christopher Wise. *Voices* 4 (2000): 55–63. Print.

Te Velde, Herman. "The God Heka in Egyptian Theology." *Jaarbericht van het Voorsaiatishch-Egyptisch Genootshap: Ex Oriente Lux* 21 (1970): 175–86. Print.

Thackway, Melissa. *Africa Shoots Back: Alternative Perspectives in Sub-Saharan Francophone African Films.* Bloomington: Indiana UP, 2003. Print.

Wise, Christopher. "Chronicle of a Student Strike in Africa: The Case of Burkina Faso, 1996–1997." *African Studies Review* 41.2 (1998): 19–36. Print.

———, ed. *The Desert Shore: Literatures of the Sahel.* Boulder: Rienner, 2001. Print.

———. "Nyama and Heka: African Concepts of the Word." *Comparative Literature Studies* 43.1–2 (2006): 17–36. Print.

Zongo, Norbert. *The Parachute Drop.* Trans. Christopher Wise. Trenton: Africa World, 2004. Print.

Shirin Edwin

Approaches to Teaching Islam in the West African Novel

Of the many themes frequently taught in a class on the African novel, Islam is either overlooked or suffers from an improper understanding. Teachers and students are often inclined to give short shrift to numerous dimensions that warrant a nuanced understanding of the religion. It is to fill this pedagogical lacuna, which is all too often symptomatic of inherent biases vis-à-vis Islam, that this essay proposes a thematic approach and foregrounds the underpinnings, both theoretical and pedagogical, for the thematic of Islam in a course on the African novel. This essay demonstrates the disservice done to Islam when the religion is inexorably associated with the politics and culture of the Arab world, where it was born and first developed before spreading to the rest of the world (Clarke 1–8).[1] This association has obscured the diversity of Islam and of African literature. Ken Harrow rightly points out that Islam has been reduced to the notion of a predetermined monolith, to an undifferentiated body of people called "Muslims" (*Faces* 3). For African literature, this myopic approach fosters pedagogical apathy and indifference toward Islam, making it perhaps last in line of the themes discussed in a classroom.

To relocate the religion on the thematic map in a classroom, four approaches suggest themselves to teaching it in the African novel. The first engages students in identifying key words that unmistakably mark the discursive presence of Islam. The second approach acknowledges the accompanying cultural systems (colonization, decolonization, immigration, capitalism, modernization, etc.) revealed through an investigation of the author's cultural and national background. The third involves studying how the religion is connected to a larger sociocultural framework. The fourth promotes a thorough understanding of Islamic practices, particularly in novels where Islam visibly manifests itself, not only spiritually but also in economic, legal, and social respects.

While these approaches are by no means exhaustive or exclusive and may vary from context to context and from one teaching style to another, they help make Islam salient and current in classroom discussions of the African novel. These recommendations for studying the religion may be viewed as meta-approaches with broad geographic and literary applications, not limited to a genre or literature from a particular region in Africa. Studying the presence of Islam through textual references, key words, allusions to politics, spiritual practices, laws, economic systems, social customs, and cultural parameters provides a pedagogical thrust to the study of literatures in every part of Africa.

First, however, we need to understand why Islam is often sidelined as a theme in African literatures. One prevalent view is that the religion is foreign and consequently inimical to fundamental African interests (*Wonders*).[2] On a number of occasions, Wole Soyinka has insisted that Islamic culture is "alien" to African culture and that it is one of the "principal enemies" of the "authentic traditions" of Africa ("Cross-Currents" 179).[3] The Nobel laureate offers a selection of West African novels to endorse the aesthetics of social justice, the universality of human values, and the human ideal as the most enduring objectives of African novelists such as Ousmane Sembène, Yambo Ouologuem, and Ayi Kwei Armah (*Myth*). His brilliant analysis is predicated on the assumption that justice and equality are necessarily divorced from religion, that many paths lead to justice but those of religious devotion and identity can lead only to oppression. Soyinka states that the Malian novelist Ouologuem, in *Le devoir de violence* (*Bound to Violence*), pronounces the Moslem incursion into black Africa to be "corrupt, vicious, decadent, elitist and insensitive" (105). Soyinka proceeds to point out that Ouologuem's novel is a direct attack on the "Islamic apologia" (104) made in *L'aventure ambiguë* (1960; *Ambiguous Adventure*), by the Senegalese novelist Cheikh Hamidou Kane.

To this perspective one may add Chinweizu's thesis on African culture in *Decolonising the African Mind*, that Islam is an Arab religion and that being Muslim or learning about Islam is naturally tethered to Arab culture, Arab beliefs, and pro-Arab sympathies. Chinweizu condemns Arab sharia and the systematic supplanting of African rites by Arabs, who consider indigenous African religions "pagan" and infidel (125). Convinced of the lack of difference between Islam and Arab culture, Chinweizu attributes the "destabilisation of African societies" to Arab Islamic expansionism (126). He also decries the impositions of "Arab genealogies on jet-black Africans" (117) and denounces Africans who are subservient toward Arab rulers from Egypt and Morocco and who promote "Islamic identity" in Senegal and Nigeria (126).

Of interest in Chinweizu's untenable connection between Arab culture and Islam is the elision of the differences between the two. His argument is untenable, since Islam has historically spread to regions as distant as China and North America, where it has been practiced for centuries without Arabization. It is of relevance to recognize that Arab culture existed long before the advent of Islam, and they are not interchangeable signifiers. Only in the seventh century AD did Islam, as a new system of spiritual beliefs and a distinct legal and economic code, transform Arab culture, in innumerable ways leaving its imprint on many features of it. But the religion, albeit a significant component of the culture, is not the only one. Moreover, in the seventh and eighth centuries AD, the Arab armies got no farther than Tunisia and northeast Sudan during the invasion of Africa (Levtzion 63).[4] It cannot be denied that Islam is foreign to Africa as opposed to practices that were born and took root on African soil; nor can it be denied that conversion to Islam substituted, displaced, and eliminated numerous African traditions. But African practices were also adapted and incorporated to develop a symbiotic relation with Islam—as later colonial policies and Christian practices led to adaptation of religious identity, creating in West Africa a space of multiple negotiations and exchanges. This process of cultural and religious co-opting may not always have been harmonious or peaceful, but it forced the recognition of difference in establishing the richness of African identity.

While it may be conceded that Soyinka's and Chinweizu's polemics are directed against an exclusive identification with Arab culture, bordering on fanaticism, by Africans who thereby run the risk of denying the African dimension of their identity, the theoretical posture of these writers does perpetuate the a priori disregard of Islam as a factor in African life. A fundamental problem with the assertion of foreignness is that it supports the dangerous idea that Muslims in Africa have no local Islamic histories. Another point is that European colonialism and neocolonialism are indeed foreign and harmful to African interests, yet it would be impossible to imagine the study of African literature, history, or society without accounting for them. Why, then, should the study of Islam be limited to the binaries of good Islam (read "moderate" and "liberal") and bad Islam (read "fanatical" and "fundamental"), of African Islam and non-African Islam, of people exclusively for or against Islam—ignoring the complexity, contradictions, and ambiguities in its practice, composition, and perception in Africa? A serious effort to study Islam without hastily depositing it in positive and negative camps could liberate the religion from a stubborn bipolar logic and neutralize the prejudices and preconceived notions about it.

More crucially, however, a teacher of African literature may productively respond to the overwhelming weight of Soyinka's and Chinweizu's arguments by enlisting a historicist approach to show that Islamic development in West Africa mapped a twofold trajectory. In the introduction to one of the most comprehensive and useful source books on Islam in Africa, *The History of Islam in Africa*, Nehemia Levtzion and Randall Pouwels describe the first phase of development of Islam through contact with clerics who preached in courts of local African rulers (3). They also attribute the expansion of Islam, in the eleventh century AD, to Manding-speaking traders who navigated across the Saharan routes to create a "commercial diaspora" (3, 64) through trade carried out by Berbers and Arabs who came into contact with the sedentary Sudanic populations and, further, into the Sahel with local West African populations in what is now Senegal, Mali, Chad, Niger, and Sudan. It should be noted that the growth of Islam through commercial contact was an urban phenomenon, limited to cities and large towns.

The second phase of Islamic expansion was marked by jihads and violent repressions. Interestingly, the violent coercion to make West Africa a part of the Dar al-Islam was carried out not by Arabs, as Chinweizu believes, but by Africans themselves: Uthman dan Fodio, who established the Sokoto caliphate in northern Nigeria; Séku Ahmadou, who founded the city of Hamdullahi; and Mohammad al-Bekkay, El Hajj Umar Tall, Nasr al-Din, Sulayman Bal, and Shaykh Umar al-Futi, to name a few revolutionary African Muslims. David Robinson notes that the holy wars or jihads sprang from the need to reform an already existing Islamic society and were funded by Sufi brotherhoods, which

> produced pedagogical systems that provided the tools to understand the faith in its original Arabic form but also in Pulaar (Fulfulde) and other languages. They were instrumental in transforming West Africa into a part of the Dar al-Islam. ("Revolutions" 131)

The existence of these brotherhoods reveals the palpable presence of Islam in African society, a presence that stems from the concomitance of political, economic, social, legal, and spiritual codes as described and ordained by Islam's central and defining text, the Qur'an. That these jihads originated not in the cities but in the countryside indicates that the influence of Islamic ideologies was not limited to the work of the ulema, the elite and religious clerics of the royal courts; it was also witnessed in rural regions, which signaled the complete immersion of African society in Islam. Through these revolutions, the practice of the faith was perceived as "attractive" to many, prompting their conversion to Islam (144). Knowledge of this twofold course in the spread of Islam is of urgent significance permitting students to explore in greater depth the various nuances in the development of Islam in Africa before eagerly dismissing it as an exclusively Arab and therefore non-African religion in Africa or a violent and oppressive faith in general.

Useful Studies on Islam in Africa

Research on the study of Islam in Africa is abundant and can be put into the categories of historical, literary, sociological, political, and anthropological. It is to the anthropological approach that we owe the term of *black Islam*, widely used to describe the composition and practice of Islam in western, eastern, central, and southern Africa as the syncretic mingling of Islam with traditional African beliefs. The term may allow immediate geographic and ethnic identification by associating the religion with the African continent or black peoples, but it is insufficient to explain Islam in West Africa. Souleymane Bachir Diagne succinctly discusses the shortcomings of using this term as the sole index to understanding Islam in West Africa. Diagne refers to Vincent Monteil's impressive study *L'islam noir: Une religion à la conquête de l'Afrique noire* (1980; "Black Islam: A Religion in the Conquest of Black Africa"), which is a revision of Monteil's "*L'islam noir*" (1964), one of the earliest projects on the religion in Africa and responsible for coining and popularizing the term.[5]

Monteil divides the study of Islam in Africa by carefully examining the nature and composition of fetishes, the Islamic pillars of faith, the role and importance of marabouts (Muslim spiritual leaders), polygamy, and dowry, among other aspects of African society and politics. He demonstrates that Islamization in Africa was in fact an Africanization of Islam and that Islam was only superficially able to impress itself on the African mind and soul. The African mind, which Monteil calls "pensée sauvage" (367 ["savage mind"]), essentially remains unchanged despite centuries of interaction with Islam. The implication is that Africans have not experienced any transformation for centuries. As a corrective, Diagne points out that African identity is not static but a product of constant re-creation through and by history (377) and that the Islamic influence in West Africa has been more than superficial. He argues that the African Muslim is no different from Muslims throughout the Islamic world, despite the ethnographic project undertaken by the French colonial enterprise to sequester West African Muslims. Studies similar to Monteil's are Alphonse Gouilly's *L'Islam dans l'Afrique occidentale française* (1952 ["Islam in French West Africa"]) and J. C. Froelich's *Les musulmans d'Afrique noire* (1962 ["The Muslims of Black Africa"]). These works grow out of the French colonial agenda to understand and control Islam in West Africa. But they are seminal in that they furnish firsthand perspectives of former officials of the French colonial government who lived and worked in close contact with Muslim communities.

To this research must be added the works of James Spencer Trimingham. Chief among them is *Islam in West Africa* (1959), a study of the different routes of Islamic penetration into African society. Trimingham gives parallels between the old religion or indigenous faiths of Africa and Islamic practices to demonstrate the mark of Islam on every sphere of African society. Drawing from both systems of belief, he discusses family structure and polygamy, dissolution of marriage, death rites and circumcision, Islamic education, kinship groups and social associations, class differentiation and election of chiefs and theocracy, Islamic and customary law. He shows both the resistance to and acceptance of the "interpenetration" of Islam and traditional faiths in West Africa (12). In *A History of Islam in Africa* (1962), he details the expansion of Islam in each geographic division of Africa, ranging from North Africa to the Sahara and Sudan (central and western Sudan states).

These early analyses help contextualize the study of Islam in Africa, but a gamut of contemporary issues are addressed in work undertaken by

Robinson, Levtzion, Jean-Louis Triaud, and Mervyn Hiskett, to name a few scholars on Islam in Africa. Peter Clarke provides a detailed account of the expansion and development of Islam in West Africa to shape an important sourcebook for students. With regard to Islam in eastern and tropical Africa, I. M. Lewis has done comprehensive scholarly work.

The study of Islam in African literature finds its way into important anthologies edited by Harrow, *The Marabout and the Muse* and *Faces of Islam in African Literature.* Attempting to redress the imbalance in scholarship on Islam in African literature, both collections provide studies on a range of topics, such as an Islamic feminist reading of Tayeb Salih's *Season of Migration to the North*, the role of sheikhs and poets in Somali literature, representation of Sufi thought in West African fiction, and the functions of marabouts, or Muslim holy leaders, in African literatures. A multidimensional prism is offered of the representation and consequently the presence of Islam in Africa. Debra Boyd Buggs's dissertation "*Baraka*: Maraboutism and Maraboutage in the Francophone Senegalese Novel" and other articles on the representations of marabouts and the Islamic community from the Franco-Senegalese panorama contribute to the research.

Ahmed Bangura's *Islam and the West African Novel: The Politics of Representation* is particularly helpful in dispelling the dangers of using black Islam or syncretism as the exclusive index for understanding Islam in West Africa. Central to his argument is the belief that the study and representation of Islam in West Africa suffers from orientalist biases that blur the crucial difference between the religious embodiment of Islam and the critical reception of the aesthetics of different West African Muslim writers, such as Ousmane Sembène, Aminata Sow Fall, Ibrahim Tahir, and Ahmadou Kourouma. Bangura demonstrates that "critical (mis)-readings" of Sembène's aesthetic have labeled it anti-Islamic and concluded that Sembène views Islam as a social evil (55). In response, Bangura analyzes the Islamic allusions in Sembène's work to prove that in fact the Senegalese novelist's oeuvre presents a dialogue among Muslims who possess varying degrees of Islamic consciousness. This dialogue, argues Bangura, debunks a fatalistic interpretation of the religion (56). He concludes that one cannot decide, by examining solely the perverse embodiments of the religion in Sembène's work, that Sembène (or any other West African novelist) denounces Islam. A proper understanding of the religion is needed before a writer's aesthetic can be judged anti-Islamic.

Most of the aforementioned research serves as the ground on which a teacher can proceed with a lesson plan attending to specific concepts vital to the study of Islam in West Africa—the birth of the religion; the life and mission of Muhammad; the fundamental practices, such as charity or *as-sadaqa*; prayer or *as-salat* and its components; the Holy Qur'an and the Hadith (the exemplary speeches, actions, and teachings of the Prophet compiled in different collections, six of which are considered most authoritative, as well as the exegetical writings on these texts);[6] the various schools and traditions of Islamic law; the vicissitudes of the spread and expansion of Islam in the West African region; the organization, function, and importance of Islamic brotherhoods as agents of political and social change;[7] the role of Muslim spiritual leaders, marabouts, and *mallams*; the practice of pilgrimage not only to Mecca but also to Touba in Senegal, as widely followed by the Mouride Muslims (O'Brien);[8] and the intersection of indigenous religions with Islamic practices, manifested for example in polygamy, which is found in both Islamic and traditional African societies. A fruitful way to approach this study is to emphasize these elements in the novels and to analyze them as well as the nuances of their presence and practice in West Africa.

Some Approaches to Teaching Islam in the African Novel

The approaches I recommend apply across literary and geographic boundaries. The works I choose to illustrate Islam in the African novel belong to a relatively familiar corpus used by teachers of African literature. The first approach involves attention to key Islamic concepts. Emphasis on key words, phrases, and practices is helpful in understanding Mariama Bâ's masterpiece *Une si longue lettre* (1979; *So Long a Letter*). Discovering the meaning and significance of terms and actions such as "Koranic school" (1), "Timiss" and "muezzin" (62), "marabouts" (48), "safara" (43), "water for ablutions and a mat on which to pray before the tomb of the ancestor" (28), "Alhaja" and "Alhaji" (10), "mirasse" (9), "Koran" (2, 8, 9), "zemzem" and "seven meters of white muslin, the only clothing Islam allows for the dead" (3), and "Bismilai!" (69) allows Islam to be approached through a spectrum of practices that resonate throughout the novel. For example, *mirasse* is the Wolof equivalent of the Arabic *al-mirath*, meaning "inheritance," as is *timiss* for the evening prayer *maghrib*. Bâ mentions this prayer again in the novel: "today I was not able to finish my evening prayer as I wanted to" (78).

The double reference to this prayer tells us that Ramatoulaye, the protagonist, regularly prays, and it leads us to an exploration of the four other obligatory prayers in Islam and to their importance in a Muslim's life. The other terms taken from Bâ's novel not only help students acquire information on various features of Islam but also signal its social and spiritual edifice. In particular, allusions to the *mirasse* as ordained by the Qur'an (9; Qur'an 4.11, 4.12, and 4.176), Ramatoulaye's evocation of verses from the Qur'an (8)), polygamy (Qur'an 4.3) as treated in the general plot of the novel, Aunty Nabou's failure to differentiate between Islam and "antiquated rites" (28), and the pilgrimage to Mecca explained by the use of the terms "Alhaji" and "Alhaja" (10) compel a teacher to attend to the discursive presence of the Qur'an in the novel.

An understanding of these terms then paves the way for deeper analysis of sociopolitical issues in the novel. Among these is the practice of polygamy, which leads readers to reflect: Why would a practising Muslim like Ramatoulaye (note her obedience to the Qur'an [8, 9]) condemn the religious dictate of polygamy (Qur'an 4.3 [Hilali and Khan])? Does Ramatoulaye denounce the practice of polygamy in general, or is she protesting the egoistical and immature behavior of her husband? Asking such questions in the context of practices described in the novel facilitates a better understanding of Islam and of the novel by preventing the elision of religious and cultural nuances in Senegalese society.

The second approach demands a look at a work's accompanying sociopolitical landscape and the author's background—that is, an awareness of factors illuminating more the context of the novel than its text, the recognition of such cultural systems as colonization, decolonization, the African diaspora, modernization, immigration, and capitalism within geographic entities like Senegal, Mali, Nigeria, and Ghana. The intersection of these systems direct the plot of a novel and influence the actions of the characters. For example, the political system in Ahmadou Kourouma's *Les soleils des indépendances* (1968; *The Suns of Independence*) is framed by the historical event of decolonization or independence of some West African nations from French colonial rule in the early 1960s. Kourouma's homeland, Ivory Coast, has a forty percent Muslim population, mainly in the northern regions of the country. Madeleine Borgamano notes that Kourouma was born in the northern part of the country and that his immediate familial and wider social influences were Islamic as he was from an influential Malinke Muslim family (14). This personal background could interact with and become part of the creative pattern of the novel. Kourouma's second novel, *En attendant le vote des bêtes sauvages* (1998; *Waiting for the Vote of the Wild Animals*), does not have an obvious or consistent Islamic thematic foundation, yet study of the author's background and social and spiritual environment shows the presence of Islam in the novel.

Many African writers are either of Muslim heritage or have been influenced by Islam. The Senegalese novelists Ousmane Sembène, Aminata Sow Fall, and Aminata Maïga Ka; the Malian author Yambo Ouologuem; the Gambian poet and writer Tijan Sallah; the Nigerian writers Ibrahim Tahir and Zaynab Alkali; the Tanzanian novelist Abdulrazak Gurnah; and the Somalian novelist Nuruddin Farah, for example, are of Muslim heritage. But non-Muslim African writers too employ Islam as a theme: Ama Ata Aidoo, David Owoyele, Calixthe Beyala, and Nadine Gordimer often depict Islamic practice in their works.

Les soleils des indépendances portrays the nexus between the politics of decolonization (the overarching cultural system in the novel) and Islam (a religious component of West African society) as an unholy alliance. Fama, a former Malinke prince, is reduced to being a scavenger in the aftermath of the euphoric and much awaited independence of his country from French colonial rule. The excessive and consistent presence of rituals, sacrifices, and consultations of marabouts made by both the underprivileged, like Fama, and powerful ministers and ambassadors to recapture and maintain political privilege (66) demonstrates the unshakable belief that Islam can defeat the corrupt political system. The religion thus assumes a political role in the novel and becomes more than a spiritual presence. Therefore, to acknowledge the effects of decolonization in the novel also demands a study of Islam as one of the political instruments used in Kourouma's fictitious country.

Knowledge of the specificity of Islam in Africa can facilitate an understanding of the text and can show the sociospiritual architecture of a society—as in Ken Bugul's *Le baobab fou*:

> We were a traditional Moslem family. The father, temporal and sacred guide, had settled in Ndoucoumane out of friendship for a great man. They had sworn to each other that they'd never abandon the other and the pact was signed . . . when the spirits stood guard. Together they devoted themselves to Knowledge and from there to Vision, inside the virtues of Islam, inside the depository of all knowledge which is the Koran. (*Abandoned Baobab* 126)

Alluding to Islamic practice, this paragraph gestures to the protagonist's Muslim identity, based on the guidance of a "great man," the Qur'an, and prayer. Since these features are not elaborated on or explained in the novel, a supplementary reading on Islam in Senegal is needed.

First, the relationship of a Senegalese Muslim to a great man points to the role and importance of marabouts. The character Ken is a Muslim whose family belongs to an Islamic brotherhood under the guidance of a marabout. The practice of Islam in Senegal is largely distributed among four brotherhoods or orders; the Mouridiyya, Tijaniyya, Qadiriyya, and Layenne (Mbacké 2). The members of these brotherhoods must pledge loyalty to the marabout, also called *serigne*, meaning "master" or "teacher." This form of devotion largely follows the Sufi practice of Islamic education with the help of a guide. The Islamic principles of a brotherhood shape a *tariqa* ("way") to eternal salvation, in which believers learn about Islam under the tutelage of a marabout as one would embark on a journey with the help of a guide to arrive at the desired goal. The father in the paragraph, who signs a "pact," witnessed by the "spirits," never to abandon this great man, is a Senegalese Muslim who takes the *wird* ("central core") of the brotherhood; his teacher in turn is bound by the *wird* to teach the student in the "virtues of Islam." The *wird* is a series of prayers transmitted through a chain or *silsila* from master to student as a means to initiate the learner into the way and to embark on the journey of knowledge and vision.

Second, the character Ken mentions the importance of the Qur'an not only as the holy text of Islam but also as the "depository of all knowledge." The Qur'an is considered by Muslims the fundamental source of knowledge, in all forms. The scientific, legal, political, and social are thus inextricably merged with the spiritual. The Qur'an is an all-encompassing text. For a practicing Muslim to obey it in matters of family inheritance, for example, is the performing of a spiritual act. In this divinely revealed text, Muslims find laws pertaining to business transactions, trade, charity, property, inheritance, banking, interest, and loans. They also find rules governing personal and family life: marriage, kinship, inheritance, personal hygiene, and eating habits. In an Islamic society, therefore, the spiritual suffuses all aspects of life. So an awareness of Ken's Muslim background allows a fuller grasp of the identity crisis she experiences in the French school and later in Belgium: the identity that existed before the brutal colonial invasion was indeed Islamic. Also helpful are allusions Ken makes to Islamic practices such as baptism (9) and her own initiative to read the Qur'an to escape solitude and trauma engendered by the French school and culture (117).

In the last approach, where Islam is more visible, an understanding of its practices and principles facilitates the study of the religion from angles not necessarily spiritual. The objective is to present the ways in which Islam suffuses every practical sphere of life. Viewing Islam from legal, economic, and political angles can also neutralize the apprehension of students who may be resistant to a religious doctrine unlike their own.

Ibrahim Tahir's *The Last Imam* is rich in possibilities for teaching Islam: it presents directly the Islamic practice of prayer and Islamic law in all its facets. Tahir's novel is one of the most important texts on Islam in West African literature. The only other novel as rich in information on the religion is Cheikh Hamidou Kane's *L'aventure ambiguë* (1960; *Ambiguous Adventure*). *The Last Imam* frames the spiritual and official struggles of Imam Alhaji Usman, described in the novel as the "Hausa or Fulani idea of Moses" (1), in an Islamic system of belief. Immediately the mention of "Hausa or Fulani" suggests the predominantly Muslim region of northern Nigeria. We are led to an exploration of information on the Sokoto Caliphate that was established through a jihad by Uthman dan Fodio. An explicit reference to this historical event also appears in the novel (12).

The novel is replete with details of spiritual, legal, and social Islamic practices: lengthy descriptions of prayer procedures and components like the *kalimat* (4, 8 ["the article and declaration of faith"]), *attahiyat* (10, 11 ["spiritual formulas"]) (see Khan, *Translation* [1994] 255 [Book of As-Salat]),[9] *sujud* (10 ["prostrations"]), the practice of Friday prayer (7, 13, 34, 150, 224), and *huduba* (150 ["the sermon"]) act as a fulcrum on which the events of the novel converge. More important, regular and constant citations from the *Book of Dreams* of the Hadith or the Sunna of the Prophet (15, 20 [Khan, *Translation* (1981) (Interpretation of Dreams, book 187)]), Qur'anic chapters such as the "Fatiha" (10), the "Surah Al-Balad" (10 ["Chapter of the City"] [Hilali and Khan 952]), as well as verse references to and from the Qur'an (8, 10, 30) weave an unmistakable and unavoidable intertextuality throughout the plot. Tahir describes the significance of the religion, the reading of the Qur'an, and the believers who listen with rapt attention to Usman reciting the holy verses:

> . . . particularly the prose poem of the holy Koran, so musical that old men and women would stand outside the school hall and listen to him with solemn admiring expressions. They did not understand the words because most of them did not understand Arabic. But they had faith, they had memory, the memory of fragments of information gathered from their scanty education about the earlier days,

> the days of the struggles of Mohammed and the victories and glories of Islam. (17)

This passage sums up the essence of Islam, for in it lies the meaning of the religion: submission to Allah and his word, the Qur'an. It is relatively unimportant if one does not understand the meaning of the verses; important is faith that the Qu'ran is indeed Allah's word and requires complete obedience to his commands. This first article of faith (*shahdah* or *kalimat*) is also considered the first pillar of Islam. The above passage could prompt a classroom discussion on the need to distinguish between blind faith and submission to the divine will in order to clarify faith in Islam and the position of the Qur'an in the Islamic religion, which is often mistaken for blind or mechanical faith bordering on fanaticism and extremism.

Consider also the legal aspect of the religion in the practice of polygamy. The character Usman cannot marry a fifth wife, because he already has four. Ironically, the fifth woman, Hasana, is the only woman he has ever loved, but Islamic law allows him to keep her only as a slave. This legal provision is justified by citing Qur'anic verses (30). Thus the psychology of the characters is shaped by religious laws. Grounding terminology from the novel in specific textual references to the Qu'ran and the Hadith gives students insight into the Islamic system of belief. Terms like "Assalamu Alaikum" (76, 77, 78), "Bismillah" (73), and "Subhana lillahi" (13) are more than salutations; students should know the purpose and reasoning behind them.

The term "Makruhi" (22) is key in understanding the varying degrees of approved acts and acts that are disapproved though not punishable, not considered *haram* ("forbidden and reprehensible"). The term "Ka'aba" (31) draws attention to the significance of pilgrimage or hajj and to the historical significance of the Black Stone, considered sacred by Muslims all over the world. Similarly, studying the months, like Ramadan and Sha'ban (90), entails a discussion of the nature, purpose, and logic of the Islamic calendar.

Each aspect of the Islamic system thus points to the fact that Islam in Tahir's novel is not merely a textual presence; it is a culture embodied in the use of expressions, words, and practices wholly integrated into the lives of the characters. The debate over the dichotomy of culture versus religion can be approached through the example of the "gwauro" (105) practice in the novel. The study of this tension can further involve the above-mentioned concept of *makruh* and the degrees of prohibited and permissible acts under Islamic law. In the process, Islam should neither be unconditionally aligned with Arab culture nor divested of its historically Arabian contexts. Either extreme would be harmful to the study of African literatures.

This essay makes the case for a context-centered instruction of Islam in the African novel. Students should see the extent to which predominantly Muslim societies in Africa incorporate in their literatures one of their most significant political, economic, and social institutions. Recognizing Islam in the African novel can often lead to a holistic understanding of African literature.

Notes

1. Clarke sketches the birth of Islam and the circumstances of its growth and expansion from Arabia in the seventh century AD to the rest of the world. His brief description stresses the relevance of the *umma* ("Muslim community") during the lifetime of Muhammad and its expansion after the Prophet's death.

2. *Wonders of the African World* is a six-part television series that shows Islam as an unfair, alien, and destructive religion that has no place in Africa. Note also the media portrayal of Islam as a monolith of fundamentalist followers. Ahmed offers an interesting argument on the inaccurate media representation of Islam, how the media cast and recast perceptions of and opinions on the religion.

3. Soyinka identifies the other principal enemy as European imperialism and views traditional values and sentimentality as incompatible with social transformation and progress.

4. Levtzion explains that in the early seventh and eighth centuries the penetration of Islam in Africa toward the Sahara by Arab expeditions occurred via two North African routes, Tripoli toward Fezzan and Sus in southern Morocco. Beyond North Africa, the Berber nomads carried Islam into the land of Bilad al-Sudan ("Land of the Blacks").

5. Diagne recognizes that Monteil's understanding of the term changed from 1964 to 1980 but that Monteil retained the original title of his book because it was familiar to many.

6. Azami explains that the Arabic word *hadith* literally means "communication," "conversation," or "story"; it can be religious or secular, historical or recent (1, 87–107). The *ahadith* (plural of *hadith*) are of special importance in Islamic practice in that they are repositories of Muhammad's sayings and actions and are followed or imitated by Muslims in an effort to be, as much as is humanly possible, like the revered Prophet. The Prophet's actions are a translation of what is recommended in the Qur'an and a model for Muslims to follow. The six accredited versions of the Hadith are the Sahih al-Bukhari, Sahih Muslim, Sunan

of Abu Dawud, Sunan of Al-Tirmidhi, Sunan of Al-Nasai, and Sunan of Ibn-Maja. The first two collections are considered authentic and therefore are the most authoritative. The last four are called *sunans* ("ways") but are not as comprehensive, since they do not contain *ahadith* concerning morality, history, or *zuhd* ("abstinence") and are only compilations of legal or codified Islamic practices, such as prayer, charity, and pilgrimage.

7. For a thorough analysis and description of Islamic brotherhoods, see Vikør.

8. Detailing the history of the Mourides; the salient features of Mouride ideology as practiced in Senegal; and the famous *magal* ("event-pilgrimage") celebrating the birth of Ahmadou Bamba, the founder of Mouride Islam, O'Brien's book is highly informative.

9. The *attahiyat*, also known as the *tashahhud*, is an important *dua* or prayer recited as part of the obligatory prayer *as-salat*. It is recommended as *sunna* ("the way of the Prophet"), for it reinforces the humility of humankind before God.

Works Cited and Recommended

Ahmed, Akbar S. *Postmodernism and Islam: Predicament and Promise*. London: Routledge, 1992. Print.

Azami, Muhammad Mustafa. *Studies in Hadith Methodology and Literature*. 1977. Indianapolis: Amer. Trust, 1992. Print.

Bâ, Mariama. *Une si longue lettre*. Dakar: Nouvelles Editions Africaines, 1980. Print.

———. *So Long a Letter*. Trans. Modupé-Odumbe Thomas. London: Heineman, 1981. Print.

Bangura, Ahmed. *Islam and the West African Novel: The Politics of Representation*. Boulder: Rienner, 2000. Print.

Borgamano, Madeleine. *Ahmadou Kourouma: "Le guerrier griot."* Paris: Harmattan, 1998. Print.

Buggs, Debra Boyd. "*Baraka*: Maraboutism and Maraboutage in the Francophone Senegalese Novel." Diss. Ohio State U, 1986. Print.

Chinweizu. *Decolonising the African Mind*. Lagos: Pero, 1987. Print.

Clarke, Peter. *West Africa and Islam*. London: Arnold, 1982. Print.

Coulon, Christian. *Le marabout et le prince*. Paris: Pedone, 1981. Print.

Diagne, Souleymane Bachir. "Islam in Africa: Examining the Notion of African Identity within the Islamic World." *A Companion to African Philosophy*. Ed. Kwasi Wiredu. Malden: Blackwell, 2004. 374–83. Print.

Edwin, Shirin. "African Muslim Communities in Diaspora: The Quest for a Muslim Space in Ken Bugul's *Le baobab fou*." *Research in African Literatures* 35.4 (2004): 75–90. Print.

Froelich, J. C. *Les musulmans d'Afrique noire*. Paris: Orante, 1962. Print.

Gouilly, Alphonse. *L'Islam dans l'Afrique occidentale française*. Paris: Larose, 1952. Print.

Harrow, Kenneth W., ed. *Faces of Islam in African Literature*. Portsmouth: Heinemann, 1991. Print.

———. *The Marabout and the Muse: New Approaches to Islam in African Literature*. Portsmouth: Heinemann, 1996. Print.

Hilali, Muhammad Taqi-ud-din al-, and Muhammad Muhsin Khan. *The Interpretation of the Meanings of the Noble Qur'an in the English Language: A Summarized Version of At-Tabari, Al-Qurtubi and Ibn Kathir with Comments from Sahih Al-Bukhari*. New Delhi: Maktaba Darul Qur'an, 1993. Print.

Hiskett, Mervyn. *The Development of Islam in West Africa*. New York: Longman, 1984. Print.

Kane, Cheikh Hamidou. *L'aventure ambiguë*. Paris: Julliard, 1961. Print.

Ken Bugul. *The Abandoned Baobab: The Autobiography of a Senegalese Woman*. Trans. Marjolijn de Jager. New York: Hill, 1991. Print.

———. *Le baobab fou*. Dakar: Nouvelles Editions Africaines, 1996. Print.

Khan, Muhammad Muhsin. *The Translation of the Meanings of the Sahih Al-Bukhari*. Medina: Dar al-Fikr, 1981. Print.

———. *The Translation of the Meanings of the Summarized Sahih al-Bukhari*. Riyadh: Maktaba Darussalam, 1994. Print.

Kourouma, Ahmadou. *En attendant le vote des bêtes sauvages*. Paris: Seuil, 1998. Print.

———. *Les soleils des indépendances*. Paris: Seuil, 1970. Print.

Levtzion, Nehemia. "Islam in the Bilad al-Sudan to 1800." Levtzion and Pouwels, *History* 63–92.

Levtzion, Nehemia, and Randall L. Pouwels, eds. *The History of Islam in Africa*. Athens: Ohio UP, 2000. Print.

———. "Introduction: Patterns of Islamization and Varieties of Religious Experience among Muslims of Africa." Levtzion and Pouwels, *History* 1–20.

Lewis, I. M., ed. *Islam in Tropical Africa*. London: Oxford UP, 1966. Print.

Mazrui, Ali A. *Islam and Acculturation in East Africa's Experience*. SwahiliOnline.com. 27 July 2004. Web. 22 Aug. 2008.

Mbacké, Khadim. *Sufism and Religious Brotherhoods in Senegal*. Ed. John Hunwick. Trans. Eric Ross. Princeton: Wiener, 2005. Print.

Monteil, Vincent. *Islam noir*. Paris: Seuil, 1964. Print.

———. *L'islam noir: Une religion à la conquête de l'Afrique*. Paris: Seuil, 1980. Print.

O'Brien, Donal Cruise. *The Mourides of Senegal: The Political and Economic Organisation*. Oxford: Clarendon, 1971. Print.

O'Brien, Donal Cruise, and Christian Coulon, eds. *Charisma and Brotherhood in African Islam*. Clarendon: Oxford UP, 1988. Print.

Ouologuem, Yambo. *Le devoir de violence*. Paris: Seuil, 1968. Print.

Robinson, David. *The Holy War of Umar Tal*. Clarendon: Oxford UP, 1985. Print.

———. "The Islamic Revolution of Futa Toro." *International Journal of African Historical Studies* 8.2 (1975): 185–221. Print.

———. "Revolutions in Western Sudan." Levtzion and Pouwels, *History* 131–44.

Robinson, David, and Jean-Louis Triaud, eds. *Le temps des marabouts: Itinéraires et stratégies islamiques en Afrique occidentale française*. Paris: Karthala, 1997. Print.

Soyinka, Wole. "Cross-Currents: The 'New African' after Cultural Encounters." *Art, Dialogue and Outrage: Essays on Literature and Culture.* Ibadan: New Horn, 1988. 179–89. Print.

———. *Myth, Literature and the African World.* London: Cambridge UP, 1976. Print.

Tahir, Ibrahim. *The Last Imam.* London: Routledge, 1984. Print.

Trimingham, J. S. *A History of Islam in West Africa.* London: Oxford UP, 1962. Print.

———. *The Influence of Islam upon Africa.* London: Longman, 1980. Print.

———. *Islam in West Africa.* Oxford: Clarendon, 1959. Print.

Vikør, Knut. "Sufi Brotherhoods in Africa." Levtzion and Pouwels 441–76.

Wonders of the African World. Narr. Henry Louis Gates, Jr. PBS. 25–27 Oct. 1999. Television.

Dosinda García-Alvite

Unveiling the African Legacy in Spanish: Novels from Equatorial Guinea

Robert Klitgaard, writing of his work as a World Bank consultant in Equatorial Guinea, relates an anecdote that is telling with regard to the place that country holds in the world's imagination. When he mentioned to officers of the United States Agency for International Development (AID) that he had an upcoming trip there, a senior representative derisively commented that Equatorial Guinea was "the armpit of the world!" The AID officer continued, "On a scale of one to ten, even an African scale, it's a zero" (15). Although an exaggeration, this comment points to the fact that Equatorial Guinea is one of the world's most isolated and forgotten countries. For decades it has been neglected by critics in the areas of both African and Spanish studies.

Recently, however, there has been an increasing awareness of Equatorial Guinea's cultural production, both in Spain, where many intellectuals went into exile after the country's independence in 1968, and in the field of Hispanic studies, as practiced in the American academy.[1] Two growing lines of research in Hispanic studies have promoted an interest in the topic. First, Afro-Hispanic studies have explored triangular connections that link Africa, America, and Spain and their cultures. Second, a cultural studies approach to the analysis of contemporary Spain has paid attention to the relation between Africa and Spain, especially in the light of such recent developments as African migration movements into the Iberian Peninsula that have put a strain on it. The cultural works from Equatorial Guinea are of interest to both areas of study, because they can establish strong bridges among the different aspects these fields cover. So they are slowly being incorporated into syllabi.

More specifically, there is a corpus of novels written by citizens of Equatorial Guinea that calls for our attention because of its political and literary value. The political strength of the writers lies in their ability to express the desire to transcend the constraints of ethnicity and national specificity, establishing a dialogue with other African postcolonial cultures and their interpretations of the colonial experience. The scholarly value of the writers derives from the fact that this topic broadens the corpus of literature written in Spanish and challenges the dominant canon, having rarely been an object of critical attention. It is necessary to remember that the meaning of *multiculturalism* in contemporary Spain is highly dependant on the different ethnic groups that have officially been considered to be established in the country for centuries (e.g., Basques, Galicians, Catalonians, Gypsies), and the field of reference for the term has only recently been expanded to incorporate African postcolonial subjects.[2] Novels by these writers emphasize the need to redefine Spain's multiculturalism by paying attention to modern historical developments of the country, such as its colonial actions on Equatorial Guinea until 1968, which are scantily mentioned either by Spanish canonical literature or by official discourse. This situation is the direct result of the Francoist regime's decree to censor in Spain all news related to the former colony from 1971 until 1976, a censorship that greatly affected the place Equatorial Guinea holds in the field of Hispanic literary studies.[3]

To provide an overview of the possibilities of incorporating Guineo-Equatorian novels in the syllabi of survey or advanced courses of Hispanic and African cultural studies and literatures, I present a chronological review of this literary production, focusing on certain works that have achieved recognition as landmarks of the period in which they were produced and of the world they represented.[4] The novels introduced here show the ways in which colonialism in Equatorial Guinea was analyzed in three different periods of its history. They also exemplify various processes of identity formation at the national and the subjective levels and how identity formation becomes distinctive depending on the stress placed on ethnic, racial, gender, and linguistic issues in each period.

According to the critic Mbare Ngom, two things differentiate the literature of Equatorial Guinea from that of other African countries. On the one hand, it is a sub-Saharan literature written in Spanish, the country's official language and the language of most of its written literary texts (French having been declared a second official language in 1997). On the other, it displays both a consciousness of being written, following all the grammar rules of the Spanish language, and an awareness of the orality of the culture of reference. As a consequence, this literature is in a strategic position to link the richness and variety of the Spanish-speaking and the African worlds (Ngom, Introduction 11).

Derived from the multiculturalism this literary production asserts, one important issue is how to best describe it and present it to students. There are basically two choices in the terms assigned to these works. Ngom prefers the phrase "Hispano-Black African literature" ("literatura hispanonegroafricana"), emphasizing that it is produced in sub-Saharan Africa (in contrast with the work of Spanish writers from Ceuta, Melilla, and Western Sahara, for example), while the Guineo-Equatorian writer and critic Donato Ndongo-Bidyogo suggests "Hispano-African literature" ("literatura hispanoafricana").[5] The reasoning behind the latter term is that "Guinea is a country both Hispanic and African at the same time, and its originality, its essence, and the guarantee of its autonomy are rooted in that symbiotic identity" (Ngom, Introduction 11). Ndongo-Bidyogo comments that the people in his country belong to the general Bantu-speaking family, but the one element that differentiates them from their neighbors in Cameroon and Gabon is that they speak Spanish. This fact also has political importance in the formation of a national consciousness (with a distinct national history) and becomes a means of warding off claims of annexation by Nigeria, Cameroon, and Gabon (Liniger-Goumaz, *Historical Dictionary* 27, 69).

One reason this literature has been rarely considered, especially in African studies, is that as a rule the literary corpus of Equatorial Guinea offers few examples of anticolonial works, even if many frequently make negative allusions to colonial power. While anticolonial movements in the rest of Africa began in the early decades of the twentieth century, in Equatorial Guinea they did not acquire strength until the 1940s. By 1959 these movements had become so widespread that in order to avoid granting independence, Spain conferred on the subjects of Equatorial Guinea all the civil rights that Spaniards enjoyed, and Guinea sent deputies to the central government in Madrid.

It is in the context of growing demonstrations in favor of self-rule in the country that the novel *Cuando los Combés luchaban: Novela de costumbres de la Antigua Guinea Española (When the Combés Used to Fight: Novel of Customs of the Old Spanish Guinea)* was first published in Madrid, in 1953, by the Institute of African Studies. A second edition was brought out in 1996, the year of the author's death, by the Spanish Agency for International Cooperation. The author, Leoncio Evita Enoy, was born in Udubuandolo in 1929. Evita Enoy, who was not formally educated beyond the elementary level, wrote this work when he was twenty-four years old, and later he added a second novel, *Alonguegue* ("I Won't Be Saved"), and a short story, "El guiso de Biyé" ("Biyé's Stew") to his oeuvre.

When the Combés Used to Fight is a short novel with illustrations by the author, who also sculpted in wood and ivory. The work is based on a traditional oral legend of the Combé people and refers to historical events that took place at the end of the nineteenth century, in and around Equatorial Guinea. It focuses on Upolo, chief of the village of Ndyebengo, which suffers attacks by the leopard people, who kidnap his son. Upolo is on good terms with John Stephen and Leona McKiver, two American Presbyterian missionaries who have opened a school and a dispensary nearby, so he enlists their help and that of some Spanish adventurers to fight the attackers. By seeking non-African help and by calling the leopards savages, Upolo seems to be quickly adopting the European lifestyle. The leopard people, who practice Bwiti and resist the presence of Western representatives, are defeated at the end of the book.

When it was first published, the novel was hailed as a clear manifestation of the positive effects Spanish colonization had in Equatorial Guinea. It showed the success of the Spanish educational system, because Evita Enoy had used the Spanish language with a high level of sophistication. Also, it showed that the colonial ideology had produced Africans who thought like Spaniards, paradoxically subverting the colonial system's stereotypes about the natives. That *When the Combés Used to Fight* received so much praise in Spain, however, has negatively affected its place in the field of Guineo-Equatorian literature: it is usually seen as an assimilationist work.[6]

While the use of the colonizers' language, which meets all the requirements of proper Spanish, favors a colonial readership, the novel also becomes an ethnographic account of the customs of the Ndowé, more specifically of the Combé people, as the title itself indicates (coinciding with socioanthropological studies published by Iyanga Pendi, Ikuga, or Creus and Nerín). The Combé people, who established themselves along the coasts of Cameroon, Equatorial Guinea, and Gabon in the thirteenth and fourteenth centuries, were accustomed to the European presence, but at the beginning of the twentieth century a number of neighboring peoples, especially the Ntumu Fang, developed an organization based on Bwiti. According to Max Liniger-Goumaz, the Bwiti were a cult of leopard men quite similar to the Mau Mau in Kenya (*Historical Dictionary* 24). Bwiti is a syncretic worship that incorporates Christianity and African tradition; it arose as a reaction to the deculturization brought on by the European presence. Bwiti was forbidden by the Spaniards, who believed it was xenophobic.

In the novel, the leopard men who under the leadership of his best friend, Penga Lengui, attack Upolo's village belong to this group, which resists the influence of the Western colonizers and resorts to open warfare. But it is not only the leopard cult that is critical of the Western presence in the territory; Upolo himself, although having a cordial relationship with Americans and Spaniards, makes a number of sharp statements about the ill effects they will have on the Combé way of life. Although Evita Enoy uses a discourse of praise for the culture of the colonizers through the words and alliances of Upolo, the architecture of the novel, in which the actions of the leopard men move the story forward, and the space given to contending views make it difficult to dismiss this work as simply assimilationist.

The problem of classifying *When the Combés Used to Fight* also stems from the specific conditions under which it first saw light. The novel was produced at a time when in Spain there was a strong interest in the culture of the indigenous peoples of Equatorial Guinea, so the colonizers promoted the collection of indigenous traditions through periodicals and magazines written by and for the natives, such as *La Guinea española*, *Poto-Poto*, and *Ebano*, very popular in the 1950s and 1960s. As commonly happened in the 1950s, however, the novel was corrected by a Spanish editor, who in the name of standardization erased some of the peculiarities and regional variations of Spanish in the Combé area. Questions can be raised too about how the work of the editor affected the exposition of the ideology the book presents.

The mixed reactions this novel provoked among ensuing generations of Guineo-Equatorian writers may partially explain the development of a rich production of poetry and short stories but few novels between the publication of Evita's novel and the 1980s. It was only after the country's first dictator, Macías Nguema, was deposed by his own nephew and the current authoritarian president, Obiang Nguema, that the novel genre was cultivated again, with impressive results.[7] Two titles deserve special attention for their focus on the processes of colonization and the search for a postcolonial identity: *Ekomo* and *Las tinieblas de tu memoria negra* ("The Shadows of Your Black Memory"). Treating different kinds of identity definition, these two novels reflect a conscious resistance to colonialism under varying degrees of exposure to it. Both are popular choices in syllabi designed to introduce Spanish students to African postcolonial studies.

Ekomo (1985) was the first novel by a Guineo-Equatorian writer to be published after the country's independence.[8] The author, María Nsué Angüe, has lived most of her life in Spain but travels regularly to her country of origin, where part of her family still lives, travels that have marked her creative endeavors. She has written more than one hundred short stories and participated in several musical recordings, both as singer and writer.

Ekomo focuses on the construction of gender by a woman, Nnanga, who narrates the story of the death of her husband, whose name figures as the book's title. The identity of the African woman living in the patriarchal Fang society is analyzed on three levels. First, the notion of womanhood defined as being a wife and mother is challenged, because she has no children but still finds an important place in her community. Second, the main female character is cast as an important actor in the preservation and maintenance of her ethnic group's traditions and in the evaluation of modern ideas, propagated mainly by the colonial powers as a tool of domination. Third, dance is analyzed as a medium of both the personal expression of the protagonist and her way of serving her people.

Although the author has expressed reservations with regard to feminist theories and writings, I believe that a feminist reading of her novel foregrounds the contributions of the protagonist in the novel and of the woman author in the field of Guineo-Equatorian literature. In fact, the work of Nsué Angüe is in ways similar to what, according to Carole Boyce Davis, African feminist writers and artists have tried to do: she offers an alternative vision to that of male writers, examining themes that are common to women writers—maternity, the experience of polygamy, the oppression of colonialism from the point of view of their gender, and the consciousness of working with forms and themes of oral literature (Boyce Davis, Introduction 14–17). Nsué Angüe's engagement with the role and social position of women in Fang groups is further enriched by presenting a protagonist who is female, an artist, and a traditional dancer who goes by the name Dove of Fire.

Apart from the incorporation of this dance element of ancestral culture, the novel reclaims religious, medical, and spiritual practices of the country's different ethnic groups, activating the historical past that preceded Spanish colonization and, more recently, the regime of Macías, who suppressed many of those practices. The pilgrimage through different parts of the country, as well as neighboring Cameroon and Gabon, in search of a cure for Ekomo's illness offers an analysis of the Fang ethnic group that inhabits these areas and allows for a recovery of their oral traditions, which often establish links with other parts of the African continent, especially the migrations from the north that connect the Fang with other Pahouin groups (Sundiata, *Equatorial Guinea* 11).

Dealing more formally and specifically with the construction of a postcolonial identity, *Las tinieblas de tu memoria negra* (1987; *Shadows of Your Black Memory*), by Donato Ndongo-Bidyogo, has become the most popular book in Guineo-Equatorian literature. It is the most popular representative of Equatorial Guinea literature in syllabi that study contemporary Spain from a cultural studies standpoint, and it is becoming increasingly known in Hispanic studies in the United States academy. In other fields of study, such as history, anthropology, and linguistics, the novel aroused such interest that it was translated into English.

Las tinieblas is a bildungsroman concerning an unnamed young African man who, after studying to become a priest in a seminary in Spain, decides not to take religious vows but instead to study law and practice it in his home country. The novel examines the educational and religious ideologies of the Franco regime in Spain as imposed on an African individual. At the same time the protagonist, a Fang colonized subject, reevaluates his ethnic traditions, thereby revealing the dignity of African history, which is usually devalued in colonial historiography.[9] In this sense, the story of the Guinean boy can be considered an example of literature of resistance. Resistance is evident in the use of humor and irony when aspects of the colonial culture are narrated and also, in a more subtle way, through a creative use of the language of empire, whereby Spanish is transformed to make room for an African reality.

The bildungsroman as the narrative form effectively explores the negotiation of identity of the colonized subject, who must consciously work out the two cultures that influence him or her. This structure allows the reader to see that the formation of identity is a process in which present living is the result of various stages of growth. It also facilitates the examination of the making and evolving of a national subject and therefore of Equatorial Guinea as a nation.

The novel offers two structural and discursive movements that allow the story to be read as a counternarrative to colonial history: first, it offers an interpretation of the colonial experience; second, it recovers the dignity of the native African culture that also informs the subject. This recovery of African practices allows a positive reading, sometimes nostalgic, of the traditions of the Fang people. But this view does not become conservative, hieratic, because it serves as the basis for the political compromise necessary to the future (the postcolonial period) of the Guineo-Equatorian subject and nation both.

Further, the novel and its title reflect the splitting of the subject, the cultural schizophrenia of which Frantz Fanon wrote, caused by the clash of two civilizations. The position of the postcolonial subject who lives between two worlds and their cultural codes, the African Fang and the European Spanish, is evident in the pervasive alternating discourses of first- and second-person narratives, the protagonist and the narrator, that present the character's evolution from child to adult in a contrapuntal movement. The autobiographical narration becomes the best representation of the instability of his identity, the most adequate form for telling the story of the Guineo-Equatorian subject, because neither authority nor closure can be achieved.

In his next novel, entitled *Los poderes de la tempestad* (1997; "The Powers of the Tempest"), Ndongo-Bidyogo focuses on the role ethnicity can play in the formation of newly independent African states, with clear references to the government of Macías Nguema (1968–79) in Equatorial Guinea. This novel depicts the difficult conditions many intellectuals and educated people endured under his dictatorship.[10] As the author himself has pointed out, the novel is "the turbulent chronicle of a double failure: that of Equatorial Guinea as a country, and of its citizens, a people victimized by the utopia of freedom and progress" (Ngom, "Autobiografía" 71). Although the Macías period is over, his successor and nephew, Obiang Nguema, has changed very little the repressive system that controls the country. Despite enjoying a time of bonanza with the discovery and extraction of oil off the island of Bioko, the government has restricted considerably the participation of intellectuals and educated citizens in the life of the country. This repression accounts for the limited production of novels in recent years. Thus *Los poderes de la tempestad* still represents life in Equatorial Guinea.

The protagonist is a Guineo-Equatorian lawyer who, after living in Spain, having married a Spaniard and sired a daughter, Rut, decides to return to his country, recently independent and ruled by Macías. This work is a continuation of *Las tinieblas*, taking from it the characters and story structure. As before, a beginning Chapter Zero establishes the main issues of the narrative, a historical fiction constructed with specific details of the dictatorship.

The lawyer, like the author, belongs to a generation of idealistic youths who, having gone to Europe to obtain advanced degrees, expected to be and were considered the future leaders of their nation after independence. The novel analyzes the destruction of those aspirations and the possibilities of the new nation-state through the use of a character whose anonymity enriches its capacity for representation. The lawyer's story is told predominantly in first- and second-person narrations that relate to each other in a dialectic exchange, broadening the reflections produced by the world to which they refer. This technique is especially effective when the lawyer repeatedly suffers torture and loses consciousness in the infamous Playa Negra prison in the capital city, Malabo. The second-person narrator relates the physical, psychological, and even sexual violence the lawyer suffers.

The structure and plot of the novel reveal the destructive power of the Macías regime and the changes it brought on society. Note that up to half the country's population was liquidated or went into exile in that period (Sundiata, "Roots" 9). Moreover, as Ngom notes, the novel is also an account of Africa in a difficult period, characterized by the consolidation of abusive and intolerant governments and the exclusion and impoverishment of large sectors of the general population ("Autobiografía" 71). Finally, the work analyzes three important aspects that shed light on the despotism the story presents: the use of the state apparatus to terrorize the population; the emphasis on ethnicity, widening disparities among clan and ethnic lines; and the consequences of Spanish colonialism, which provoked Macias's extreme de-Europeanization and the promotion of a cult of his personality.

As can be seen, these novels show a commitment to the citizens of Equatorial Guinea in the way they reflect on and represent their different ethnic groups (Ndowé, Benga, Bubi, the Fang majority); their political history (the Spanish colonial period, independence movements, the country's becoming a province of Spain, the dictatorship of Francisco Macías and the autocracy of Teodoro Obiang Nguema); and the economic, social, religious, and cultural experiences (British, American Presbyterian, Spanish Catholic) that the inhabitants have experienced up to the present. Additionally, some characteristics that define the novels of Equatorial Guinea are the importance they place on memory, being faithful to the wisdom of the ancestors, a flexible understanding of the different ethnic traditions that enrich the country's history, a questioning attitude toward Spanish colonialism that does not exclude resistance and protest, and a socially committed rewriting of the history of the nation.

Just as in the African context the novel is a foreign artistic form, so in these novels the manipulation of the colonizer's language becomes a vehicle of communication and expression of the realities of the characters. Here Spanish is put to the test and enriched by the continuous references to the worldview of various ethnic groups. In this respect, Spanish has grown beyond its usual fields of reference, offering different assumptions and ways of relating to the world. The ability to incorporate many types of African cultural manifestations, such as legends, stories, and regional expressions, have made the novel a popular form for engaging in active representation and definition of the country's culture.

The cultural expansion that these novels represent for the Hispanic world is much enhanced by the revision they offer of the African colonial period of Spanish history, which has been forgotten in Spain itself. Concomitantly, these works establish links with peoples of other African countries, with whom Guineo-Equatorians have ethnic, economic, and historical ties. Because of its cultural richness and unique situation, Equatorial Guinea deserves a place in the fields of both Hispanic and African studies.

Notes

1. Donato Ndongo-Bidyogo, probably the most important writer of Equatorial Guinea, has commented on the problem that very few critics of Spanish literature incorporate Guinean literary production in their syllabi ("Interview" 227). He pointed out that interest in this literature is growing in the university system of Spain, but usually it is found outside the official curriculum.

2. African subjects too have lived in Spain for centuries, but their presence has been erased from the contemporary historical and cultural canon. For example, Carter G. Woodson traces their presence in Spain's literature from the fifteenth to the eighteenth century as one with frequent, varied, and sometimes conflicting representations. A fact rarely commented on in textbooks and therefore little known by teachers and students of Spanish is that the dominant literary figure in Spain at the time Cervantes started writing his *Don Quixote* was Juan

Latino (1518–96?), a former African slave who raised himself from the ranks of servitude to be a literary model and teacher at the University of Granada.

3. For a more detailed analysis of this censorship, see Liniger-Goumaz, *Small* 117, 164).

4. Although the adjective *Equato-Guinean* has been common, I use instead *Guineo-Equatorian*, as it was preferred and recommended by some of the writers whose work I comment on in the First International Hispano-African Congress of Culture, celebrated in Bata, Equatorial Guinea, 1984. They considered *Equato-Guinean* to have a less positive meaning (Evita Enoy 24).

5. These differences are discussed in detail in several articles by Ngom and in the books he published in collaboration with Ndongo-Bidyogo.

6. This evaluation is common among other critics and readers. See, for example, the negative review Sanford Berman wrote in the United States soon after the publication of the novel.

7. In 1962, Daniel Jones Mathama wrote *Una lanza por el boabí* ("A Spear for the Boabí"), in which Spanish colonialism is seen in a positive light. This may be why the novel is rarely referred to by later generations of Guineo-Equatorian writers.

8. The interest this novel has raised in general is reflected by the fact that it was translated into French in 1995.

9. Ndongo-Bidyogo's *España en Guinea* presents an account of Spain's colonialism from the perspective of a Guineo-Equatorian.

10. *El párroco de Niefag* (1996; "The Priest of the Niefag Parish"), by Joaquín Mbomío, examines the same topic from the point of view of a Catholic Guineo-Equatorian priest who suffered persecution under Macías. Mbomío's next novel, *Huellas bajo la tierra* (1999; "Traces under the Earth"), is more ambitious in its coverage of a period of forty years, analyzing Spanish colonialism, exile during the dictatorship, and return to the country. Interestingly, it looks at less commonly represented issues, such as Catalonian economic investments in Guinea and exile in France, Germany, and other European countries.

Works Cited

Berman, Sanford. Rev. of *Cuando los Combés luchaban: Novela de costumbres de la Guinea Española*, by Leoncio Evita. *Journal of Negro History* 44.3 (1959): 272–74. Print.

Boyce Davis, Carole. Introduction. Boyce Davis and Graves 1–23.

Boyce Davis, Carole, and Ann Adams Graves, eds. *Ngambika: Studies of Women in African Literature*. Trenton: Africa World, 1986. Print.

Creus, Jacint, and Gustau Nerín, eds. *Estampas y cuentos de la Guinea española*. Madrid: Clan, 1999. Print.

Evita Enoy, Leoncio. *Cuando los Combés luchaban: Novela de costumbres de la Antigua Guinea Española*. 2nd ed. Malabo: Agencia de Cooperación Española, 1996. Print.

Fanon, Frantz. *Black Skin, White Masks*. New York: Grove, 1963. Print.

Ikuga Ebombebombe, Nganwe. *Cómo se habla, se escribe y se lee el ndowé.* Barcelona: Asociación Cultural Rhombe, 1993. Print.

Iyanga Pendi, Augusto. *El pueblo ndowé: Etnología, sociologyía e historia.* Valencia: Nau Llibres, 1992. Print.

Jones Mathama, Daniel. *Una lanza por el Boabí.* Barcelona: Casal, 1962. Print.

Klitgaard, Robert. *Tropical Gangsters: One Man's Experience with Development and Decadence in Deepest Africa.* New York: Basic, 1990. Print.

Liniger-Goumaz, Max. *Historical Dictionary of Equatorial Guinea.* Metuchen: Scarecrow, 1979. Print.

———. *Small Is Not Always Beautiful: The Story of Equatorial Guinea.* Totowa: Barnes, 1989. Print.

Mbomío Bacheng, Joaquín. *Huellas bajo tierra.* Malabo: Centro Cultural Hispano-Guineano, 1998. Print.

———. *El párroco de Niefang.* Malabo: Centro Cultural Hispano-Guineano, 1996. Print.

Ndongo-Bidyogo, Donato. *España en Guinea: Construcción del desencuentro, 1778–1968.* Toledo: Sequitur, 1998. Print.

———. "Interview with Donato Ndongo." By Michael Ugarte. *Arizona Journal of Hispanic Cultural Studies* 88 (2004): 217–34. Print.

———. *Los poderes de la tempestad.* Madrid: Morandi, 1997. Print.

———. *Shadows of Your Black Memory.* Trans. Michael Ugarte. Chicago: Swan Isle, 2007. Print.

———. *Las tinieblas de tu memoria negra.* Madrid: Fundamentos, 1987. Print.

Ndongo-Bidyogo, Donato, and Mbare Ngom, eds. *Literatura de Guinea Ecuatorial: Antología.* Sial: Madrid, 2000. Print.

Ngom, Mbare. "La autobiografía como plataforma de denuncia en *Los poderes de la tempestad* de Donato Ndongo-Bidyogo." *Afro-Hispanic Review* 19.1 (2000): 66–71. Print.

———. Introduction. Ndongo-Bidyogo and Ngom 11–29.

Nsué Angüe, María. *Ekomo.* Madrid: U Nacional de Educación a Distancia, 1985. Print.

———. *Ekomo.* Paris: Harmattan, 1995. Print.

Sundiata, Ibrahim K. *Equatorial Guinea: Colonialism, State Terror, and the Search for Stability.* Boulder: Westview, 1990. Print.

———. "The Roots of African Despotism: The Question of Political Culture." *African Studies Review* 31.1 (1988): 9–31. Print.

Woodson, Carter G. "Attitudes of the Iberian Peninsula (in Literature)." *Blacks in Hispanic Literature: Critical Essays.* Ed. Miriam DeCosta-Willis. Port Washington: Kennikat, 1977. 36–47. Print.

Fernando Arenas

Teaching Lusophone African Fiction

Teaching lusophone African fiction entails teaching about some of the least known nations from the least known and perhaps most misunderstood continent. This essay addresses a series of issues—historical, geopolitical, and conceptual, among others—that are crucial in developing courses that include lusophone African material. It stresses the need for cultural, historical, and geopolitical contextualization. At the same time, it highlights the interrelatedness among lusophone African countries, their connections to both Portugal and Brazil, and their links to the African continent as a whole. A main problem I consider is the very term *lusophone Africa*. What is the actual status of the Portuguese language in Angola, Cape Verde, Guinea-Bissau, Mozambique, and São Tomé and Príncipe? Who writes in it and for whom? What is the future of Portuguese in Africa? In addition, I touch on a number of subthemes to provide a framework in which to situate lusophone Africa: the subaltern character of Portuguese colonialism; the preponderance of creole cultures in various parts of lusophone Africa and its impact on the definitions of race in these countries; the longevity of Portuguese colonialism and its violent end in Guinea-Bissau, Mozambique, and Angola; the aftermath of independence; Marxist nationalism; the experience of civil wars; the advent of market economies, multiparty politics, and globalization.

Despite the focus on the genre of the novel in this volume, we cannot understand lusophone Africa from a literary point of view without paying close attention to poetry, which has been in the history of lusophone African literature the primary genre, especially during the decades leading to independence between 1973 and 1975. Poetry was the privileged medium through which to imagine the budding nations of Portuguese-speaking Africa before independence; it was also the ideal means, given its succinct, immediate, and lyrical qualities, to communicate the importance of the struggle against colonialism.

Even though African writing in a Europhone language first occurred in Portuguese, in sub-Saharan Africa during the sixteenth century, as pointed out by the pioneering critic Gerald Moser, this writing was the last to be discovered outside the Portuguese-speaking world (1).[1] After the sixteenth century, a consistent flow of African literature written in Portuguese began only in the mid-nineteenth century, emanating mostly from Angola and Cape Verde. This flow is attributable to the fact that in both these former colonies during this period, and even more so in the early twentieth century, there were important urban economic centers (Mindelo in Cape Verde, Luanda in Angola) where clusters of highly educated people (overwhelmingly male) of European and Euro-African descent (together with a few black Africans) created a great deal of intellectual synergy by publishing mostly poetry, short fiction, and anthropological as well as linguistic studies. From this synergy a discernible protonationalist consciousness emerged.[2] Since the mid–twentieth century, the bulk of African literary output in Portuguese has been produced in Angola, Mozambique, and Cape Verde.

One reason for the belated discovery of the rich literary corpus produced in lusophone Africa is the colonizing power's chronic state of economic underdevelopment. This underdevelopment affected the colonies of the Portuguese empire and made its geopolitical location in the world precarious. The peripheral status of Portugal and its former colonies has lowered the visibility of their cultural production and the ability of that production to circulate internationally. Except for a brief period of global maritime supremacy (alongside Spain) between the late-fifteenth and mid-sixteenth centuries, the Portuguese empire remained largely on the margins and at the mercy of historical and geopolitical developments on a global scale. In effect, the Portuguese empire in its various arenas—Asia, Africa, and Brazil—became subordinate to the imperial powers of Spain, Holland, England, and France. Meanwhile, its relation to its most important colony, Brazil, was characterized by economic dependence. Indeed, even before Brazilian independence, the Brazilian economic output and natural resource base were far greater than that of the mother country, making the relation between former colonizer and former colony exceptional.[3] However, it was the British Ultimatum of 1890 in the context of the scramble for Africa by European colonial powers that sealed the subordinate character of Portuguese colonialism in the world.[4]

Brazil, for its part, played a major role in the transatlantic slave trade, before and after its independence in 1822. Slave labor imported from West Africa, the Gulf of Guinea region, as well as west-central Africa (particularly Angola) was crucial to the economic survival and development of colonial and postindependence Brazil. Both the Portuguese and the Luso-Brazilian elites therefore had much at stake in the preservation of the slave trade. In the struggles against the Dutch occupation of the Brazilian Northeast and Angola during the first half of the seventeenth century, they acted as co-colonizers in their quest to recover the Angola-Brazil lifeline that the Dutch had wrested from them. Continued dependence on slave labor during the nineteenth century meant that even after independence Brazil was inextricably linked to the colonial black Atlantic matrix, until the abolition of slavery. According to the historian Luiz Felipe de Alencastro, Brazil emerged from an economically and socially bipolar space located in the south Atlantic, a space created by Portuguese colonialism, largely based on slave labor, and encompassing an area of slave reproduction centered in Angola and an area of slave production in various enclaves throughout Portuguese America (9). An understanding of the emergence and development of the various nations that compose Portuguese-speaking Africa today must bear in mind the early interdependence between Portugal and Brazil as well as the central role of Africa in that relation.

After Brazilian independence, Portugal gradually focused its attention and energies on the effective colonization of its African territories. A series of "pacification campaigns" ensued between 1841 and 1920 in the hinterland of Mozambique, Angola, and Portuguese Guinea against rebel and independent kingdoms.[5] Meanwhile, after the abolition of slavery in the Portuguese colonial territories in 1878, a system of indentured labor was introduced in the agriculturally rich areas of São Tomé and Príncipe as well as of Angola. Cape Verdeans, who suffered through cyclically devastating droughts, bore the brunt of the indentured labor system. Tens of thousands of people were forced to work in the cocoa plantations of São Tomé and to a lesser extent in the cotton plantations of Angola (many Angolans were also sent to work in São Tomé and to other regions in Angola itself). Mozambicans were subjected to forced labor practices in agriculture; they were also forced, in coordination with South African authorities, to mine gold in the Rand. The system of forced labor practices in the Portuguese African colonies was officially abolished in 1961, and during its peak at the turn of the century it was vehemently condemned by the international community. This tragic episode in the history of Portuguese colonialism has been widely thematized by poets from Cape Verde, Angola, Mozambique, and São Tomé.[6]

Both the first Portuguese republic (1910–26) and the subsequent Salazar fascist regime (1926–74) were equally committed to empire building, and as a result Africa figured high on the list of national priorities. There were various attempts at systematizing the administrative structure of the Portuguese African empire, in addition to legally codifying the ontological status of the colonial subjects into *indígenas* ("indigenous") and *assimilados* ("assimilated") (the latter were black Africans who had formal education and fluency in Portuguese; the former did not), a system that was similar to that implemented in the French colonies that divided African societies into *evolués* and *paysans* (resp., "evolved" and "peasants"). Yet despite the political initiatives undertaken by the Portuguese government, together with meager attempts at economic development, according to figures offered by Armelle Enders, by 1950 more than ninety-seven percent of the African population in the Portuguese colonies was illiterate, while the percentage of illiteracy in the Portuguese metropole totaled forty-four percent (89).

In the mid–twentieth century and in the face of these great odds, a group of assimilated Africans studying in Portugal launched the nationalist movement that eventually led to independence. These students congregated in Lisbon around the Casa dos Estudantes do Império (between 1949 and 1964; "Empire Students' House") and the Center for African Studies, where they organized a flurry of social, cultural, and political activities that were pivotal for all those involved in gaining a national as well as pan-African and anticolonial consciousness. The literary output resulting from this historical juncture was published in several esteemed journals and publication series and is today considered an integral part of the canon of African literatures written in Portuguese.[7] Key figures of this important moment were the founding political or literary fathers and mothers of independent Angola (Agostinho Neto, Mário Pinto de Andrade), Mozambique (Marcelino dos Santos, José Craveirinha, Noémia de Sousa), Cape Verde and Guinea-Bissau (Amílcar Cabral and Vasco Cabral), and São Tomé and Príncipe (Francisco José Tenreiro and Alda do Espírito Santo).

The independence of the five former Portuguese colonies in Africa took place as a result of the collapse of the stubbornly long-lasting fascist-colonialist regime of Salazar and Caetano. The collapse took place under the pressure of a protracted three-front national liberation war in Guinea-Bissau, Angola, and Mozambique and because of the strong dissent in the Portuguese military. A direct consequence of the colonial wars in Africa, this dissent eventually led to the Revolution of 1974, which signaled the beginning of the end of Portuguese colonialism. The collapse of the Salazar-Caetano regime[8] brought about a peculiar postcolonial scenario: a short-lived and belated Marxist regime in Western Europe and the emergence of Marxist-nationalist parties to govern in every single former Portuguese colony (even in briefly independent East Timor before the Indonesian invasion of 1975). These single-party and economically centralized regimes lasted until the early 1990s, when there was a shift to multiparty systems and market-oriented economies. Angola and Mozambique, the largest and richest of the five lusophone African states, sank into two of the most tragic human conflicts of the late twentieth century, conflicts in part driven by the cold war, with devastating consequences for both nations.

In the context of contemporary globalization, Portugal and all its former colonies—Brazil, Angola, Mozambique, Guinea-Bissau, Cape Verde, São Tomé and Príncipe, as well as newly independent East Timor—today occupy, in differing degrees and at times simultaneously, core, semiperipheral, and peripheral positions, either in the world system at large or in their respective regions or subregions. Angola, one of the chief players in the "global geopolitics of hydrocarbons" (Mbembe 45), has its center of gravity in the Gulf of Guinea and is one of the world's primary diamond suppliers; it continues to be, potentially, a rich country. However, after the civil war that ended in 2002, a main obstacle for the materialization of wealth for the benefit of the whole national community is widespread government corruption. Cape Verde, a Creole-speaking nation in its entirety and a culturally homogeneous society, remains a hopeful case in the African context: despite a substantially limited natural resource base, its economy has been managed with a minimal amount of corruption (according to aid experts) and in the framework of a democratic political culture. São Tomé and Príncipe, on the other hand, a culturally creole society though less so linguistically, is undergoing a period of political and social instability, largely because of its enormous potential as an oil-exporting country. Guinea-Bissau, where Guinean Creole is the most widely spoken language among more than ten different West African languages, has a tenuous democracy in a weak state that today is still mired in economic stagnation and political uncertainty. Finally, Mozambique, much like Angola and other partners in the southern African region, is a nation of great linguistic, ethnic, and racial heterogeneity. After its brutal civil war, which ended in 1992, it has embarked on a relatively successful course of redemocratization, national reconstruction, and peace.

Today, the linguistic designator *lusophone* is a reality in Angola, Cape Verde, Guinea-Bissau, Mozambique, and São Tomé and Príncipe. Yet the role of Portuguese is relative: although the official language, it exists in national spaces that are bilingual or multilingual. Its use is decidedly expanding, through national and international radio and television via satellite; through the printed media; in the school system, as a vehicle for social mobility; or as the lingua franca in Angola, Mozambique, and to a certain degree in São Tomé and Príncipe. At the same time, the Creoles of Cape Verde and Guinea-Bissau continue to develop and consolidate themselves in their respective national spaces, and there have been concerted attempts at standardizing various national languages in Mozambique and Angola. Most of the literary production in these countries is written in Portuguese, by members of the elites, many of them either white descendants of Portuguese or of mixed African and Portuguese heritage.[9]

Since independence there has been a steady increase in the number of black African writers, both male and female. While Portuguese remains the privileged language in the realm of high culture (particularly literature), the preference in the domain of popular culture (e.g., music) is for the national languages (including the Creoles of Cape Verde, Guinea-Bissau, and São Tomé and Príncipe). However, among the youth of the Angolan capital, Luanda, Portuguese is fast becoming the dominant tongue in pop music, though it is used in a distinctively Angolan fashion, peppered with words and expressions in Kimbundu.[10]

Most critics agree that before political independence a sense of national identity in lusophone Africa separate from Portugal emerged first and foremost in the realm of literature (poetry being the dominant genre) in Angola, Cape Verde, São Tomé, and Mozambique.[11] For some writers, acquiring a national consciousness occurred after a period of ideological deassimilation in relation to European culture.[12] Many writers during the nationalist period (1940s–60s) were also informed and influenced by the cultural, intellectual, and political legacy of pan-Africanism and negritude. Francisco José Tenreiro is considered the first lusophone African author to incorporate pan-Africanist and negritudinist themes in his poetry (e.g., "Negro de todo o mundo" [41–44] [1942; "Negro of the Whole Wide World"]). Yet, Tenreiro nuanced these themes with an acute "mulatto consciousness" or "mulattitude," as Russell Hamilton suggests (16), which resulted from the travails of being a person of mixed racial heritage (see the poem "Canção do mestiço" [27–28] ["The Mulatto Song"]).[13]

With the advent of independence in most French and British African colonies and the beginning of the liberation wars in Angola (1961), Portuguese Guinea (1963), and Mozambique (1964), there was a radicalization of the political stance, represented by such writers as the Angolans Mário Pinto de Andrade and Agostinho Neto. They not only condemned living conditions under colonialism, as the San Tomean Alda do Espírito Santo did in the 1950s, and called for solidarity with Africa and its diaspora, as the Mozambican Noémia de Sousa did in the 1940s, but also called for national liberation. This radical turn is generally described by critics as combat literature. Andrade, better known as an essayist, editor of *Présence africaine* (1951–58), cofounder of the Angolan liberation movement MPLA (Movimento Popular de Libertação de Angola ["Popular Movement for the Liberation of Angola"]), and editor of the first anthology of lusophone African poetry (1958), also called for debunking powerful myths, such as lusotropicalism, that legitimated Portuguese colonialism in the intellectual and diplomatic fields. Lusotropicalist ideology proved to be a tenacious obstacle to the liberation cause, in that it attempted, consciously or unconsciously, not only to validate Portuguese colonialism on the basis of the well-known relatively wide racial intermixing, especially in Brazil, Cape Verde, São Tomé, Goa, and parts of Angola and Mozambique, but also to obscure the fact that the overwhelming majority of the population in the Portuguese African colonies was indeed black and living for the most part in dismal conditions.[14]

Literary journals and magazines became an important vehicle to disseminate knowledge about the various Portuguese African colonies among well-educated Africans based either in the metropole or on the African continent. There were a number of publications in Lisbon, Luanda, Lourenço Marques (the former colonial name for Maputo, the capital of Mozambique), and Mindelo, featuring poetry, essays, and short fiction, that circulated widely among the lettered elites. The earliest translated African literary texts from Portuguese into English were poems included in anthologies of African poetry (e.g., Moore and Beier), at a time when the world was closely following developments that unfolded in the period between the liberation struggles in the Portuguese African colonies and the dawn of independence.[15]

Despite the dominance of poetry during this period, there were several prose masterpieces that emerged in Angola and Mozambique, written by José Luandino Vieira (*Luuanda*) and Luís Bernardo Honwana (*We Killed Mangy Dog*), respectively. Vieira, the son of poor Portuguese migrants to Angola, grew up in Luanda's shantytowns (or *musseques*). He revolutionized Angolan literary language by combining the oral expression of the *musseques* imbued with Kimbundu words, idiomatic expressions, syntax, and neologisms to produce a highly original and idiosyncratic prose.[16] He wrote most of his works at Tarrafal Prison in Cape Verde during the 1960s, documenting life under colonialism at the margins of Luandan society where most of the population lived. Since independence, he has mostly ceased publishing. Many critics suggest, on the basis of statements made by the author, that his disillusionment with the path taken by Angola in the postindependence era prevented him from writing until recently.[17]

A prevalent theme in postcolonial lusophone African literature (though more so in Angola than in Mozambique or Guinea-Bissau) is profound disenchantment with the political establishment that emerged after independence.[18] The triumphant Marxist-nationalist parties converted to capitalism after the fall of the Berlin Wall and the collapse of the Soviet Union. Many writers feel that the ideals of a truly egalitarian and democratic state were betrayed once the liberation movements came to power and that, with the advent of the market economy, not only did the Marxist-nationalist parties remain entrenched, especially Angola's MPLA, but political and economic corruption also became more endemic. Hence narrative strategies were devised to represent this confluence of events and sentiments, by writers such as Pepetela, Manuel Rui, José Eduardo Agualusa, and João Melo (in Angola), Mia Couto (in Mozambique), and Abdulai Sila (in Guinea-Bissau). These strategies range from postmodern historiographical metafiction and animistic realism to allegory, humor, irony, and biting social satire.[19]

Even though the state of the nation—in this case, the postcolonial nation—is still a major concern for lusophone African writers, fiction and poetry no longer serve exclusively the interest of a grand national cause such as independence, during the period of armed struggle. The heavy utopian investment by writers in the creation of a free and just society under a Marxist-nationalist banner has receded in favor of a multiplicity of macro- and microcultural, sociopolitical, and historic concerns. In effect, there has been a veritable explosion in themes: the interweaving of literature with oral folklore; the recovery of precolonial historical memory; the tension between modernity and tradition, between city and country, and among local, national, and global forces; the civil wars in Angola and Mozambique; and emigration, which continues to be a key experience, especially in Cape Verdean culture.

An important development has been the emergence of women's writing from a self-consciously feminist perspective that overtly explores concerns related to sexuality and gender (male writers have ventured in this direction as well, particularly João Melo, Pepetela, and Couto). The works of women writers such as Paula Tavares (Angola), Vera Duarte (Cape Verde), Paulina Chiziane (Mozambique), Dina Salústio (Cape Verde), Conceição Lima (São Tomé and Príncipe), and Odete Semedo (Guinea-Bissau) deal with the female body, women as subjects of erotic desire, women as historical subjects, gender relations, motherhood, domestic violence, the experience of women and children in war, the importance of preserving ancestral memory as a strategy for cultural survival, and traditional cultures' oppression of women. In her remarkable novel *Niketche: Uma história de poligamia* (2002; "Niketche: A Story of Polygamy"), Paulina Chiziane offers a scathing critique of informal and formal polygamy in Mozambican culture. Of all women writers today in lusophone Africa, Paula Tavares and Chiziane have been the most critically celebrated, even though none of the women writers currently active, except for the Mozambican authors Lina Magaia and Lília Momplé, have had their work translated into English as of 2009.[20]

Arguably, there is as much prose as poetry being produced in lusophone Africa today. Given the relatively low literacy levels in most countries in question (a situation that is slowly improving), the widespread poverty, and the high cost of books, the readership is limited. Yet there are a handful of publishing houses in Luanda, Maputo, Mindelo, and Praia.[21] African authors writing in Portuguese depend on a Western readership (i.e., in Portugal, and increasingly in Brazil) to disseminate their literary goods—a scenario that exemplifies the continuing neocolonial dependency of Africa vis-à-vis the West. Couto is an exceptional case of an author who enjoys a market outside the Portuguese-speaking world; in Europe, some of his books have become best sellers. Since the late 1980s, there has been a wider recognition of lusophone African literature in Portugal and Brazil.[22] The quality and originality of African works have increased sales, won critical reception, gained author visibility, and garnered major literary awards for José Craveirinha, Pepetela, Couto, and Tavares.[23] There has been growing interest in lusophone African literatures and cultures in the Portuguese and Brazilian academy. A variety of college-level courses are offered on the subject, and there are graduate degrees with a lusophone African concentration.[24]

English-language translations of lusophone African literary works are available mostly in several titles published by Heinemann.[25] Yet the teaching of lusophone African literature has grown in United States, British, and Canadian universities where Portuguese is currently taught. Language and culture courses include African materials; in some cases, undergraduate and graduate courses focus partially or exclusively on lusophone Africa. At the same time, lusophone African materials are occasionally included in African history courses or courses in anthropology and African and African American studies. Despite the greater recognition of and interest in the literatures and cultures of lusophone Africa, as well as the salutary and yet modest growth of lusophone African studies as a field of scholarly inquiry, the field remains peripheral, much like that of African studies as a whole.

However, lusophone Africa is bound to benefit from the increased demand for Portuguese-language courses at United States universities as an indirect result of the Spanish explosion in the United States due to demographic factors but, more important, due to the geopolitical and economic rise of Brazil as a world power. This favorable situation is likely to bring more attention to the five Portuguese-speaking nations in Africa and their rich cultural production, where literature stands out as one of the most remarkable manifestations.

Notes

1. According to Moser, the first writings in Portuguese in sub-Saharan Africa were letters written by the converted Kongo princes addressing the Portuguese monarchs of the time. During the reign of the Portuguese king João II in the early sixteenth century, the king of the Kongo converted to Christianity after extensive amicable contacts with the Portuguese (3).

2. Between 1866 and 1923 there was an extraordinarily dynamic intellectual and cultural scene in Angola that revolved around fifty different newspapers. Luanda was the site where members of the *mestiço* ("mulatto"), white (Portuguese- and Angolan-born alike), and black elite engaged in a well-informed and forceful critique of the living conditions under colonialism while also defending the right of native Africans (i.e., non-Westernized) to an education. Aside from journalistic writing, many wrote poetry and prose; some also developed ethnographic and linguistic studies on Angolan Bantu cultures. The first major work in prose, a novella, was written by Alfredo Troni, *Nga Muturi* (1882). The most prolific figure to emerge during this period was Joaquim Dias Cordeiro da Matta, who wrote a collection of Angolan proverbs entitled *Philosophia em provérbios angolanos* (1891), poetry in Portuguese, the first Kimbundu-Portuguese dictionary (1893), and a Kimbundu textbook. In Cape Verde the most important literary and cultural movement revolved around the magazine *Claridade* ("Clarity"), which was published irregularly between 1936 and 1966. Even though it went through various phases and did not necessarily offer a monolithic view of Cape Verdean culture, *Claridade* provided a platform through which to disseminate knowledge regarding a nation that was distinct from Portugal. Hence, Cape Verde's constitutive creole identity was an object of investigation and celebration through short stories, poetry written in Portuguese and in Kriolu, ethnographic accounts, linguistic studies, and oral folklore. The founding figures were Manuel Lopes, Baltasar Lopes, and Jorge Barbosa. Other major contributors were Arnaldo França, Félix Monteiro, Gabriel Mariano, and Teixeira de Sousa.

3. Throughout the history of European colonialism, no other colonial power transferred its capital from metropole to colony as Portugal did between 1808 and 1821 because of the Napoleonic Wars. This transfer led to the emergence of Rio de Janeiro as the center of the Portuguese empire.

4. Portuguese ambitions to claim the hinterland of southern Africa between Angola and Mozambique (roughly today's Zambia, Malawi, and Zimbabwe) were dashed by Britain's greater ambitions for claiming African territories from Cape Town to Cairo. With such logic in mind, Britain threatened to take Portuguese African colonial territories by force if Portugal insisted on occupying the coveted hinterland.

5. See the work of the French historian René Pélissier on the Portuguese "campaigns of pacification" in Africa: *Guerres grises, Naissance*, and *Campagnes*.

6. See the poetry of Agostinho Neto and António Jacinto (Angola), Ovídio Martins (Cape Verde), Noémia de Sousa and José Craveirinha (Mozambique), and Alda do Espírito Santo (São Tomé).

7. The CEI (Casa dos Estudantes do Império) published the newsletter *Mensagem* ("Message") between 1948 and 1952 and between 1957 and 1964 and a series of poetry anthologies *(Antologias de Poesia)* divided by countries (Angola, Mozambique, and São Tomé and Príncipe). These publications were key in bringing about a heightened consciousness of a common identity as colonized Africans. In short, the margins of empire were visualized from the center (as pointed out by the critic Laura Padilha).

8. The term "Salazar-Caetano regime" refers to the reign of António de Oliveira Salazar, Portugal's dictator from 1933 until 1968 (the year he suffered a stroke that rendered him unable to govern), and of his successor, Marcelo Caetano, who remained in power until 1974.

9. In the Creole-speaking nations of Cape Verde and Guinea-Bissau, a few novels, short fiction, poetry, and transcriptions of oral tradition have been written in their respective variants of Creole. In Cape Verde, some poetry and transcription of songs since the late nineteenth century were published in the *Almanach luso-africano para 1899* (Hamilton 248). In the early twentieth century, the poet and lyricist Eugénio Tavares published his collected *Mornas* (1931), and the poet Pedro Cardoso published transcribed oral tradition in *Folclore caboverdeano* (1933) and his own poetry in *Morna e saudade: Versos em crioulo e em português* (1940). Among members of the *Claridade* group, Gabriel Mariano, Jorge Pedro, Mário Macedo Barbosa, and Sérgio Frusoni transcribed oral tradition or wrote poetry in Kriolu. Among the post-*Claridade* generation, Kauberdiano Dambará and Tomé Varela stand out for their poetry written in the Kriolu of Santiago. A more recent example is the pioneering novel by the linguist Manuel Veiga *Odju d'agu* (1987), written in the Cape Verdean Creole variants of the islands of Santiago, São Vicente, and Fogo. Kaká Barboza and Danny Spínola have written poetry and short fiction in the Kriolu of Santiago. In Guinea-Bissau, the Instituto Nacional de Estudos e Pesquisa ("National Research Institute") has published an anthology of poetry written in Guinean Creole, *Kebur: Barkafon di poesia na kriol* (1996). The publishing house Ku Si Mon in Bissau has printed a series of transcribed oral stories simultaneously in Creole, Portuguese, and French. In Angola there is at least one contemporary example of a novel translated from Portuguese into Umbundu, *Nda Nda Kaile Ekimba / Quem me dera ser onda* ("I Wished I Were a Wave"), by Manuel Rui (2000).

10. While the Angolan national music genre, *semba,* tends to be sung in Kimbundu or in a mixture of Kimbundu and Portuguese, more recent urban musical genres such as *kizomba* (a style of music heavily influenced by French Caribbean *zouk)* and *kuduro* (semba-based rhythmically but couched in an electronic and uniquely Angolan rap format) are performed mostly in Portuguese.

11. New historical studies point to the emergence of a sense of national identity since the 1940s beyond the realm of lettered elites and in the realm of popular culture in Luanda's *musseques* (or shantytowns), particularly through music. This reality has been ignored by canonical accounts of the emergence of Angolan nationalism (see Moorman).

12. During the final decades of Portuguese colonialism, African writers belonged to the class of assimilated colonial subjects, which allowed them access to

higher education, civil service jobs, and sometimes even a political career in the metropole, as in the case of the San Tomean Francisco José Tenreiro.

13. The *Claridade* movement in Cape Verde was an exception among African intellectual and cultural movements in that it claimed not an African identity for Cape Verde but a creole identity, which in the early years of the movement emphasized the country's European roots. Several writers distanced themselves from the Eurocentric inclinations of the early *claridosos* (the nickname given to members of *Claridade),* thus emphasizing the Africanness of Cape Verdean culture: Manuel Duarte, Gabriel Mariano, and Onésimo Silveira. At the political level—through the liberation movement and subsequent postindependence party in power, the PAIGC (the African Party for the Independence of Guinea-Bissau and Cape Verde)—Cape Verde underwent an identity shift that brought it more in alignment with the rest of Africa, even though today Kriolu identity still cannot be separated from Cape Verdean national identity as a whole.

14. The concept of lusotropicalism, developed by the Brazilian anthropologist Gilberto Freyre, became—and still is, to an extent—one of the most powerful and controversial metanarratives to explain (or, some would argue, justify) Portuguese colonialism. Lusotropicalism argues that because of a series of interrelated climatological, geographic, historical, cultural, and genetic factors, the Portuguese have been more inclined to intermix racially with peoples of the tropics, and this inclination would have somehow made the Portuguese a softer, more benign colonizing nation. The epistemological basis for lusotropicalism is laid out in Freyre's magnum opus, *Casa-grande e senzala* (1933; *The Masters and Slaves*). As Freyre elaborated his lusotropicalist theorization in various lectures and publications, its reach would be extended to the African colonies as well as to the various Asian enclaves that were part of the Portuguese empire. Ultimately, he provides a discursive nexus of cultural exceptionalism in order to explain Portuguese, Brazilian, as well as lusophone individualized and collective identities. The Freyrean lusotropicalist nexus, despite its many detractors and critics, proved to be quite resilient: it migrated from the intellectual field to that of politics and attitudes. It endures today, particularly with regard to notions such as miscegenation, *mestiçagem,* and hybridity, which are key to understanding the lusophone world.

15. The first major critical work in English on lusophone African literature was published during this critical period. See Hamilton's groundbreaking *Voices from an Empire* (1975).

16. João Guimarães Rosa, considered one of the most original writers in the history of Brazilian literature, took the early-twentieth-century linguistic experimentation of the Brazilian avant-garde and cultural exploration of Brazilian Northeast regionalism to the highest level by inventing a new literary language that was at the same time deeply Brazilian, modern, archaic, metaphysical, and uniquely personal. The influence of Rosa's work was felt, across the Atlantic, by the Angolan Vieira in the 1960s and decades later by the Mozambican Mia Couto. Thus Rosa helped shape the emerging literary languages of both Angola and Mozambique. Cape Verdean writers belonging to the *Claridade* movement were also

profoundly inspired by the Brazilian search for a quintessentially national literary language as well as content matter.

17. In 2006 Vieira published his first novel in decades, which is part of a trilogy entitled *De rios velhos e guerrilheiros* ("Of Old Rivers and Guerrillas").

18. For a critical survey written in English on postcolonial lusophone African literatures until the mid-1990s, see Chabal.

19. The term *animistic realism* was coined by the Angolan authors Pepetela and Henrique Abranches (Laranjeira 316).

20. For a thorough English-language discussion of Paulina Chiziane and other Mozambican women writers (de Sousa, Momplé, and Magaia), see Hilary Owen's *Mother Africa, Father Marx* (2007).

21. The most publishing activity takes place in Luanda, with presses such as Nzila and Chá de Caxinde (subsidiaries, resp., of the Portuguese presses Caminho and Campo das Letras; in Maputo, Njira is also a subsidiary of Caminho). In Mindelo and Praia (Cape Verde) and to a much lesser degree in São Tomé, the Centro Cultural Português ("Portuguese Cultural Center") publishes irregularly literary and nonliterary titles. In Bissau, Ku Si Mon and the Instituto Nacional de Estudos e Pesquisa ("National Institute for Research Studies") have published a number of volumes on an irregular basis.

22. The main presses in Portugal that publish lusophone African material are Caminho, Cotovia, Campo das Letras, D. Quixote, and Edições 70. In Brazil they are Nova Fronteira, Companhia das Letras, Record, and Ática Língua Geral.

23. Both Craveirinha and Pepetela received the most prestigious literary prize in the Portuguese-speaking world, Prémio Camões (in 1991 and 1997, resp.). Couto was awarded the Vergílio Ferreira prize in 1999 for the body of his work. He and Paula Tavares were awarded the Mário António prize for lusophone African literature sponsored by the Gulbenkian Foundation in Lisbon (in 2001 and 2004, resp.).

24. In Brazil, universities in Rio de Janeiro, São Paulo, and Belo Horizonte offer such courses and degrees; in Portugal, they are offered in Lisbon, Coimbra, and Oporto.

25. The lusophone African writers most translated into English are Couto, Pepetela, Vieira, and Ondjaki. See the appendix for a list of translated works of these and other authors. For English-language critical studies on Vieira, see Hamilton; Peres. For English-language critical studies on Couto, see Rothwell; Madureira.

Works Cited

Alencastro, Luiz Felipe de. *O trato dos viventes: Formação do Brasil no Atlântico sul.* São Paulo: Companhia das Letras, 2000. Print.

Andrade, Mário Pinto de, ed. *Antologia da poesia negra de expressão portuguesa.* Paris: Oswald, 1958. Print.

Cardoso, Pedro. *Folclore caboverdeano*. Porto: Maranus, 1933. Print.

———. *Mornas e saudade: Versos em crioulo e em português*. Cabo Verde, 1940. Print. Self-published.

Chabal, Patrick, ed. *The Postcolonial Literature of Lusophone Africa*. London: Hurst, 1996. Print.

Chiziane, Paulina. *Niketche: Uma história de poligamia*. Lisboa: Caminho, 2002. Print.

Claridade: Revista de arte e letras. Linda-a-Velha: ALAC, 1986. Print.

Cordeiro da Matta, Joaquim Dias. *Philosophia em provérbios angolanos*. Lisboa: Typographia e Stereotypia Moderna, 1891. Print.

Enders, Arnelle. *História da África lusófona*. Trans. Mário Matos e Lemos. Lisboa: Inquérito, 1997. Print.

Freyre, Gilberto. *Casa-grande e senzala*. 1933. 30th ed. Rio de Janeiro: Record, 1992. Print.

Hamilton, Russell. *Voices from an Empire*. Minneapolis: U of Minnesota P, 1975. Print.

Honwana, Luís Bernardo. *Nós matámos o cão-tinhoso*. 1964. São Paulo: Ática, 1980. Print.

Kebur: Barkafon di poesia na kriol. Bissau: Instituto de Estudos e Pesquisa, 1996. Print.

Laranjeira, Pires. *Literaturas africanas de expressão portuguesa*. Lisboa: U Aberta, 1995. Print.

Madureira, Luís. *Imaginary Geographies in Portuguese and Lusophone-African Literature: Narratives of Discovery and Empire*. Lewiston: Mellen, 2006. Print.

Magaia, Lina. *Dumba nengue: Histórias trágicas do banditismo*. São Paulo: Ática, 1990. Print.

Mbembe, Achille. "At the Edge of the World: Boundaries, Territoriality, and Sovereignty in Africa." Trans. Steven Rendall. *Globalization*. Ed. Arjun Appadurai. Durham: Duke UP, 2001. 22–51. Print.

Momplé, Lília. *Neighbours*. Maputo: Associação dos Escritores Moçambicanos, 1995. Print.

Moore, Gerald, and Ulli Beier. *Modern African Poetry*. London: Penguin, 1963. Print.

Moorman, Marissa J. *Intonations: A Social History of Music and Nation in Luanda, Angola, from 1945 to Recent Times*. Athens: Ohio UP, 2008. Print.

Moser, Gerald. "The Origins of an African Literature in the Portuguese Language." *Pennsylvania State University Studies* 26 (1969): 1–11. Print.

Owen, Hilary. *Mother Africa, Father Marx: Women's Writing of Mozambique, 1948–2002*. Lewisburg: Bucknell UP, 2007. Print.

Padilha, Laura. "As vozes poéticas femininas no percurso da formação das literaturas africanas em língua portuguesa." U of Minnesota, Minneapolis. 25 Sept. 2002. Lecture.

Pélissier, René. *Les campagnes coloniales du Portugal, 1844–1941*. Paris: Pygmalion, 2004. Print.

———. *Les guerres grises: Résistances et révoltes en Angola, 1845–1941*. Orgeval: Pélissier, 1977. Print.

———. *Naissance du Mozambique: Résistance et révoltes anti-coloniales, 1854–1918.* Orgeval: Pélissier, 1984. Print.

Peres, Phyllis. *Transculturation and Resistance in Lusophone African Narrative.* Gainesville: UP of Florida, 1997. Print.

Rothwell, Phillip. *A Postmodern Nationalist: Truth, Orality, and Gender in the Work of Mia Couto.* Lewisburg: Bucknell UP, 2004. Print.

Rui, Manuel. *Nda Nda Kaile Ekimba / Quem me dera ser onda.* Luanda: Nzila, 2000. Print.

Tavares, Eugénio. *Mornas: Cantigas crioulas.* Lisboa: Rodrigues, 1931. Print.

Tenreiro, Francisco José. *Obra poética.* Lisboa: Imprensa Nacional; Casa da Moeda, 1991. Print.

Troni, Alfredo. *Nga Muturi: Cenas de Luanda.* 1882. Lisboa: 70, 1973. Print.

Veiga, Manuel. *Odju d'agu.* Praia: Instituto Caboverdiano do Livro, 1987. Print.

Vieira, José Luandino. *Luuanda.* 1964. São Paulo: Ática, 1990. Print.

———. *De rios velhos e guerrilheiros.* Lisboa: Caminho, 2006. Print.

Appendix: Bibliography of Lusophone African Literature in English Translation

Agualusa, José Eduardo. *Creole.* Trans. Daniel Hahn. London: Arcadia, 2002. Print.

Couto, Mia. *Everyman Is a Race.* Trans. David Brookshaw. Oxford: Heinemann, 1994. Print.

———. *The Last Flight of the Flamingo.* Trans. David Brookshaw. London: Serpent's Tail, 2004. Print.

———. *A River Called Time.* Trans. David Brookshaw. London: Serpent's Tail, 2008. Print.

———. *Sleepwalking Land.* Trans. David Brookshaw. London: Serpent's Tail, 2006. Print.

———. *Under the Frangipani.* Trans. David Brookshaw. London: Serpent's Tail, 2001. Print.

———. *Voices Made Night.* Trans. David Brookshaw. Oxford: Heinemann, 1990. Print.

Ellen, Maria M., ed. *Across the Atlantic: An Anthology of Cape Verdean Literature.* Dartmouth: Center for the Portuguese-Speaking World, 1988. Print.

Honwana, Luís Bernardo. *"We Killed Mangy Dog" and Other Stories.* Trans. Dorothy Guedes. London: Heinemann, 1969. Print.

Magaia, Lina. *Dumba Nengue, Run for Your Life: Peasant Tales of Tragedy in Mozambique.* Trans. Michael Wolfers. Trenton: Africa World, 1988. Print.

Momplé, Lília. *Neighbours: The Story of a Murder.* Trans. Richard Bartlett and Isaura de Oliveira. Oxford: Heinemann, 2001. Print.

Neto, Agostinho. *Sacred Hope.* Trans. Marga Holness. Dar es Salaam: Tanzania, 1974. Print.

Ondjaki. *Good Morning Comrades.* Trans. Stephen Henighan. Emeryville: Biblioasis, 2008. Print.

———. *The Whistler.* Trans. Richard Bartlett. Laverstock: Aflame, 2008. Print.

Pepetela. *Jaime Bunda, Secret Agent: Story of Various Mysteries.* Trans. Richard Bartlett. Laverstock: Aflame, 2006. Print.

———. *Mayombe.* Trans. Michael Wolfers. London: Heinemann, 1983. Print.

———. *Return of the Water Spirit.* Trans. Luís Mitras. Oxford: Heinemann, 2002. Print.

———. *Yaka.* Trans. Marga Holness. Oxford: Heinemann, 1996. Print.

Rui, Manuel. *Yes, Comrade.* Trans. Ronald Sousa. Minneapolis: U of Minnesota P, 1993. Print.

Sunflower of Hope: Poetry from the Mozambican Revolution. Trans. Chris Searle. London: Allison, 1982. Print.

Vieira, José Luandino. *The Loves of João Vêncio.* Trans. Richard Zenith. San Diego: Harcourt, 1991. Print.

———. *Luuanda.* Trans. Tamara L. Bender and Donna S. Hill. London: Heinemann, 1980. Print.

———. *The Real Life of Domingos Xavier.* Trans. Michael Wolfers. London: Heinemann, 1978. Print.

Louise Bethlehem

The Pleasures of the Political: Apartheid and Postapartheid South African Fiction

"It is clear to me," declared Chinua Achebe to an audience at Makerere University College, Kampala, in August 1968, "that an African creative writer who tries to avoid the big social and political issues of contemporary Africa will end up being completely irrelevant—like that absurd man in the proverb who leaves his burning house to pursue a rat fleeing from the flames" ("African Writer" 78). The timing of this address, delivered at the height of the Biafran War, which had already claimed the life of the poet Christopher Okigbo, amplifies the call to engagement that Achebe is issuing. But it is central to Achebe's argument that the war, for all its urgency, intensifies the writer's orientation toward political commitment and social relevance but is not a precondition for engagement. "The fact of war," in his words, "merely puts the matter in sharper focus" (78).

Certainly, the deep involvement of African writers in the process of decolonization, as reflected in the spectacular malleability of the boundary between writer and politician for Jomo Kenyatta, Kwame Nkrumah, Léopold Sédar Senghor, and Agostinho Neto, to note only the most visible instances, would seem to provide concrete evidence for Achebe's statement. On the one hand, becoming a writer constituted "one of the most important sources of legitimacy for the political class in Africa," as

Simon Gikandi has noted ("Theory" 1). On the other hand, decolonization and its long aftermath appear to render engagement less a choice in the African context than a structural constraint, as if the writer's house were always burning, to revisit Achebe's proverb, or as if history itself were constantly called on to underwrite the politicization of African writing.

For all the confidence of Achebe's pronouncement however, the very need for its enunciation betrays his understanding that political or historical necessities do not become aesthetic ones without certain discernible interventions. His support for the frank instrumentalism of the African writer—evident for instance in his declaration that "the involvement of the Biafran writer today in the cause for which his people are fighting and dying is not different from the involvement of many African writers . . . in the big issues of Africa" ("African Writer" 78)—certainly speaks directly to his specific historical emplacement. But, as Achebe well knows, his exhortation also subtends the history of the art-versus-politics debate in Western literary culture and its relevance for an African literature that is enfolded in a global (i.e., a Western and capitalist) cultural and pedagogical system (see Amoko 23; Brown 832; Mudimbe).

"It is clear to me," says Achebe. Yet his claims are not self-evident. They must implicitly be defended against the preference for autonomy, self-referentiality, formal experimentation, and anti-instrumentalism that marked the ascendancy of Western modes of literariness in post-Romantic thought, culminating in literary modernism with its distinctive critical apparatus (see Attwell, "Experimental Turn" 158; Brown 833–38; Soyinka 62–63). In classroom settings, I have found it useful to draw attention to these trends as a way of contextualizing the African debate on aesthetics versus politics in relation to broader historiographic issues concerning the construction of literariness.

Regarding Western literariness, Achebe is succinct and polemical: "Some time ago, in a very testy mood, I began a lecture with these words: *Art for art's sake is just another piece of deodorized dog-shit*" ("Africa" 19). This flamboyantly transgressive gesture anticipates yet another of Achebe's interventions: the calculated and well-known provocation that would term that preeminent modernist, Joseph Conrad, "a bloody racist" ("Image" 788). His protest, for such it is, arises in the course of demonstrating how the literary achievements of "one of the great stylists of modern fiction" (783) are vitiated by ethical and epistemological failures. Literary worth, for Achebe, can no longer be allowed to inhabit the sanctuary of aesthetic form. Rather, its criteria are redirected to take in the material and discursive dimensions of Conrad's colonial complicity, its pointedly social and political parameters. A different accommodation of the aesthetic consequently becomes possible. Elsewhere Achebe will declare that "art is, and was always, in the service of man" ("Africa" 19). Art "in the service of," or art as what Louis James once termed the "protest made by affirmation" (109), adjoins the rationale of the more militant nationalist or anticolonialist protest literatures, whether we choose to direct our students' attention in this respect to tendencies in negritude in francophone West Africa, to the political ferment of lusophone writing (particularly poetry) in Angola and Mozambique between the years 1960 and 1975 (Chapman, *Southern African Literatures* 286), or to the writing that emerged from the black consciousness movement in post-1976 South Africa.

Achebe has been credited with the "invent[ion of] African literature" (Gikandi, "Chinua Achebe" 6), no less. His standing may be exemplary, but his negotiation of the opposition between the political and the aesthetic is far from unique. The reach of the debate over literary engagement, whether viewed in temporal or spatial terms, speaks to central issues of authority and legitimacy arising from the uneven and often conflicted institutionalization of African literatures in various locations. No doubt our students will recognize similar moments in the contestation of the canon conducted by, say, African American or feminist critics. In pointing to the wide circulation of the debate, however, I do not intend to homogenize its terms. The particular inflections it attains across different arenas are no less significant than its diffusion. When Oswald Mtshali asserts that the English used by black South African writers "is not the Queen's language that you know as written by say Wordsworth and Coleridge. It is the language of urgency which we use because we have got an urgent message to deliver to anyone who cares to listen to it" (127), it is surely possible to position him near Achebe. But it is equally useful to continue to unravel what is particular to his context of utterance. He adds:

> We have not got the time to embellish this urgent message with unnecessary and cumbersome ornaments like rhyme, iambic pentameter, abstract figures of speech, and an ornate and lofty style. We will indulge in these luxuries which we can ill-afford . . . when we are free people. (127)

Mtshali's qualification stages a contrast between the ready consolation of political engagement and the supposed self-indulgence of an ornamental formalism: an opposition that has been a staple of the call to engagement by African writers and critics in general. But the terms in which Mtshali addresses this debate, his particular foregrounding of a "rhetoric of urgency," which, I have argued elsewhere, is symptomatic of dissident literary culture under apartheid (Bethlehem 368), might profitably be taken as a point of entry into a more situated history (and historiography) of the anglophone South African novel. Such a turn folds the debate concerning the relative merits of political versus aesthetic commitment back into the regime of meaning in which it occurs, and in so doing affords access to the effects, as well as to the affective dimensions, of precisely this complicity. Accordingly, my own interest in the discussion that follows does not lie in charting a taxonomy of responses on the part of the African writer regarding the (in)commensurability of aesthetics and politics; it consists in reckoning with the texture—indeed, the textuality—of the debate within the specific parameters of apartheid South Africa.

South Africa constitutes a peculiarly overdetermined instance of analysis for our purposes, precisely because the consequences of literary engagement were heightened, sometimes lethally so, by the extremely repressive politics of the state. This much is obvious. But instead of taking the politicization of the literary as self-evident, even in a context as determinate as apartheid South Africa, I suggest that we challenge our students to ask what is foreclosed and what facilitated by premature submission to the claims a politicized literature makes for itself. What collusions between the political and the aesthetic are misrecognized when the relation between the two is represented as one of necessary collision? How do the negotiations concerning the appropriate means of literary representation in South Africa intersect the economy of literary forms displayed there, and what relation do they bear to the predominantly "realist dominant" (Bethlehem 365) of South African literature in English?[1]

Apartheid affected every aspect of the social and political constitution of South Africa from its inception. The segregationist doctrines of the Afrikaner ideologues who came to power in May 1948 soon translated into a barrage of discriminatory laws restricting freedom of movement, of residence, of land ownership, of access to education, even of sexual congress, for black, colored (mixed-race), and Indian South Africans. No less significantly, apartheid guaranteed the ongoing economic servitude of black South Africans and ensured the rigid demarcation of class boundaries along racial lines. The trajectory of nonracial resistance to apartheid, proceeding through the Defiance Campaign of the early 1950s, the adoption of the Freedom Charter at the Congress of the People in June 1955, the Soweto Student Revolt of 1976, and the mass democratic mobilizations of the 1980s and early 1990s, was met by the state with the increasingly severe repression of formal political opposition, leading culture eventually to be proclaimed a weapon of the antiapartheid struggle.

Well before this particular slogan was put into circulation, however, considerable consensus existed regarding the role of literature under apartheid. This uniformity was doubtless one of the consequences of the regime of meaning that apartheid generated. The euphemisms of the state were a notorious component of its social engineering. Thus, the Natives (Abolition of Passes and Coordination of Documents) Act of 1952, for instance, could function in defiance of its apparent meaning to extend rather than to curtail the punitive reach of the Pass Laws. "Apartheid," wrote the novelist Harry Bloom, "a word with a potent appeal to the longing for racial exclusiveness. A word with a thousand meanings and no meaning, but with a curious power to change the meaning of other words" (200). South African literary culture unfolded within, and against, the cooption of the sign that Bloom foregrounds—an annexation of discourse that was itself integral to the material violence of apartheid. The desire to "reveal the lie behind the moral sanctimony of separate development" became imperative. It was, the poet and literary scholar Leon de Kock suggests, "an immediate, primary need as strong as hunger" (230).

This commitment to a literature of revelation was a fundamental principle of South African literary culture, in ways that went beyond exposure of the regime's specific lies. The act of depiction in a broader sense, the literary rendering of life under apartheid, was held to constitute a call to conscience. As the influential critic of African literature Bernth Lindfors once put it, "the picture alone indicts the society which permits such inhumane conditions to exist" (17). The statement arose in the course of a discussion of anglophone fiction in an article Lindfors entitled "Robin Hood Realism in South African English Fiction." The attribution is telling. The white South African writer Rose Moss was party to a similar understanding when she declared some years after Lindfors, "Telling the truth is bad for apartheid"—then added, "The primary obligation is to tell the truth" (48–49).

To oppose apartheid through the devices of literature, these scholars and writers suggest, is fundamentally to expose it. This assumption was prevalent in apartheid South Africa as writers grappled with the need to translate the pernicious effects of apartheid into a decipherable script. Literary scholar and state prosecutor, censor and critic joined together in undisguised regard for the mimetic fidelity of the literary text (see Cronin 13; Bethlehem 366). That the depiction of life under apartheid could, and often did, trigger punitive state reprisals merely heightens the paradox of this shared adherence by bitter political adversaries to a resolutely stenographic view of literature. Revelation befits revolution, we might gloss in their aftermath. The formula would prove to be robust. Novelists like Alan Paton and Nadine Gordimer lent their moral authority and growing canonical standing to the truth-telling priorities of literary dissidence, as did the Afrikaans writers Breyten Breytenbach and André Brink. Brink's corroboration of the position taken by his lesser-known counterpart Moss was particularly blunt. For Brink, the writer's function under apartheid was to ensure that "the terrible excuse of Nuremberg is not heard again" (152).

For all its importance, the emphasis on revelation could translate at times, in the hands of its more conservative white adherents, into apolitical forms of discourse that tended to deflect the act of writing away from engagement and toward more transcendental or universalist notions of the poet as seer. This tendency was forcefully challenged by black writers who reinterpreted the poetics of revelation as an explicit politics of representation. "We need a writing that records exactly the situation we live in," stated Mothobi Mutloatse, a polemical writer and editor associated with the radical *Staffrider* magazine, which rose to prominence in the period following the 1976 Soweto Revolt, "and any writing which ignores the urgency of political events will be irrelevant" (qtd. in Seroke 305). Black writing is called on to further the political objectives of the constituencies in whose name it has come into being. In this view, the writer as victim of or witness to injustice is simultaneously a political delegate bound to the articulation of an alternative politics on behalf of precisely those South Africans whom apartheid bars from access to democratic representation.

Mutloatse's declaration, and many others like it, may be analyzed in the terms that the postcolonial scholar Gayatri Chakravorty Spivak makes available to us in the reading of Marx that she conducts in her well-known "Can the Subaltern Speak?" Recall that Spivak attends there to the two different meanings of the word *representation* that are held apart in the original German of Marx's *The Eighteenth Brumaire*: "representation as 'speaking for,' as in politics, and representation as 're-presentation,' as in art or philosophy"; *Vertretung* and *Darstellung*; proxy and portrait (275).

The attempt to invest the act of writing with political force in apartheid South Africa is typically founded on a willed conflation of these two senses. Clear evidence of this conflation is to be found in some of the commentary offered by the influential writer and scholar Es'kia Mphahlele, who draws "portrait" into pointed alignment with "proxy" when he characterizes black South African writing as "a response to the immediate, to the instant, and a direct, urgent confrontation with the dominant political morality" ("South African Literature" 14). But this alignment assumes that a particular model of semiosis is already in place. Mphahlele's recourse to notions of immediacy and directness help us unearth for our students the ideology of literary production implicit here. The priorities of political representation are held by its proponents to require a mode of artistic re-presentation that is as transparent as possible: *Vertretung*, in other words, seems to call for a rigidly circumscribed *Darstellung*.

That Mphahlele regards such transparency as both feasible and politically effective is apparent from the ongoing course of his discussion of Mtutuzeli Matshoba, a contributor to Mutloatse's post-1976 volume of black protest literature *Forced Landing*. Matshoba, says Mphahlele, exemplifies those black writers who

> wrench the spiked cactus from the ground with bare hands, so to speak, in their attack on the system. [Matshoba] extracts experience from raw life and does little to impose an aesthetic structure on the material. . . . Writers like Mtutuzeli feel called on to range their words against the oppressor. They resist that intrinsic tendency for words to weave themselves into metaphor and allegory to express high seriousness in a memorable diction, and prefer a prose that goes straight to the visible target. ("South African Literature" 14)

These claims are forceful, but their presuppositions are largely undeclared. Part of our students' investment in adjudicating such claims in the context of the wider debate on the politicization of literature might consist in coming to terms with the underlying assumptions here—whether these bear on theories of signification or on perceptions of writers and literary critics regarding the distinctive constitution of the social in apartheid-era South Africa.

A number of observations are in order here. The first regards the extreme politicization of the everyday in apartheid South Africa. As Mphahlele demonstrated in his autobiography *Down Second Avenue*, no aspect of black experience was insulated from the seepage of apartheid. The concept of raw life in Mphahlele's work subsumes its own politicization, given the saturation of the social by the political in apartheid South Africa (see also Watson 18–19). This understanding remains implicit in Mphahlele's statement but is rendered considerably more explicit in the literary scholar Malvern van Wyk Smith's characterization of black writing published a few years after Mphahlele's article. Black writers, van Wyk Smith states,

> often write from harrowing personal experience. The mere transcription of such experience does not always make a passable play, novel or poem, but the everyday experiences of humiliation, harassment, displacement and sheer violence that every black can bear witness to are such as to require often no more than an honest record. (98)

The notion of transcription is a crucial one, I would argue. The everyday, the nexus of political dispossession, appears in some accounts of the role of literature under apartheid almost to write itself, by annexing, as it were, the ontological being rather than mediatory agency of the writing subject. An honest record suffices to fulfill the truth-telling priorities of the literary culture. Yet the understanding that every representation is necessarily predicated on some form of mediation is all but absent. Instead, we find a sustained investment in notions of verisimilitude or mimetic adequation: the very assumptions that inform Mphahlele's invocation of raw life, to return to his part in our discussion. Mphahlele's use of *raw life* as a kind of shorthand for *verisimilitude* is prefigured by the mobilization of such terms as *immediacy* and *directness*, themselves key markers of the rhetoric of urgency. In discussion of these issues in the classroom, I engage in close readings of the essay by Mphahlele ("South African Literature") and the interviews conducted by Jaki Seroke to make the claim that oppositional South African literary culture recurrently invokes a model of signification in which language effaces itself to produce radical proximity to the lived world.

To cast the issues at stake here in a different theoretical vocabulary, we might say that the trope of truth, the commitment to the "honest record" that underpins the South African writer's ethical investment in the politicization of literature, is sustained by pervasive recourse to the trope as truth—by an instrumentalist or stenographic attitude to meaning production that yearns for a prose that might, in Mphahlele's terms "go straight to the visible target." Yet the assimilation of trope (rhetorical figure, but equally literary topos) to truth is never complete. The trope-truth tension can be isolated in Mphahlele's contributions to the rhetoric of urgency that we have been examining. Accordingly, I ask students to pay attention to his use of figurative language. The thoroughly corporeal figure ("bare hands") that he employs in order to lend affective force to his declaration is persuasive, but its impact cannot be dissociated from a lingering awareness of the difference between the literal and the figurative registered in the tell-tale phrase "so to speak." To attend to Mphahlele's language, however, is to begin to see the manner in which a residual awareness of the gap between the word and the world may be retrieved from his text at the very moment that Mphahlele champions Matshoba for the seeming ability to overcome that gap. In other words, I encourage students to consider how Mphahlele disrupts the literary orthodoxy that he recirculates: the raw life he invokes is as much a literary construct as the bare hands whose figurative status he acknowledges, even as he registers Matshoba's repudiation of the metaphoric. Mphahlele's investment in the politicization of quotidian black experience naturalizes—renders axiomatic—a certain set of aesthetic principles.

Expanding this insight, we might state that the very craving for the raw life of experience that Mphahlele and others make manifest in the South African context dissimulates the extent to which the politicization of literature there relies on a thoroughgoing investment in instrumentalist views of language. The craving obeys the codes of a representational literalism (Grant 14–15) that is associated with realism in its most habitual Western forms.

Literary realism is a nineteenth-century movement that accompanied the rise of industrial capitalism. Its philosophical underpinnings are deeply indebted to notions of representational authenticity, the ability to represent actuality as common sense assumes it to be. Erich Auerbach's *Mimesis* famously charts the realist tradition in European literature, identifying the emergence of modern tragic realism with Stendhal and Balzac (408, 413). High realism, Auerbach claims, is directed at the "mimetic imagination of the reader" (115). It does not obey the flights of "free imagination" but is subservient to "real life, as it presents itself everywhere" (424)—that is to say, to real life perceived in relation to social and historical determinants. Thus, "the serious realism of modern times cannot represent man otherwise than as embedded in a total reality, political, social and economic, which is concrete and constantly evolving" (408; see also 433–34). Auerbach's intervention reminds us that the assumption that literature properly refers to the real in its sociohistorical manifestations is an ideology that emerges in South Africa on the basis of continental European as well as British realist precedents.

The politicization of writing in South Africa, as elsewhere in Africa, cannot be dissociated from questions relating to the fraught intersection of mimesis and form on the Continent. But in South Africa, this indebtedness is seldom recognized for the aesthetic structuring that it entails. On the contrary, the imperative of revelation relies on a thoroughgoing elision of the discursive codes that mediate between realism in its various genealogies and the overdetermined social reality of apartheid. It is accordingly a constitutive paradox of apartheid-era writing in English that what casts itself as need—immediately compelling, compellingly unmediated, given the political exigencies—can more properly be seen as evidence of a certain desire (Bethlehem 382). The otherwise divergent agendas of liberalism, radicalism, and populism in South African literary culture all manifest the will to close the gap between the word and the world.

It is in this suturing that oppositional literary culture in South Africa imagines its own seizure of political and symbolic agency. Its "essentially outward or moral or worldly thrust," in David Attwell's words ("Problem" 594), is a profoundly ethical reflex. There is, undeniably, consolation to be had here: the solace of morality; the certainty of moving in step with history on the road to liberation; a certain pleasure, even, despite what Lewis Nkosi once termed the "breadline asceticism" of the black aesthetic credo ("Postmodernism" 77). So I propose that the pleasure of the literal be repositioned as a major, if occluded, constituent of the aesthetic orientation of politically engaged writers in South Africa.

It is yet another paradox of South African literary culture that the pleasure of the literal often coincides with a kind of attrition of pleasure—for its addressee, that is. Nkosi, a writer and scholar who like Mphahlele rose to visibility out of the literary ferment of the 1950s, has been consistent and outspoken over the course of three decades in his criticism of this tendency (see his "Fiction," *Tasks* 76–106, "South African Writers," and "Postmodernism"). For Nkosi, who initiated a far-reaching debate concerning politics and aesthetics in South African fiction in the mid-1960s, the black writer's "mere concern with *telling* the story" reflects the shortcomings of a literary tradition where "the journalistic fact [parades] outrageously as imaginative literature" ("Fiction" 110). What is found in South African literature, continues Nkosi, is

> a type of fiction which exploits the ready-made plots of racial violence, social apartheid, interracial love affairs which are doomed from the beginning, without any attempt to transcend or transmute these given "social facts" into artistically persuasive works of fiction. (110)

He regrets that the political saturation of the everyday under apartheid leads to a homogenization of the quotidian in the set repertoires of South African literary representation. He laments that a certain trivialization or flattening of the particulars has kept politically engaged literature in apartheid South Africa from fulfilling its estranging or defamiliarizing role, to draw on the terms of the Russian formalists (see Shklovsky). It is in this light that we might read Nkosi's criticism that Richard Rive's novel *Emergency* (1964) presents

> no real full-blooded characters with real blood to spill; no characters whose fighting or love-making has the stench of real living people: they are cardboard pieces and cardboard pieces don't spill any blood. Embarrassingly, what comes out of the apartheid machine when it has ground to a standstill is not human flesh but cardboard pulp. ("Fiction" 115)

Some twenty years later, Njabulo Ndebele, an influential writer and intellectual, would amplify Nkosi's precedent as a call for a thoroughgoing "rediscovery of the ordinary"—the title of an important volume of essays on South African literature and culture, published in 1991. Ndebele redefines received notions of "relevance" to suggest that "what has been called protest literature may have run its course in South Africa" ("Redefining" 58). He criticizes an emaciated literary tradition that stakes too much on documentation, since "an art that is grounded in the negation of social debasement" leads to mere recognition instead of a transformation of the reader's consciousness ("Turkish Tales" 27). His objections are similar to those raised by James Baldwin in his well-known critique of Richard Wright in "Everybody's Protest Novel." Baldwin points to the continuity between *Uncle Tom's Cabin* and

> the novels of Negro oppression written in our own, more enlightened day, all of which say only: "This is perfectly horrible! You ought to be ashamed of yourselves!" (Let us ignore, for the mo-

> ment, those novels of oppression written by Negroes, which add only a raging, near-paranoiac postscript to this statement and actually reinforce . . . the principles which activate the oppression they decry.) (14)

Although Ndebele does not refer to Baldwin, it is instructive to read the two essays (Ndebele's "Rediscovery," Baldwin's "Everybody's Protest Novel") side by side in the classroom as a way of illuminating the contours of the South African and African American protest traditions, respectively. I have found it effective to assign to students the task of producing short oral reports on the similarities and differences between Ndebele and Baldwin, in order to clarify the range of issues addressed here.

It is important to point out that Ndebele's intention is not to depoliticize literary practice so much as to encourage a reorientation of the interrogation of power conducted by black writers in the late-apartheid state away from its public exposition as "spectacle" ("Rediscovery" 43). Anthony O'Brien sees in this shift a movement toward the private sphere and reads it as evidence of Ndebele's implicit alliance with other forms of contestation, such as a nascent black South African feminism, whose political challenge was grounded in the particularities of subject position, along axes of class or gender (52; see 36–75 for further discussion).

For Attwell, Ndebele's fiction, like Ndebele's theoretical and literary-historical essays, institutes an epistemological shift in black South African writing that opens it to a more reflective engagement with the structures of selfhood made possible by, for example, modernist experimentalism. Attwell stresses that the engagement with what he terms "the experimental turn" is not derivative or epigonic, since it repositions the concern with selfhood, which is a recognizable legacy of modernism, in a politicized, post–black consciousness setting that coincides, at least for Ndebele, with "the conditions of modernity defined by the apartheid city" ("Experimental Turn" 160; see 159–69). Attwell's argument, an impressive one, is sustained in his readings of Zakes Mda's fiction as well. His analysis is a useful corrective to South African literary culture's conceit that a literature of urgency could be realized as an exhaustive program. The prescriptions and proscriptions of a politicized aesthetic, as it is constructed under apartheid, not only fail to confront the contradictions internal to the model of realist signification that they espouse but also seem to predispose us toward a less than adequate reading of the literary corpus that came into being there, a corpus more stratified, more experimental, Attwell rightly claims, than the critical discourse is prepared to concede (156).

Once the debate surrounding the politicization of the South African novel has been grounded in this fashion, my classroom interventions now consider an important counterexample. For the alternative of an explicit literary experimentalism, a "late modernist" (Attridge 2) regard for the aesthetic does, of course, have a forceful advocate elsewhere in South African literary culture. The Nobel Prize–winning author J. M. Coetzee has long offered a sustained and powerful challenge to the realist dominant of English-speaking South African literature, as many of our students will surely know.

Coetzee's early fiction is striking in its avoidance of the repertoires that a politically committed realism might have afforded him, along the lines of Alan Paton's path-breaking *Cry, the Beloved Country* (1948) or some of Nadine Gordimer's early works—*The Lying Days* (1953), *A World of Strangers* (1958), and *Occasion for Loving* (1963). Coetzee uncompromisingly rejects the staple components of the "liberal novel of stricken conscience," in Benita Parry's trenchant phrase (149). The coordinates of a contemporary South African setting that might denote urgency are consistently deferred in his early novels. The fictional world is self-consciously relegated to the past in both "The Narrative of Jacobus Coetzee," the second novella in *Dusklands* (1974), and the subsequent work, *In the Heart of the Country* (1976). It is suspended in the no-time of an apocalyptic future in *Life and Times of Michael K* (1983). It is stripped, in *Waiting for the Barbarians* (1980), of external markers of time and space other than those generated by the fiction itself. What results is a highly allegorical oeuvre that is nevertheless, Attwell ("Problem" and *J. M. Coetzee*), Derek Attridge, and others have argued, deeply responsive to the troubled politics of the late-apartheid state.

A well-known passage in *Life and Times of Michael K*, where the Medical Officer reflects on the protagonist's incarceration in a prison camp, exemplifies the challenge that Coetzee's knowingly self-reflexive poetics posed for the literary culture in which it was emplaced. I usually begin my positioning of Coetzee within, and against, the protest tradition with a close reading of this passage:

> Your stay in the camp was merely an allegory, if you know that word. It was an allegory—speaking at the highest level—of how scandal-

> ously, how outrageously, a meaning can take up residence in a system without becoming a term in it. Did you not notice how, whenever I tried to pin you down, you slipped away? I noticed. (228)

The extract can easily be interpreted as Coetzee's metafictional commentary on his own poetics. I use it to point out to my students that Coetzee has widely been seen as using allegory himself in order to resist incorporation into a determinate narrative of history, where *history* resonates with the political freight it was made to carry in radical intellectual discourse in South Africa of the 1970s and 1980s. He is on record as seeking to elude—or, better still, to resist—gestures that might render his fiction a mere supplement to the discourse of history.

In the now notorious *Weekly Mail* Book Week address delivered in 1987, Coetzee would argue:

> In times of intense ideological pressure like the present, when the space in which the novel and history normally coexist like two cows on the same pasture, each minding its own business, is squeezed almost to nothing, the novel, it seems to me, has only two options: supplementarity or rivalry. ("Novel" 3)

As his argument unfolds, he rejects a novel constrained to provide readers with "vicarious first-hand experience of living in a certain historical time, embodying contending forces in contending characters and filling our experience with a certain density of observation" (3). The dismissal of supplementarity clearly stages a breaking of ranks with the realist allegiances of a politically committed South African fiction. Nor is it surprising that Coetzee's embrace of the option he terms "rivalry" is simultaneously a call for the relative autonomy of fiction, an autonomy that is at least partly formal in nature. He advocates

> a novel that operates in terms of its own procedures and issues in its own conclusions, not one that operates in terms of the procedures of history and eventuates in conclusions that are checkable by history (as a child's school-work is checked by a schoolmistress). (3)

The preference for a self-reflexive and formally innovative form of writing is clearly articulated.

This preference was not without its consequences for Coetzee's early reception in South African literary culture. His failure to submit to what Damian Grant once called "the purifying ravishment of fact" (14) was highly controversial for its time and place. Coetzee was accused, with increasing vehemence over the course of the early 1980s, of dehistoricizing the real and of evading political responsibility. Gordimer's scathing review of *Life and Times of Michael K* in the *New York Review of Books*, well known for its judgment that "revulsion against all political and revolutionary solutions rises with the insistence of the song of cicadas to the climax of this novel" ("Idea" 6), conveys the tone of much of this condemnation. The very terms in which the attack on his knowingly antimimetic poetics were formulated speak eloquently of the instrumentalist orientations of South African literary culture—a point that I use the reading of Gordimer's review in the classroom to make.

Gordimer was not alone in her position; it was widely shared by literary authorities in both radical and revisionist circles in South Africa at the time. For the Marxist critic Michael Vaughan, who championed Mtutuzeli Matshoba's poetics against Coetzee's, Coetzee's self-reflexive language "can say next to nothing, and certainly nothing reliable, about experiences outside the modality of its own racial-historical dialectic" (128). Michael Chapman similarly lamented Coetzee's evasion of the "responsibility of action" (in Arthur Koestler's phrase), which laid Coetzee open to the charge of being lost to history ("Writing" 336). Chapman went on to identify the theoretical debate surrounding the publication of Coetzee's novel *Foe* (1986) as yet another context in which the evasion of historical responsibility might be registered—this time by the poststructuralist critic. Whereas "history may certainly be regarded, poststructurally, as discourse," he proclaimed, "it is more likely to manifest itself, concretely, as low wages or the police cell" (327).

The premises of Chapman's argument should be familiar by now. Given the urgency of the political situation, Chapman implies, the enjoyment that Coetzee's texts afford those readers who are prepared to countenance the "demythologizing" of history (Coetzee's phrase ["Novel 3]) is highly suspect. Chapman's disapproval culminates in his condemnation of Teresa Dovey's Lacanian analysis of Coetzee published in 1988, which Chapman holds to "confirm the suspicions of many black writers that literary pursuit in white South Africa has rather more to do with the gratifications of libidinal language than the fulfillments of fighting political injustice" (338). Pleasure bifurcates once again into its sanctioned and illicit forms, along the familiar binary that Mtshali delineated a decade earlier.

But is Coetzee's practice as a novelist really antithetical to the political? Attwell, in his exemplary reading of Coetzee's early corpus, claims that that corpus as *"situational metafiction"* (*J. M. Coetzee* 20) does not detract from its political importance; on the contrary, the metafiction is integral to it—whether or not Coetzee himself is prepared to concede this dimension of his work. Attwell is fully cognizant of the nonmimetic aspects of Coetzee's writing. Far from constituting an evasion of responsibility, he claims, it is the very self-reflexivity of the oeuvre that draws attention to "the historicity of discourses, to the way subjects are positioned within and by them" (20). Such deconstruction is a necessary prelude to the informed contestation of the authority of narratives of colonial power, apartheid prominent among them. It is for this reason that Attwell can confidently maintain Coetzee's novels to be directed, in their (and his) reflexivity, "at understanding the conditions—linguistic, formal, historical and political—governing the writing of fiction in contemporary South Africa" (Attwell, "Editor's Introduction" 3). Drawing on the work of Attwell and his successors, we might conclude that if Coetzee's preference for formal experimentalism is intransigent, his poetics is neither intransitive nor hermetic. His fiction, and the protocols of reading generated in response to it, has helped deflect contemporary South African literary culture away from a rigidly mimetic conceptualization of the relation between the literary and the political.

This flexibility was amplified by the transition to democracy that has reshaped the social and political constitution of South Africa. In April 1994, the African National Congress came to power under the leadership of Nelson Mandela in an election victory that was the successful culmination of decades of collective struggle against apartheid. The country reinvented itself as a constitutional democracy and committed itself to a program of national reconciliation. The Truth and Reconciliation Commission (TRC) was set up to investigate human rights violations that occurred in apartheid South Africa between the years 1960 and 1994. Perpetrators of human rights abuses were offered amnesty in return for full disclosure of their deeds, while victims gave public testimony in a cathartic engagement with the trauma of the recent past. "Healing Is Revealing," suggested one of the publicity banners under which public hearings of human rights violations often unfolded.

The emphasis on revelation that was the moral signature of the TRC is clearly aligned with some of the major presuppositions of the oppositional literary culture that preceded the TRC. The testimonies delivered there, in the first-person voices of both victims and perpetrators, have been regarded by some scholars as discrete components of a collective autobiography that often coalesces around the scarred body of the apartheid subject. "The autobiographical act in South Africa, more than a literary convention," state Sarah Nuttall and Cheryl-Ann Michael, "has become a cultural activity" (298). But if the boundaries of the literary have become more permeable, as these insights suggest, it is also true that the political has itself shifted. The public terrains of struggle that defined politics under apartheid have been renegotiated through the initiatives of feminist and homosexual constituencies in South Africa (O'Brien 185–214; Jones 114–17) or through the interventions of human rights activists, particularly those who have challenged the "denialism" that has been a lamentable feature of postapartheid politics and public discourse on HIV/AIDS (Sitze 780–90). Postapartheid novels accordingly show a new intimacy with forms of fiction and of self-writing that are located at a certain remove from politics in its designated apartheid-era forms. In the classroom, I use the cumulative close reading of a number of novels to illustrate this shift.

Ndebele's most recent work, *The Cry of Winnie Mandela*, is a text I have found useful in demonstrating that the debate on the seeming incommensurability of the political and the aesthetic has been resolved in contemporary South Africa through the novelist's decision to suspend the antagonism that formerly bound the two in an illicit and much repudiated embrace. Ndebele's opening ploy is explicitly metafictional:

> Let's begin with the blurb of an imaginary book about a South African woman during the long years of struggle against apartheid. It reads:
>
> *So what does a woman do in the absence of her husband who is in jail, or in the mines, in exile, or is dead, or away studying, or spends most of the time on the road as a salesman, or who, while not having gone anywhere in particular is never at home because he is just busy fooling around? . . . Departure, waiting, and return: they define her experience of the past, present, and future. They frame her life at the centre of a great South African story not yet told.* (1)

The life of South African women is resolutely politicized. Its temporality of deferral lies at the core of the author's quest to weave together "*the stories of four unknown women, and that of South Africa's most famous woman, who waited*" (1). Viewed in terms of continuity with Ndebele's commitment to a poetics of the ordinary, this weaving is no surprise. The scandal of the text lies elsewhere: in the sympathetic, first-person invocation of the politically discredited figure of Winnie Madikizela Mandela, who appears alongside Homer's Penelope in a distinctly contemporary incarnation, as a hitchhiker.

The fictionalization of the real contours of Winnie Mandela's biography draws attention to its own artifice and is allied in this respect to Ndebele's placing of the Homeric text *en abîme* in his own. But the playfulness that suspends the illusion of the transparency of the literary medium is allied to a serious political purpose. Ndebele's rehabilitation of Winnie Mandela is not capricious; it allows Ndebele to stage, in her name, a searing criticism of the discourses of reconciliation that have shaped public culture in the aftermath of the TRC. "There is one thing I will not do," proclaims the Winnie Mandela of the fiction. "It is my only defence of the future. I will not be an instrument for validating the politics of reconciliation. For me, reconciliation demands my annihilation" (113). She offers scant consolation, but in withholding it, she becomes emblematic of the skepticism of a politically responsive postapartheid literature caught in the long duration of transition in South Africa, where the rhetoric of the new does not always fulfill its promise.

In Mda's novels, the exuberance of magic realist conceits or of a reworked oral tradition pits imagined agency against the intractable and often violent legacies of apartheid. Attwell reads Mda's poetics as staging an engagement that "renders history—colonialism, apartheid—as a process of creeping death which necessitates modes of aesthetic production—the professional mourner, the dancer, *ritual*, in general—which are offered as sources of hope" ("Experimental Turn" 171). I ask my students to elaborate on the manner in which the artists and performers who populate Mda's texts—Toloki, the theatrical "Professional Mourner" of *Ways of Dying* (1995); the artist Father Frans Claerhout, whose painting are enfolded into the text of *The Madonna of Excelsior* (2002); the singers and musicians of *The Whale Caller* (2005), particularly the title figure himself—can be seen as allegorical entries in a discourse on aesthetics that emerges between the lines of contemporary postapartheid fiction.

A kind of fecundity emerges in the new interface between the political and the aesthetic, one that the magic realist protagonist of Achmat Dangor's remarkable novel *Kafka's Curse* celebrates and interrogates:

> This continent [Africa] is fecund—yes, fecund—with the kind of foliage which gives birth to the secret lives that are the very substance of magical parable. We spring our heroes on you when you

> least expect it, conjure them up from dusty townships, bring them old and wizened to your doorstep in order to defeat you with their wisdom. (30)

The metafictional interjection arises in the course of a magic realist fable, which like many of Mda's texts is skeptical about the possibility of change, viewed as the cleansing suspension or heroic overthrow of the past.

In *Kafka's Curse*, Dangor interrogates the resurgence of the past in the present, through the return of a peculiarly South African repressed. His protagonist, Oscar Kahn—or Omar Khan—is a colored Muslim who passes as a Jewish Johannesburg architect. Omar's becoming a tree in the wake of his mother's death gives the lie to his failed social metamorphosis, as the secret of his colored birth stands revealed. The familiar topos of passing is given a distinctly innovative turn, through its grafting onto the Arab myth of Leila and Majnoen. But the traditional positions of the gardener and the princess are translated into a South African syntax in which race determines the extent of the "life's station":

> Imagine a man turning into a tree as he waits for a lover who will never arrive. A well-deserved fate, if you ask me, for a lowly gardener waiting for a princess. . . . You see, the myth really warns against the madness of Majnoen, or is it against majnoen the Madness. An insanity that strikes those who dare to stray from their "life's station," that little room which you are told at birth is yours. You may expand it a bit, add a loft or garden, build a bigger fence than the one you inherited. But you leave it at your peril. (30, 31)

The extract is haunted by Dangor's firsthand knowledge of what the literary scholar and novelist Stephen Gray mordantly terms the "accident of birth" in his apartheid-era autobiography of the same name. But confronting the traumatic legacies of South African history—in those "plots of racial violence, social apartheid, interracial love affairs" lamented by Nkosi—need no longer entail recourse to the "ready-made" ("Fiction" 110). Dangor's hyperbolic deviance from the codes of a social or socialist realism in favor of a magic realist fable is a powerful index of the distance traveled by contemporary South African literary culture.

Dangor's novel shares the certainty of haunting, the unpredictable claims of past on present, with Zoë Wicomb's *David's Story* (2000), whose interrogation of colored identity spectacularly disrupts the realist code. The female frame narrator's attempts to render the biography of a political activist into writing are frustrated by its subject, David, who has commissioned her. Her failures as David's "amanuensis" (3)—a writer from dictation—surely underscore Wicomb's suspicions concerning the traditional realist project of struggle-era fiction, particularly when the narrator's task of representation is broadened to include the elusive figure of Dulcie, beloved and betrayed, David's comrade in the underground guerrilla movement: "Dulcie and the events surrounding her cannot be cast as story" (150). This skepticism culminates in the novel's dissolution of the privileged signifier of the politicized literature of the struggle era: truth. "Truth, I gather, is the word that cannot be written" (136). The unwritten word resonates beyond its erasure, nevertheless, honed in declension to what Wicomb's narrator calls the

> palindrome of Cape Flats speech—TRURT, TRURT, TRURT, TRURT—the words speed across the page, driven as a toy car is driven by a child with lips pouted and spit flying, wheels squealing around the Dulcie obstacles. [David] has, hauling up a half-remembered Latin lesson, tried to decline it.
>
> Trurt, oh trurt, of the trurt, to the trurt, trurt, by, with, from the trurt. (136)

The deformation of the word, the foregrounding of its hurt ("trurt") materiality, can be read as a precarious displacement of the scarring of Dulcie's body by torturers. The certainty of her violation is one of the few givens of the work. Wicomb's typographic disfigurement of the signifier dismisses the position that truth may be apprehended outside its circulation, its voiced inflection, by the living bodies who lay claim to it. Wicomb's gesture of deformation declines in a second sense—that is to say, refuses—the confident appropriation of truth by a political project, even a liberatory one. Renewed debate on the aesthetics of a politically responsive (South) African literature that takes its orientation from the critique that Wicomb performs promises to exceed the mutual foreclosure of the political by the aesthetic, of the aesthetic by the political, a foreclosure that has long structured the African novel.

Note

1. I am using "dominant" in Jurij Tynjanov's sense, mediated through Roman Jakobson, to denote the focusing component of a work or synchronic literary system that governs, determines, and transforms the remainder (Jakobson).

Works Cited

Achebe, Chinua. "Africa and Her Writers." Achebe, *Morning* 19–29.

———. "The African Writer and the Biafran Cause." Achebe, *Morning* 78–84.

———. "An Image of Africa." *Massachusetts Review* 18 (1977): 782–94. Print.

———. *Morning Yet on Creation Day.* London: Heinemann, 1975. Print.

Amoko, A. O. "The Problem with English Literature: Canonicity, Citizenship, and the Idea of Africa." *Research in African Literatures* 32.4 (2001): 19–43. Print.

Attridge, Derek. *J. M. Coetzee and the Ethics of Reading: Literature in the Event.* Chicago: U of Chicago P, 2004. Print.

Attridge, Derek, and Rosemary Jolly, eds. *Writing South Africa: Literature, Apartheid, and Democracy, 1970–1995.* Cambridge: Cambridge UP, 1998. Print.

Attwell, David. "Editor's Introduction." Coetzee, *Doubling* 1–13.

———. "The Experimental Turn in Black South African Fiction." *South Africa in the Global Imaginary.* Ed. Leon de Kock, Louise Bethlehem, and Sonja Laden. Pretoria: U of South Africa P; Leiden: Koninklijke Brill, 2004. 154–79. Print.

———. *J. M. Coetzee: South Africa and the Politics of Writing.* Berkeley: U of California P; Cape Town: Philip, 1993. Print.

———. "The Problem of History in the Fiction of J. M. Coetzee." *Poetics Today* 11.3 (1990): 579–615. Print.

Auerbach, Erich. *Mimesis: The Representation of Reality in Western Literature.* New York: Doubleday, 1957. Print.

Baldwin, James. "Everybody's Protest Novel." *Notes of a Native Son.* 1955. Boston: Beacon, 1963. 13–23. Print.

Bethlehem, Louise. "'A Primary Need as Strong as Hunger: The Rhetoric of Urgency in South African Literary Historiography." *South Africa in the Global Imaginary.* Ed. Leon de Kock, Bethlehem, and Sonja Laden. Spec. issue of *Poetics Today* 22.2 (2001): 365–89. Print.

Bloom, Harry. *Transvaal Episode.* Berlin: Seven Seas, 1959. Print.

Brink, André. "After Soweto." 1976. *Mapmakers: Writing in a State of Siege.* London: Faber, 1983. 128–53. Print.

Brown, Nicholas. "The Eidaesthetic Itinerary: Notes on the Geopolitical Movement of the Literary Absolute." *South Atlantic Quarterly* 100.3 (2001): 829–51. Print.

Chapman, Michael. *Southern African Literatures.* Pietermaritzburg: U of Natal P, 2003. Print.

———. "The Writing of Politics and the Politics of Writing: On Reading Dovey on Reading Lacan on Reading Coetzee on Reading . . . ?" *Journal of Literary Studies / Tydskrif vir Literatuurwetenskap* 4.3 (1988): 327–41. Print.

Coetzee, J. M. *Doubling the Point: Essays and Interviews.* Ed. David Attwell. Cambridge: Harvard UP, 1992. Print.

———. *Dusklands.* 1974. Johannesburg: Ravan, 1982. Print.

———. *Foe.* Johannesburg: Ravan, 1986. Print.

———. *In the Heart of the Country.* 1976. London: Vintage, 1999. Print.

———. *Life and Times of Michael K.* Johannesburg: Ravan, 1983. Print.

———. "The Novel Today." *Upstream: A Magazine of the Arts* 6.1 (1988): 2–5. Print.

———. *Waiting for the Barbarians.* New York: Penguin, 1982. Print.

Cronin, Jeremy. "'Even under the Rine of Terror . . .': Insurgent South African Poetry." *Research in African Literatures* 19.1(1988): 12–23. Print.

Dangor, Achmat. *Kafka's Curse.* New York: Vintage, 1999. Print.

de Kock, Leon. "A Prison-House of Mirrors? Discussion Contribution." *Journal of Literary Studies / Tydskrif vir Literatuurwetenskap* 5.2 (1989): 229–31. Print.

Dovey, Teresa. *The Novels of J. M. Coetzee: Lacanian Allegories.* Johannesburg: Donker, 1988. Print.

Gikandi, Simon. "Chinua Achebe and the Invention of African Culture." *Research in African Literatures* 32.3 (2001): 3–8. Print.

———. "Theory, Literature and Moral Considerations." *Research in African Literatures* 32.4 (2001): 1–18. Print.

Gordimer, Nadine. "The Idea of Gardening." *New York Review of Books* 2 Feb. 1984: 3+. Print.

———. *The Lying Days.* London: Gollancz, 1953. Print.

———. *Occasion for Loving.* London: Gollancz, 1963. Print.

———. *A World of Strangers.* London: Gollancz, 1958. Print.

Grant, Damian. *Realism.* 1970. London: Methuen, 1985. Print.

Gray, Stephen. *Accident of Birth: An Autobiography.* Johannesburg: Congress of South African Writers, 1993. Print.

Jakobson, Roman. "The Dominant." *Readings in Russian Poetics: Formalist and Structuralist Views.* Ed. Ladislav Matejka and Krystyna Pomorska. Cambridge: MIT P, 1971. 105–10. Print.

James, Louis. "The Protest Tradition: *Black Orpheus* and *Transition.*" 1969. *Protest and Conflict in African Literature.* Ed. Cosmo Pieterse and Donald Munro. London: Heinemann, 1982. 109–24. Print.

Jones, Tim Trengove. "Fiction and the Law: Recent Inscriptions of Gayness in South Africa." *Modern Fiction Studies* 46.1 (2000): 114–36. Print.

Lindfors, Bernth. "Robin Hood Realism in South African English Fiction." *Africa Today* 15.4 (1968): 16–18. Print.

Mda, Zakes. *The Madonna of Excelsior.* Oxford: Oxford UP, 2002. Print.

———. *Ways of Dying.* 1995. Oxford: Oxford UP, 2002. Print.

———. *The Whale Caller.* London: Penguin, 2005. Print.

Moss, Rose. "'Telling the Truth': Interview by Jean Marquard." *Contrast* 47 (1978): 48–55. Print.

Mphahlele, Es'kia. *Down Second Avenue.* London: Faber, 1959. Print.

———. "South African Literature vs. the Political Morality (1)." *English Academy Review* 1 (1983): 8–28. Print.

Mtshali, Oswald. "Black Poetry in South Africa." *Aspects of South African Literature.* Ed. Christopher Heywood. London: Heinemann, 1976. 121–27. Print.

Mudimbe, V. Y. "African Literature: Myth or Reality." *African Literature Studies: The Present State / L'état present.* Ed. Stephen Arnold. Washington: Three Continents, 1985. 7–15. Print.

Mutloatse, Mothobi, ed. *Forced Landing: Africa South, Contemporary Writing.* 1980. Johannesburg: Ravan, 1981. Print.

Ndebele, Njabulo S. *The Cry of Winnie Mandela: A Novel.* Cape Town: Philip, 2003. Print.

———. "Redefining Relevance." Ndebele, *Rediscovery* 58–73.

———. *Rediscovery of the Ordinary: Essays on South African Literature and Culture.* Johannesburg: Congress of South African Writers, 1991. Print.

———. "The Rediscovery of the Ordinary: Some New Writings in South Africa." Ndebele, *Rediscovery* 37–57.

———. "Turkish Tales and Some Thoughts on South African Literature." Ndebele, *Rediscovery* 11–36.

Nkosi, Lewis. "Fiction by Black South Africans." 1966. *African Writers on African Writing.* Ed. G. D. Killam. London: Heinemann, 1973. 109–17. Print.

———. "Postmodernism and Black Writing in South Africa." Attridge and Jolly 75–90.

———. "South African Fiction Writers at the Barricades." *Third World Book Review* 2.1–2 (1986): 43–45. Print.

———. *Tasks and Masks: Themes and Styles of African Literature.* Harlow: Longman, 1981. Print.

Nuttall, Sarah, and Cheryl-Ann Michael. "Autobiographical Acts." *Senses of Culture: South African Culture Studies.* Ed. Nuttall and Michael. Oxford: Oxford UP, 2000. 298–317. Print.

O'Brien, Anthony. *Against Normalization: Writing Radical Democracy in South Africa.* Durham: Duke UP, 2001. Print.

Parry, Benita. "Speech and Silence in the Fictions of J. M. Coetzee." Attridge and Jolly 149–65.

Paton, Alan. *Cry, the Beloved Country.* 1948. New York: Simon, 1995. Print.

Seroke, Jaki. "Black Writers in South Africa." *Ten Years of* Staffrider, *1978–1988.* Ed. Andries Walter Oliphant and Ivan Vladislavić. Johannesburg: Ravan, 1988. 303–09. Print.

Shklovsky, Victor. "Art as Technique." *Russian Formalist Criticism: Four Essays.* Ed. Lee T. Lemon and Marion J. Reis. Lincoln: U of Nebraska P, 1965. 3–24. Print.

Sitze, Adam. "Denialism." *South Atlantic Quarterly* 103.4 (2004): 769–811. Print.

Soyinka, Wole. "Ideology and the Social Vision (I): The Religious Factor." 1976. *Myth, Literature and the African World.* Cambridge: Cambridge UP, 1990. 61–96. Print.

Spivak, Gayatri Chakravorty. "Can the Subaltern Speak?" 1985. *Marxism and the Interpretation of Culture.* Ed. Cary Nelson and Lawrence Grossberg. Urbana: U of Illinois P, 1988. 271–313. Print.

van Wyk Smith, Malvern. *Grounds of Contest: A Survey of South African English Literature.* Wynberg: Juta, 1990. Print.

Vaughan, Michael. "Literature and Politics: Currents in South African Writing in the Seventies." *Journal of Southern African Studies* 9.1 (1982): 118–38. Print.

Watson, Stephen. "Poetry and Politicization." *Contrast* 16.1 (1986): 15–28. Print.

Wicomb, Zoë. *David's Story*. Cape Town: Kwela, 2000. Print.

Brenda Cooper

Language, Multiple Worlds, and Material Culture in the Teaching of African Migrant Fiction

Many African writers instill the echoes of their other languages, universes, and knowledges into the European languages in which they write their fiction. The corollary of this proposition is that we, as teachers of this fiction, have to learn how to hear those echoes. There are many angles to the fierce debate about the use of language in African writing, the most publicized one being whether to write in a European language, like English, or in an indigenous African language. This debate is not new. Over half a century ago, Frantz Fanon, in a paper entitled "The Negro and Language," spelled out some of the consequences of the hegemony of French, which meant that "the Negro of the Antilles" only became "a real human being in direct ratio to his mastery of the French language" (18). From the beginning of the debate, the language weapon was seen to be double-edged. French may dehumanize, but mastery of it "affords remarkable power" (18) and "the Negro wants to speak French because it is the key that can open doors" (38).

French may open doors, but some African writers and thinkers do not wish to go through them. Obiajunwa Wali, in a conference paper published in 1963, caused a furor by warning writers against using European languages and by asserting that the European language has "no chance of advancing African Literature" but makes it "only a minor appendage in the mainstream of European literature" (13).

Chinua Achebe took issue with Wali and insisted that "the English language will be able to carry the weight of my African experience" (62). However, Achebe emphasized that the English that is necessary in order to express African experience is a new tongue, a different language. In effect, he was saying that you need to make English an Africanized language—"But it will have to be a new English, still in full communion with its ancestral home but altered to suit its new African surroundings" (62).

Ngũgĩ wa Thiong'o took issue with Achebe and deeply regrets the decision that he and other writers made to opt for European languages (7), which he sees as colonizing their minds: "the bullet was the means of the physical subjugation. Language was the means of the spiritual subjugation" (9). He therefore insists that to produce African literature, as opposed to "Afro-European" literature, to liberate their psyches from European neocolonial interests and worldviews, African writers must write in their indigenous languages (27). In opposition, Ali Mazrui enters the debate with the quite categorical suggestion that "any language can be a weapon of either colonization or liberation" (71).

Beyond doubt is that from the beginning of African fiction written in English, writers, like Achebe and others, have struggled with the fact that English is saturated with metaphors and meanings linked to imperialism. The exemplary metaphor is, of course, Africa as the dark heart of Conrad's classic. Writers struggle against the tentacles of this language of their colonizers, a language through which Africans have been constituted as reluctant, ambivalent subjects. They therefore seize this language, for which they have both love and hatred, and attempt to manipulate its tropes and symbols in a variety of ways.

This essay suggests that some migrant African writers experiment with English, in the diaspora, in the tradition of Achebe, to contest the hegemony of European culture. It proposes that one way they do this is to anchor their fictions in the concrete, visceral material realities of their previous lives and of their new lives in the diaspora. This anchoring involves infusing into their English the sounds, words, and worldviews of the other languages into which they were born and socialized, whether Arabic, Igbo, or Yoruba.

Bill Ashcroft has referred to this infusion as the "metonymic gap," which he identifies as "a crucial feature of the transformative function of post-colonial writing" (75). The metonymic gap, which accomplishes this installation of difference, occurs when postcolonial writers "insert unglossed words, phrases or passages from a first language, or concepts, allusions or references which may be unknown to the reader." What then happens is that

> such words become synecdochic of the writer's culture—the part that stands for the whole. . . . Thus the inserted language "stands for" the colonized culture in a metonymic way, and its very resistance to interpretation constructs a "gap" between the writer's culture and the colonial culture. (75)

The rhetoric of metonymy, albeit entwined as it always is with metaphor, has proved to be a useful postcolonial language device, enabling some African writers to depict their multiple worlds and material daily realities as well as to incorporate the rhythms of other languages into their fictions. Metonymy holds the potential to interrogate the hierarchical law of dominant metaphors.

While metaphors are based on meaningful comparisons between different dimensions, metonymic connections are often based on the chance ordering of elements that find themselves next to each other—on contiguity. By contrast, the bonds of metaphor are deep, symbolic, and figural. Rhymes and jangles, songs, the rhythmic, and happenstance are all the stuff of metonymy. Ashcroft observes that this harnessing of metonymy flies in the face of the law of the powerful, Western center: "in the European tradition the contiguous and accidental, those characteristics which seem to accrue to the metonymic, will never have the power of truth," and truth, of course, "is the province of the metropolitan" (75).

Metonymy also lends itself to the depiction of concrete cultural realities. As George Lakoff and Mark Johnson put it, metonymy, unlike metaphor, "usually involves direct physical or causal associations" rather than symbolic connections (39), therefore "experience with physical objects provides the basis for metonymy" (59). And so "the structure of the world, sustained by an authoritative and legitimating metaphor," may be challenged through the use of the metonymic" (Durham and Fernandez 209).

I am not defining the rhetoric of these writers in terms of metonymy, which has been available and used by postcolonial writers through the generations and from both their countries of birth and the diaspora. All I demonstrate here is that migrant writers find metonymy useful, as they express in English and in their fiction their multiple lives, cultures, and languages. The metonymic seems to fit their purposes, given that they, by definition, have been uprooted from their routines and familiar environments. They seek to capture the reality of their new environments as well as hold on to the visceral feel of their old homes, lives, and selves.

A cleansed metonymic, concrete language, freed of symbols, culture, and discourse, of course, does not exist. However, what we often have is not a privileging of the figurative but more than one universe and dimension, operating side by side and contesting the binaries between worlds. Multiple cultures, traditions, and languages may emerge, which Achille Mbembe attempts to capture when he refers to African imaginary worlds as predicated on "simultaneous multiplicities" (145). The visible and the occult are not regarded as opposed to each other; they need to be interpreted simultaneously. "More precisely," Mbembe enlarges, "the invisible was not only the other side of the visible. . . . The invisible was in the visible and vice versa." These worlds were "part and parcel" of each other and provide the basis for "the inseparability of . . . the being and the nonbeing of persons and things" (145).

This multiplicity demands of African fiction new kinds of poetic troping, within a syncretism of the literal and the figurative. This syncretism could be precisely what Lakoff and Johnson refer to when they use the concept of "symbolic metonymies" as forging the "critical links between *everyday experience* and the coherent metaphorical systems that characterize religions and cultures." These symbolic metonymies are figurative but also "are grounded in our physical experience" (40; my emphasis). Or, as Mbembe emphasizes, what is being abolished is "the distinction between being and appearance, the world of the living and the world of spirits" (145).

This focus on the everyday, material, and concrete, which is imbricated with the spiritual and unseen, links to my earlier work on magic realism in a West African context. There I described how, by definition, magic realism renders the magical-supernatural religious worlds as mundane and ordinary, as part of the daily lives of ordinary people. Along similar lines, Harry Garuba attempts to come to grips with the parallel worlds of the living and the spirits, and with the language of their representation in fiction, using a concept he terms not magic realism but "animist materialism," in which everyday objects are "the physical and material manifestations of the gods and spirits" (268, 267). Animist thought "spiritualizes the object world, thereby giving the spirit a local habitation."

This spiritualization entails a refusal of binaries and hierarchies, such as the growth from the literal to the figurative, given that we have "the 'locking' of spirit within matter or the *merger of the material and the metaphorical,* which animist logic entails" (267; my emphasis). The blended language refuses the binary between the metaphoric and metonymic. The narrative device is "a representational strategy that involves giving the abstract or metaphorical a material realization" (284). In other words, the play with language, with metonymy, which both undoes and reconstructs symbols; the paradoxical manipulation of happenstance, rhymes, slogans, songs; and the use of untranslated Arabic or Igbo words is all a carefully constructed artifice.

The journeys between worlds and languages are not always smooth or safe. To capture some of their peril for her students, Sneja Gunew introduces them to what she calls, after Gilles Deleuze, a "stammering pedagogy." She explains that "when there are several languages the body sometimes transits from one to the other less than gracefully." Interesting for our purposes is her link between a form of teaching and migration, where "displaced from home, we are thus unable to feel at home because we are too aware of the alternative and parallel worlds we could be inhabiting equally well" (125). Deleuze, in the essay to which Gunew refers, entitled "He Stuttered," also defines stuttering as a narrative device, a construction of the writer whose intention it is to invent "a *minor use* of the major language" (109). English is taken and turned partly into a strange and foreign language—a mechanism that relates precisely to Ashcroft's metonymic gap.

I demonstrate the importance of this manipulation when I touch briefly on three migrant novels: Biyi Bandele's *The Street*, Chimamanda Ngozi Adichie's *Purple Hibiscus*, and Leila Aboulela's *The Translator.* Bandele's strange fantasy words, Adichie's Igbo, and Aboulela's Arabic render "the native language foreign," as Gunew puts it, in the context of Deleuze's theory (126). She emphasizes the relation between this linguistic device and the politics of teaching such works in North America, turning "the stammer into a pedagogical model" that "is attuned to the ghostly dimension of other meanings." A language made foreign disrupts "the gathering menace . . . of monolithic models of knowledge" (132).

But how does this narrative device function in some recent African novels? And, if we know the function, how may we better teach these novels? Multiple universes, twinning, the literal, material culture of the everyday, embedding and anchoring the figurative and spiritual abound in many novels in general and migrant novels in particular. Teaching them provides a way into the fiction.

The street referred to in Bandele's *The Street* is Brixton High Street, where the action takes place. This statement is true but simplistic: the novel occupies parallel universes—the worlds of the living and the dead, the lands of reality and of dreams, the Nigeria of Bandele's birth and growing up and the London of his chosen home. In the process of spanning these universes, of mixing and mingling these dimensions, Bandele Africanizes Lewis Carroll's *Alice in Wonderland* mode of metonymic nonsense writing and flies Amos Tutuola's West African oral tradition of *The Palm-Wine Drinkard* to London. Bandele's tools for this great transposition between cultures, his bags of tricks, are, among other things, words themselves, words in all their fleshy, powerful, and solid materiality.

The wild, weird, and unhinged words that scurry along *The Street* draw attention to its nomadic narrative structure as surely as do the metonymic gaps embodied in another language like Arabic or Yoruba. As the Undead ramble and rave on the street, appearing and disappearing throughout the book, crazy words weave across the book, dictating its style and even its purpose—words like "Trustafarians," "Afro-Saxon" (17), "Nowheresville" (34), "hebetude" (48), "coruscating" (103), "spindling" (125), "prestidigitation" (133), "pauciloquence" and "underwhelmed" (136), "lactovegetarian activist" (145), "bizarrerie" (167), "omphaloskepsis" (174), "copacetic folk" (175), "oenomaniac" (187), "absquatulated" (195), "exercitation" (202), "Black Blandiloquence" and "irrefragable claim" (203), "parannoying" (217), "diseconomies" (225).

A strange, enigmatic character in the novel is Mr. Bill, a peddler of words:

> [He] was to be found every weekday during the morning rush hour standing outside the tube station, touching commuters for money by enacting one or more of his specialities, which included reciting and offering the meanings, origins, synonyms, antonyms and, where applicable, the usage and abusage of every single word under the letter H in the Oxford English Dictionary. (181)

Why H? Why not? It could be the H of happenstance of metonymy that enables Mr. Bill, who "gifted" words with wings "and sent them flying into the great void beyond sound or silence, where all words uttered in the universe, and in all languages on the planet, are stored for all time, or forgotten for ever" (182). Not always, however, are words sucked into the abyss and forgotten. Mr. Bill mends words that become damaged, such as the one that had "suffered from a fractured syllable." He repairs it "with a needle and thread." He even raids rubbish bins "for stray, homeless or discarded words" (182). One time, he bought words cheaply from a "second-hand words seller" because they had been damaged by rain—"he laid them out in the sun to dry" (183).

Mr. Bill occupies multiple universes. He is one of Bandele's liminal Undead who live on the street. At the same time, if he looks deep into his heart, he "may spot the Pleiades, that dazzling cluster of small stars in the constellation Taurus" (287).

Back on earth, to what purpose all these planets, detonating words, and traveling tales? In this novel, Bandele is seeking, playing with, and hiding his identity, as a Nigerian living in London. He is doing so by means of the here and now of daily life on the High Street of Brixton. He is determined not to seek his identity in the depths of his psyche, in deep symbols, metaphors, and figurative language. He wishes to discover a language and an urban landscape in all its material reality, such that he might find a concrete place as a writer and artist in the place in which he lives and works.

Adichie's *Purple Hibiscus* is the story of Kambili, the first-person protagonist. Fifteen years old, she lives in the violent and repressive atmosphere of her father, who physically abuses her meek mother and also herself and her brother, Jaja, by beating them into submission. Yet he is a pillar of the community, an avid Catholic churchman. What we witness in the novel, as part of Kambili's spiritual awakening and finding of her voice, is the attempt to reenchant solid objects, linked to precolonial rituals but syncretized with a Catholicism unlike her father's. This Africanized Catholicism is integrated into a global modernity, because Adichie is writing the novel from America, where she was a student. On a return visit to Nsukka, she feels that she is "re-seeing Nsukka with [her] Americanized eyes" ("Heart" 1). Writing from America but, unlike Bandele, setting her fiction mainly in Africa, she views her life through the lens of her new abode.

Adichie attempts to capture Nsukka by giving a thick description of its material, of its daily reality. At the same time, this concreteness is a portal to other worlds, and the multiple dimensions are enacted as flesh and objects meld and as spirits contest the boundary between the animate and the inanimate. Everyday objects, such as tables and chairs, grains of rice and ceramic ornaments, syncretize with bodies and are infused with life. The *mmuo* are spirits who integrate into objects, inhabiting baskets and chairs and animating them. With minimal explanation, Kambili's grandfather, Papa-Nnukwu, points to "our *agwonatumbe*," which is "the most powerful *mmuo* in our parts, and all the neighboring villages fear Abba because of it" (86). As Kambili watches a huge *mmuo* float past, she observes that "it was eerie, watching it, and I thought then of chairs running, their four legs knocking together, of water being held in a basket, of human forms climbing out of ant holes" (87).

The *mmuo*, and the untranslated Igbo to describe their material manifestations, light the path to a more hybrid religion, in which African spirits enter Catholic ritual. They enter through the Igbo language and songs, and these echo throughout the novel. Adichie sometimes translates Igbo words and phrases, sometimes makes their meaning clear in the context, and sometimes lets the Igbo speak for itself without clarification. These three different modes have been classified by Ismail S. Talib as "overt cushioning," "covert cushioning," and "no cushioning at all" (128–29) or metonymic gaps. In all cases, whether a translation is provided or not, the use of words from another language indicates a frame of reference outside the dominance of English.

For example, there are times that the English is echoed into a sentence, as in " '*Nne, ngwa*. Go and change," Mama said to me, startling me although her Igbo words were low and calming" (8). The words may be explained, but the timbre of the language is metonymically communicated. Later, and likewise, she says of Father Amadi that she "did not fully comprehend his English-laced Igbo sentences at dinner because my ears followed the sound and not the sense of his speech" (135). In the same vein, part of Adichie's rich and concrete description is of food and the rhythm of its preparation:

> Lunch was fufu and onugbu soup. The fufu was smooth and fluffy. Sisi made it well; she pounded the yam energetically, adding drops of water into the mortar, her cheeks contracting with the *thump-thump-thump* of the pestle. The soup was thick with chunks of boiled beef and dried fish and dark green onugbu leaves. . . . I molded my fufu into small balls with my fingers, dipped it in the soup, making sure to scoop up fish chunks, and then brought it to my mouth. (11–12)

The thump thump of the pestle replicates the rhythm of the dance or the soothing tones of Igbo in Mama's voice—the thick description of the smells, sights, sounds, and rhythm of life buttresess the narrative frame of the novel. The detail here is important, since the novel takes pains to create the texture of a life that is unfamiliar to the Western reader. Local food and Igbo songs—senusal pleasure in taste and music—are chorused throughout, and often the choruses are not translated, as in the repeated "*I na-asi m esonaya! I na-asi m esonaya!*" (179). These songs and their metonymic choruses are crucial accompaniments to the growth of Kambili's identity and ability to find her voice.

The Translator, by Aboulela, tells of the tempestuous love between a Muslim woman, Sammar, from the Sudan and a Scotsman, Rae. He is "a Middle-East historian and a lecturer in Third World Politics" (5), and her job is to translate between English and Arabic for him. In addition to this linguistic communicating, she has to find a way of communicating between different cultures. The language that writers like Aboulela are crafting must be malleable to depict multiple cultures, experiences, and spiritualities. It must capture the rich detail of daily life for travelers like Sammar, who walk about in a strange city—here, Aberdeen.

Aboulela's fiction tirelessly plays with everyday items that give the visceral feel of ordinary life. The novel bulges with a kettle, glowing coals, a bicycle lamp, a cat, and smells of every kind, good and bad. Wool, socks, cushion, floorboards. There is repeated reference to soap and body creams: glycerine, Vaseline, precious imported Nivea. There are Miranda bottles and 7-Up and Coke, and in the house of Sammar's aunt constant "boiling water for tea, special trays for guests, an elegant sugar bowl" (123). The computer and printer of Sammar's brother are described in detail; they are precious—in fact, "everything was precious in Khartoum, even ink and paper, because it was all imported, so hard to replace" (140).

There is profound imbrication between the everyday of buses, buildings, and bricks and deeper meanings, symbols, and subjectivity, which is why Slavoj Žižek "incorporates the everyday within his work and includes in his deliberations both "toilets and Tarantino" (Myers 2). Objects like toilets and computer screens translate, or fail to translate, realities between worlds. Aboulela portrays very literally the workings of the toilet in the apartment of Sammar's brother in Khartoum. The pump that lifts the water to his floor is electrical and thus at the mercy of power failures. The old toilet handle has to be yanked a few times, and Sammar's niece is embarrassed and anxious until "it finally flushe[s]" (136). When the power fails and later comes on again, it brings with it the relief of "the loud television, the purr of the air cooler, and from the bathroom [Sammar] could hear the toilet filling up with water" (14). This is part of daily life in Khartoum, and its vicissitudes anchor the novel.

As always, words themselves are the solid building blocks on which to raise an edifice around different cultures, words like those from the Qur'an, which are metonymic mantras that protect and shield by repetition:

> [She] began to say silently, *All praise belongs to Allah, Lord of all the worlds, the Compassionate, the Merciful* . . . and the certainty of the words brought unexpected tears, something deeper than happiness, all the splinters inside her coming together. (66)

Without these weighty words, Sammar slips into the terror of hallucinations that are felt on her body as fits or migraine headaches.

The lack of a common understanding between Sammar and Rae of concrete words could be summed up by Rae's comment that in the secular West, "God is out playing golf" (37). For him, this flippant metaphor describes the hedonism of Western culture, a hedonism that amounts to a new religion. Sammar, however, taking words seriously and literally, is puzzled: "'But why golf?' she asked. 'Why specifically golf?'" (37). For Sammar, golf, like toilets and buildings, is concrete, and she cannot follow the idiomatic and iconoclastic inflections in Rae's use of words.

Arabic words in the novel, not only from the Qur'an, signal the existence of another language and a different spiritual and knowledge base. These are metonymic gaps that draw attention to themselves and alter the sound of the English. Arabic sayings, meanings, wordplay, and names are small signposts, always invested in the minutiae of daily life. In Khartoum, Sammar hears "the sunset *azan*," which she had missed in Aberdeen and which sends her "to make *wudu*" with "*Allah akbar. Allah akbar* . . . " (130) reverberating rhythmically in her head.

The English that emerges from these migrant writers is always different, given that it has been "appropriated, taken apart, and then put back together with a new inflection, an unexpected accent, a further twist in the tale" (Chambers 23). These writers have transported worlds, cultures, and knowledges into the West along with their suitcases and boxes, recipes and accents. They transform the streets of London or Aberdeen with their manipulation of language and of the ethics and aesthetics of the everyday. As Iain Chambers puts it, "the urban script is rewritten," and the European city moves "according to different rhythms, making it move to a diverse beat," which involves speaking "the languages—linguistic, literary, cultural, religious, musical—of the dominator, of the master" (Chambers 23). These rhythms, beats, mantras, metonymic gaps, and material realities contest the hegemony of the master, even as they accede to aspects of the master's power.

Sometimes, the tension between this acceding and this contesting makes for the stutter that we saw Gunew earlier turn into the basis of a postcolonial pedagogics. The protagonists of many, although not exclusively, women African writers struggle to find their voices, their words, in these novels. Kambili, Adichie's protagonist, stutters, chokes on her words, stammers, and whispers: " 'I . . . I . . .' I stopped to take a breath because I knew I would stutter even more if I didn't" (49). Aboulela's Sammar is often rendered speechless, or sucked into the torment of a debilitating migraine headache, "pain greater than childbirth," and "the silence, the absence of pain would not come. *Ya Allah, Ya Arham El-Rahimeen*. . . . She thought she must have had something between a migraine and a fit" (20). The physical pain is foregrounded by the metonymic gap of the untranslated Arabic, which highlights the abyss between the worlds that she is attempting to negotiate.

Gayatri Chakravorty Spivak suggests that women postcolonial writers are "necessarily *fighting to write the body* in the normative, privative, rational abstractions of a uniform civil law" (30; my emphasis). Trinh T. Minh-ha in another context refers to "linguistic flesh" (33). This goal is not the old stereotype of woman as instinct, as body, as nonrational and babbling prelanguage. It is a new language, and if we listen to it more carefully, we will be better, more empowering teachers in our culturally mixed classrooms. We may not hear the whole script, understand the Arabic or Yoruba references, or follow all the multiple cultural signs and signals and be able to communicate all their complex dimensions and nuances to our students. But if we ourselves are prepared to stutter and stumble, we may begin to hear the silences and absences in our own arsenals of knowledge, along with our contributions and insights. Being aware of those other sources, languages, and knowledges will profoundly mediate the way we teach such texts. As Vilashini Cooppan puts it, you may "lose something in translation in order to gain something in transformation" (30).

Mr. Bill, Bandele's word seller, mended one of the words that had come into his care, a word that "had a broken wrist," and with this word I end my essay. The word had "healed into a fist unable to open." Once

Mr. Bill nursed it, "it shook hands and opened doors" (183). English words and stories have imprisoned and oppressed some people, but, once healed and warmed, perhaps still stuttering from the aftershock of their wounds, they may open doors for writers, readers, and teachers. These solid words, whose "average price . . . is ten pence" (181), flying between Lagos and London, the worlds of the living and the dead, are both literal, solid objects and spirits on whose wings we may also fly, if we listen to them carefully enough.

Works Cited

Aboulela, Leila. *The Translator.* Edinburgh: Polygon, 1999. Print.

Achebe, Chinua. *Morning Yet on Creation Day.* London: Heinemann, 1975. Print.

Adichie, Chimamanda Ngozi. "Heart Is Where the Home Was." *Topic Magazine* 3 (2003): 1–5. Print.

———. *Purple Hibiscus.* London: Fourth Estate, 2004. Print.

Ashcroft, Bill. *Post-colonial Transformation.* London: Routledge, 2001. Print.

Bandele, Biyi. *The Street.* London: Picador, 1999. Print.

Chambers, Iain. *Migrancy, Culture, Identity.* London: Routledge, 1994. Print.

Cooper, Brenda. *Magical Realism in West African Fiction: Seeing with a Third Eye.* London: Routledge, 1998. Print.

Cooppan, Vilashini. "Ghosts in the Disciplinary Machine: The Uncanny Life of World Literature." *Comparative Literature Studies* 4.1 (2004): 10–36. Print.

Deleuze, Gilles. *Essays Critical and Clinical.* Minneapolis: U of Minnesota P, 1997. Print.

Durham, Deborah, and James W. Fernandez. "Tropical Dominions: The Figurative Struggle over Domains of Belonging and Apartness in Africa." *Beyond Metaphor: The Theory of Tropes in Anthropology.* Ed. Fernandez. Stanford: Stanford UP, 1991. 190–210. Print.

Fanon, Frantz. "The Negro and Language." *Black Skin, White Masks.* New York: Grove, 1967. 17–40. Print.

Garuba, Harry. "Explorations in Animist Materialism: Notes on Reading/Writing African Literature, Culture, and Society." *Public Culture* 15.2 (2003): 261–85. Print.

Gunew, Sneja. *Haunted Nations: The Colonial Dimensions of Multiculturalisms.* London: Routledge, 2004. Print.

Lakoff, George, and Mark Johnson. *Metaphors We Live By.* Chicago: U of Chicago P, 1980. Print.

Mazrui, Alamin. "Relativism, Universalism, and the Language of African Literature." *Research in African Literatures* 23.1 (1992): 65–72. Print.

Mbembe, Achille. *On the Postcolony.* Berkeley: U of California P, 2001. Print.

Myers, Tony. *Slavoj Žižek.* London: Routledge, 2003. Print.

Ngũgĩ wa Thiong'o. *Decolonising the Mind: The Politics of Language in African Literature.* London: Currey; Nairobi: Heinemann, 1986. Print.

Spivak, Gayatri Chakravorty. "Echo." *New Literary History* 24 (1993): 17–43. Print.

Talib, Ismail S. *The Language of Postcolonial Literatures: An Introduction*. London: Routledge, 2002. Print.

Trinh T. Minh-ha. *Woman, Native, Other*. Bloomington: Indiana UP, 1989. Print.

Tutuola, Amos. *The Palm-Wine Drinkard*. London: Faber, 1952. Print.

Wali, Obiajunwa. "The Dead End of African Literature?" *Transition* 10 (1963): 13–16. Print.

Peter Kalliney

East African Fiction and Globalization

Most academic writing on modern African fiction works within the broad theoretical premises of postcolonial criticism. In recent years, however, the emergence of globalization, as both a material reality and a body of scholarly knowledge, has exerted subtle pressure on the field of postcolonial studies. The concept comes to literary theory from the social sciences, where thinkers such as Anthony Giddens, Saskia Sassen, Anthony King, Manuel Castells, and Arjun Appadurai have used the term since the early 1990s to describe and critique the forces of globalization in its economic, political, and cultural guises. If the major assumptions of globalization are true—that we now live in a world where individual states are no longer able to regulate the movement of capital, commodities, ideas, and people across national borders—postcolonial theory is rapidly becoming a historical enterprise, no longer capable of analyzing contemporary political conditions.[1] Where does this leave the vast majority of African fiction courses, the syllabi of which were undoubtedly constructed in the context of postcolonial theory? How do we frame questions about the relation between imperialism and globalization when we teach African novels?

In this essay, I situate two contemporary East African novelists—Abdulrazak Gurnah and M. G. Vassanji—in the midst of this incipient debate between postcolonial criticism and globalization theory. First, I suggest that postcolonial studies, with its special focus on historical relations, may have something to teach students and critics of globalization. Most globalization theory posits European imperialism as a nascent, undeveloped form of transnationalism: Euroimperialism serves as the main precursor of economic and political globalization. Likewise, the moment of strong, relatively autonomous postcolonial nation-states of the 1960s and 1970s (such as those in Tanzania, Kenya, and Uganda) has passed, an unstable product of the cold-war balancing act. In this historical account, the current form of globalization, shaped to fit the insidious demands of international capital, gradually displaces imperialism and the postcolonial nation-state as the dominant geopolitical category of analysis. With its more supple forms of economic and political coercion, globalization breaks down the fairly rigid geographic boundaries thought characteristic of both high imperialism and postcolonial nationalism.

But an attentive reading of East African history and fiction may suggest that this account of globalization tends to flatten out the multivalent applications of power that were operational during imperialism, and those that now exist under the banner of global capital. In East Africa, for instance, European imperialism was not the only, and certainly not the most important, precursor to globalization. Novels such as Gurnah's *Paradise* and Vassanji's *The Gunny Sack* remind us that the basic principles of transnational economic and cultural exchange existed in the Indian Ocean region well before the imposition of colonial rule by European powers. The east coast of Africa was as culturally diverse and commercially interconnected as any European capital during the nineteenth century. By emphasizing this precolonial history, these novels contest the lingering ideological preeminence of Euroimperialism in narratives about the rise of globalization. Academic histories of globalization, these texts imply, grant too strong and unequivocal a presence to European imperialism when they describe the historical development of contemporary international political systems.

Although these novels turn to the precolonial era to complicate recent accounts of transnational exchange, neither text finds much comfort in East Africa's multicultural history. Gurnah and Vassanji are both strong critics of imperialism in its various forms, yet they steadfastly refuse to romanticize precolonial Swahili culture. Similar to *Things Fall Apart*, the only African novel with which many undergraduate students may be familiar, the narratives of Gurnah and Vassanji reach back to a time before European rule. Unlike Chinua Achebe's classic text, however, their novels continually emphasize the polyglot nature of East Africa before and during the imposition of colonialism. These writers do not gesture toward a racially or culturally uniform society—in fact, they go out of their way to illustrate the inherent hybridity of Swahili culture.

More important, perhaps, is that these novels alert us to the fact that Euroimperialism was not a unitary force: it applied power differentially, often exploiting and exacerbating local economic, ethnic, religious, and cultural differences. Refusing to homogenize African or colonial forms of subjectivity, they offer strong critiques of imperialism while categorically rejecting nationalist models of cultural production that celebrate the past as an imaginative form of resistance. As such, these novels also go far beyond the colonizer/colonized dichotomy, a pedagogical paradigm that tends to homogenize the study of African fiction. This realization permits us, however provisionally, to interrogate the concept of *the* African novel while teaching a course bearing that very name. The project of imaging an African literary tradition is itself a fraught endeavor, marked by debates about the status of regional history, imperialism, and even globalization.

Trading Culture

Gurnah's *Paradise* depicts the changes in Swahili culture just as the Germans began to stamp their political and economic authority on the colony of Tanganyika. Like *Things Fall Apart*, Gurnah's novel fictionally records the decline of indigenous cultural institutions during early confrontations with European rule. The novel's young protagonist, Yusuf—an allusion to the Qur'anic and biblical figure of Yusuf/Joseph—travels several hundred miles from the coast to the interior of the continent as part of a caravan organized by his "uncle" Aziz, a wealthy and unscrupulous merchant.

Such trading caravans were the foundation of East Africa's robust commercial culture throughout the nineteenth century, fully operational long before the imposition of Euroimperial control. On foot, along well-established routes, caravans of dozens of men—the largest numbered well over one hundred—would travel deep into the interior over the course of several months, ranging as far as the Great Lakes region and the Congo. The fictional caravan in *Paradise*, numbering nearly fifty men, is not as grand as the expeditions of yore, but it is still an impressive sight, replete with musicians, storytellers, guides, cooks, porters, guards, and overseers. Staples of commerce included beads, mirrors, wire, textiles, agricultural implements, and guns. Ivory, skins, and slaves were the main objects sought by Swahili merchants; these were transported back to the coast for trade with Zanzibar, the Middle East, India, and Europe. Such ventures involved a high degree of uncertainty—caravans were exposed to various environmental dangers, bandits, avaricious competitors, and the unpredictability of trade itself—but successful journeys could be immensely profitable. Workers were willing to absorb some of the risk because they were normally vested in the journey, paid with a share of the proceeds rather than with a fixed wage.

As the work of both Abdul Sheriff and Andre Gunder Frank suggests, this caravan trade, gradually destroyed by the arrival of German and British imperialism in East Africa, was only one specialized branch of an incredibly complex system of commercial exchange throughout the Indian Ocean region. Reliable monsoon winds made trade possible between Africa, the Middle East, the west coast of India, and beyond. Large dhows, Arab sailing vessels, plied these waters for centuries, and there is evidence of trade with India and even China going back over a millennium (Chami). Zanzibar, one of the world's wealthiest cities in the nineteenth century, was the commercial and cultural hub of Indian Ocean trading networks. The islands of Zanzibar and Pemba, otherwise known as the Spice Islands, were home to extremely profitable plantations specializing in clove, cinnamon, pepper, and cardamom production. Such plantations, worked largely by slaves, were owned predominantly by descendants of an Omani aristocracy (Zanzibar was even the capital of the Omani sultanate for a time in the mid-1800s). By the latter part of the nineteenth century, Zanzibar had the largest slave market in the world; some slaves were exported to the Middle East and occasionally to India, illegally, but the vast majority remained in Zanzibar and Pemba to work in agriculture.

Vassanji's novels, especially *The Gunny Sack* and *The In-Between World of Vikram Lall*, describe how migrants from South Asia flocked to East Africa, fabled for its wealth, throughout the nineteenth and early twentieth centuries. Many Indians came to escape British imperialism, caste differences, or familial and communal conflicts. Initially, Asians played a crucial part in developing the region's commercial identity. Many opened shops or worked as small merchants, while the wealthiest supplied credit to Omani planters and Swahili caravans (in *Paradise*, Aziz's large expedition is heavily mortgaged to Indian financiers). Mobilizing vast, intercontinental social networks to facilitate trade, many Indians brought financial acumen to East Africa. Later, when the British established control over Zanzibar, Kenya, and Uganda (and eventually Tanganyika), Indians came as indentured laborers, brought to build East Africa's railways. Vassanji repeatedly emphasizes the heterogeneity of the Asians who settled throughout East Africa. They were a mix of Muslims, Hindus, and Sikhs, speaking a variety of languages and dialects; vast differences in wealth and status divided the Asian population further. Some profited by and were sympathetic to imperial governance; many were ambivalent; and still others were actively hostile, working alongside indigenous Africans in efforts to end European dominance. South Asians and Omanis, of course, were not the only immigrants to come to East Africa during this period: flourishing trade brought Greeks, Turks, Lebanese, Syrians, Persians, and other Europeans and Africans.

In *Paradise*, the daunting shadow of European rule looms progressively longer as the narrative develops. Yusuf first learns the life of trade and travel in the service of Aziz (like the biblical-Qur'anic Yusuf, he is pawned by relatives into slavery). As one of his patron's caravan leaders explains, commerce is the foundation of Swahili society:

> We go to the driest deserts and the darkest forests, and care nothing whether we trade with a king or a savage, or whether we live or die. . . . You'll see some of the places we pass, where people have not yet been brought to life by trade, and live like paralyzed insects. There are no people more clever than traders, no calling more noble. It is what gives us life. (119)

In this account, at least, commerce gives Swahili culture purpose, autonomy, and structure. As their European counterparts who engaged in civilizing missions, these coastal traders believe that their way of doing business brings vitality, enlightenment, and even a sort of crude democracy to the backward interior: traders recognize no essential difference between kings and savages. But the days of the great caravans, Aziz explains to Yusuf, are drawing rapidly to a close: the Germans, building a railway all the way to the lakes, will soon make the trading routes obsolete. Moreover, Europeans conspire to restrict and control commerce wherever they go: the

Belgians are closing up the Congolese border to itinerant traders; the British, who control Zanzibar, have abolished the slave trade; the Germans, wanting the best land for cultivation, confiscate Omani plantations and expel their owners from the colony; while all the Europeans establish punitive systems of taxation on commercial activity (130–33). By the end of the novel, a confused Yusuf, denied the chance to join further expeditions and weary of his life of servitude in Aziz's household, submits himself to a platoon of German soldiers looking for local conscripts, trading one form of oppression for another.

The Gunny Sack takes up the themes of travel and trade by fictionally recording four generations of a South Asian family. The narrator's great-grandfather comes to East Africa in the 1880s; the itinerant family moves throughout the region for the next eight decades. The text self-consciously reflects the region's multicultural history. The narrator's grandfather comes from a mixed union; he is the son of an African concubine given to the narrator's great-grandfather. The narrator himself, in the exuberant wake of Tanzanian independence, falls in love with a black African woman, a relationship doomed from the start. The novel's working language is English, but the text is peppered with fragments of Swahili, Cutchi, Gujarati, and Arabic.

As far as these novels are concerned, the basic principles of globalization—sophisticated patterns of intercontinental economic and cultural traffic—are hardly new to East Africa, and they most certainly are not the result of European rule in the area. The material building blocks of globalization, the existence of a multicultural society and extensive transnational trading networks, were in place long before the establishment of Euroimperialism. If anything, it was Europeans who learned something about global commerce from their colonial subjects around the Indian Ocean.

In general, both British and German imperialists were more interested in straightforward extraction than in existing forms of free trade, the central premise of economic globalization. The Germans, more or less uninterested in the caravan trade, consistently attempted to lure (or force) porters away from their mobile occupations and set them to work on coastal plantations for cash wages (Illiffe; Sunseri). The British, who used banning the slave trade as a pretext for assuming control of Zanzibar, were slow to exploit the region's commercial potential. Sheriff argues that the British effectively learned the principles of ivory and spice trading from South Asian merchants, but they were frustrated in their attempts to trade with East Africa directly, forced to rely instead on the less direct Zanzibar-Bombay-London route (90–91). Both novels reflect European indifference to the Indian Ocean commerce by representing the precolonial era as the high point of the area's immersion in a multinational trading culture.

This special literary interest in East Africa's polyglot character can be read as a subtle criticism of the tendency to imagine globalization as either fundamentally new or the product of Euroimperialist exploration, conquest, and rule. Steeped in regional history, these novels complicate the idea that European imperialists were the first to bring the techniques of global trade—or international forms of political domination—to East Africa and elsewhere. Beyond this, however, these novels contest historical narratives that read imperialism as the main precursor of the contemporary world order. If East Africa is now or in the process of becoming part of this new international system, we should not unilaterally install European imperialism as the first stage of this ineluctable process. Such texts imagine East Africa as an important site of—not just a place subject to—globalization at work.

Instead of conceding the academic discourse about globalization to European and American intellectuals, these novels suggest that East Africans have a stake in debates over the past, present, and future of transnational systems of exchange. Teachers of African fiction, and postcolonial scholars more generally, should not be too quick to grant European imperialism pride of place in stories about how globalization came to be. If anything, Euroimperialism absorbed, redirected, and then destroyed the Indian Ocean trading routes of the nineteenth century. Suppressing or not acknowledging this history might even be described as a quasi-imperialist act: perhaps globalization is not as different from its predecessor as both its proponents and critics would like to believe. At the very least, such historical assumptions give Euroimperialism an epistemological and hermeneutic power that it may not have achieved on its own terms. As many postcolonial theorists emphasize, Euroimperialism was constrained by its own hesitations, ambivalences, and limitations. When we retroactively read imperialism as a coherent form of political domination, we may be downplaying some its internal contradictions, many of which undoubtedly contributed to its dissolution. While globalization theory sometimes glosses over the fine details of imperialism, the best postcolonial histories leave room for the many inconsistencies and ambivalences that shaped imperial applications of power.

Literature without Borders

In contrast to *Things Fall Apart* and many nationalist African novels, both *Paradise* and *The Gunny Sack* emphasize the heterogeneity of East Africa on the eve of European colonialism. This is not to say that they present precolonial East African culture as idyllic, peaceful, and equitable. Both novelists show the various points of tension and inequality that were engrained in this way of life; they systematically refuse tropes of nostalgia and mourning for a golden age irretrievably destroyed by imperialism. Published more recently, these novels respond to a very different cultural moment: they neither capture rising anticolonial sentiment nor respond to the rush of enthusiasm generated by the newly independent postcolonial nation. Instead, they reflect growing concerns with the current condition of East Africa. They are highly critical of European imperialism, yet they also suggest that opposition to imperialism does not necessarily produce an equitable postcolonial society.

Paradise is quite ambivalent about the region's historical legacy. Yusuf's life mirrors many of East Africa's political tensions during the transition to colonial rule. At the age of twelve, he becomes an object of commercial exchange between his feckless father and the crafty Aziz; he learns that his father cleared his debts to the merchant by offering up his son. This painful realization is intertwined with the history of Swahili trading culture. In the novel's unlikely closing scene, Yusuf takes charge of his own life by volunteering for the German army. German imperialism, of course, is not depicted in a favorable light in the novel, but then neither is the system of labor and exchange it comes to replace. The novel thus stands at odds with many narratives that use the bildungsroman to announce the triumphant (or disappointing) establishment of the postcolonial nation-state. Neither Swahili trading culture nor Euroimperialism represents a desirable prospect in this rather pessimistic account. In Gurnah's later work, novels such as *Admiring Silence* and *By the Sea*, the postcolonial nation-state also becomes an instrument of oppression. Resisting, escaping, or overcoming imperialist domination guarantees neither political liberty nor personal autonomy.

Similarly, *The Gunny Sack* emphasizes the many sources of friction among European, South Asian, and various indigenous communities in East Africa. The novel's Asian characters often find themselves caught in the midst of competing interests. The novel repeatedly criticizes Asians for their patronizing, sometimes overtly racist attitudes toward black Africans. Though most of the community members maintain a scrupulous social distance from their non-Asian compatriots—acknowledging black ancestry, for example, comes with the risk of instantaneous ostracism—the narrator improbably decides to name himself after his "renegade half-caste ancestor," his mixed-race grandfather (108). He also criticizes Asians for collaboration with British authorities and their reluctance to put down firm roots in and commit to the future of East Africa, especially during the self-governance movement. As the narrator reports in a chatty aside:

> Among the trading immigrant peoples, loyalty to a land or a government, always loudly professed, is a trait one can normally look for in vain. Governments may come and go, but the immigrants' only concern is the security of their families, their trade and savings. (52)

Many families depended on an exceptional degree of mobility—in *The Gunny Sack*, the family seems to move every couple of chapters—yet this flexibility becomes a curse, especially when Asians get caught in the crosshairs of imperialism and independence movements.

These various refusals of nostalgia and invocations of a tense multicultural society complicate any neat, unequivocal distinction between imperialist oppressors and colonial subjects. The overarching message is that personal opposition to European imperialism does not automatically translate into belonging in the postcolonial nation. And because both writers belong to a minority group—Vassanji is of South Asian descent, while Gurnah is a Zanzibari Arab—most critical treatments of these texts hinge on the difficulty of placing their work in national literary traditions. Simon Lewis and Rosemary Marangoly George both argue that Vassanji and Gurnah belong to the emerging genre of immigrant literature, not fitting easily into any other category. That they repeatedly use the figure of the refugee or immigrant is telling: the history of East Africa is filled with arrivals, departures, and expulsions. Both novelists, moreover, are highly critical of their own communities. Lewis claims that such texts "complicate the assumption that being a colonized native of a place implies a sense of national belonging in the postcolonial state" (218), while George provocatively insists that the work of writers like Vassanji "*unwrites* nation and national projects" (186). Being an opponent of imperialism, they imply, does not guarantee citizenship in the postemancipation nation. As these readings make clear, such novels are the product of a global, diasporic, even postnational imaginary, maintaining at best an ambivalent relation with the nation at large. Although Vassanji and Gurnah are deeply invested in the history of East Africa, they are less sanguine about the present and future of East Africa.

Skepticism about the viability of the postcolonial nation-state puts these novelists outside the boundaries of nationalist literary paradigms. As May Joseph argues, the early days of independence saw the state asking Tanzanian Asians to "perform citizenship" through ritualized public displays in order to demonstrate their loyalty to the nation, an affiliation always under suspicion. Yet she also notes that the relation between the modern state and such minorities inevitably "transpires through transnational networks." The existence of visible minority communities tends to "interrupt the coherence of the state and the privileging of national boundaries" (154).

The work of Gurnah and Vassanji is therefore global in two very different senses. Both writers call attention to East Africa's precolonial history as a site of international exchange, and they foreground the ramifications of that history on contemporary patterns of cultural traffic. By highlighting the travails of East Africa's minority groups—especially minorities who were in a position of relative power before or during the colonial period—Gurnah and Vassanji challenge any simple theoretical dichotomy between colonizer and colonized, foreign imperialist and African subject. This challenge does not mean, however, that such novels can be easily dismissed as the product of elite cosmopolitan writers who are politically disengaged from and contemptuous of the plight of East Africa. Gurnah and Vassanji, now residents of England and Canada, respectively, are very much the product of our global world and a diasporic imagination, yet they have an abiding interest in their place of origin. Their regular fictional returns to East Africa force readers to confront the particularity of the region, especially its cultural diversity.

In this respect, it is difficult to label these writers African, nationalist, or global. Their work clearly falls beyond the scope of pan-African or negritude movements. Nor can one call their texts, premised as they are on global migration, nationalist in even a loose sense of the term. By contrast, it could be argued that many of the continent's most influential writers, including Achebe and Ngũgĩ wa Thiong'o, have relied extensively, at different points in their careers, on nationalist models to address problems of political emancipation and cultural autonomy from Europe. Gurnah's and Vassanji's writings are also quite different from the typical postcolonial novel of disillusionment—texts such as *The Interpreters*, by Wole Soyinka;

The Beautyful Ones Are Not Yet Born, by Ayi Kwei Armah; and *Flowers and Shadows*, by Ben Okri spring to mind—because the source of discontent goes well beyond corrupt national elites or undemocratic regimes. Moreover, neither Gurnah nor Vassanji finds solace in a smaller, disaffected minority group: both writers begin and end with strong criticism of East Africa's minority communities. Yet fitting them under rubrics like global, diasporic, or postnational elides their specific investment in East African history and culture. Placing such texts in a geographically or culturally indeterminate space, such as the global, mitigates the sense of regional specificity and historical awareness with which they approach the problems of belonging and difference.

Together, these three tendencies—Gurnah's and Vassanji's nonconformity with national models of literary production, their insistent unsettling of the colonizer/colonized dichotomy, and their continuing interest in minority communities—combine to raise questions about the catchall category of African fiction. Both novelists, working with themes of dissidence and exile, are deeply invested in the project of redefining the relation between fiction and African history, yet neither slots comfortably into the schemata of courses bearing a generic title. Their narratives remind us that ideas about African culture and African literature—vague yet still operational in our globalized world—may themselves be holdovers from the imperialist moment, when the political boundaries of the continent could be determined willy-nilly around a conference table in Europe, when the geographic and cultural specificity of Africa was hardly a concern for its would-be rulers. The broad category of Africa, when applied to the study of literature, tends to conceal more than it reveals. It is a category that continues to organize our syllabi and even governs the way we think about the canon and curricular issues in this supposedly global, postimperial moment, but it is clearly a relic from the imperial age.

Raising the issue of labels, classifications, and literary categories has important epistemological consequences for courses on the African novel—in fact, for courses on national or regional literatures of any variety, including British and American. By reading postcolonial historiography as a contested intellectual practice, these novels encourage students and teachers to replace the blanket categories of African fiction or African culture with a more regionally specific, theoretically rigorous set of concepts. They promote, in other words, attentiveness to particularity and may frustrate readers who expect to find affinities with other African writers, especially those who organize their texts around the problem of the nation. This articulation of regional specificity effectively pulls at the seams of African fiction syllabi; it directly affects the way we discuss the value of minor literatures in a North American pedagogical context.

My observations are not a plea to disband courses on African fiction any more than their British or American counterparts. Instead, by introducing debates about historiography, regional specificity, and globalization to the study of the African novel, I suggest that students can begin to consider the way access to knowledge is situated, mediated, and regulated by a host of global factors. When we study African fiction, we study not only a collection of individual texts but also how the concept of African culture gets mobilized in the broader field of literary studies. The idea of African literature is the product not simply of a neutral, abstract, disembodied African culture but also of academic institutions and the global market for letters. A recent special issue of *PMLA* on globalization provides an interesting example of how many scholars approach the question of teaching minor literatures from around the world. Most of its articles, with one notable exception, broadly encourage faculty members to teach more texts of non-Western provenance.[2] This goal is all well and good, but students should also be aware of how North American academic institutions work firmly within—and help to create—a global literary marketplace. Continually introducing more minor literatures *as* minor literatures may have the paradoxical effect of reinforcing the hierarchies that already exist, even the hierarchies that such strategies were designed to challenge or disrupt.

The basic premise of opening up an impoverished, little-known corner of the world through the study of fictional texts—an important way that globalization discourse has been incorporated into literary theory—necessarily positions readers at the center of a self-important critical apparatus, one that too easily reinforces and repositions problematic distinctions between center and periphery. Some of this exoticizing tendency is perhaps unavoidable in many academic situations, but instructors can at least seize the chance to initiate discussions about the techniques and assumptions of the field as a whole. When students take a course about African fiction, it presents an opportunity to read texts by a variety of African writers from many distinct regions, but it also allows teachers to introduce questions about how the study of literature in the North American academy is organized. And because such courses are typically upper-division and elective, they may allow students to consider the contours of the entire discipline from a fairly informed perspective. Enabling students to challenge or defend the requirements of their subject is a worthwhile endeavor in any setting, but such enabling seems particularly urgent in a class on the African novel, which tends to promise the study of marginality at many different levels. Introducing discussions about globalization into the classroom should encourage us to do more than expand the types of courses we offer: it should allow us to consider the relation between academic knowledge production and the global market for cultural products.

Including conversations about globalization during a course on African fiction can be a productive way to stage debates about the academic status of different literary traditions. As the examples of Gurnah and Vassanji demonstrate, East African writers are participating directly in discussions about the history of globalization as well as about the organization of literary studies. Beyond questioning the historical premises of globalization theory, these novels also foreground the presence of minority communities in East Africa. This special emphasis on marginality calls attention to the limitations inherent in pedagogical terms such as *African fiction*. Labels of this variety promise a form of marginality at the expense of intellectual particularity. It may be impossible to escape the use of such regional categories and terms altogether, but encouraging students to consider how they function within the parameters of the discipline can be productive. Teachers of African fiction are uniquely positioned to make their students aware of this dilemma.

Notes

1. Michael Hardt and Antonio Negri make precisely this critique of postcolonial studies. Contemporary forms of sovereignty, embedded in the workings of global capital, refuse to respect long-standing distinctions between imperial center and colonial periphery or between metropolitan and subaltern subjects, distinctions that are staples of postcolonial criticism. Still relying on such defunct categories, postcolonial theorists typically espouse a "very confused view" of international politics, remaining "fixated on attacking an old form of power" and consequently proposing strategies of liberation "that could be effective only on that old terrain" (146).

2. See *Globalizing*. Ian Baucom criticizes the idea that globalization in literary studies means teaching more minor literature. By implication, his article criticizes nearly every other essay in the issue. As he points out, sometimes "expansion

contracts" (160): when those of us in the North American academy call for teaching ever more minor literatures, it can have the paradoxical effect of consolidating power to judge literary merit and pedagogical utility. See also Amoko.

Works Cited

Achebe, Chinua. *Things Fall Apart.* Oxford: Heinemann, 1996. Print.

Amoko, Apollo. "*PMLA* and the Limits of 'Anglo-American' Literary Globalism." MLA Annual Convention. Sheraton New York Hotel and Towers. 29 Dec. 2002. Address.

Appadurai, Arjun. *Modernity at Large: Cultural Dimensions of Globalization.* Minneapolis: U of Minnesota P, 1996. Print.

Armah, Ayi Kwei. *The Beautyful Ones Are Not Yet Born.* London: Heinemann, 1969. Print.

Baucom, Ian. "Globalit, Inc.; or, The Cultural Logic of Global Literary Studies." *Globalizing* 158–72.

Castells, Manuel. *The Rise of Network Society.* Cambridge: Blackwell, 1996. Print.

Chami, Felix. "People and Contacts in the Ancient Western Indian Ocean Seaboard or Azania." *Man and Environment* 27 (2002): 33–44. Print.

Frank, Andre Gunder. *ReOrient: Global Economy in the Asian Age.* Berkeley: U of California P, 1998. Print.

George, Rosemary Marangoly. *The Politics of Home: Postcolonial Relocations and Twentieth-Century Fiction.* Berkeley: U of California P, 1999. Print.

Giddens, Anthony. *The Consequences of Modernity.* Stanford: Stanford UP, 1990. Print.

Globalizing Literary Studies. Spec. issue of *PMLA* 116.1 (2001): 16–188. Print.

Gurnah, Abdulrazak. *Admiring Silence.* New York: New, 1996. Print.

———. *By the Sea.* New York: New, 2001. Print.

———. *Paradise.* New York: New, 1994. Print.

Hardt, Michael, and Antonio Negri. *Empire.* Cambridge: Harvard UP, 2000. Print.

Illiffe, John. *A Modern History of Tanganyika.* Cambridge: Cambridge UP, 1979. Print.

Joseph, May. *Nomadic Identities: The Performance of Citizenship.* Minneapolis: U of Minnesota P, 1999. Print.

King, Anthony. *Global Cities: Post-imperialism and the Internationalization of London.* London: Routledge, 1990. Print.

Lewis, Simon. "'Impossible Domestic Situations': Questions of Identity and Nationalism in the Novels of Abdulrazak Gurnah and M. G. Vassanji." *Thamyris: Mythmaking from Past to Present* 6 (1999): 215–29. Print.

Okri, Ben. *Flowers and Shadows.* Harlow: Longman, 1989. Print.

Sassen, Saskia. *Losing Control? Sovereignty in an Age of Globalization.* New York: Columbia UP, 1996. Print.

Sheriff, Abdul. *Slaves, Spices, and Ivory in Zanzibar: Integration of an East African Commercial Empire into the World Economy.* Athens: Ohio UP, 1987. Print.

Soyinka, Wole. *The Interpreters.* London: Heinemann, 1970. Print.
Sunseri, Thaddeus. *Vilimani: Labor Migration and Rural Change in Early Colonial Tanzania.* Portsmouth: Heinemann, 2002. Print.
Vassanji, M. G. *The Gunny Sack.* Oxford: Heinemann, 1989. Print.
———. *The In-Between World of Vikram Lall.* New York: Knopf, 2004. Print.

Part III

Pedagogical and Institutional Contexts

S. Shankar

The African Novel in a Course on the Twentieth-Century Novel in English

The sub-Saharan African novel is one of the most important—and instructive—literary innovations of the twentieth century. Largely, but not exclusively, written in English and French, this genre represents a startlingly diverse and original response to the challenges of writing in a literary context multiply fractured in readership, publishing venues, influences, and critical reception. Throughout the twentieth century, but especially from the 1950s onward, African novelists have struggled to adapt the dominant conventions of the novel genre as inherited from European sources to their particular writing situation. Surely the most widely discussed example of such innovation is Chinua Achebe's *Things Fall Apart*. But a similar struggle is to be observed in a variety of other extraordinary works, such as Achebe's *A Man of the People*, Ngũgĩ wa Thiong'o's *Petals of Blood*, Buchi Emecheta's *Joys of Motherhood*, and Nadine Gordimer's *July's People*.

That these struggles of African novelists are instructive not only to students of African literature but also to students of the novel in general is demonstrated by an upper-division course I teach entitled The Twentieth-Century Novel in English. The course is restricted to anglophone writing, but the lessons to be drawn from it are not. I place African novelists such as those mentioned above alongside William Faulkner, Joseph Conrad, Robert Graves, Anita Desai, R. K. Narayan, E. M. Forster, Toni Morrison, Jamaica Kincaid, and others. The main purpose of the course is to introduce students to the way literature in English grows to a global phenomenon during the twentieth century. Yet in teaching the course, I also emphasize the variety of ways in which novelists not only contribute to this globalizing tendency but also resist it by a deliberate accommodation and articulation of opposing vernacular impulses in their works.[1]

At its best, the sub-Saharan African novel is an especially effective response to the globalizing-antiglobalizing tension, which requires it to bend and extend the conventions of the novel genre. In a course on the anglophone twentieth-century novel in general, one contribution it makes is how, in so doing, it throws into critical relief the possibilities as well as limitations of the novel. Thus it can play a crucial pedagogical role in posing otherwise underarticulated questions to the genre—regarding the politics of language, the ideological content of point of view, the opposition of the aesthetic to the ethnographic in discussions of the novel.

English and the African Novel in English

In the introductory chapter of his influential work *Aspects of the Novel*, E. M. Forster takes up briefly the question of English, for, despite his title, he means really to confine his study to the novel in English. He observes:

> "English" we shall of course interpret as written in English, not as published south of the Tweed or east of the Atlantic, or north of the Equator: we need not attend to geographical accidents, they can be left to the politicians. (3)

In the course of his work, Forster does discuss Herman Melville's *Moby-Dick* but otherwise confines himself to British literature. Thus, despite the apparent catholicity of his initial understanding of *English*, he is able quickly to pass on to "more important" matters, such as that of periodization, and thence return to an understanding of the novel in English as part of a more or less conventionally regarded "English literature" (5). It is true that he did not have the many well-known examples of "postcolonial" fiction in English to work with that we have now, though given his association with India, it might not have been too much to expect that he be aware of the novels written in English in Bengal toward the end of the nineteenth century (see Iyengar 314–15; Mukherjee, *Twice-Born Fiction* and *Perishable Empire*). His expansive understanding of English, then, is undermined by the narrowness of the tradition to which he ultimately lays such easy claim.

Only a few decades later the matter of language is altogether more complicated, altogether more political, for an anglophone writer from Africa like Achebe. Achebe's conflicted relation to the language in which he writes—and therefore also to the tradition that is carried by the language—is evident in his essay "The African Writer and the English Language," where he suggests that the African writer in English should "aim at fashioning out an English which is at once universal and able to carry his peculiar experience" (100). The objective is to use the English language because of its versatility and its status as a global language, while accommodating it to the particularities of African experience. The African writer in English, Achebe suggests, should not hesitate to make a sacrificial offering of English in the pursuit of his own ends (100–01). The balance Achebe wishes to maintain—between the utility of English as a received language for cross-cultural communication and its transformation into an Africanized medium—may be regarded as an attempt to weigh the claims of the transnational against those of the vernacular. Earlier in the essay, he notes the role of English as national language in Africa: "If you take Nigeria as an example, the national literature, as I see it, is the literature written in English; and the ethnic literatures are in Hausa, Ibo, Yoruba, Efik, Edo, Ijaw, etc., etc." (93). The African writer writing in English, then, has the obligation to extend the resources of English in multiple directions, even if this extension requires the sacrifice, to return to Achebe's telling simile, of the language itself.

Achebe's approach to the English language is not dissimilar to that of R. K. Narayan, an Indian writer in English who once noted on behalf of his kind of writer:

> English has proved that if a language has flexibility any experience can be communicated through it, even if it has to be paraphrased rather than conveyed, and even if the factual detail . . . is only partially understood. . . . We are still experimentalists. I may straightway explain what we do not attempt to do. We are not attempting to write Anglo-Saxon English. . . . (23)

The anxieties of this passage are similar to those of Achebe: they are those of an author writing in a multilingual context where the role of English is itself contested. Like Achebe, Narayan identifies what he considers the great suppleness of English as a literary language, even as he acknowledges its limitations—sometimes paraphrase is necessary and sometimes there can be only partial understanding of factual details. Despite these limitations, he finds the language adequate to his purpose, because he says, "We are still experimentalists." His manner of expression is less extravagant than Achebe's, but the implications are the same: we will use English, but it will be an English transformed; if necessary, sacrificed.

In the African literary context, even Achebe's qualified advocacy of English as a literary language has been challenged by writers like Ngũgĩ wa Thiong'o. Framing the question of language in a sociohistorical context, Ngũgĩ noted in *Decolonising the Mind*:

> The literature it [the petite bourgeoisie] produced in European languages was given the identity of African literature as if there had never been literature in African languages. Yet by avoiding a real confrontation with the language issue, it was clearly wearing false robes of identity: it was a pretender to the throne of the mainstream of African literature. (22)

He went on to assert, "African literature can only be written in African languages, that is, the languages of the African peasantry and working class" (27).

Internationalism, nationalism, ethnicity, class: even this brief review of the interventions made by Achebe and Ngũgĩ in the debate over the status of English as a medium for African fiction (for the list of literary figures making such interventions is much longer) is refracted through all these categories.[2] Thus, in the classroom, it becomes one of the sites around which pedagogical questions can be raised regarding these very categories as they relate to the twentieth-century novel in English. Clearly, Forster's relation to English is not the same as that of Achebe's or, certainly, Ngũgĩ's. Forster's *Passage to India* and Achebe's *Things Fall Apart* may both be about the colonial encounter (albeit in different locations) but, whatever the merits of Forster's depiction of this encounter, in the classroom the contrasts between the two texts can become an occasion to explore the linguistic medium in which the anglophone novel is written. An African example can draw attention to the question of the language in which the twentieth-century novel in English is written.

The particular ways in which such attention is drawn are diverse. In *A Man of the People*, for example, Achebe repeatedly makes various characters speak in pidgin, leaving the passage "untranslated" for the uninitiated reader. The worldly Chief Nanga, discussing women, says at one point, "Any person wey tell you say woman no get sense just de talk pure jargon. When woman no want do something e go lef am, but make you no fool yourself say e left the thing because e no get sense for do am" (61). "How true," the young narrator, Odili, thinks to himself in response. It is an important moment for Odili as he is initiated into the ways of the world by Chief Nanga. In the United States classroom, most students are unable to gloss this passage to their satisfaction. But these moments of incomprehension and frustration become occasions to consider why Achebe might have chosen to insert such passages into a novel in English. What is he conveying about himself as an anglophone novelist through such passages? What relationship to his transnational readers is he signaling here?

Achebe's famous Africanization of English through the importation of African proverbs and idioms in *Things Fall Apart* (examples of which might be shared with the students through photocopied passages) can reveal to students the ways in which African writers denaturalize the English language. At its most successful, such denaturalization makes it possible to go back to novels like *A Passage to India* and ask fresh questions of it. It becomes pertinent to ask in what ways passages such as the dialogue among Aziz, Hamidullah, and Mahmoud Ali in chapter 2 of *A Passage to India* or the presentation of the thoughts of the devoutly Hindu Narayan Godbole in the final section of the novel strive to capture a cultural location foreign to the English language as Forster uses it. And if there is not in Forster the kind of sacrifice of language that Achebe writes of, how does that lack affect his representation of the consciousness of Aziz and his fellow Indians?

Ideology and Point of View

In the classroom, Gordimer's South African novel *July's People* (written in 1981, that is, before the actual fall of apartheid) makes possible other kinds of denaturalization. The novel examines apartheid through the mechanism of a reversal. It depicts the relationship between a white "madam" and her black "boy" in a fictional future South Africa in the midst of a revolutionary situation. The flight of Bam Smales and Maureen

Smales with their children from their urban home to the village of their servant July places them, for the first time, in a role subservient to their black servant. Suddenly their liberal ideas are put to the test. In the isolation of July's village, July as well as Bam and especially Maureen, whose story this really is, confronts the implications of a reversal of roles.

July's People challenges through this mechanism of reversal the natural association of power or ability to rule with the white race. As the days pass in July's village, it becomes increasingly clear that Bam and Maureen's assumed superiority in prerevolutionary South Africa was grounded largely on their greater knowledge of the cultural codes they lived by. Confronted with the alien cultural codes of July's world, their helplessness becomes apparent. Most tellingly, they are unable to recognize the true sources of power in the village, mistaking the headman for the chief (111–12).

The reversal of roles in the novel is the plausible result of the Smales' displacement into a society of which they know virtually nothing, in a time when their own center of authority has been undercut by the revolutionary situation. July himself is hardly a revolutionary. Maureen finds herself challenged not so much by him as by her realization that he has an independent existence that she knew nothing about. The novel traces her journey from that moment at the beginning of the novel when "July broke into snickering embarrassment at her ignorance of a kind of authority not understood—his" (3) to the moment at the end of the novel when July disclaims responsibility for Daniel's taking the gun and speaks to her in his own language—the question of language again!—and we are told, "She understood although she knew no word" (152). What she has understood now and did not understand before is precisely that authority of his, an authority grounded in his own culture, society, and language.

In bringing Maureen—and the reader—to this realization, Gordimer exploits one of the most versatile resources available to the novelist: point of view. Although the protagonist is Maureen and it is her transformation that is mostly told, the point of view in the novel is not confined to her. In various sections, the narrative is presented from the point of view of other characters—Bam, July, July's wife. When the novel adopts the perspective of July or his wife, alternatives to Maureen's white liberalism are uncovered. A different world, with its own cultural and social codes, stands revealed through this shift, and consequently Maureen's own world and values are placed under interrogation.

While any novel can make use of shifts in point of view to explore versions of reality (as Faulkner did so famously in *The Sound and the Fury*), the exploitation of this particular resource in African novels like *July's People* is often much more easily legible as determined by history and politics—that is, it is closely linked to questions of power, race, and social control. Thus an opportunity is opened up in the classroom to push discussions of novelistic structure beyond questions of technique and into the realm of ideology. What sets of values does the concatenation of points of view convey in a novel? Through novels like *July's People*, the question becomes easier to pose in a class on the twentieth-century novel in English. In the process, the novel as a literary form is denaturalized again.

Art and Ethnography

In her critical work *The Black Interpreters*, Nadine Gordimer asserted:

> African writing is writing done in any language by Africans themselves and by others of whatever skin colour who share with Africans the experience of having been shaped, mentally and spiritually, by Africa rather than anywhere else in the world. One must look at the world *from* Africa, to be an African writer, not look *upon* Africa from the world. (5)

As a statement of critical intent, the passage is impeccable. In practice, however, African novels cannot always be said to fulfill the "requirement" articulated here. African novels in English are often written by writers not resident in Africa and published by European and American presses for readers the majority of whom are outside Africa. This transnational publishing situation can make it difficult for authors to maintain the stance of writing *from* Africa. A good illustration of what is at issue here is offered by Emecheta's novel *The Joys of Motherhood*.

The Joys of Motherhood is the account of Nnu Ego, an Igbo woman who sets out to make a place for herself in the world as a mother. She is convinced that it is only as a mother of male children that she will have the traditional respect and goodwill she craves. She spends a lifetime in the pursuit of this goal, in the process enduring enormous hardships piled on her both by her husband and by her children, only to wonder at the end whether it was all worth it. Emecheta's novel is historical in its narrative sweep if not in its narrative mode, starting early in the twentieth century, from before Nnu Ego's birth, and ending decades later with her death. Through the life of her unlikely protagonist, Emecheta presents the changes that Nigeria as well as Igbo society underwent through the decades. As Igboland and Nigeria change, Nnu Ego too is forced to change, though she remains, to her ultimate detriment, unable to give up her desire to find fulfillment as a wife and mother. In this fashion, Emecheta not only presents a novel of character but also explores through this specific mode of presentation both Nigeria's history during the twentieth century and marriage as an institution.

But knowledge of neither this history nor the institution of marriage as it exists in Igbo society is something that Emecheta can assume on the part of all her readers. In various passages, then, she is forced to adopt what can only be called an autoethnographic narrative mode: explaining one's cultural mores and customs to outsiders. Speaking of Nnu Ego's imposing father, Nwokocha Agbadi, for example, Emecheta writes:

> In his young days, a woman who gave in to a man without first fighting for her honour was never respected. To regard a woman who is quiet and timid as desirable was something that came after his time, with Christianity and other changes. (10)

In another passage on Agbadi, Emecheta writes:

> Nwokocha Agbadi was not only a chief but an important one, therefore the disclosure of his death would have to comply with certain cultural laws—there must be gun shots, and two or three goats must be slaughtered before the announcement. Anyone who started grieving before the official proclamation would be made to pay fines equivalent to three goats. (13–14)

And even more directly, during a key scene when Nnu Ego attempts suicide, the reader is told:

> However a thing like that is not permitted in Nigeria; you are simply not allowed to commit suicide in peace, because everyone is responsible for the other person. Foreigners may call us a nation of busybodies, but to us an individual's life belongs to the community and not just to him or her. So a person has no right to take it while another member of the community looks on. He must interfere, he must stop it happening. (60)

In each of these passages the narrative voice may position itself in Nigeria or in the Igbo community, but the audience being addressed is clearly outside. Why would an Igbo readership need the kind of elucidation of customs and history provided by the first two passages? In the third passage, the identification of an external audience is even clearer. The narrator identifies herself as Nigerian, but the mode of address indicates that readers who are not Nigerian are intended here. There is in the passage a sharing of cultural knowledge (about the nature of an "individual's life") and also a criticism of "foreigners" and their opinions, which might itself be a symptom of anxiety about the adequacy of the Africanness of the text.

It cannot always be assumed that the African novel in English is primarily speaking to Africa. Even as it sets out to speak *from* Africa, it may not find itself speaking *to* Africa. This is one of the chief complaints Ngũgĩ wa Thiong'o lodges against African literatures written in European languages. Like a great deal of contemporary African cinema, an African novel may find itself more widely distributed outside Africa than inside. So no matter what vantage point novelists choose to adopt in presenting the story, they must also negotiate the question of where the readers are mainly located. On the one hand, this necessity often requires an ethnographic or autoethnographic approach to narration, where certain kinds of cultural knowledge, routine to those raised in that culture, have to be described in some detail. On the other hand, a readership constructed as foreign may push the narrative voice to claim a specific ethnic or national identity as a way of insisting on the Africanness of the novel. The three passages from *The Joys of Motherhood* cited above illustrate this tension in the African novel in English—which is not to say that African novels in English in general are replete with such passages, for authors have a variety of different strategies to respond to the problem.

In the classroom, such passages from African novels in English open up questions of authorial vantage point and readerly location. How does the "from" in the Gordimer passage above relate to the "to"? If the "to" is outside Africa for all practical purposes, to what extent can the "from" remain unaffected? What kinds of editorial changes are imposed by the disjuncture between "from" and "to"? What kinds of transformations must the narrative voice undergo in an attempt to suture this disjuncture? Can it rigorously maintain the distinction between "from" and "upon" that Gordimer desires in attempting this suturing? Out of such questions flow others: How does the ethnographic content of such passages comport with notions of the novel as a work of art? Are such novels compromised as works of art because of such passages? Or must we revise our understanding of what a work of art is and how a novel becomes a work of art?

Once again, the special position of the African novel in English, where it is at once heir to a certain literary tradition and language and perforce a traitor to them, catalyzes a series of questions about the genre of the novel. The pedagogical utility of such a catalytic effect in an introductory class on the twentieth-century novel in English cannot be overstated.

At the beginning of the twentieth century, the novel in English was mainly a British and American phenomenon. At the end, arguably, some of the most exciting writing was coming from elsewhere—Africa, South Asia, the Caribbean. In this context, the African novel in English represents a vital literary development of the twentieth century. It is part of the cultural history of decolonization; it represents one of the ways in which the colonized wrested control over their own lives from their erstwhile masters. While the popularity the novel in English enjoyed during the nineteenth century in Britain and the United States was steadily eclipsed through the twentieth by the rise of mass media, the novel remained a cultural form of considerable prestige. Part of the reason for this continuing prestige was the extension of the novel's reach into other parts of the world. Thus it could be said that the cultural prestige of the novel in English was perpetuated by the contributions of writers like those discussed here, even as its influence was circumscribed by other developments.

In his essay "Why the Novel Matters," a defense of the novel early in the twentieth century, D. H. Lawrence called the novel "the book of life," suggesting through that phrase that the novel had a unique capacity to depict the changeable flow of the experiences of men and women alive, as opposed to men and women dead inside—that is, fixed and in thrall to received ideas (105). In a class on the twentieth-century novel in English, I have used this essay in conjunction with a novel like Lawrence's *Women in Love*, first, to ask the question if and in what ways the novel is a "book of life"; second, later in the semester, to ask the class to return to Lawrence's assertions about the novel during a discussion of Achebe's *A Man of the People.* This journey to Africa and back is facilitated by close readings of a passage each from the two novels.

In the first passage, early in *Women in Love*, Birkin, Gerald, and their companions are discussing an African sculpture Gerald finds ugly and Birkin defends as high art for the purity with which it abstracts what he regards as mindless sensuousness and physicality (81–82). The racialism of this passage is not hard to recognize for most students. However, when juxtaposed with Achebe's recourse to the example of African sculpture in *A Man of the People*, the discussion is pushed into even more complex and rewarding territory. In his passage, Achebe's intention is to challenge the notion that non-African readers can have easy access to African artistic realities; the false interpretations of the statue offered by a non-African viewer are satirized (50–51). By comparing the two metafictional passages in the two novels—passages in which the two novelists offer highly condensed and not at all facile ideas about art and, by extension, novels—we are able to open up the novel in English for discussion in radically new ways.

Lawrence believes that the novel matters, because through it, as a "book of life," "the whole of me shall tremble in its wholeness" ("Why" 105). The racialism and sanctioned ignorance of Africa through which the notions behind this theory of the novel are purchased are made clear by juxtaposition of the two passages. Further questions can be posed to students: In this light, what are we to make of Lawrence's assertion that the novel as "the book of life" is meant to set "the whole of me" trembling? What is "life" or "whole" or "me" here? And what do they have to do with race?

The processes that took the English language to the African colonies also brought the novel there. Neither the language nor the novel could remain untransformed in the process. The accommodation to African realities and lives necessitated the rethinking of many received ideas about the novel. This rethinking was neither systematic nor unanimous. Where Achebe demonstrated a desire to fashion certain kinds of remedies in his work, Ngũgĩ wa Thiong'o declared the very notion of writing novels in English a dead end. The rethinking of the novel in African contexts proceeded not only through the generation of numerous examples by the kinds of authors discussed above but also in lively critical debate surrounding the production of actual novels. In a class on the twentieth-century novel in English, the examples of African fiction can serve both to denaturalize the novel in general and to render visible the implicitly, and sometimes explicitly, ideological choices made by novelists everywhere.

I conclude by insisting that in a class such as the one described here an African novel be appreciated both on its own merits and in terms of its conversation with other African and postcolonial novels. I never teach an African novel by itself in such a class. If there is a Ngũgĩ, there will also be an Emecheta, in addition to a Narayan or a Kincaid. The African novel in English is pedagogically useful, because it turns canonical metropolitan novels like Forster's *A Passage to India* and Lawrence's *Women in Love* inside out, but this utility is not its only one, and the African novel should not be taught as if it were.

Notes

1. I explore these distinctions in greater detail in "Midnight's Orphans."

2. For other writers weighing in on this debate, see Wali; Chinweizu and Madubuike, especially 8–16; Bishop, especially chapter 2; and Onwuemene.

Works Cited

Achebe, Chinua. "The African Writer and the English Language." *Morning Yet on Creation Day.* New York: Anchor, 1975. 91–104. Print.

———. *A Man of the People.* New York: Anchor, 1967. Print.

———. *Things Fall Apart.* New York: Anchor, 1994. Print.

Bishop, Rand. *African Literature, African Critics: The Forming of Critical Standards, 1947–1966.* New York: Greenwood, 1988. Print.

Chinweizu, Onwuchekwa Jemie, and Ihechukwu Madubuike. *Toward the Decolonization of African Literature.* Washington: Howard UP, 1983. Print.

Emecheta, Buchi. *The Joys of Motherhood.* Oxford: Heinemann, 1994. Print.

Faulkner, William. *The Sound and the Fury.* New York: Vintage, 1990. Print.

Forster, E. M. *Aspects of the Novel.* London: Arnold, 1974. Print.

———. *A Passage to India.* New York: Harcourt, 1984. Print.

Gordimer, Nadine. *The Black Interpreters.* Johannesburg: Ravan, 1973. Print.

———. *July's People.* New York: Penguin, 1982. Print.

Iyengar, K. R. Srinivasa. *Indian Writing in English.* Rev. ed. New Delhi: Sterling, 1985. Print.

Lawrence, D. H. "Why the Novel Matters." *Selected Literary Criticism.* London: Heinemann, 1955. 102–07. Print.

———. *Women in Love.* New York: Bantam, 1996. Print.

Melville, Herman. *Moby-Dick.* New York: Columbia UP, 1998. Print.

Mukherjee, Meenakshi. *The Perishable Empire: Essays on Indian Writing in English.* New Delhi: Oxford UP, 2000. Print.

———. *The Twice-Born Fiction: Themes and Techniques of the Indian Novel in English.* New Delhi: Pencraft, 2005. Print.

Narayan, R. K. "English in India." *A Story-teller's World: Stories, Essays, Sketches.* New Delhi: Penguin, 1989. 20–23. Print.

Ngũgĩ wa Thiong'o. *Decolonising the Mind: The Politics of Language in African Literature.* London: Currey, 1986. Print.

———. *Petals of Blood.* New York: Dutton, 1978. Print.

Onwuemene, Michael C. "Limits of Transliteration: Nigerian Writers' Endeavors toward a National Literary Language." *PMLA* 114.5 (1999): 1055–66. Print.

Shankar, S. "Midnight's Orphans; or, A Postcolonialism Worth Its Name." *Cultural Critique* 56.1 (2004): 64–95. Print.

Wali, Obiajunwa. "The Dead End of African Literature?" *Transition* 10 (1963): 13–15. Print.

Mohamed Kamara

The Francophone African Novel in the French-Language Classroom

The history of francophone African literature dates back to the time before Africans started writing about themselves in French. Jonathan Ngate observes:

> By the time Francophone African writers came on the scene and started producing their own literature, theirs was, chronologically, only the second African literature in French, which is also a way of pointing out that the general context of Francophone African literature is not just Africa itself but also, and primarily, the long French tradition of literary and other discourses on Africa and Africans. (20)

It seems appropriate, then, that any suggestion of ways to teach the francophone African novel should be accompanied by a presentation of the major debates, issues, events, and discourses that have shaped its trajectory. What I seek to do in this essay, therefore, is to delineate briefly the historical, cultural, conceptual, and discursive contours of the francophone sub-Saharan novel, from its origins to its present,[1] while suggesting specific courses that highlight some aspects of its historiography and thematic evolution.

French colonization of sub-Saharan Africa started officially with the establishment of the town of Saint-Louis du Sénégal in 1659. However, before official colonies were established, the French, like other Europeans, had been in significant contact with Africans, mostly through the slave trade and the so-called legitimate trade that replaced it (Munro 42). As a result, Africa began to occupy a significant space in the European imaginary. In the nineteenth century, the image of the black African, which had already appeared in pre-Enlightenment French literature (see Masse), began taking more serious form in the works of Claire de Duras (*Ourika* [1823]), Victor Hugo (*Bug-Jargal* [1826]), and Prosper Mérimée (*Tamango* [1829]), among many others. *Ourika* is about a Senegalese girl who is brought to France to live in an aristocratic family whose members treat her like one of their own. She dies of a broken heart when she realizes that because of her skin color she cannot be with the one she loves. Both Hugo and Mérimée confront the question of slavery. Whereas Mérimée criticizes what he sees as the corruption and perfidy of Western civilization and the savagery of the black man, Hugo manages to portray interracial friendship and rivalry between a Frenchman and one of the leaders of the 1791 black slave revolt of San Domingo. By far one of the best, or worst, examples of this type of literature is Pierre Loti's *Le roman d'un spahi* (1881; "The Romance of a Spahi"). In Loti's novel, the representation of the black African as a gratuitous savage, sexually promiscuous, irrational being incapable of thought reached its paroxysmal zenith.

This *littérature exotique* was followed by the *littérature coloniale.* The colonial period, from the 1910s to the late 1930s, produced two kinds of novels: one written by non-Africans, the other by Africans. Whereas for Ngate the writers of this period were only "precursors of francophone African literature" (29), for Ngandu Nkashama, their works represented "la première étape de la littérature africaine proprement dite" (*Littérature* 48; "the first stage of African literature in the strict sense of the term"). The difference in classification of the literature of this period is of little significance. What matters is the relevance of the production, whether by Africans or non-Africans, for the development of francophone African literature as a whole. As Ngate notes, "the colonial literature that emerged sought to distinguish itself from the exotic literature that had preceded it" through its claim to greater accuracy (19). Notable examples of colonial novels by non-Africans in this period are Paul Adam's *La ville inconnue* (1911; "The Unknown Town"), Jérôme Tharaud and Jean

Tharaud's *La randonnée de Samba Diouf* (1922; "The Long Walk of Samba Diouf"), and Jean Francis-Boeuf's *La soudanaise et son amant* (1924; "The Sudanese Woman and Her Lover"). Regardless of whether the writer lived in the colonies for a considerable period of time (Adam) or never even set foot in the French African territory written about (the brothers Tharaud), the general purpose seemed the same: the portrayal of Africans and the so-called "âme nègre" (Senghor, *Liberté 1* 23; "Negro soul") in such a way as to lend justification to the French colonial enterprise. Much of the so-called *littérature coloniale* was a reaction to "le facile et le faux exotisme des passants" (qtd. in Ngate 22; "the easy and false exoticism of passers-by"). As it were, the colonizer, probably to give order and rational justification to his colonial mission, preferred a more scientific (read: documented), albeit exotic, discourse on Africa.

Among Africans who contributed to *la littérature coloniale*, the following stand out: Amadou Mapaté Diagne (*Les trois volontés de Malic* [1920; "Malic's Three Wishes"], a children's story considered to be the first fictional text in French by an African),[2] Bakary Diallo (*Force-Bonté* [1926; "Benevolent Force"]); Félix Couchoro (*L'esclave* [1929]), and Paul Hazoumé (*Doguicimi* [1938]). Although not necessarily anticolonialist,[3] these writers were avant-garde in their own right. They were different from their white contemporaries in the colonial literature category by the simple fact of showing that African peoples actually had organized societies and institutions before the arrival of the white man:

> Il s'agit de réfuter les arguments de la littérature coloniale, arguments selon lesquels le colonisateur européen débarquant en Afrique se serait trouvé en face de sociétés inorganisées sans aucuns passés historiques. (Nkashama, *Littérature* 49)
>
> It is a question of debunking arguments put forward in the colonial literature that, upon his arrival in Africa, the European colonizer was greeted by disorganized societies devoid of history.

Hazoumé's ethnographic novel, which presents a Dahomian (Beninois) society—with specific focus on the royal court—in all its complex human relationships and political machineries and machinations, is a particularly good case in point. With the notable exception of Paul Lomami-Tshibamba's *Ngando* (1948) and Joseph Saverio Naigiziki's *Escapade rouandaise: Journal d'un clerc en sa trentième année* (1949; "A Rwandan Adventure: Diary of a Thirty-Year-Old Clerk"),[4] francophone African fiction, after Hazoumé's *Doguicimi*, practically entered a phase of nonexistence.

The period of drought in fiction production coincided with the halcyon days of European Africanist ethnography, as well as with the negritude movement it helped inspire. Christopher Miller reminds readers of African literature of the importance of anthropology in understanding the literature: "a fair Western reading of African literatures demands engagement with, and even dependence on, anthropology . . ." (4–5). The history of African literature itself reveals the significant role played by anthropologists in its development. In this light, the work of two European anthropologists, Leo Frobenius and Maurice Delafosse, merit special mention.

Frobenius's *Histoire de la civilisation africaine* (1936; "History of African Civilization") and *Le destin des civilisations* (1940; "The Future of Civilizations") were particularly influential among black intellectuals and students of the time. Through extensive travels and research in Central and West Africa, the German ethnologist set out to prove the originality, historicity, and autonomy of African civilizations. Both Aimé Césaire and Léopold Sédar Senghor, cofounders of the negritude cultural and political movement, praised Frobenius for his objectivity and seriousness while showing their indebtedness to him. Senghor, for example, notes:

> C'est Leo Frobenius qui nous donna, et la vision, et l'explication au moment même où, les études terminées, nous entrions dans la vie active, militante, le mot et l'idée de la *Négritude* dans notre gibecière. (*Liberté III* 399)

> It was Leo Frobenius, at the very moment we were entering an active life of militancy at the end of our studies, who gave us, in addition to the vision and explanation, the word and idea of *négritude*.

The other European anthropologist to whom Senghor and his fellow black students express their gratitude is the French colonial functionary and indefatigable researcher Maurice Delafosse.[5] Senghor refers to him as "le plus grand des africanisants en France—je veux dire le plus attentif" (*Liberté I* 26; "the greatest of researchers in France interested in Africa–I mean the most conscientious"). Senghor and other black students in France used the findings of Frobenius and Delafosse not only as raw material for their poetry and cultural essays but also as a political weapon against French colonial policy of assimilation founded on the claim that Africa was a *terra nullius* and Africans a *tabula rasa*.[6] The rise of negritude is also attributable to two factors: the influence and contribution of diaspora Africans from the United States and the Caribbean and black newspapers and journals published in Paris.[7]

The works of intellectuals of the Harlem Renaissance, such as the novel *Banjo* (1929), by Jamaican-born Claude McKay, and the poetry of Countee Cullen and of Langston Hughes, as well as the Back to Africa movement spearheaded by Marcus Garvey, greatly impressed the future founders of negritude. Senghor singled out W. E. B. DuBois's *Souls of Black Folk* as one of the most important books he ever read and, in a letter to Mercer Cook, referred to Langston Hughes as "the greatest Negro-American poet. . . . [T]he most spontaneously Negro poet" (qtd. in Guillaume 272). The contribution to the conception and birth of negritude, and thus to the early development of modern francophone literature, by newspapers and journals run by Caribbeans and by Africans, mostly students in Paris, cannot be overemphasized.

The first such journal was *La revue du monde noir / Review of the Black World*, founded in 1931 by Leo Sajous and the Nardal sisters, Andrée and Paulette. "Despite its middle-class and assimilationist orientation," observes Lilyan Kesteloot in her groundbreaking work on the literary history of negritude, "*La Revue du Monde Noir* nonetheless launched two of the major themes of negritude: the ennoblement of the Negro race and the reevaluation of African civilizations" (4). The radical *Légitime défense* ("Self-Defense") came out in June 1932, published by Etienne Léro, René Menil, and Jules Marcel Monneret. The journal-manifesto's attack on the French and Franco-Caribbean bourgeoisies was so vehement that a combination of lack of funds, suspension of scholarships for its student founders, and threats from disgruntled French authorities ensured that its first issue would be its last (Kesteloot 83). Nonetheless, the journal had made its impact on the black community in Paris and abroad. On its ashes rose *L'étudiant noir* ("The Black Student"), a more cautious newspaper that brought together, for the first time, black students from Africa and the diaspora. From its founding in 1934, the newspaper would continue publication until the start of World War II. *Présence africaine* ("African Presence"), founded by Alioune Diop, virtually replaced *L'étudiant noir*. It released its first edition in both Paris and Dakar in 1947. What started as a magazine aimed at the "rehabilitation of the Black world" (C. Diop xiv), Présence Africaine has become today one of the leading publishers of African writing.

It was in this context that negritude was born and grew. During this time, Senghor published the landmark *Anthologie de la nouvelle poésie nègre et malgache de langue française* (1948, pref. Jean-Paul Sartre; "Anthology of the New Black and Malagasy Poetry in the French Language") and three volumes of his own poems: *Chants d'ombre* (1945; "Shadow Songs"), *Hosties noires* (1948; "Black Hosts"), and *Chants pour Naett* (1949; "Songs for Naett").[8] The politics and poetics of negritude left its imprint on the novelistic production that took place during the 1950s, the last decade of French colonization of black Africa. With the failure of the policies of assimilation and association, the end of World War II and the attendant exposure of France's fallibility, and the relative success of negritude's cultural campaign, the demands for political autonomy became louder and more frequent, both in France and in the colonies. The stage was thus set for the arrival of what could be effectively called the anticolonial novel.

Whereas the novels written before 1953 were intended almost entirely for a European readership, the anticolonial novel seems to be addressed to both Europeans and Africans. Even when they eschew direct criticism of colonialism, the novels of this period can be regarded as anticolonial for the simple reason that they present Africans not as effaceable and reinscribable slates but as a people with a complex past and present. Some of the major writers of this period are Camara Laye (*L'enfant noir* [1953; "The Dark Child"]), Ferdinand Oyono (*Une vie de boy* and *Le vieux nègre et la médaille* [1956; "Houseboy" and "The Old Man and the Medal"]), Mongo Beti (*Ville cruelle* [1954; under pseud. Boto; "Cruel City"] and *Le pauvre Christ de Bomba* [1956; "The Poor Christ of Bomba"]), and Cheikh Hamidou Kane (*L'aventure ambiguë* [1961; "Ambiguous Adventure"]). With the exception of *L'enfant noir*, all these novels provide explicit criticisms of the colonial system.[9]

If the novelists of colonialism's last decade focused the barrel of their pen on what Abdul JanMohamed has called the "Manichean allegory" of white/black, Occident/Africa, Christianity / African animism, modernism/tradition, and so on (59), those writing in the postcolonial period turned the critical gaze inward. Consequently, direct criticism of colonization ceased to occupy any significant place in the works of Africans. The novelists, especially of the first decade of independence, register their disenchantment with the stewardship of the new African states; they also begin to question earlier assumptions about Africa's so-called idyllic precolonial past. The intended audience here is clearly African, despite the fact that most Africans do not have access to the texts. *Dramouss* (1966), by Camara Laye; *Le devoir de violence* (1968; "Bound to Violence"), by Yambo Ouologuem; *Les soleils des indépendances* (1968; "The Suns of Independence"), by Ahmadou Kourouma; and *Le mandat* (1969;

"The Money Order"), by Ousmane Sembène are some examples. In Camara Laye's *Dramouss*, for example, the protagonist, Fatoman, returns to his native land after six years in Paris, only to realize that the traditional family and social values of Africa (as celebrated in such works as *L'enfant noir*) no longer have relevance amid the political violence that now reigns supreme in the postcolonial state. Ouologuem's novel, for its part, presents one of the most unflattering representations of Africa's precolonial history, which was romanticized in such texts as *Soundjata ou l'épopée mandingue (*Niane*;* "Sundiata: An Epic of Old Mali"). With spiritual concerns giving way to narratives of material anguish, the lyricism characteristic of many of the novels of the 1950s all but disappeared in the novels of the 1960s.

While, thematically speaking, the novels of the 1970s are not very different from those of the 1960s, many of them chose a slightly different orientation and idiom. Furthermore, with scenes of increasing confrontation between dictatorial regimes and their target populations, many of the novels move beyond the mere critique of the postcolonial incubus to ask questions and postulate political and ideological solutions. Alioum Fantouré's *Le cercle des tropiques* (1972; "Tropical Circle"), Emmanuel Dongola's *Un fusil dans la main, un poème dans la poche* (1973; "A Gun in the Hand, a Poem in the Pocket"), and Beti's *Remember Reuben* and *Perpétue et l'habitude du malheur* (1974; "Perpetua and the Habit of Unhappiness") point toward one form or another of a people's uprising as an antidote to postcolonial aberrations. Sembène, in *Xala* (1973), especially with the possibility that the dispossessed and marginalized beggars may hold the cure to the impotence of El Hadji Bèye at the end of the novel, also seems to be casting his lot with the dispossessed masses.

According to Ngate, "[f]rancophone African literature has been, in effect, a continuous attempt at fleeing its Western models" (18). V. Y. Mudimbe observes that the African "has gone from the situation in which he or she was perceived as a simple functional object to the freedom of thinking of himself or herself as the starting point of an absolute discourse" (*Invention* 200). If Ngate's and Mudimbe's observations are true of the above novels by Fantouré, Dongala, Beti, and Sembène, they apply even more to William Sassine's *Saint-Monsieur Baly* (1973), Makombo Bamboté's *Princesse Mandapu* (1972), Mudimbe's *Le bel immonde* (1976; "Before the Birth of the Moon"), and Sony Labou Tansi's *La vie et demie* (1979; "Life and a Half").[10] In these novels, the writers seem to operate in a discursive realm different from that of their predecessors. The African and

African subject matter have become, as it were, the be-all and end-all of novelistic reference. The flight of which Ngate speaks, and which Mudimbe confirms, takes place at both the thematic and stylistic levels. In Sassine's *Saint-Monsieur Baly*, for example, the focus is on the failed philanthropic effort of a retired schoolteacher who decides to build a private school for dropouts and abandoned children. Thematically speaking, there is no direct criticism of colonialism or postcolonialism in the novel. Similarly, in *Princesse Mandapu*, *Le bel immonde*, and *La vie et demie*, even when Bamboté, Mudimbe, and Labou Tansi make references to or directly engage the corruption and excesses of the postcolonial dispensation, they not only adopt a new language but also focus on narratees who are clearly African, who are called on often to delve into their "regional archives" to help in the creation of meaning (Mudimbe, *Invention* 99).

New meanings, new relations, and new realities in the dehumanizing world of postindependent Africa occasioned the need for a new kind of fictional language to capture them. Consequently, the need has become more evident to approach African texts as raw material that can be engaged more fully by using exegetical tools fashioned by Africans themselves. The work of such francophone African intellectuals as Paulin Hountondji and Mudimbe is remarkable in that regard. Speaking of the contribution made by Hountondji and Mudimbe, Miller notes that their work has made it "possible for readers to conceptualize Africa and its cultures using models that are proposed by Africans . . . [thus] breaking down the wall between 'theory' as exclusively Western and 'information' as all that Africa can provide" (3). Mudimbe calls on African intellectuals to break away from "Western epistemological order," revisit Africa's "traditional systems of thought" with the aim of extracting from them the raw material necessary for the creation of an "African *gnosis*" (*Invention* x). In the same vein, the work of Achille Mbembe is valuable. In his book *On the Postcolony*, he offers new analytic models for engaging what he describes as the "banality of power" and "excess" characteristic of the geopolitical entity he calls the African "postcolony" (102).

The 1980s and 1990s saw no decline in novel production by African male writers.[11] There was the much-anticipated return of such living legends as Kourouma (*Monnè, outrages et défis* [1990; *Monnew*], *En attendant le vote des bêtes sauvages* [1998; "Waiting for the Vote of the Wild Animals"], and *Allah n'est pas obligé* [2000; "Allah Is Not Obliged"]) and Kane (*Les gardiens du temple* [1997; "Guardians of the Temple"]). Other writers, like Tierno Monénembo (*Les écailles du ciel* [1986; "Scales of the

Sky"] and *Un rêve utile* [1991; "A Useful Dream"]), Massa Makan Diabaté (*Le coiffeur de Kouta* [1980; "The Barber of Kouta"], *Le boucher de Kouta* [1982; "The Butcher of Kouta"],[12] and *Le lion à l'arc* [1986; "The Lion with the Bow"]), Nkashama (*Le pacte de sang* [1984; "The Blood Pact"]), and Amadou Koné (Les coupeurs de têtes [1997; "The Decapitators"]), never stopped writing. Some relatively new faces as far as novel writing is concerned, such as Bernard Nanga (*Les chauves-souris* [1980; "The Bats"] and *La trahison de Marianne* [1984; "Betrayed by Marianne"]) and Boubacar Boris Diop (*Les tambours de la mémoire* [1990; "The Drums of Memory"], *Le cavalier et son ombre* [1997; "The Horseman and His Shadow"]), also made their mark. Diaspora writers also flourished during this period. Nonetheless, it is fair to say that the 1980s and 1990s belonged to women writers. Indeed, the efflorescence of novelistic activity by women that began then continues to this day. Francophone sub-Saharan women novelists are now such a veritable force to reckon with that a discussion of the trajectory of the francophone African novel cannot be complete without an acknowledgment of their contribution to it.

Because of Africa's patriarchal ethos and the colonizer's lack of interest in the education of women, women were excluded from the space of intellectual activity for a long time. The two earliest recorded examples of francophone sub-Saharan women's prose writing are both from Cameroon: Marie-Claire Matip's short autobiography *Ngonda* (1958) and Thérèse Kuoh-Moukoury's *Rencontres essentielles* (1968; *Essential Encounters*).[13] One would have to wait until the mid-1970s to see any significant incursion by francophone women writers into that male-dominated realm. This "prise d'écriture" ("taking of writing") by women was first given book-length attention by Irène Assiba D'Almeida in her seminal work *Francophone African Women Writers: Destroying the Emptiness of Silence* (1994) (1). The 1970s produced such landmark novels as Nafissatou Diallo's *De Tilène au Plateau: Une enfance dakaroise* (1975; "From Tilène to Plateau: A Dakar Childhood"); Aoua Keita's voluminous *Femme d'Afrique: La vie d'Aoua Kéita racontée par elle-même* (1975; "An African Woman: The Autobiography of Aoua Kéita, Told in Her Own Words"; it won the Grand Prix Littéraire); Aminata Sow Fall's *La grève des battus* (1979; "The Beggars' Strike"); and Mariama Bâ's *Une si longue lettre* (1979; "So Long a Letter"), by far the best known of them.[14] In her novel, Bâ documents, among other concerns, the plight of women in modern African societies still controlled by patriarchal traditions.

The 1980s and 1990s gave us Ken Bugul's *Le baobab fou* (1982; "The Abandoned Baobab"), Werewere Liking's *Elle sera de jaspe et de corail* (1983; "It Shall Be of Jasper and Coral") and *L'amour-cent-vies* (1988; "Love-across-a-Hundred Lives"), Calixthe Beyala's *Tu t'appelleras Tanga* (1988; "Your Name Shall Be Tanga"),[15] Véronique Tadjo's *Á vol d'oiseau* (1986; "As the Crow Flies") and *Le royaume aveugle* (1991; "The Blind Kingdom"), Monique Ilboudo's *Le mal de peau* (1992; "The Scourge of the Skin"), and Fatou Keita's *Rebelle* (1998; "Rebel"). With the notable exception of Fall, whose works examine mostly larger cultural and political concerns, francophone women novelists have generally focused their attention on issues affecting women. In *Tu t'appelleras Tanga*, for instance, Beyala presents a scathing commentary on the so-called phallocentric universe of men. All the men in this iconoclastic novel are identifiable almost entirely by their phallus and the corporeal regions and activities associated with it.

From the foregoing, many curricular possibilities for courses on the francophone sub-Saharan novel become evident. One could, for example, offer an introductory or survey course at both the undergraduate and the graduate levels that provides a glimpse of the historical and thematic evolution of the francophone sub-Saharan novel.[16] Taking into account the level of the students, it is always a good idea to begin with a quick overview of the history of Africa, with focus on precolonial Africa and such historical subjects as the slave trade, colonization, the two World Wars, decolonization and independence, and the postcolonial period. The primary reading list for an undergraduate introduction to the francophone African novel could feature the following. Djibril Tamsir Niane's *Soundjata ou l'épopée mandingue* ("Sundiata, an Epic of Old Mali") or Diabaté's *L'aigle et l'épervier ou la geste de Soundjata* ("The Eagle and the Sparrow Hawk; or, Sundiata's Exploit"), both on the legend of Sundiata Keita, founder of the Mali Empire, can provide a fine introduction to precolonial Africa. For a depiction of black-white relations in the colonial period, at the personal, spiritual, and political levels, one might use Oyono's *Une vie de boy* or Beti's *Le pauvre Christ de Bomba*. For a portrayal of colonial education and its impact on the African, I would recommend Pierre Sammy-Mackfoy's bildungsroman *L'odyssée de Mongou* ("Mongou's Odyssey") or Beti's *Mission terminée* ("Mission to Kala"). Regarding the tradition/modernism debate, Seydou Badian's *Sous l'orage* ("Caught in the Storm"), Abdoulaye Sadji's *Maïmouna*, or Fall's *L'appel des arènes* ("The Call of the Arenas") is a good choice. For postcolonial Africa, I would recommend

Francis Bebey's lighthearted *Le ministre et le griot* ("The Minister and the Griot") or Nanga's mordantly critical *Les chauve-souris.* This course could be rounded out by a discussion of Kuoh-Moukoury's *Rencontres essentielles* or Angèle Rawiri's *Fureurs et cris de femmes* ("Furies and Cries of Women"), for an introduction to women's issues.

For an introductory course at the graduate level, the following texts provide material for more complex intellectual engagement. The texts are proposed on the assumption that graduate students, or upper-level undergraduate students, have already had some exposure to francophone African literature and history. On the subject of precolonial Africa, Camara Laye's *Le maître de la parole* ("The Guardian of the Word") is highly recommended. Hazoumé's *Doguicimi* or even Niane's text on Sundiata can be a good alternative. For a comprehensive representation of French colonial presence in sub-Saharan Africa, there is hardly a better text than Amadou Hampaté Bâ's 1973 *L'étrange destin de Wangrin* (*The Fortunes of Wangrin*). According to Abiola Irelé, Bâ's novel is "one of the most significant texts in all of African literature. . . . A compelling reconstruction of the colonial experience, and as such, a social document of great significance" (vii). The novel can also be used as the basis for a discussion of the intersection between orality and the novel form, between history and anthropology, and between biography and fiction. Bernard Dadié's autobiographical novel *Climbié*, like *L'odyssée de Mongou*, addresses the question of colonial education. However, where Sammy-Mackfoy seems almost eulogistic about the Westernizing tendency of the colonial school, Dadié spares no opportunity to criticize what he sees as the depersonalizing effects of the French policy and practice of assimilation that the school represented. Kane's *L'aventure ambiguë* exploits the education motif but also focuses on the pragmatic debate of whether to stay oneself and risk irrelevance and death or gain new life through adopting the ways of the colonizing other. Camara Laye's *Dramouss* or Kourouma's *Les soleils des indépendances* provides a very convincing picture of the disillusionment, corruption, and political violence that quickly replaced the optimism of the early years of African independence. Fall's *L'ex-père de la nation* ("The Former Father of the Nation"), which interrogates the question of the origins and growth of dictatorial regimes, is also a good alternative. Any text from either the later postcolonial period, including texts by women writers on matters germane to the feminine condition, can be used to crown the list.

Survey courses will also benefit tremendously from the use of secondary readings and films. For material dealing with the colonial period, one could bring in Bassek ba Kobhio's film *Le grand blanc de Lambaréné* (1995; "The Great White Man of Lambaréné") or Jean-Marie Téno's film *Afrique, je te plumerai* (1992; "Africa, I Will Fleece You"). Excerpts from Albert Memmi's *Portrait du colonisé, précédé de portrait du colonisateur* ("The Colonizer and the Colonized"), Aimé Césaire's *Discours sur le colonialisme* ("Discourse on Colonialism"), or Frantz Fanon's *Peau noire, masques blancs* ("Black Skin, White Masks") can make for good supplementary readings. Depending on the length of the semester or whether the course is graduate or undergraduate, either Memmi's or Césaire's text can be assigned in its entirety. To accompany the postcolonial texts, at least one chapter from Fanon's *Les damnés de la terre* (*The Wretched of the Earth*)—for example, "Mésaventures de la conscience nationale" ("Misadventures of National Consciousness")—and Achille Mbembe's "Provisional Notes on the Postcolony" could be assigned. Kobhio's film *Sango Malo* (1991) or Dani Kouyaté's film *Keita ou l'héritage du griot* (1995; "Keita: The Heritage of the Griot") can be used to enhance any discussion of the problem of education, tradition, and the heritage of colonialism in modern Africa.

The African postcolony has been marked by many important events that deserve attention in the classroom: the cold war, civil wars, the fall of the Berlin Wall, and the subsequent wind of change that swept across Africa and other nondemocratic regions of the world and removed the remnants of many dictatorial regimes. The cold war, which began on the morrow of World War II, made much of Africa the battleground for superpower political and economic rivalries. It can be blamed, at least partially, for the proliferation of military coups and failed states, widespread corruption, and civil wars, which have stigmatized Africa's sociopolitical landscape since the 1960s. Kourouma's *En attendant le vote des bêtes sauvages*, a novel that chronicles the rise of the late Gnassingbé Eyadéma of Togo, underlines the role of the cold war in postcolonial Africa. Many of the problems associated with it have in turn provided, directly or indirectly, thematic nourishment for the postindependence African novel. Moreover, even though wars have plagued sub-Saharan Africa since the 1960s (the two Congos, Casamance in Southern Senegal, Angola, Mozambique, Nigeria, and so forth), those that took place in the 1990s and early 2000s (Liberia, Sierra Leone, Rwanda, Côte d'Ivoire) attracted the most attention in francophone literature. The scale of the conflicts as well as the amount of media coverage of them partly account for this difference. It is therefore entirely possible to teach an undergraduate seminar or graduate course on the francophone African novel that focuses on civil war and genocide.

The reading list for such a course could include Kourouma's *Allah n'est pas obligé*; *La mort ne veut pas de moi* ("Death Does Not Want Me"), by the Rwandan genocide survivor Yolande Mukagasana; Tanella Boni's *Matins de couvre-feu* ("Curfew Mornings"); at least two of the novels that came out of the 1998–2000 Fest'Africa-sponsored project Rwanda: Écrire par devoir de mémoire, *L'aîné des orphelins* ("The Oldest Orphan"), by Monénembo, and *Murambi, le livre des ossements* (2000; "Murambi, the Book of Bones"), by Boubacar Boris Diop.[17] Narrative voice and point of view, the representation of violence, ethnic politics, nationalism and sovereignty, women and body politics, poverty and class relations, power relations, issues of postcolonial citizenship, precolonial and colonial relations, the cold war, and the phenomenon of the child soldier are among the topics that can be addressed in the course. An analysis of the genocide texts will further reveal such themes as memory and memorialization, the roots and banality of evil, and the racialization of difference and the role of theory in it. The novel *Transit* (2003), by Abdourahman Waberi, can be included in the list for its focus on the theme of war and exile. Mahmood Mamdani's *When Victims Become Killers: Colonialism, Nativism, and the Genocide in Rwanda* (2002) can be an indispensable companion to the course. A film like *Sometimes in April* or even *Hotel Rwanda* will be a valuable resource as well.

There is also a significant and growing body of literature by a generation of Africans living and writing in the diaspora, especially in France, that merits attention in the francophone literature classroom. These are novels produced mainly by the children of first-generation immigrants or by African immigrants in France. Most are writers born after 1960, the landmark year for francophone Africa's political independence from France. Abdourahman Waberi, a diaspora writer from Djibouti, has referred to them as "les enfants de la postcolonie" ("children of the postcolony") (Waberi, "Enfants" 11). Immigration, migrancy, exile, identity, nomadism, vagrancy, and otherness are some of the themes addressed by these novels, from a perspective and in a language different from those manifested in the so-called mainstream francophone African novel. Among diaspora writers, Beyala has been the most prolific—and the most controversial. Others include Alain Mabanckou, from Congo-Brazzaville; Sami Tchak, from Togo; and Sandrine Bessora, from Gabon. For many of these writers, at least for their protagonists, Africa is an imaginary landscape seen through the life and reminiscences of their parents. The narrator-protagonist of Tchak's *Place des fêtes* (2001), for example, lives a particularly tenuous existence. Unlike his parents, who have an Africa to go to or at least to reminisce about, he is a stranger even in Paris, his place of birth. Even though he has been to Africa, Paris is the only geographic and cultural space he has ever really known. The language in *Place des fêtes* is slangy and scatological, each chapter beginning with the expression "Putain de . . ." ("Fucking . . ."). A novel from this group of writers could be added to the list of the survey courses suggested above, or a special course could be taught entirely on diaspora writers. Kandioura Dramé's seminal study "Bwanapolis or Africa-on-the-Seine" is indispensable to the student and instructor looking for a deeper appreciation of this new category of francophone African literature.[18]

Finally, I discuss briefly the symbiotic relation between novel and film. If properly exploited, this relation can be a valuable component in the teaching of the francophone African novel. The importance of francophone film as a corollary genre is highlighted in the works or oeuvre of Ousmane Sembène, the most important filmmaker from sub-Saharan Africa. While film adaptation of literary works is nothing new in Africa (e.g., the adaptation of a part of Niane's *Soundjata ou l'épopée mandingue* by Kouyaté in his film *Keita où l'héritage du griot*), Sembene is unique in that he adapted four of his own literary works into film. A social critic, Sembene decided to go into filmmaking in order to reach out to his people, most of whom had limited or no access to his novels in French. This desire is further exemplified in his use of Wolof in his second feature-length film, *Mandabi* (based on his short novel *Le mandat*).

A senior or graduate film seminar could focus not only on the points of convergence and divergence of the two different media used by Sembene but also on their limits and possibilities. Take for example the film *Xala* and the novel of the same name.[19] Both novel and film focus on the theme of the *xala* ("sexual impotence," both real and symbolic) that has befallen the main character, El Hadji Abdou Kader Bèye, a member of the comprador postcolonial bourgeoisie that is the target of Sembene's searing criticism. Even more interesting are the differences between film and novel.[20] The film's stunning visuals (dress, Senegalese mannerism, and other aspects of local color), the use of Wolof and French by different characters according to their class appurtenances, and characterization (for example the reduction in the number of characters and the prominent role of women) are some of the ways in which the film differs from the novel.

The francophone African novel has had a long and interesting journey. In the course of its rich and varied trajectory, probably more than any other area of African studies it has helped delineate and interpret the relations among the continent, its peoples, and the rest of the world. While we cannot claim that the novel, despite its length and breadth of coverage, has fully captured the history, geography, civilizations, and cultural and mental evolutions and manifestations of black Africa, it has successfully presented, and continues to present, credible vignettes of the trials, travels, travails, hopes, and aspirations of a people and continent. The teacher of Africa, professional or occasional, who seeks to teach the continent or any of its myriad regions and peoples, will find in the novel enough material to instruct, entertain, awe, and encourage.

Notes

1. It must be noted that the temporal boundaries that emerge in my discussion are fluid. For instance, it is not uncommon for texts written in the postcolonial period to deal with precolonial or colonial subject matters. Two very good examples are Djibril Tamsir Niane's *Soundjata ou l'épopée mandingue,* which chronicles, through the memory of a griot, the eighteenth-century founding of the Mali Empire, and Ahmadou Kourouma's *Monnè, outrages et défis*, which focuses on the French military conquest and eventual domination of the Mandinka empire of Samory Touré.

2. René Maran's novel *Batouala*, published a year after Diagne's narrative and subtitled "veritable roman nègre," occupies a special place in the annals of African literature. Maran was a Caribbean working for the colonial administration in Ubangi-Shari, French Equatorial Africa. Senghor refers to Maran as "le Précurseur de la Négritude" (*Liberté 1* 410). *Batouala* is probably the only fictional work of its time that constitutes an unequivocal rebuke of colonialism. Though the novel won the Prix Goncourt, its anticolonial stance quickly earned the author stern disapproval from some French colonial authorities and citizens (Kesteloot 75).

3. In fact, in *Les trois volontés de Malic* and *Force-Bonté*, for example, we see an explicit endorsement of the colonial *mission civilisatrice*. This type of novel is referred to as "le roman assimilé" (Bonn et al. 246).

4. The novel, the first of two volumes of a monumental autobiographical novel of five hundred pages that would be published in 1955 as *Mes transes à trente ans*, was awarded a literary prize when it came out in Brussels. It addresses questions of urbanization, modernity, and religious identity.

5. Among other works on Africa, Delafosse published *Haut-Sénégal-Niger* (1912), *Les noirs de l'Afrique* (1922), and *Les nègres* (1927).

6. The appeal of Frobenius and Delafosse can only be fully appreciated if their works are read against the background of fashionable exotic literature on Africa as well as the racist theories propounded by such anthropologists as Joseph de Gobineau (*Essai sur l'inégalité des races humaines* [1853–55]) and Lucien Lévy-Bruhl (*La mentalité primitive* [1922]).

7. The term is believed to have been first used by Césaire in a 1935 issue of the student newspaper *L'étudiant noir*. Senghor defined it as "l'ensemble des valeurs culturelles du monde noir" (*Liberté 1* 26).

8. The complete volumes of Senghor's poetry are found in *The Collected Poetry*, a bilingual edition.

9. Mongo Beti, who had specific expectations of the African writer, was disappointed by Camara Laye's novel: "Laye ferme obstinément les yeux sur les réalités les plus cruciales, celles justement qu'on s'est toujours gardé de révéler au public d'ici. Ce Guinéen, mon congénère, qui fut, à ce qu'il laisse entendre, un garçon fort vif, n'a-t-il donc rien vu qu'une Afrique paisible, belle, maternelle? Est-il possible que pas une seule fois, Laye n'ait été témoin d'une seule exaction de l'administration coloniale?" (qtd. in M. Kane 89).

10. According to Lydie Moudileno, Labou Tansi's novel "gave African letters and its critics the spectacular literary event it needed in order to confirm institutionally the advent of a new generation of francophone sub-Saharan African writers" (28). The novel is able to do this, adds Moudileno, thanks to a "revolutionary aesthetic in the representation of the postcolonial that breaks structurally from nineteenth-century European models" (29).

11. The novels of this period are not very different from those of the 1970s. They generally deal with the same themes of corruption and violence, especially those that result from the breakdown of social and political values and structures. Many of the novels published in the 1990s and after but that are not mentioned above—Florent Couo-Zotti's *Charly en guerre* (2001) and Dongola's *Johnny, chien méchant* (2002)—portray extreme violence, especially that perpetrated by children during Africa's many civil wars. However, some novels, like Nanga's *La trahison de Marianne*, deal with existentialist concerns in which individual identity and the personal quest for freedom play a major role.

12. These are the last two novels of Diabaté's trilogy, the first being *Le lieutenant de Kouta* (1979).

13. Africa's first published woman novelist was Nigeria's Flora Nwapa, whose first novel, *Efuru*, was published by Heinemann in 1966. Nwapa would go on to write two other novels and many children's books.

14. It was during this time that Awa Thiam published her very controversial *La parole aux négresses* (1978), in which she confronts polygamy and such taboo subjects as genital excision and infibulation.

15. Beyala was the first black writer to be awarded the prestigious Grand Prix du Roman de l'Académie Française.

16. At the graduate level, a course can also focus on a specific theme: resistance and power, traditionalism versus modernism, women's issues, colonization, and the like.

17. Dongola's *Les petits garçons naissent aussi des étoiles* (1998), Alain Mabanckou's *Les petit-fils nègres de Vercingétorix* (2002), and Véronique Tadjo's prose-poetry *L'ombre d'Imana* can be alternative texts on the reading list.

18. Waberi's "Les enfants de la postcolonie" and Odile Cazenave's *Afrique sur Seine* (which also exists in English) are also good studies focusing on this phenomenon.

19. According to Gugler and Diop, "the film successfully marries the seductive lure of the medium to the director's didactic purpose . . . [and] offers an excellent opportunity to compare Sembène's approaches to his two chosen media" (147).

20. Note that *Xala* was first a film script, then a novel, before finally becoming a film.

Works Cited

Adam, Paul. *La ville inconnue.* Paris: Flammarion, 1911. Print.

Bâ, Amadou Hampaté. *L'étrange destin de Wangrin ou les rouéries d'un interprète africain.* Paris: Union Générale d'Éditions, 1992. Print.

Bâ, Mariama. *Une si longue lettre.* Dakar: Nouvelles Éditions Africaines, 1997. Print.

Badian, Seydou. *Sous l'orage.* 1963. Paris: Présence Africaine, 1972. Print.

Bamboté, Makombo. *Princesse Mandapu.* Paris: Présence Africaine, 1972. Print.

Bebey, Francis. *Le ministre et le griot.* Saint-Maur-des-Fossés: Sepia, 1992. Print.

Beti, Mongo. *Mission terminée.* Paris: Buchet, 1957. Print.

———. *Le pauvre Christ de Bomba.* Paris: Lafont, 1956. Print.

———. *Perpétue et l'habitude du malheur.* Paris: Buchet-Chastel, 1974. Print.

———. *Remember Reuben.* Paris: Union Générale d'Éditions, 1974. Print.

Beyala, Calixthe. *Tu t'appelleras Tanga.* Paris: Stock, 1988. Print.

Boni, Tanella. *Matins de couvre-feu.* Paris: Serpent à Plumes, 2005. Print.

Bonn, Charles, et al., eds. *Littérature francophone 1: Le roman.* Paris: Hatier; AUPELF-UREF, 1997. Print.

Boto, Eza [Mongo Beti]. *Ville cruelle.* Paris: Présence Africaine, 1954. Print.

Camara Laye. *Dramouss.* Paris: Plon, 1966. Print.

———. *L'enfant noir.* Paris: Plon, 1953. Print.

———. *Le maître de la parole.* Paris: Plon, 1978. Print.

Cazenave, Odile. *Afrique sur Seine: Une nouvelle génération de romanciers africains à Paris.* Paris: Harmattan, 2003. Print.

Césaire, Aimé. *Discours sur le colonialisme.* Paris: Présence Africaine, 1989. Print.

Couchoro, Félix. *L'esclave.* Paris: Dépêche Africaine, 1929. Print.

Couo-Zotti, Florent. *Charly en guerre.* Paris: Dapper, 2001. Print.

Dadié, Bernard. *Climbié.* Paris: Seghers, 1953. Print.

D'Almeida, Irène Assiba. *Francophone African Women Writers: Destroying the Emptiness of Silence.* Gainesville: UP of Florida, 1994. Print.

Delafosse, Maurice. *Haut-Sénégal-Niger.* Paris: Maisonneuve, 1912. Print.

———. *Les nègres.* Paris: Rieder, 1927. Print.

———. *Les noirs de l'Afrique.* Paris: Payot, 1922. Print.

Diabaté, Massa Makan. *L'aigle et l'épervier ou la geste de Soundjata.* Paris: Oswald, 1975. Print.

———. *Le boucher de Kouta.* Paris: Hatier, 1982. Print.

———. *Le coiffeur de Kouta.* Paris: Hatier, 1980. Print.

———. *Le lieutenant de Kouta.* Paris: Hatier, 1979. Print.

———. *Le lion à l'arc.* Paris: Hatier, 1986. Print.

Diagne, Amadou Mapaté. *Les trois volontés de Malic.* Paris: Larose, 1920. Print.

Diallo, Bakary. *Force-Bonté.* Paris: Rieder, 1926. Print.

Diallo, Nafissatou. *De Tilène au Plateau: Une enfance dakaroise.* Dakar: Nouvelles Éditions Africaines, 1975. Print.

Diop, Boubacar Boris. *Le cavalier et son ombre.* Paris: Stock, 1997. Print.

———. *Murambi, le livre des ossements.* Paris: Stock, 2000. Print.

———. *Les tambours de la mémoire.* Paris: Harmattan, 1990. Print.

Diop, Christiane Yandé. "Foreword: Présence Africaine." *The Surreptitious Speech: Présence Africaine and the Politics of Otherness.* Ed. V. Y. Mudimbe. Chicago: U of Chicago P, 1992. xiii–xvi. Print.

Dongola, Emmanuel. *Un fusil dans la main, un poème dans la poche.* Paris: Michel, 1973. Print.

———. *Johnny, chien méchant.* Paris: Serpent à Plumes, 2002. Print.

———. *Les petits garçons naissent aussi des étoiles.* Paris: Serpent à Plumes, 2000. Print.

Dramé, Kandioura. "Bwanapolis or Africa-on-the-Seine." *Research in African Literatures* 26.1 (1995): 97–110. Print.

DuBois, W. E. B. *The Souls of Black Folk.* New York: Vintage; Lib. of Amer., 1990. Print.

Duras, Claire de. *Ourika.* Paris: Des Femmes, 1979. Print.

Fall, Aminata Sow. *L'appel des arènes.* Dakar: Nouvelles Éditions Africaines; Sepia, 1993. Print.

———. *L'ex-père de la nation.* Paris: Harmattan, 1987. Print.

———. *La grève des battus.* Dakar: Nouvelles Éditions Africaines, 1979. Print.

Fanon, Frantz. *Les damnés de la terre.* Paris: Maspero, 1961. Print.

———. *Peau noire, masques blancs.* Paris: Seuil, 1995. Print.

Fantouré, Alioum. *Le cercle des tropiques.* Paris: Présence Africaine, 1972. Print.

Francis-Boeuf, Jean. *La soudanaise et son amant.* Paris: Michel, 1924. Print.

Frobenius, Leo. *Le destin des civilisations.* Paris: Gallimard, 1940. Print.

———. *Histoire de la civilisation africaine.* Paris: Gallimard, 1936. Print.

Gobineau, Joseph de. *Essai sur l'inégalité des races humaines.* Paris: Belfond, 1967. Print.

Gugler, Josef, and Oumar Cherif Diop. "Ousmane Sembène's *Xala*: The Novel, the Film, and Their Audiences." *Research in African Literatures* 29.2 (1998): 147–58. Print.

Guillaume, Alfred J., Jr. "Negritude and Humanism: Senghor's Vision of a Universal Civilization." *The Harlem Renaissance: Revaluations.* Ed. Amritjit Singh et al. New York: Garland, 1989. 271–80. Print.

Hazoumé, Paul. *Doguicimi.* Paris: Larose, 1938. Print.

Hotel Rwanda. Dir. Terry George. Perf. Don Cheadle, Xolani Mali, and Desmond Dube. United Artists, 2004. Film.

Hugo, Victor. *Bug-Jargal.* Paris: Hughes, 1888. Print.

Ilboudo, Monique. *Le mal de peau.* Paris: Serpent à Plumes, 2001. Print.

Irele, Abiola. Introduction. *The Fortunes of Wangrin.* By Amadou Hampaté Bâ. Trans. Aina Pavolini Taylor. Bloomington: Indiana UP, 1999. vii–xvi. Print.

JanMohamed, Abdul R. "The Economy of Manichean Allegory: The Function of Racial Difference in Colonialist Literature." *Critical Inquiry* 12.1 (1985): 59–87. Print.

Kane, Cheikh Hamidou. *L'aventure ambiguë.* Paris: Julliard, 1961. Print.

———. *Les gardiens du temple.* Paris: Stock, 1997. Print.

Kane, Mohammadou. *Roman africain et tradition.* Dakar: Nouvelles Éditions Africaines, 1982. Print.

Keita, Aoua. *Femme d'Afrique: La vie d'Aoua Kéita racontée par elle-même.* Paris: Présence Africaine, 1975. Print.

Keita, Fatou. *Rebelle.* Paris: Présence Africaine, 1998. Print.

Ken Bugul. *Le baobab fou.* Dakar: Nouvelles Éditions Africaines, 1982. Print.

Kesteloot, Lilyan. *Black Writers in French: A Literary History of Negritude.* Trans. Ellen Conroy Kennedy. Philadelphia: Temple UP, 1974. Print.

Kobhio, Bassek ba, dir. *Le grand blanc de Lambaréné.* LN Productions, 1995. Film.

Koné, Amadou. *Les coupeurs de têtes.* Saint-Maur: Sépia, 1997. Print.

Kourouma, Ahmadou. *Allah n'est pas obligé.* Paris: Seuil, 2000. Print.

———. *En attendant le vote des bêtes sauvages.* Paris: Seuil, 1998. Print.

———. *Monnè, outrages et défis.* Paris: Seuil, 1990. Print.

———. *Les soleils des indépendances.* Paris: Seuil, 1970. Print.

Kouyaté, Dani, dir. *Keita ou l'héritage du griot.* Afix Productions, 1994. Film.

Kuoh-Moukoury, Thérèse. *Rencontres essentielles.* Paris: Harmattan, 1995. Print.

Labou Tansi, Sony. *La vie et demie.* Paris: Seuil, 1979. Print.

Lévy-Bruhl, Lucien. *La mentalité primitive.* Paris: Alcan, 1922. Print.

Liking, Werewere. *L'amour-cent-vies.* Paris: Polisud, 1989. Print.

———. *Elle sera de jaspe et de corail.* Paris: Harmattan, 1983. Print.

Lomami-Tshibamba, Paul. *Ngando.* Bruxelles: Deny, 1948. Print.

Loti, Pierre. *Le roman d'un spahi.* Paris: Calman-Lévy, 1881. Print.

Mabanckou, Alain. *Les petit-fils nègres de Vercingétorix.* Paris: Serpent à Plumes, 2002. Print.

Mamdani, Mahmood. *When Victims Become Killers: Colonialism, Nativism, and the Genocide in Rwanda.* Princeton: Princeton UP, 2002. Print.

Maran, René. *Batouala: Véritable roman nègre.* Paris: Michel, 1938. Print.

Masse, Fernand. "The Negro Race in French Literature." *Journal of Negro History* 18.3 (1933): 225–45. Print.

Matip, Marie-Claire. *Ngonda*. Paris: Bibliothèque du Jeune Africain, 1958. Print.
Mbembe, Achille. *On the Postcolony*. Berkeley: U of California P, 2001. Print.
———. "Provisional Notes on the Postcolony." *Africa: Journal of the International African Institute* 62.1 (1992): 3–37. Print.
McKay, Claude. *Banjo*. Fort Washington: Harvest, 1970. Print.
Memmi, Albert. *Portrait du colonisé, précédé de portrait du colonisateur*. Paris: Gallimard, 2002. Print.
Mérimée, Prosper. *Tamango*. Paris: Larousse, 1986. Print.
Miller, Christopher L. *Theories of Africans: Francophone Literature and Anthropology in Africa*. Chicago: U of Chicago P, 1990. Print.
Monénembo, Tierno. *L'aîné des orphelins*. Paris: Seuil, 2000. Print.
———. *Les écailles du ciel*. Paris: Seuil, 1986. Print.
———. *Un rêve utile*. Paris: Seuil, 1991. Print.
Moudileno, Lydie. "Magical Realism: 'Arme Miraculeuse' for the African Novel." *Research in African Literatures* 37.1 (2006): 28–41. Print.
Mudimbe, V. Y. *Le bel immonde*. Paris: Présence Africaine, 1976. Print.
———. *The Invention of Africa: Gnosis, Philosophy, and the Order of Knowledge*. Bloomington: Indiana UP, 1988. Print.
Mukagasana, Yolande. *La mort ne veut pas de moi*. Paris: Fixot, 1997. Print.
Munro, J. Forbes. *Africa and the International Economy, 1800–1960: An Introduction to the Modern Economic History of Africa South of the Sahara*. Totowa: Rowman, 1976. Print.
Naigiziki, J. Saverio. *Escapade rouandaise: Journal d'un clerc en sa trentième année*. Bruxelles, 1949. Print.
———. *Mes transes à trente ans*. Astrida: Groupe Scolaire, 1955. Print.
Nanga, Bernard. *Les chauves-souris*. Paris: Présence Africaine, 1996. Print.
———. *La trahison de Marianne*. Dakar: Nouvelles Éditions Africaines, 1984. Print.
Ngate, Jonathan. *Francophone African Fiction: Reading a Literary Tradition*. Trenton: Africa World, 1988. Print.
Niane, Djibril Tamsir. *Soundjata ou l'épopée mandingue*. Paris: Présence Africaine, 1960. Print.
Nkashama, Pius Ngandu. *La littérature africaine écrite*. Issy les Moulineaux: Classiques Africaines, 1979. Print.
———. *Le pacte de sang*. Paris: Harmattan, 1984. Print.
Nwapa, Flora. *Efuru*. Portsmouth: Heinemann, 1966. Print.
Ouologuem, Yambo. *Le devoir de violence*. Paris: Seuil, 1968. Print.
Oyono, Ferdinand. *Une vie de boy*. Paris: Julliard, 1956. Print.
———. *Le vieux nègre et la médaille*. Paris: Julliard, 1956. Print.
Rawiri, Angèle. *Fureurs et cris de femmes*. Paris: Harmattan, 1989. Print.
Sadji, Abdoulaye. *Maïmouna*. Paris: Présence Africaine, 1958. Print.
Sammy-Mackfoy, Pierre. *L'odyssée de Mongou*. Paris: Hatier, 1977. Print.
Sango Malo. Dir. Bassek Ba Kobhio. Perf. Jerom Bolo, Marcel Mvondo II, and Edwidge Ntongon a Zock. Diproci, 1991. Film.
Sassine, William. *Saint-Monsieur Baly*. Paris: Présence Africaine, 1973. Print.

Sembène, Ousmane. *Le mandat.* Paris: Présence Africaine, 1969. Print.
———. *Xala.* Paris: Présence Africaine, 1973. Print.
Senghor, Léopold Sédar, ed. *Anthologie de la nouvelle poésie nègre et malgache de langue française.* Paris: PUF, 1948. Print.
———. *The Collected Poetry.* Trans. Melvin Dixon. Charlottesville: UP of Virginia, 1991. Print.
———. *Liberté 1: Négritude et humanisme.* Paris: Seuil, 1964. Print.
———. *Liberté III: Négritude et civilisation de l'universel.* Paris: Seuil, 1977. Print.
Sometimes in April. Dir. Raoul Peck. Perf. Idris Elba and Oris Erhuero. HBO, 19 Mar. 2005. Television.
Tadjo, Véronique. *Á vol d'oiseau.* Paris: Nathan, 1986. Print.
———. *L'ombre d'Imana.* Arles: Actes Sud, 2000. Print.
———. *Le royaume aveugle.* Paris: Harmattan, 1991. Print.
Tchak, Sami. *Place des fêtes.* Paris: Gallimard, 2001. Print.
Téno, Jean-Marie, dir. *Afrique, je te plumerai.* Films du Raphia, 1993. Film.
Tharaud, Jérôme, and Jean Tharaud. *La randonnée de Samba Diouf.* Paris: Lapina, 1927. Print.
Thiam, Awa. *La parole aux négresses.* Paris: Denoël, 1978. Print.
Waberi, Ali Abdourahman. "Les enfants de la postcolonie: Esquisse d'une nouvelle génération d'écrivains francophones d'Afrique noire." *Notre Librairie* 135 (1998): 8–15. Print.
———. *Transit.* Paris: Gallimard, 2003. Print.
Xala. Dir. Ousmane Sembene. Perf. Makhouria Gueye, Thierno Leye, and Dieynaba Niang. Films Domireew, 1974. Film.

Cora Agatucci

Introducing African Novels in a Web-Enhanced Community College Survey Course

Humanities 211, Culture and Literature of Africa, is a one-quarter introduction to sub-Saharan African oral arts, literature, and film offered at Central Oregon Community College (COCC). One among many options that our degree-seeking transfer students can elect, Humanities 211 satisfies lower-division humanities general education and cultural diversity requirements. I regularly teach Chinua Achebe's *Things Fall Apart* and Tsitsi Dangarembga's *Nervous Conditions* in this multigenre introductory survey, and I recently added J. M. Coetzee's *Disgrace* to the reading list. Web-enhanced and proficiency-based instruction has helped me meet the special challenges of teaching African novels to community college students in a time-constrained general education course.

Contextualized study of African texts is particularly important for my students, who typically enter Humanities 211 with no prior course work and little unbiased knowledge of sub-Saharan African history, cultures, and language arts. Effective study of African novels requires reading guides and glossaries, historical and cultural contextual materials, and accessible secondary criticism, integrating African perspectives as much as possible. While Heinemann's Classics in Context "Expanded Edition with Notes" of Achebe's novel meets most of these needs, the dearth of suitable multigenre survey anthologies and of enriched editions of other African novels has required that I generate and compile contextual materials myself as well as construct a historical framework to organize course study. Fortunately, my college's prescient investment in instructional technology has supported development of my Humanities 211 course Web site to house these contextual materials, link to other freely accessible and increasingly valuable World Wide Web resources, publish student writing (with student permission), and foster international educational exchanges. Steady expansion of the COCC library's subscriptions to online databases and interlibrary loan capabilities has also helped us overcome the disadvantages of Central Oregon's geographic isolation in conducting African studies research.

While COCC, like other community colleges, accords high priority to teaching effectiveness, accreditation-driven imperatives over the last decade have forced us to redefine student-centered pedagogy in the rigorous new terms of proficiency-based instruction. A measurable set of student learning outcomes had to be defined for Humanities 211 (see "HUM 211 Syllabus—Fall 2004" in Agatucci for a list of these outcomes); and, because the course was approved to satisfy general education and cultural diversity transfer requirements, course-specific outcomes had to be explicitly aligned to program and college core degree outcomes. Implementation of outcomes-based instruction has helped me sharpen the focus, objectives, and organization of Humanities 211, affecting where I place African novels in the course plan and what I emphasize when I teach them. For example, the primacy of contextualized study of African novels as well as of other texts is embedded in general outcome A ("Build knowledge of language arts and cultures different from one's own") and learning outcome 2 ("Situate individual African texts in their historical, national/regional and cultural contexts, and analyze significant ways that these texts reflect or represent those contexts [e.g., cultural values and beliefs, intellectual and creative traditions, historical and biographical backgrounds, social and political realities]").

I adapted a literary-historical introductory survey model in my organizing of the course and found that placing African texts in the course plan by the historical periods they treat rather than by their dates of publication or distribution worked best with my introductory students. Thus, *Keita: Heritage of the Griot* (1994) is studied in unit 2 (Traditional African Oral Arts, weeks 1–3) because the film dramatizes the oral epic of the thirteenth-century Mande hero Sundiata, while *Things Fall Apart* (1958) is assigned in unit 4 (weeks 4–6) because the novel dramatizes late-nineteenth-century traditional Igbo society at the incursion of British colonialism. However, my students also study the contemporary contexts of these works, modeled on Simon Gikandi's "Chinua Achebe and the Invention of African Literature," which insightfully parallels the historical, literary, and biographical crises that produced the novel. Formal writing assignments asked students to explain and demonstrate the value of studying African works in their contexts.

Humanities 211 is divided into six instructional units, following a roughly historical progression anchored by assigning successive chronological parts of my online "African Timelines: History, Orature, Literature, and Film," the broad period subtitles and embedded mini-essay topics of which were inspired by Molefi Kete Asante and Abu S. Abarry's *African Intellectual Heritage*. The first African novel, *Things Fall Apart*, is not assigned until unit 4, because earlier units provide essential preparation for its study. *Nervous Conditions* is assigned in unit 5 ("Film and Literature of African Colonialism"). In the fall 2004 version of Humanities 211, the final unit 6 ("South Africa") concentrated on *Disgrace*. I highlight here the instructional approaches, materials, and experiences relevant to teaching these particular African novels. My online "HUM 211 Course Pack—Online Index—Fall 2004" offers a complete list of required and recommended readings, and "HUM 211 Course Plan—Fall 2004" links to student assignments and writing examples.

Unit 1: Introduction to Humanities 211 (week 1)

Correcting Central Oregon students' limited knowledge of Africa and misperceptions derived from Western media is a term-long process that begins with multimedia presentations of basic maps and facts of contemporary Africa and introductory discussions of Africa's cultural history based on assigned reading of part 1 ("Ancient Africa") and part 2 ("African Empires") of my online "African Timelines: History, Orature, Literature, and Film." But corrective knowledge building alone is insufficient to clear other obstacles from the path to open-minded, empathetic, and academically informed study of different cultures. Most COCC students elect Humanities 211 because they are interested in the subject matter. Even so, prejudices (however unconscious) and ethnocentrism, the inevitable lens through which cross-cultural knowledge is filtered, had to be addressed explicitly and students given analytic tools to help them detect and counter, if not erase, these obstacles.

Informed by the goals and methods of multicultural education (see Walsh and Agatucci), the following "HUM 211 Course Pack" readings are assigned: (1) common negative images of Africa and African history, identified and analyzed by various Africanist scholars, including Achebe ("African Voice"), help students acknowledge and understand sources of prejudices embedded in their images of Africa; (2) insights of cultural anthropology, comparative religious studies, and myth theory, offered in "Culture, Religion, and Myth: Interdisciplinary Approaches," encourage students to understand and respect cultural differences as creative adaptations to survival in divergent circumstances rooted in common human needs, to suspend immediate judgment based on their own ethnocentric values, and to seek informed ethnorelative perspectives when examining and evaluating the values and behaviors of other cultures; and (3) "Cross-Cultural Study: Some Considerations" explains enabling attitudes and approaches to cross-cultural studies, including more testimony by the invaluable Achebe, excerpts and summaries of Reed Way Dasenbrock's predicted stages of learning and change in these sometimes threatening but ultimately rewarding journeys and of Jacqueline Jones Royster's recommended code of conduct for strangers crossing cultural boundaries.

If my Pacific Northwest students are predominantly white, they are by no means so culturally homogeneous that they cannot bring to bear multicultural frictions and fusions inhabiting their own identities and past experiences. Topics for follow-up seminars and midterm papers require students to apply these course materials and learning experiences with the primary texts to self-reflective analysis of what obstructs and what facilites cross-cultural study of sub-Saharan language arts.

Unit 2: Traditional African Oral Arts and *Keita: Heritage of the Griot* (weeks 1–3)

Unit 2 begins with "In Praise of the Word: Traditional Oral Arts," featuring sections on orality and literacy, derived from Walter Ong's well-known analysis of the epistemological power and characteristics of each modality, and on "Ikemefuna's Song," from *Things Fall Apart*, to illustrate how indigenous orature is incorporated into African literature. Unexamined assumptions about the superiority of Western literate-based cultures are challenged by comparative analysis of the strengths and weakness of orality and of literacy. Students are prepared for more open-minded study and appreciation of the wisdom traditions, communal values, and aesthetic beauties manifested in genres and formal attributes of performance-based African oral arts. ("African Timelines," like the rest of the course, provides examples of Western ways of knowing the world and organizing study of its cultures.) The section on "Ikemefuna's Song" reprints Achebe's untranslated Igbo version from *Things Fall Apart* (42; ch. 7), accompanied by Emmanuel Obiechina's English translation and by excerpts from his explication of relevant Igbo cultural concepts (130–31). As Obiechina has demonstrated, *Things Fall Apart* provides some of the best examples of embedding traditional oral narratives in African literature "for diverse formal, thematic, and aesthetic purposes" (127).

My students quickly grasp that literal translation alone is insufficient. Obiechina's contextual cultural explication is necessary to understand the cautionary and thematic function of Ikemefuna's song-proverb. When students later read the novel in its entirety and encounter Ikemefuna's untranslated Igbo song in chapter 7, they are better prepared to analyze Achebe's use of African English and to tackle issues of language choices, intended audiences, and authorial purposes, in *Things Fall Apart* as well as in film and other novels.

My selection of novels written in English rather than translated from other languages removes at least one layer of mediation from the complexities of cross-cultural interpretation for my students. Key translation issues, targeted by Humanities 211 learning outcome 3, are introduced and viscerally experienced by listening to indigenous language recordings of African praise songs and epics and by viewing the English-subtitled francophone African films *Keita! L'héritage du griot* (in French and Jula) in unit 2 and *Afrique, je te plumerai* and *Chocolat* in unit 5, on Africa under European colonialism.

Unit 3: African Holocaust and African Diaspora (weeks 3–4)

Knowing little of African history, students are introduced to the African holocaust and African diaspora in "African Timelines Part III: African Slave

Trade and European Imperialism." Selections from the slave narrative of Olaudah Equiano and contextual materials on my Web page "Olaudah Equiano" enable me to present this important genre and Achebe's Igbo countryman. Film clips from *Amistad* (the "Middle Passage" segment) and research into the true story (see my "*Amistad*: The True Story and the Film"), highlighting United States involvement, deeply affect my students. African and African Caribbean griot traditions and female experiences of the holocaust and diaspora are dramatized by *I Is a Long-Memoried Woman*, Frances-Anne Solomon's unique film, and by the powerful diasporan poetry of Grace Nichols.

In Humanities 211, much class time is devoted to instruction in discipline-specific writing and documentation. When students publish their writing on the Humanities 211 course Web site, they avoid plagiarism, follow MLA documentation style, and review the commentary that their work stimulates not only from other students in the class but also from Internet visitors. World Wide Web publication breaks the boundaries that traditionally limit instructional discourse to self-contained learning communities of known students and teachers in protected classroom spaces. That our Web materials are regularly accessed and scrutinized by a wide, heterogeneous audience—including people who are the subjects of our Humanities 211 publications—has sensitized both me and my students to the necessity of adhering to a "respectful, reciprocal, and responsible" code of conduct in cross-cultural discourse (Royster 29).

Unit 4: *Things Fall Apart*, by Chinua Achebe (weeks 4–6)

In the canon of African literature, *Things Fall Apart* is central. The novel's placement in unit 4 is dictated by its subject matter: "Achebe's evocation of the precolonial Igbo culture of southeastern Nigeria—and of the impact of the [Western] colonial intrusion on that culture—makes a number of crucial points" about that confrontation (Booker x). Contextual study is invaluably aided by Don C. Ohadike's "Igbo Culture and History" and Gikandi's "Chinua Achebe and the Invention of African Literature." My students never fail to be fascinated and impressed when they meet the author through *Chinua Achebe: A World of Ideas*, Bill Moyers's short videotaped interview, including Achebe's account of writing the novel to challenge racist depictions of Africa and Africans in classic Western literature, such as Joseph Conrad's *Heart of Darkness*. Achebe's views on the value and functions of literature and storytelling are reiterated in excerpts and summaries from his essays, collected in my online handout "Chinua Achebe: In His Own Words."

Unit 2 prepares students for close study of Achebe's use of African English and orature. His discussion of Igbo oral traditions, worldview, gender roles, and griots is a valuable supplement ("If One Thing"). Close reading for students with little experience of literary study is directed by a study guide into which I have invested chapter-by-chapter reading and discussion questions and much commentary and research. In its entirety, the study guide can be overwhelming for some students, so I typically highlight key sections to direct discussion, and I mine the guide for seminar and paper topic choices. Amid the rich array of critical studies and guides for teachers, I recommend Bernth Lindfors's *Approaches to Teaching Achebe's* Things Fall Apart and M. Keith Booker's *The African Novel in English: An Introduction*. Themes and issues important to the study of anglophone African novels are elucidated in chapter 1 of Booker's book, introducing questions of relevance, cultural difference, background, language, genre, and history important to reading the African novel (1–28). Chapter 2 offers a brief historical survey of the African novel (29–64), and the next eight chapters are devoted to individual authors and novels—including *Things Fall Apart* (ch. 3)—with criticism and historical and biographical background.

Unit 5: Film and Literature of African Colonialism (weeks 6–8)

Nineteenth- and twentieth-century developments, covered by "African Timelines, Part IV: Anti-colonialism and Reconstruction" and "Part V: Post-independence Africa and Contemporary Trends," are dramatically brought to life by Jean-Marie Téno's genre-bending antidocumentary *Afrique, je te plumerai* ("Africa, I Will Fleece You"). Téno indicts colonialism and neocolonialism as one hundred years of cultural genocide, and my *Afrique* film guide and resources directs students to comparisons with Achebe and *Things Fall Apart*. *Afrique*'s attention to the impact of colonialist education and the themes of cultural forgetting and remembering also raises valuable comparisons to *Nervous Conditions*, Dangarembga's engaging and provocative bildungsroman.

Several years ago, to diversify regional representation, I replaced Buchi Emecheta's *Joys of Motherhood* (Nigeria) with Dangarembga's *Nervous*

Conditions (Zimbabwe) to present emergent female perspectives on gender issues complicating the politics of race and nation in colonial and postcolonial Africa. (Both novels receive valuable chapter treatments in Booker's *The African Novel in English.*) "*Nervous Conditions* Study Guide: Characters, [Shona] Family Relationships, Places, Reading and Study Questions," included in my "African Authors: Tsitsi Dangarembga and *Nervous Conditions*," directs student contextual study and close reading. The four main female characters present provocative studies in contrast. Correspondences between Dangarembga and her fictional characters, particularly Nyasha, are addressed in Jane Wilkinson's valuable interview with Dangarembga, excerpts and summaries of which are also available on my Web page. In the later weeks of Humanities 211, with a substantial body of work under their belts, students are prepared to address comparison-contrast topics for seminars and final essays required to meet relevant course learning outcomes.

Unit 6: South Africa (weeks 8–10)

In my time-constrained course, adopting Coetzee's postapartheid novel *Disgrace* in fall 2004 required that I drop *African Short Stories*, by Achebe and C. L. Innes, and abridge my multimedia presentation on apartheid resistance arts, thus reducing the number of periods, regions, and genres represented by required Humanities 211 primary texts. However, after Coetzee was awarded the 2003 Nobel Prize in Literature, the inclusion of *Disgrace* provided a unique occasion to examine not only this but other African Nobel Prize winners, as part of the global dissemination and evaluation of world literature today.

Teaching such a disturbing yet fascinating novel for the first time was a risky but interesting adventure. Not having completed all the contextual materials I had planned to produce by week 8, I shared what I had and invited my students to contribute their own chapter summaries, analysis of themes and narrative elements, and contextual research, to compile a collaborative *Disgrace* study guide. This class project proved to be a refreshingly different and challenging assignment that actively engaged students and resulted in a stimulating diversity of readings, sources, and discussion topics.

Works Cited

Achebe, Chinua. "An African Voice." Interview by Katie Bacon. *Atlantic Unbound.* Atlantic Monthly Group, 2 Aug. 2000. Web. 1 Jan. 2003.

———. "'If One Thing Stands, Another Will Stand beside It': An Interview with Chinua Achebe." By Rob Baker and Ellen Draper. *Parabola* 17.3 (1992): 19–27. Print.

———. *Things Fall Apart.* Expanded ed. London: Heinemann, 1996. Print. Classics in Context.

Achebe, Chinua, and C. L. Innes, eds. *African Short Stories: Twenty Short Stories from across the Continent.* Oxford: Heinemann, 1985. Print.

Afrique, je te plumerai ["Africa, I Will Fleece You"]. Dir. Jean-Marie Téno. California Newsreel, 1992. Videocassette.

Agatucci, Cora. *HUM 211: Culture and Literature of Africa.* Central Oregon Community Coll, 1 Sept. 2008. Web. 19 Feb. 2009.

Asante, Molefi Kete, and Abu S. Abarry, eds. *African Intellectual Heritage: A Book of Sources.* Philadelphia: Temple UP, 1996. Print.

Booker, M. Keith. *The African Novel in English: An Introduction.* Portsmouth: Heinemann, 1998. Print. Studies in African Lit.

Chinua Achebe: A World of Ideas. 1989. [Bill] Moyers Collection. Films for the Humanities, 1994. Videocassette.

Chocolat. Dir. Claire Denis. Perf. Guilia Boschi, Isaach de Bankole, and Francois Cluzet. 1988. Orion Classics–MGM Home Entertainment, 2001. DVD.

Coetzee, J. M. *Disgrace.* 1999. New York: Penguin, 2000. Print.

Dangarembga, Tsitsi. *Nervous Conditions.* 1988. 3rd ed. New York: Seal, 2002. Print.

———. "Tsitsi Dangarembga." Interview by Jane Wilkinson. *Talking with African Writers: Interviews with African Poets, Playwrights and Novelists.* By Wilkinson. London: Currey, 1992. 189–98. Print.

Dasenbrock, Reed Way. "Teaching Multicultural Literature." *Understanding Others: Cultural and Cross-Cultural Studies and the Teaching of Literature.* Ed. Joseph Trimmer and Tilly Warnock. Urbana: NCTE, 1992. 35–46. Print.

Gikandi, Simon. "Chinua Achebe and the Invention of African Literature." Achebe, *Things* ix–xviii.

I Is a Long Memoried Woman. Dir. Frances-Anne Solomon. Prod. Ingrid Lewis. 1990. LedaSerene-Yod Video, 1991. Videocassette.

Keita! L'héritage du griot ["Keita: Heritage of the Griot"]. Dir. Dani Kouyaté. Perf. Seydou Boro, Hamed Dicko, Abdoulaye Komboudri, and Sotigui Kouyaté. Afix Prod.; California Newsreel, 1994. Videocassette.

Lindfors, Bernth, ed. *Approaches to Teaching Achebe's* Things Fall Apart. New York: MLA, 1991. Print.

Nichols, Grace. *I Is a Long Memoried Woman.* London: Caribbean Cultural Intl. Karnak House, 1983. Print.

Obiechina, Emmanuel. "Narrative Proverbs in the African Novel." *Research in African Literatures* 24.4 (1993): 123–40. Print.

Ohadike, Don C. "Igbo Culture and History." Achebe, *Things* xix–xlix.
Ong, Walter J. *Orality and Literacy: The Technologizing of the Word.* 2nd ed. New York: Routledge, 2002. Print.
Royster, Jacqueline Jones. "When the First Voice You Hear Is Not Your Own." *College Composition and Communication* 47.1 (1996): 29–40. Print.
Walsh, Kathleen, and Cora Agatucci. *Multicultural Goals: 1. What Are the Goals of Multicultural Education?* Central Oregon Community Coll., 1 Nov. 2001. Web. 1 Aug. 2005.

Harry Garuba

Between Three African Locations: Teaching Chinua Achebe's *Things Fall Apart* at the Universities of Ibadan, Zululand, and Cape Town

Despite the continual assertion that *Arrow of God* is the more accomplished of the two novels, the fascination with *Things Fall Apart* and its centrality to discussions of Chinua Achebe's work and of modern African literature in general remain unassailable. There is, it appears, no stopping the reputation of *Things Fall Apart* as the novel most closely associated with the emergence of modern African literature and the protocols of reading that have developed around it. As Simon Gikandi quite correctly points out in the very first sentence of his book *Reading Chinua Achebe*, "For many students and scholars of African literature, the inaugural moment of modern African literature was the publication of Chinua Achebe's *Things Fall Apart*" (1). Not only does this novel broadly signal this "inaugural moment," it also marks the conceptual and theoretical questions and the literary-critical practices that have gained ascendancy in the reading of this literature. In the first sense, its inaugural significance lies in its projection of an image of Africans as subject and agent of their own history, a subjectivity and agency previously erased or denied by discourses of empire; in the second sense, the novel raises the issues and questions that are necessary for accounting for this subjectivity in the domain of literary discourse. The novel thus fulfills a dual function: it presents African subjects in an African world, carefully, ethnographically, and graphically, and it gives expression to a group of critical categories and practices that have become foundational in the study of African literature.

I have elsewhere commented on the consequences of this historical and discursive placement:

> Certainly more than any other text, this novel has come to be seen as central to the evolving canon of African literature and, lately, of postcolonial literatures. Indeed, the innumerable critical essays on the novel and its ubiquitous presence in the curricula of different academic departments all over the world is evidence that in this novel, what we are dealing with is the phenomenon that Jonathan Arac describes as "hypercanonization." Apart from simply being a literary text, it is made to bear the burden of providing documentary evidence for anthropological studies and sociological speculations, corralled to perform other functions in the history of colonialism and decolonization and, in general, made the representative text of the African response to colonialism and modernity. Being overburdened with so large a freight of functions and thus critically reconstituted as the representative countercanonical text results in an "unarticulated stigmatization" that, in this case, often delegitimizes other avenues of inquiry beyond those consecrated in the counterdiscursive agenda. (146)

Thus a particular reading of the text—based on its celebration of an African culture and its counterdiscursive relation to discourses of empire—becomes something of an authorized version, and this reading is given such hegemony that it tends to prevent other readings from emerging, which cannot be appropriated into this framework. A generalized template of reading is erected in which colonialism, representation and difference, indigenous tradition and European modernity, subject formation and culture, nation and narration, orality and literacy, and so on are the privileged items. In this template, *Things Fall Apart* becomes the text that depicts the struggle for narrative authority between empire and the self-representation of the colonized, presenting a simple binary of resistance to colonial domination. Valid as this template is, this historical and discursive placement makes it difficult for us "to see the object as in itself it really is," to use Matthew Arnold's (in)famous words (249).[1]

Teaching a text of this nature thus presents its own peculiar challenges, because of the hegemony of one kind of reading and also because the text is overinvested with a necessary and valid desire, a desire that acquires an even greater immediacy and resonance when the text is studied in the West or outside Africa in general. But my essay focuses on what it is like to teach this novel in contexts where—supposedly—the pressures of its counterdiscursive power and its status as the iconic text of anticolonial nationalist desire are not exactly overwhelming. I attempt to reflect on a personal, pedagogic experience: teaching, in three African contexts, a canonical text that has come to be globally read as the representative countercanonical text of the colonial experience, written from the viewpoint of the colonized. From this narrative I try to draw specific conclusions about, on the one hand, the ways in which the reading and reception of postcolonial texts is overdetermined from without by the power of dominant discourses and reading practices that refigure the text into a consumable product (Huggan) in the global market of cultural commodities and, on the other, the ways in which the material and discursive geography of its circulation through different places modifies this authorized reading.

Drawing on the common background of colonialism in the three African locations of my narrative and the social and historical specificities of each, I speculate on the reasons for the inclusion of the text in the curriculum in each circumstance, the overall framing of the courses in which it appears, and the approach to teaching that this framing implicitly calls forth—readings that may or may not necessarily follow the dominant, universal template. My purpose is not to show, as travel theories do, the mutations and transformations that texts undergo as they travel. Rather my intention is to show how locality and the contingencies it imposes struggle against the hegemonic power of the global reading of the text. I endorse this struggle and recommend it as an empowering approach in the face of the onslaught of the more generalized, univocal postcolonial reading.

Background

In the mode of personal reflection, I begin with an account of my first introduction to *Things Fall Apart*, because it has a significant bearing on my subsequent relation to the text. My encounter took place through the medium of oral storytelling. In the mid-1960s, my mother was attending a teachers' training college, and one of the texts on the required reading list for her English literature course was *Things Fall Apart*. This was a time before television came to our part of Nigeria, then known as the

Midwest State. During holidays, when my mother returned from this boarding college, she would tell us stories in the evenings, in the same way that an uncle of ours, Akande, known by us all as the master storyteller, always did when he came visiting. One of the stories that she told was the tale of a champion wrestler and great farmer known as Okonkwo, who overreaches himself and meets his downfall as a result. Although she explicitly told us that the title of this story was "Things Fall Apart," we were not old enough to recognize the significance of this novel in the cultural history of colonialism and decolonization and so could not fit it into that frame of reference. Our immediate frame of reference was constituted by oral discourses of great, superhuman wrestlers (always men) or women of otherworldly beauty who, regularly in these tales, meet disastrous ends precisely because of the hubris that came with their endowments. It is worth noting that such stories were also finding their way into the popular culture of the day in magazines, chapbooks, and songs. In fact, the Edo-speaking musician known as Sir Victor Uwaifo had just popularized one version of the famed master wrestler tale with the song "Joromi," which was so hugely successful that it became his signature tune, and his double-headed guitar and his own club became known as Joromi. Stories of this nature found a ready audience even in an emergent urban culture, because they tapped into an already available discursive space provided by the oral tradition.

The pervasiveness of such stories guaranteed that once the narrative of Okonkwo began with his wrestling prowess—the details of which, if my memory serves, were extensively portrayed in my mother's telling of it—we immediately knew what to expect. In the context of these expectations, sanctioned by the oral discourses we were familiar with, Okonkwo's suicide at the end of the story is only one version of the tragic end that befalls such figures of folklore, a version that is of no greater significance because it occurred after he killed the messenger of the white man. In the regular folktale, the wrestler usually defeats all available opponents in the human world and then proceeds to the spirit world, where he also wins all the contests, until he meets a tiny spirit who throws him, breaks his back, and kills him. The inevitability of the disastrous end is often highlighted in the songs that accompany the wrestler as he moves from one opponent to the other, songs of caution containing dire warnings and allusions to the consequences of hubris. In the oral narrative of Okonkwo's life that my mother told, we heard (or thought we heard) these words of caution again and again from his friends and the community: in his participation in the killing of Ikemefuna, at the scene of the beating of his wife during the peace week, during the near-fatal shooting of his wife, and so on. These ominous events and the fatal shooting that leads to his exile and then his longing to return to the battlefield of his egotistical ambitions in Umofia seemed to us to reproduce a pattern that echoed the lineaments of the oral tale.

Achebe himself seems to have a fondness for this tale, because it not only appears in his novels, he has also expounded on it in his commentaries. In the essay "*Chi* in Igbo Cosmology," for example, he dwells on it:

> There is a story of how a proud wrestler, having thrown every challenger in the world, decides to go and wrestle in the world of spirits. There he throws challenger after challenger, including many multiple-headed ones—so great was his prowess. At last there is no one left to fight. But the wrestler refuses to leave. The spirits beg him to go; his companion praise-singer on the flute pleads with him. But it is all in vain. *There must be someone left; surely the famed land of spirits can do better than this,* he said. Again everyone begs him to collect his laurels and go, but again he refuses. Finally his own *chi* appears, thin as a rope. The wrestler laughs at this miserable-looking contender and moves forward contemptuously to knock him down, whereupon the other lifts him clear off the ground with his little finger and smashes him to death. (163)

So my mother's rendering of the Okonkwo story in the context of this oral frame of reference was not exactly off the mark, despite the often remarked-on realism of *Things Fall Apart.* Perhaps she gave so much rein to the oral tales in the novel, the prodigious feasts, the songs and dances, and invocations of the seasons, and the supernatural that we lost the realism of the story and its sense of historical time. She may have unwittingly cast it in the mode of another story, one called "Animal Farm," which she also told us at a different time. But then the animal story also fitted into oral discourses of animal tales of disguise and trickery that we knew. Whether realism was denied or not, what I think is significant is that there was a template of oral storytelling into which we could fit this tale almost effortlessly. In a truer sense than anyone steeped in colonial and postcolonial discourses can imagine, the colonial factor was not an overwhelming one, nor was it narrated in such a way as to make it the dominant point of reference. There is no better way to convey this than to invoke Wole Soyinka's characterization of the District Officer's intervention in the ritual suicide of Elesin in *Death and the King's Horseman*, as incidental but not central to the drama that the play enacts. In Soyinka's words, "[t]he Colonial Factor is an incident, a catalytic incident merely" (3). In my mother's oral telling of "Things Fall Apart," the killing of the messenger was merely a catalytic incident.

Is it possible to read and teach *Things Fall Apart* in a manner that makes the colonial factor merely an incident in the larger drama of the Igbo world and its history? I return to this question later. What I want to highlight now from this narrative of my first encounter with *Things Fall Apart* is not only the possibility of another frame of reference for reading the novel but also that this possibility rests on a different kind of positioning in relation to the text. This different kind of reading, along with many other possible kinds, was largely repressed as a consequence of the hegemony of what I have been calling the authorized version. Therefore, in studying and teaching the text in different contexts, I have always been aware of other possible approaches. This oral reader response to the text, acquired from my mother's narration of it, has always been in the background, conditioning my subsequent study and teaching of the text.

My mother's narrative of this story is not a fluke instance of a practice unique to her. The rendering of written texts in an oral medium is fairly widespread in Nigeria. Such oralization of written texts is not just a matter of a low degree of literacy; it is a cultural practice that emerged at a period when literacy was not the dominant mode of communicating and transmitting ideas and that endured to become a new way of creating various kinds of publics around issues deemed important to particular groups.[2]

The University of Ibadan

In teaching *Things Fall Apart* at the University of Ibadan in Nigeria, could I assume that my students also had access to this oral reading tradition, since for several years the novel had been a required text in the secondary school syllabus? The culture of television had intervened, and the storytelling practices of the past were no longer what they used to be. Very likely, the teachers of literature in the schools, who had come from institutions that taught the authorized version of anticolonial resistance and cultural self-affirmation, had erased whatever memory they had of the expectations generated by the oral rendition of the text and of its validity as another approach to the text. What was clear beyond question was that they had come with a knowledge of the text acquired from school learning. Even though I could assume that the students had been equally interpellated to some degree with an orality that reconfigured written texts through the process of oral reproduction and reinscribed them in the discursive world of oral textuality, I could not assume that the interpellation would apply to this particular novel. The novel's canonical status had become so established by the 1980s that it would be unwise to suggest that the power of the canonical reading of the text was less effective in Nigeria than elsewhere.

But it is also true that the allegory of colonialism and nationalist resistance was gradually losing its power in the Nigerian context of the 1980s and 1990s, when the failures of several postindependence governments led not only to civil war but also to economic collapse. The sense of disillusionment was so strong that, in one symptomatic instance, after the rigged national and state elections of 1983, a state governor, Sam Mbakwe, openly wondered in public if it wouldn't be better for the British to return. In these circumstances, the imperative of teaching the novel as a straight allegory of nationalist resistance and a counterdiscourse to colonialism was not as overwhelming as it had been. While this reading should not be discounted, a more appealing option lay in another direction. But a brief review of the place of the text in the course in which it appears and in the overall design of the curriculum of English majors at the university then will help give context to the discussion that follows and put my argument into a proper perspective.

By the 1980s, the nationalist cultural and institutional struggles of the 1960s and 1970s and the decolonization of the English curriculum that followed had come to be taken for granted in many Nigerian universities.[3] The most famous description of this struggle in postcolonial English departments on the continent is presented in Ngũgĩ wa Thiong'o's account of the Nairobi Memo in his book of essays *Homecoming*. In the spirit of that struggle for decolonizing English studies, English departments in some Nigerian universities changed their names to "Department of Literature" or "Department of Literature in English." This renaming marked the reorganization of course offerings to reflect the centrality of African literature in whatever language it was produced. In fact, the designation "Literature in English" was extended to translations into English, often of novels and poetry originally written in French or Portuguese (see Adesanmi, "Europhonism"). To use the metaphor of center and periphery that characterized these debates, African literature was now truly at the center of the curriculum. There were full-length courses on the African novel, African drama, African poetry, and so on, and these were no longer merely optional offerings but constituted the bulk of the required courses.

The immediate consequence of this shedding of marginal status was that more African texts could, for the first time, be included in the courses taught. More significant than this show of numbers was that there was now a greater responsibility for textual exploration than would otherwise have been possible if one or two African texts were featured in a curriculum dominated by the Western canon. In a curriculum dominated by the English canon, the relational placing of African texts often signals the possibility of another way of seeing or an alternative canon, defined by its difference from the Western canon. The texts therefore become representative of this alternative, this otherness. The Africanization—if I may use a contentious word—of the curriculum thus becomes the first step in displacing or erasing this binarism, by reducing the influence of binarism on reading and interpretation. At this purely structural level of curriculum design, an opening emerges for a more detailed exploration of local subjects and subjectivities, indigenous practices and poetics, institutions and epistemologies, in the context of local history. The overwhelming focus on difference is replaced by a focus on the constitutive elements of the cultural norm in this social order. Normativity rather than the otherness becomes the subject of exploration. This foregrounding of the local as an object of study in its own right, outside a binary framing in relation to Europe, is perhaps the most important consequence of these changes.

To use an analogy from Soyinka's author's note, the curriculum design allowed us to move beyond the colonial factor to focus on "the far more difficult and risky task of eliciting the [novel's] threnodic essence" (3). What did this change mean for teaching *Things* in the context in a Nigerian university in the 1980s and 1990s? Basically it meant directing greater attention inward, to Okonkwo and his culture and society, rather than outward, to the colonial factor, the less difficult and less risky option. Since the curriculum had already been designed in such a way as to make this inward approach possible, it was somewhat easier to highlight an oral reading, by drawing attention to the construction of the character of Okonkwo along the lines of the heroic wrestler narrative. This reading involved not simply thinking of him as the embodiment of anticolonial resistance but also examining the nature of his insertion as heroic wrestler figure into the culture of his society.

As many have noted, Okonkwo is portrayed in the novel as a culture hero; he is the embodiment of the values that the community reveres and the primary defender of its tradition and customs. However, a close examination of his character shows that he is unevenly inserted into the culture of his society. He is not just a flawed character in the novelistic sense of an individual with personal quirks and individual failings that are due to his personal history and psychological complexes. Beyond this idiosyncratic understanding is a larger question that can be said to be epistemic, in the sense of a specific cultural understanding of the world. Okonkwo, like the wrestler in the tale, seeks to enthrone the supremacy of one cultural value or principle over all others, and this attempt goes against the foundational principle of multiplicity and relationality that guides the culture. How does one bring this understanding to a class of students conditioned to see the character as simply having "personality issues," as one student so aptly described it?

Again, I found the solution in Achebe's essay "*Chi* in Igbo Cosmology":

> It is important to stress what I said earlier: the central place in Igbo thought of the notion of duality. Wherever Something stands, Something Else will stand beside it. Nothing is absolute. *I am the truth, the way, and the life,* would be blasphemous or simply absurd, for it is well known that a man may worship Ogwugwu to perfection and yet be killed by Udo. (161)

While it is undeniable that Okonkwo has "personality issues" that the novel depicts in deference to novelistic convention, the ways in which the culture consolidates and reproduces itself are also foregrounded. One of the primary modes of cultural reproduction, as the novel shows, is narrative. It is through narrative that the transmission of cultural values takes place, and it is through narrative that the culture engages in autocritique.

The principle of masculinity, bravery, prowess, and so on may be valorized by the culture, but it is blasphemous to elevate this principle to the status of an absolute. Therefore the culture in its narratives regularly engages in the kind of autocritique that the wrestler tale represents as a cautionary balance to the reification of one value. The monocentric pursuit of a single ideal, no matter how important the ideal, goes against the grain of the polycentric orientation of this society. Thus Achebe, in his characteristically folksy manner, reiterates the well-known saying that a man may worship one god to perfection and yet be slain by another. This dimension of cultural autocritique is often lost in the authorized reading of *Things Fall Apart*.

By foregrounding the oral generic approach I have outlined, it was possible to draw attention to this dimension. It also became easier to show that the narrative's criticism of Okonkwo's monomaniacal pursuit is of the same order as the community's milder criticism of his father's, Unoka's, elevation of the pleasure principle, the love of music and poetry, above every other. The paradoxical similarity of the fate that befalls them in the end becomes eminently more meaningful in the context of this reading. The portrayal of several other characters and events in the novel, such as the priestess Chielo's kidnapping of Okonkwo's daughter, an event that inscribes the authority of the female principle, and Nwoye's defection to the Church, can then be seen as representations of the necessary balance called forth by Okonkwo's inflexible adherence to one ideal. Even the folktale of the tortoise and the feast in heaven further consolidates this generic pattern. The tortoise, it is important to recall, is the creature of folklore that is often celebrated for its cunning and trickery and usually figures as the embodiment of the wisdom of the small over the strength and power of the big. But here the warning rings out clear and loud that even that celebration of the subversive wisdom of the small should be conducted within limits—certainly in relation to other values the community also prizes.

Teaching *Things Fall Apart* at the University of Ibadan in this way proved to be more rewarding than focusing on its counterdiscursive relation to colonial discourse. Not only did the design of the course and the curriculum make this approach possible, but the historical circumstance of postcolonial governance that was the lived reality of the students called for other ways of reading *culture* and *tradition* that did not simply turn them into reified objects demanding unquestioned celebration or that validated themselves only in relation to colonialist culture. Drawing the students' attention to these issues by way of oral narrative genres and ideology served as a good way to balance the hegemonic narrative of nation and empire.

The University of Zululand

Between 1998 and 2000, I taught *Things Fall Apart* every year to a class of first-year undergraduate students at the University of Zululand, South Africa. Most of the students were from rural backgrounds in northern KwaZulu-Natal and therefore, to some extent, had a knowledge of the practices of traditional culture and the ways in which it produces local subjects and subjectivities. They could understand Okonkwo as the product of a particular culture. So ideologically interpellated is he by the culture, that he has naturalized its understanding of the world. Though they were broadly familiar with the practices of cultural reproduction in rural, traditional settings, the specificities of Igbo ways were not so familiar. Unlike most Nigerian students, who knew the customs, rituals, and mores described in the novel either directly from personal experience or indirectly from a knowledge of the social life of another major ethnic group in the country, the students at Zululand were fascinated with the ethnographic details of the novel. They wanted to know what yams looked like, what pounded yam tasted like, and I struggled to find local equivalents. The kola nut was also a source of great curiosity. What did it look like? Did it have an appealing taste? And why was it so significant to social life and interaction in the community? It was a pleasure to discover that the cocoyam—another food mentioned in the novel—is found in Zululand and goes by the local name *madumbe*.

Beyond this interest in local Igbo foods and cultural practices, there was a major investment in Okonkwo's status as a hero of the anticolonial struggle. In 1998, just four years after the first South African black majority government came to power, the memory of the apartheid era and the liberation struggle was still very fresh in the minds of the students. Okonkwo's struggle against colonial imposition resonated strongly at the political level with the antiapartheid struggle. Furthermore, his ideal of masculinity seemed identical to local notions of Zulu masculinity and its warrior ethos cultivated in various narratives since Shaka's imperial wars and consolidated in the ideology of the major Zulu cultural organization and political party, Magosuthu Buthelezi's Inkatha Freedom Party (the IFP). In short, the students could almost effortlessly tie together the question of political resistance and a culturalist celebration of the values held sacrosanct by tradition. There was thus a powerful desire to read the novel for its counterdiscursive agenda as an allegory of empire and nationalist struggle. Recognizing these circumstances, I asked myself how I could teach this novel in a way that struck a balance between the authorized version and the novel's elements of cultural autocritique? In the light of the political uses and abuses of tradition and culture that were prevalent in the community, a balanced approach, I believed, was even more needed.

In general, English departments in South African universities had not undergone the same kind of decolonization and Africanization that had happened in other parts of the continent. For reasons of South Africa's different history, African literature was still a marginal subject in the curriculum, though there was a heavy dose of South and southern African literature. African literature was still framed as an alternative to the English canon. This framing, as I have observed, often calls for a reading that emphasizes the literature's otherness, its enactment of a national allegory, as Fredric Jameson once said in reference to Third World literatures. The University of Zululand was no different in this respect, except that the dangers of a reading that emphasized only this aspect of the novel, without the critique, were more obvious on the ground in the everyday life where the reification and politicization of culture were taking such a toll in human lives.

In introducing *Things Fall Apart* to the students at the first-year level, the English department adopted a comprehension-and-writing framework focused on reading selected passages from the text and answering questions based on them. A course guide had been developed for this purpose, and selected passages from the novel were printed in this guide, followed by the questions that the students were supposed to respond to in class and in their writing assignments. The guide had been in use before I joined the university in January 1998 and proved quite useful in instructing students on the rudiments of writing, logic, and argumentation. It focused on how to write a paragraph and develop paragraphs into complete essays; it dealt with such things as generalization and evidence-proof, topic sentences and elaboration, linking paragraphs, maintaining a logical sequence and moving on to a conclusion.

The course guide featured passages that attempted to give an idea of the whole story when strung together and also sought to bring out something of Okonkwo's character. In this regard, the selected passages dealt with Okonkwo's wrestling prowess and achievements and his relationships with his father; with his household, especially his wives and children; and finally with his community. Other passages focused on the murder of Ikemefuna, the defection of Nwoye, the priestess Chielo, the arrival of the missionaries, and the climactic murder and suicide. In short, the passages provided enough material for the ethnographic stuff (the cultural affirmation and the anticolonial national allegory) and the novelistic stuff (Okonkwo's personality issues, their source in his temperament, his internalized fear of failure, his stuttering speech, and so on). The conventional staple of a psychological reading of character in the novel was thus provided. But room was also provided for an oral generic reading and thus an opening for the cultural autocritique. The passages provided enough material to plot the movement in the novel from celebration to lament. One could highlight the contradictions, paradoxes, and reversals that follow Okonkwo on his journey from humble birth to achievement of the status of culture hero to ignoble end. On the whole, the course guide with its passages and questions was commendably well put together, and one could use it—as I did—to provide a reading beyond the authorized version.

The course was jointly taught by all lecturers in the department. Large numbers of students, both English majors and nonmajors, registered for the course as a way of improving their English and their writing skills. These numbers necessitated splitting the class into several groups. At least one group was assigned to a lecturer—some had more than one lecturer, depending on numbers—and the lecturer's task was to see the students through the course with an eye on their comprehension and writing skills. Using this course guide was meant to ensure uniformity, as much as possible in such a context.

Year after year, following the established format of question and answer, I would ask one final question at the end of the course, a question not provided in the course reader. In the spirit of the sequence of question, answer, and evidence that we had developed during the semester, I would remind students to begin with a one-sentence answer and then provide evidence to support it. My question was, For whom do things fall apart in this novel? Expecting that everyone would first identify Okonkwo before mentioning the community, I was surprised: the imaginative students in the class almost always identified the community or Igbo society or Igbo culture and, by extension, Africa. When the less imaginative students chose the obvious but more literal example of Okonkwo, I was somewhat disappointed and doubted the effectiveness of my attempt to provide other ways of reading the text. I would rationalize their response: it was due to the power of the authorized version, or it was a result of the lure of allegorical interpretation in literary studies.

However, when it came to providing evidence for this interpretation, the evidence was almost always adduced from outside the text—in the institution of colonialism and apartheid in the continent. When I asked for evidence from the text, my attention was often brought—in true tautological fashion—to the novel's epigraph taken from William Butler Yeats's poem or to Obierika's statement about the white man's having put a knife to the things that bound the community together. In search of evidence beyond these statements, some students mentioned the establishment of the Christian church on the piece of land the community called the evil forest, others recalled the strife that the ways of the new converts brought, and still others pointed to the treatment of the Umuofia elders by the white man and his messengers.

While granting the validity of their interpretations, I would draw their attention to the paragraph immediately following Okonkwo's killing of the messenger and ask what it told us about the community:

> The waiting backcloth jumped into tumultuous life and the meeting was stopped. Okonkwo stood looking at the dead man. He knew that Umuofia would not go to war. He knew because they had let the other messengers escape. They had broken into tumult instead of action. He discerned fright in that tumult. He heard voices asking: Why did he do it? He wiped his matchet and walked away. (182)

Did this passage show that the community had fallen apart? The students agreed that the community seemed united. There is evidence of unity in the collective disapproval—even if, as some pointed out, that disapproval was a consequence of fear. Was there any evidence thereafter that the ways of the community and its institutions, beliefs, and practices of everyday life as prescribed by tradition had irretrievably fallen apart? Not really. In deference to tradition, the community does not bury Okonkwo; they have to ask strangers to do it. We must concede that the dynamics have changed because of the presence of the white man.

I suggest that students place this ending in the context of the structure of the heroic wrestler narrative and think of lessons apart from the anticolonial that the narrative is trying to inscribe through its criticism of monocentricism. I follow on this by suggesting that they read Achebe's other novel, *Arrow of God*, and compare the fate of the community and its religious and social institutions at the end of that novel with what occurs in *Things Fall Apart*. In *Arrow*, it would appear, the narrator is unequivocal that things have fallen apart for the community. In *Things Fall Apart,* we conclude, things fall apart for the hero, and the dynamics have changed because of the presence of the white man, but things really fall apart for both hero and community only in *Arrow of God*, a later novel set at a later historical period.

The template of passage, question, and answer proved more rewarding for my teaching of the novel than I had thought it would.

The University of Cape Town

My general comments about the status of African literature in English departments in South African universities also apply at the University of Cape Town. To reiterate the points: comparatively little African literature north of the borders of southern Africa, a good dose of South and southern African literature, curriculum framing in ways that invoke the English canon and its others. However, the cultural and institutional location is very different from that of the University of Zululand: the University of Cape Town is not a historically black university (HBU); its student population is not predominantly rural and Zulu. The university is historically white, having a student population that was and is still largely white and of the middle and upper classes. There is now a fair percentage of students who are considered colored (in the South African racial designation of the apartheid years) and who also fall in the middle- and upper-class brackets. Black students remain a minority. In the African literature course in the English department, a sizable proportion of the class is made up of American study-abroad students.

As can be expected from this demographic composition, most of the students do not have much familiarity with African literature, nor do they have personal experience of the ways in which traditional cultures produce and reproduce their subjects. Thus for both the English majors and the other students, local and foreign, a great attraction was the expectation that the course would present literature and literary tradition different from the ones they were conversant with. They also expected the course to provide, from an insider perspective, an insight into African traditional culture and its workings. It was therefore important for me to underline this difference, literary and cultural, and to map out the dynamics of empire and nationalist resistance as it is played out in the text. The counterdiscursive agenda was much more significant here than at Ibadan or Zululand.

Since 2002, I have jointly taught this course—ELL 210S: African Literature and Language Studies 11—with Brenda Cooper. The course description summarizes how we have designed the lectures and approached the teaching:

> The lectures are organized around four themes, which will provide some basic theoretical tools. In other words, these four themes split the lecture series into four blocks of six lectures each. These tools are applied to the three selected texts—that is, the three texts are referred to under all four themes: "Orality and Written Narrative," "The Language Debate," "Power, Knowledge, and Discourse," and "Gender."

The three texts are Achebe's *Things Fall Apart,* Ama Ata Aidoo's *Our Sister Killjoy,* and Ngũgĩ wa Thiong'o's *A Grain of Wheat.* The idea is to provide the students of this second-year course with a sense of the major themes of intellectual discourse in the field and to show them how these themes have become key concepts in the analysis of the literature. This focus on the intellectual and discursive rather than on a host of primary texts has served us well in introducing students to the field, especially since this may well be the only African literature (apart from South African) course that they will take in their undergraduate studies. The emphasis on theoretical tools conveys the idea of applying a critical vocabulary of situated discourse in a field instead of theory in the abstract.

I have been responsible for the first two blocks of lectures, "Orality and Written Narrative" and "The Language Debate." "Orality and Written Narrative" may seem to provide ample space for the insertion of what I have been calling an oral reading of *Things Fall Apart.* But the difficulty of inserting this reading immediately arises when one examines the critical literature in this section. The emphasis on difference, discursively consolidated into rigid dichotomies and binaries, that runs through the literature on orality and written narrative, from Milman Parry to Walter Ong, makes it almost impossible to discuss orality without a contrastive positioning to writing. Such positioning, important in leading students to a discussion of why orality has become such a privileged concept in African literature, is also constraining, because an examination of its foregrounding invariably invokes the notion of counterdiscourse, even before counterdiscourse becomes a topic in the third section.

The literature on orality inscribes this dichotomy, and when you proceed to consider why the dichotomy is important for African literature, you reinscribe its significance as an instrument of counterdiscourse in the context of the nationalist poetics that governed the emergence of the literature. Coming to the text of *Things Fall Apart* with this background of readings, you end up squarely in the territory of the authorized version. That the tool of orality as historically and intellectually deployed bears the indelible signature of difference and dichotomy tends to block other approaches to reading the novel—or it renders them secondary. Inserting a reading that focuses on the narrative genres of oral societies and the ways they function as carriers of specific ideologies then becomes a struggle.

However, at the end of the lectures for this section, I devote some time to problematizing the notion that oral and written are binary opposites. I focus on the distinction usually drawn between the fluidity of the oral and the fixity of the written. I draw students' attention to genres of oral literature such as the Ifa divination verses of the Yoruba, which are as fixed as you can get. The Ifa priest or *babalawo* recites these verses as handed down by tradition; the priest uses his or her own words only when it comes to interpreting the import of the verses for the client. The relation between fluid and fixed in this instance is complementary rather than oppositional, a continuum rather than a dichotomy. I suggest that a fair amount of the material of oral narratives is quoted or recited in this manner and is recognized as such by the community, in the same way that the community recognizes proverbs, idioms, and other genres that announce their quotedness or fixity whenever they are used. Asking students to read Emevwo Biakolo's "On the Theoretical Foundations of Orality and Literacy" and Karin Barber's "Quotation in the Constitution of Yoruba Oral Texts" has been particularly helpful in making this point clear to them.

By deconstructing the binarism that inheres in the discourse of orality and writing and highlighting the ways in which oral genres are constituted, I find an opening for other readings of Achebe's novel. My literature students are familiar with the idea of genres and how genres function as instruments of ideology at particular times. To move from this understanding to the heroic wrestler narrative and its ideological function and to fit Okonkwo's story into it proved not to be as huge a step as it would otherwise have been. I hesitate to speculate on how successful this effort has been in this instance, because for the more radical students, the attractions of Okonkwo as an icon of anticolonial resistance and the novel as one that truly writes back can make no space for any other reading.

For a text, like *Things Fall Apart*, that is read as weaving the narrative of a particular group or nation, it is important not to see that national story only as an anticolonial story. It is an anticolonial story but also the story of a nation taking stock of itself, of its values, history, and orientation to the world. The narrative of the nation emerges fully not in the struggle against colonial domination but in the struggle to assert its values in their complexity and complementarity. This wholeness is denied when the story is seen to be determined by only one factor—European colonialism. That denial reinscribes what Neil Lazarus describes as "the fetish of the West" in postcolonial studies, by making the encounter with the West the primary determinant of a nation's history.

We need to encourage continually readings of *Things Fall Apart* that see the novel not only as a product in the global market of cultural commodities determined by the West, readings that also understand its situatedness in a local world that has other ways of narrating its history beyond that authorized by capitalist modernity and its cultural institutions.

Notes

1. I must immediately say that my invocation of this quotation here does not necessarily mean that I agree with Arnold's point of view. I find the statement useful as a way of drawing a contrast between it and readings of a different kind.

2. A particularly important example of this practice, which has yet to be studied, developed around newspaper stands in Nigeria. Usually, a group of readers gathers where the newsvendor has spread the daily and weekly papers and magazines. The objective is to browse through as many papers as possible before buying one or two or not buying any at all. As one reader finds a news story he is excited about, he narrates it to the other readers, who are busy with other papers. If they are sufficiently moved by it, a discussion arises among them about it. If the degree of interest is great, the discussion may evolve into a full-blown debate. If a critical mass of opinion is generated, the group may take away this story—that only one person has read—together with all the other facts that were flying around, and pass it on to others—acquaintances, friends, family, and so on—who also retell it, creating a relay chain from this one story as told by one person, who purportedly read it in a newspaper. These kinds of written-oral chain stories were frequently used to create various publics during the Babangida and Abacha dictatorships.

3. For other accounts of this curriculum change, see Garuba; Adesanmi, "Europhonism." See also Adesanmi, "Colonialism."

Works Cited

Achebe, Chinua. *Arrow of God*. London: Heinemann, 1986. Print.

———. "*Chi* in Ogbo Cosmology." *Morning Yet on Creation Day*. New York: Anchor-Doubleday, 1975. 159–75. Print.

———. *Things Fall Apart*. London: Heinemann, 1958. Print.

Adesanmi, Pius. "Colonialism, Ecriture Engagee, and Africa's New Intellectuals." *The Dark Webs: Perspectives on Colonialism in Africa*. Ed. Toyin Falola. Durham: Carolina Acad., 2005. 269–85. Print.

———. "Europhonism, Universities, and Other Stories: How Not to Speak for the Future of African Literatures." *Palavers in African Literature: Essays in Honor of Bernth Lindfors*. Ed. Toyin Falola and Barbara Harlow. Trenton: Africa World, 2002. 105–36. Print.

Arac, Jonathan. "Why Does One Care about the Aesthetic Value of *Huckleberry Finn*?" *New Literary History* 30.4 (1999): 769–84. Print.

Arnold, Matthew. "On Translating Homer." *Essays Literary and Critical*. London: Dent, 1906. 210–75. Print.

Barber, Karin. "Quotation in the Constitution of Yoruba Oral Texts." *Research in African Literatures* 30.2 (1999): 17–41. Print.

Biakolo, Emevwo. "On the Theoretical Foundations of Orality and Literacy." *Research in African Literatures* 30.2 (1999): 42–65. Print.

Garuba, Harry. "*The African Imagination*: Postcolonial Studies, Canons, and Stigmatization." *Research in African Literatures* 34.4 (2003): 145–49. Print.

Gikandi, Simon. *Reading Chinua Achebe: Language and Ideology in Fiction*. London: Currey, 1991. Print.

Huggan, Graham. *The Postcolonial Exotic: Marketing the Margins*. London: Routledge, 2001. Print.

Jameson, Fredric. "Third World Literature in the Era of Multinational Capitalism." *Social Text* 15 (1986): 65–88. Print.

Lazarus, Neil. "The Fetish of 'the West' in Postcolonial Theory." *Marxism, Modernity and Postcolonial Studies*. Ed. Crystal Bartolovich and Lazarus. Cambridge: Cambridge UP, 2002. 43–64. Print.

Ngũgĩ wa Thiong'o. *Homecoming: Essays in African and Caribbean Literature and Politics*. London: Heinemann, 1972. Print.

Ong, Walter. *Orality and Literacy: The Technologizing of the Word*. London: Methuen, 1982. Print.

Parry, Milman. *The Making of Homeric Verse: The Collected Papers of Milman Parry*. Ed. Adam Parry. Oxford: Clarendon, 1971. Print.

Soyinka, Wole. *Death and the King's Horseman*. 1975. Ed. Simon Gikandi. New York: Norton, 2003. Print.

Neville Hoad

The Blank Maps of Difficult Desires: Sexuality and African Literature in the Classroom

To start, two caveats:

1. *Africa* (or *African*) can never be a singular designation, although it references places and people with shared but diverging histories in a global economic system, although it is the subject of passionate identifications for a variety of historically changing interested parties, although it is currently a net exporter of capital and the favored recipient of aid, and although it is the privileged object of many ideas about race.
2. I do not really know what sexuality is, besides a discourse connecting bodies to each other and to systems of social reproduction and death, of biopolitics and necropolitics, of moral economies and pleasures, of experiences and abstractions, of narratives and truths: a particularly dense point in multiple codings of value.

Field Formation

I think it important for students to know something about how what they are studying came to be a sanctioned area of inquiry: the contests and struggles that allowed a class on sexuality and African literature to be on the curriculum. Coupling Africa and sexuality compounds the difficulties suggested in my two caveats, and in the classroom I let institutional definitions hold even as I inevitably work against them. The fields of African studies and sexuality studies in the United States academy are complex and contested disciplinary and interdisciplinary formations. African studies in the United States emerged out of the cold-war Title VI area studies programs and willy-nilly bears the traces of the aspirations of United States global power. However the African Studies Association, helped by some significant controversies along the way, from the start has made meaningful attempts to engage the scholarly output of scholars based in Africa, and the formation of African studies has been available for insurgent knowledge production against its embedded origins in United States imperial power (Martin and West). Some commentary also needs to be made about the ongoing relation between African studies and cognate fields like African American studies, African diasporic studies, and postcolonial studies more generally.

Sexuality studies has been institutionalized in United States universities in a more piecemeal manner, lacking a central professional organization like the African Studies Association, growing out of and having to distinguish itself from the contested terrain of women's studies and then gender studies (Wiegman). Often a kind of euphemism for the expanding identitarian knowledge practices of lesbian and gay studies tending to the LGBTQ umbrella formation, sexuality studies is more often than not a shorthand for a focus on a set of questions that could find a home in a variety of more historically established academic disciplines.

The relation between African studies and sexuality studies has been fraught with difficulties for a variety of reasons, despite their shared investment in the figure of the scholar activist and despite their shared notion of accountability to popular, community, and political constituencies (Undie and Benaya). The essays in Signe Arnfred's recent anthology *Rethinking Sexualities in Africa* (2004) provide carefully historicized ethnographic materials on some African sexualities, though the risk of assigning such materials is that one invites the reality testing of fictional representations against them, allowing the fiction to be nothing but realism in the face of race and sexuality as powerful social fantasies—and I am not saying here fantasy is not real. There has been in recent years an almost overwhelming proliferation of social science scholarship on the HIV/AIDS pandemic in sub-Saharan Africa from a variety of disciplinary and political perspectives. I still find Cindy Patton's "Inventing African

AIDS" (1997) more than useful for its sustained problematizing of apparently simple descriptions of the disease, in view of deep histories of racism and exploitation—allowing one, once again, to think *Africa* as a relational rather than merely a referential designation. More recent work looks specifically at the challenges of prevention programs on a range of scales (Campbell; Kalipeni et al.).

These broad institutional histories will be nuanced by the specificities of the institution in which we teach. At the University of Texas, Austin, I informally discuss with my students other Africa and sexuality curricula offerings and campus-wide resources for the study of African and sexuality issues. I teach in an English department, so the texts from Africa—out of Africa, if you like—are written in English, which renders their representativity extremely marginal. My interest in questions of sexuality in these texts is produced by a sense of political urgency around the current HIV/AIDS pandemic in certain parts of sub-Saharan Africa, though the slippage between sexuality with its identitarian implications and sexual practices requires constant attention. Nevertheless, I think reading fiction can allow these different figurings of sexuality, identity, and politics to become visible.

Imagining Students of Africa, Literature, and Sexuality

When I teach any course with predominantly African material, I begin by handing out a contemporary blank political map of Africa and asking students to fill in the names of as many countries as they can. The point of this exercise is twofold: first, it is a simple way of gauging the degrees of knowledge and ignorance of my students; second, it brings home forcibly the staggering diversity of experiences, languages, cultures, and histories held under the sign of Africa. The map also allows a gesture toward the colonial histories and attendant artificialities of political boundaries across much of the continent. I sometimes despair at the returned maps—in a few cases left blank, Egypt where Nigeria should be—and wonder what to make of the odd übernerd perfection.

Interestingly, the map exercise confounds many of my students' interests in and fantasies and preconceptions of the continent. These investments are often as numerous as the names of the countries they do not know. Usually, however, the classes are a mix of recognizable constituents. There are two kinds of Anglo peace-corps type, who have been or want to go to Africa: secular and missionary. For these groups, who often vehemently disagree with each other in classroom discussion, Africa represents a kind of atrocity exhibition where they can help. Next, there are various kinds of what could be called heritage students. In this group, there are students on ancestral cultural quests in search of their imagined forebears. (In my South African literature classes, I sometimes have to remind the Afrocentric African American student that South Africa was a slave-importing, not slave-exporting, colony.) There are some students from the continent studying abroad and assorted members of diasporic and exile groupings with different histories—white South Africans and Zimbabweans, Asian students with parents or grandparents from East Africa. The two African literature classes I teach with some regularity are entitled Introduction to South African Fiction in English and The Literature and Culture of the HIV/AIDS Pandemic in Sub-Saharan Africa. I am sure the particularities of the student body at the University of Texas, Austin, go some way to produce the above-mentioned constituencies of students, but I suspect that in other classrooms African literature draws students who would not necessarily take a Melville or Shakespeare course, and they come with competing understandings, desires, and expectations of a continent and its literature. The singularity of the life and learning experiences of my students means that they invariably exceed, refute, and contest my typologies of them.

I find this map exercise vaguely embarrassing, too rudimentary or punitive, but it bears powerful and inescapable resonances of interest in Africa that are not that easily disavowed. The still most famous novel about Africa, Joseph Conrad's *Heart of Darkness* (1902), understands its own desire as something like the prompt of a blank map:

> At that time there were many blank spaces on the earth, and when I saw one that looked particularly inviting on a map (but they all look that) I would put my finger on the map and say, "When I grow up I will go there." The North Pole was one of these places I remember. Well I haven't been there yet and shall not try now. The glamour's off. Other places were scattered about the equator, and in every sort of latitude over the two hemispheres. I have been in some of them, and . . . well we won't talk about that. But there was one yet, the biggest, the most blank, so to speak that I had a hankering after.
>
> True, by this time it was not a blank space any more. It had got filled since my boyhood with rivers and lakes and names. It had ceased to be a blank space of delightful mystery—a white patch for a boy to dream gloriously over. It had become a place of darkness. But there

> was in it one river especially, a mighty big river that you could see on a map, resembling an immense snake uncoiled, with its head in the sea, its body at rest curving afar over a vast country, and its tail lost in the depths of the land. And as I looked at the map of it in a shop window, it fascinated me as a snake would a bird, a silly little bird. (70–71)

The names that my students must add to the palimpsest of Africa have also changed since Conrad's time, and the meanings of the blanknesses persist unevenly (Mbodj). I see my first work as engaging these understandings, desires, and expectations as critically as possible, while trying to recognize that these interests, as partial and overdetermined as they are, represent modes of care and attention that must be nurtured in a process that can look like demystification. The fantasy shared by teacher and student that knowledge is something like filling in a map persists—but filling in the map with what? Something more and other than the names of the countries? Kinds of imaginative identifications and disavowals that displace the contours of the map itself, that can supplement my shaming geography quiz?

Achille Mbembe problematizes *Africa* succinctly for me, albeit in a social science rather than literary context, and without explicit consideration of pedagogy in the United States tertiary institution classroom:

> I wish I could have made it clearer that what is called Africa is first and foremost a geographical accident. It is this accident that we subsequently invest with a multitude of significations, diverse imaginary contents, or even fantasies, which, by force of repetition, end up becoming authoritative narratives.
>
> As a consequence of the above, what we call "Africa" could well be analyzed as a formation of desires, passions and undifferentiated fantasies. It is a subjective economy that is cultivated, nurtured, disciplined and reproduced. To nurture it, to police it and to reproduce it involve an intensive work of the imagination. But it also entails a tremendous labor of bad faith social science discourse does not know how to deal with.

Teaching Africa—which also means unlearning Africa—through literature nuances Mbembe's warning in that the dominant mode of reading I find in my students is a very difficult to shake, characterologically driven projective identification, often in the negative. For example, a common student judgment is, "Catherine Njeri in Carolyne Adalla's *Confessions of an AIDS Victim* is a slut." That the narrative voice in the novel seems to share this opinion is immaterial here. I can assign readings on transactional intimacy in neoliberal Africa, slow down students' rush to assimilate the elsewhere of Kenya to their own naturalized moral values around sex and gender, often with unintended consequences in the line of the simplest kinds of cultural relativist arguments. They respond to the arguments in these materials with, "Oh you mean it is normal for Kenyan girls to be sluts." No. The attempt to suggest an alterity to African sexual norms continually risks reinscribing imperialist and racist stereotypes in which the sexual African is always and already a self-consolidating other for the figure of European civilization. This problem is never merely one of literary interpretation. The notorious AIDS denialism by the former South African president Thabo Mbeki operates precisely in this discursive field:

> And thus does it happen that others who consider themselves to be our leaders take to the streets carrying their placards, to demand that because *we are germ carriers, and human beings of a lower order that cannot subject its passions to reason, we must perforce adopt strange opinions, to save a depraved and diseased people from perishing from self-inflicted disease.*

We are in competing accounts of the consequences of the history of racism tending to no common historiographical ground. How can reading literature teach us something else here? Gayatri Spivak's aphorism, "Literature contains the element of surprising the historical" (55), must be held in place even as one yields to the seduction of broaching the historical through literature, and the students' and teacher's versions of African sexual histories are ideologically overdetermined in ways that defy any reliable demystification. I have written elsewhere how Phaswane Mpe's 2001 novel *Welcome to Our Hillbrow* simply refuses the figuration of African sexuality present in Mbeki's denialism, by focusing on the sex lives of young, urban, respectable Africans and revealing a vulnerability to AIDS as an almost arbitrary consequence to being human.

If I can use a blank political map as a way of beginning to teach Africa, I can imagine no such equivalent exercise for beginning to teach sexuality. The utility and the risk of using the common-sense assumptions about sexuality that a teacher finds in the classroom seem unavoidable here.

Two Literary Readings

In a wide variety of contexts, narratives of sexuality are useful for representing more than themselves. The now decade-old controversy over the un-Africanness of homosexuality is an obvious case in point, where sexuality is used to police national, if not racial, authenticity and representations of sexuality. *Normative* and *ideal* or *deviant* and *abhorrent* are strong figures for *corruption* and *decadence*, *resistance* and *progress*. Fredric Jameson clearly overstated his case when arguing that all Third World literature is national allegory, but elements of narratives of sexuality as national allegory have proved irresistible to some writers sometimes.

Mark Behr's *The Smell of Apples,* written in Afrikaans in 1993 and translated into English by the author, is a double narrative by the same narrator. It received several awards, including the Art Seidenbaum Award from the Los Angeles Times (1996); the Betty Trask Award from the British Society of Authors (1995); and, in South Africa, the Eugene Marais Prize, the M Net Award, and the CNA Literary Debut Award. I think the novel's success can partly be attributed to its shrewd staging of South Africa's racial struggle in allegorically sexual terms. The bulk of the book is set in 1974, when our narrator, Marnus, is eleven years old. This narrative is counterpointed by the voice of Marnus as a young adult fighting in the South African defense force in covert operations in Angola in the late 1980s. Two pedagogical interventions emerge almost immediately: the double narration allows for a discussion of the duplicities involved in fighting a covert war and for a recognition that all history writing is revisionist in the interests of an ever-changing present.

Marnus is raised in a racist and loving family, and the novel describes an Edenic childhood in Cape Town that begins by suggesting a contrast with the wider brutal social world of apartheid, but ultimately Marnus's childhood proves entirely congruent with that world. The trope that shows this congruence, indicating that the white family is corrupted by the evil system that sustains it and that the pervasive national shame of apartheid is not just national but also familial and personal, is homosexual child abuse by Marnus's father, a general in the South African army, of Frikkie, Marnus's best friend. In the classroom, we begin to talk about the representational uses of sexuality, how representations of different kinds of sex can be deployed to make arguments about wider social and political issues.

In the literally climactic scene of the novel, our spying narrator, peering through holes in his bedroom floor, initially misrecognizes his father as a miscegenated Chilean general. Marnus's attempt to displace the scene of desire and perversion forcefully beyond the frame of the nation and family only highlights the trauma of the subsequent recognition of the rapist, molester, and possible object of desire as the white father:

> Upstairs I tiptoe to the holes. I will die if the floor makes a sound now. Carefully I lie down. . . . [The general] pulls Frikkie's legs apart and it looks as if he is rubbing something into Frikkie's bum. Then he goes onto his knees between Frikkie's legs and I can see his mister. It's too dark to see everything, but it seems like he pushes his mister into Frikkie's bum, and then he lies down on top of him. He starts moving around. It is just like the Coloured with the girl in the dunes. He uses his one hand to hold himself up on the bed. With the other he keeps the pillow down over Frikkie's head. With all the moving around, the pyjama-shirt is pushing up. It seems as though the sun is about to come up, because downstairs the room is turning light pink. Even before the pyjama-shirt has moved halfway up, I can see: the scar is gone from the General's back. (176–77)

Marnus thus gets an illicit glimpse into the web of lies, hypocrisy, and brutality that is the world of his father. The scene, given the double narrative of the novel, is easily readable as national allegory of sorts. The white fathers are fucking and fucking up their sons, first literally and then by sending them to die defending the indefensible in Angola. I find the description of the moment of recognition that the molester is Marnus's father and not the Chilean general fascinating. "Even before the pyjama-shirt has moved halfway up, I can see: the scar is gone from the General's back." I stress the value of close reading in a discussion of this scene by asking why the scar is the identifying marker of the father and what are the implications of the way the narrative requires us to share the voyeurism of Marnus.

Earlier in the novel, Marnus has asked the general, who is passing as a certain Mr. Smith in South Africa:

> "Is everyone in Chile Spanish, Mr. Smith?" I ask. He laughs. Then he says: "We are not really Spanish. Most of us are Chilenos, but we all speak Spanish." "Most Chilenos have Spanish and Indian ancestors, don't they Mr. Smith" Ilse asks. (153)

Later Marnus ponders the problem that the Chilean general in South Africa helping to defend white supremacy would himself be "coloured" in South African racial taxonomy. This comparative moment in the novel can be opened up into a discussion of the geographic and historical differences in racial formation. I often find that United States students want to assimilate the apartheid category *coloured* into *black*, because they have difficulty imagining *partly black* as a legally sanctioned racial designation. This insistence on the differences in racial classification between South Africa and the United States can also help in showing students that the antiapartheid struggle is not simply an extension of the United States civil rights struggle. The general is identifiable in Marnus's spying throughout the novel—Marnus's vision is limited by what Marnus can see through the hole in the floor—by the scar on the general's back, which is miraculously healed in this scene, a drama of misrecognition turned into recognition. In the molestation, the Chilean general becomes the white father, losing his scar—violence written on his skin—in the act of inflicting violence on a young boy. Sex for Marnus already has a racial history. What his father does to Frikkie is like the "Coloured with the girl in the dunes." The novel renders achingly clear, in a child's voice, the obsessive regulation of sex in the name of racial purity by the apartheid regime.

This is not the only scene of eroticized violence against young male bodies in the novel. Little-Neville, the son of Doreen, the domestic servant of Marnus's family, suffers the following fate, which Marnus hears about rather than observes:

> Mum gets up from her haunches and leans against the basin. She presses her lips together and starts speaking slowly: "Little-Neville and one of his cousins went to the railway yard in Touwsrivier—to steal some charcoal. They wanted to take it to Doreen's sister, before he came to Cape Town." She closes her eyes before going on: "Then someone caught him. They took off his clothes and rubbed lard or something all over his back. And then . . . they held him up in front of the locomotive furnace." Now Mum is crying and I have also got tears in my eyes. I don't know what to do. If only Mum and Ilse would stop crying I'll be able to think. (130–31)

It would appear that little white boys are lubed up to be fucked and little colored boys are lubed up to be burnt, and mixed-race identity seems to have something to do with scars on the back, inflicted and healed by sexualized violence. Here is the description of Little-Neville in the hospital bed:

> He is completely naked and his arms are tied to the bed with strips of plastic to stop him scratching his burns. His legs are drawn wide apart so they won't rub together. Between his thighs across his bum and all over his back it looks like a big piece of raw liver. (189)

I find this scene an awkward one to teach, but it can be used to broach the difficulties in respresenting atrocity—how the novel's deployment of the child's voice can do another kind of cultural work compared with the language of testimonial found in the South African Truth and Reconciliation Commission (TRC).

We see Little-Neville next in a dream of Marnus's:

> And for the first time, I dream the dream of me and Frikkie galloping along Muizenberg Beach. We're in uniform, and the horses are right up against the water. It sounds as if somewhere a woman is singing. In the distance I can see someone running from the horses. It sounds as if somewhere a woman is singing. Now it sounds like the woman's voice is coming from the red waves, or from under the horses' hoofs or from the dunes. Then we get closer to the person who is running away from us. Slowly the horses are catching up. Through the mist I can see that it is someone wearing a hat, and when she turns around and screams, it's Zelda Kemp. She tries to get away, but the horses are almost on top of her. When she sees we are going to catch her, she runs up the beach towards the dunes. I laugh and turn to look at Frikkie. But it is not Frikkie on the horse next to me. It's Little-Neville. (199)

An aside: Zelda Kemp is a local poor white girl, recipient of Marnus's family's charity in the form of Ilse's hand-me-down dresses, and so on. Her last name is not without resonance for any South African who grew up in the 1970s. Glenda Kemp was the national stripper—so to speak—an erotic dancer who continually graced the tabloids with her python, running her own legal battles with a sexually puritan regime. With some texts, the teacher is able to deal with cultural ephemera in a deeper reading. With other texts, one tries to imagine the kinds of cultural literacies that mere erudition cannot reach.

In the climactic scene of the other half of the double narrative, the adult Marnus is frantically running away from someone he assumes to be a terrorist in the bush in Angola. Eventually he makes it back to base camp:

> The black section leader comes over and asks whether I have any instructions. No, I answer, let every man sleep until he wakes. He lies down on his back next to me in the grass. "Lieutenant?" he asks. "Yes?" "Why did you keep on running, Lieutenant? Didn't you hear me calling?" I look him in the face and slowly shrug my shoulders. I turn over to sleep. (178)

Not even the enemy is recognizable anymore. War is rendered as men chasing men, and our narrator collapses at the terror of being chased by a black man, even one fighting on the side of white South Africa. In a novel about spying, the figure of the black collaborator with apartheid is an important one, and one that often baffles students, so we spend some time talking about this scene as a face-to-face encounter in contrast with the younger Marnus's voyeurism-spying.

Bits of biographical information consolidate and disrupt the allegorical reading of sex and sexuality here. In 1995, shortly before he left South Africa for graduate study at Notre Dame, Behr confessed to having been on the payroll of the South African Security Forces as a spy on leftist student organizations. He had been a member of such an organization at Stellenbosch University in the western Cape. In this confession, he gave two explanations: he wanted to preempt revelations about his being a spy before they came to the TRC, and he spied because his homosexuality was a blackmailable secret.[1] He was never called before the TRC, which had many and more serious matters to deal with. This revelation was widely viewed as a publicity stunt for *The Smell of Apples* and his second novel, *Embrace,* being written at the time of his announcement.

Although I think *The Smell of Apples* is both more interesting and disturbing than its author, Behr's going public marks forcibly how the claim of shame is a way for white male South Africans to enter the new nation: it allows their experience to claim a certain centrality and moral capital. They were bad because they were fucked over by history, raped but not burned by apartheid. Their victimization is more interesting because they were perpetrators too. They stage scenes of charged voyeurism for us in order to explain themselves: Mea culpa, but it is not really my fault, if you saw what I saw or did what I had to do, you would be as shameful as me. In the deferred logic of a dream, Behr will substitute a molested white brother with a burnt colored one, and they will ride horses on the beach and chase abject poor white girls into the sea, into the dunes. In another time, he will realize that the black soldier that he thinks has been chasing him, turning him into a version of Zelda Kemp, and trying to kill him in Angola is on his side after all and will still call him lieutenant if not baas. We may be in the birth pangs of white male homosexuality in the imagining of a new South Africa here.

A very different novel also works sexuality through ideas of national, racial, and masculine identity. Wole Soyinka's first novel, *The Interpreters* (1965), is occasionally criticized for its homophobic representation of Joe Golder, a homosexual African American. Though this fact is not part of the racial taxonomy of the novel, Golder is usually referred to as three-quarters white. I do not discuss Golder here but instead argue that a focus on Egbo, the male character most disgusted by the revelation of Golder's queerness, allows one to read sexuality in the novel in a more convoluted, less allegorical way. What follows is a reading of a scene where sexuality and race appear not only as vectors of power but also as potential resources in an ethics of self-fashioning.

If, as Lee Edelman suggests, queerness is a problem for normative social imaginaries because it messes with the figure of the child as a route to a future that is more social reproduction than change, *The Interpreters* suggests that the postcolonial African has similar but divergent difficulties in getting a future started. I stage a risky dialogue here. Much queer theory has rightly been accused of Eurocentrism, especially Edelman's *No Future: Queer Theory and the Death Drive* (2004). Nevertheless, there is something useful here about identity and futurity that can be unevenly transposed. (One of the significant challenges of the African Sexuality Literature classroom—let the awkwardness of that imagined place remind us of the not quite established institutional and interdisciplinary place of these questions—is to bring texts and critical modalities into conversation with texts and critical modalities that they do not and perhaps cannot imagine.)

The Interpreters struggles to imagine social continuity for all its protagonists in the world of a disintegrating nation, an African cosmopolitanism, and a wider postcoloniality. Paddling on a creek with his friend Kola, Egbo remembers an encounter with his grandfather. He feels the contact of a terrifying virility and a redeeming grace in the touch of his grandfather's hands, hands that seem to penetrate his skull and touch the very bumps and crevices of his brain. This encounter is obviously not homosexual, but it is powerfully homosocial. One can also, at this place, point students to continuum rather than binary understandings of sexuality and its diffusions. What follows is a long series of passages, but they are key, exemplifying the continued necessity of close reading, particularly in a pedagogical situation where the providing of historical context can become a substitute for actual reading:

> "I've brought your son." And Egbo could remember the sudden transformation of the ancient strong man, his laughter of menace changed to true delight and a sudden incomprehensible strength which lifted him clean above the dwarfs and onto his knees. Egbo felt again the contact of a terrifying virility, of two hands which felt him all over the face and head, the head especially, of fingers which pressed beneath the hair and into the skull as if [they] would feel into the bumps and crevices of his brain. (10–11)
>
> He knew and despised the age which sought to mutilate his beginnings. . . . If the fight were only political, nothing more. But Egbo had felt a virile essence, a redeeming grace in the old man and in that existence. And this was being destroyed he knew, and by cozening half-men who came bloated on empty wind. There is also my pride of race Egbo said, I am after all, an Egbo. . . . Egbo had begun to wonder and to set the warlord of the creeks against dull grey file cabinet faces of the Foreign Office. (12)
>
> Affecting innocence, Kola asked, "How many wives has the old man?"
>
> For a moment Egbo was deceived, then he laughed. "I've admitted that's a powerful consideration. . . . Just think, not only to be able to fill my house with women but to have it regarded as befitting and manly. I don't know how many he has but I won't be skimpy, I tell you." . . .
>
> "Oh I've dreamt of me and a household like that dozens of times. And the future prospects for the country's traditions. By example to convert the world."
>
> "You are the first genuine throw-back of this generation."
>
> "On the contrary. Polygamy is an entirely modern concept. Oh I don't deny the practice is old, but whoever thought it was polygamy then. . . . What choice, I ask myself, is there between the ugly mudskippers on this creek and the raucous toads of our sewage-ridden ports? What difference?"
>
> "None."
>
> "That is the answer I dread to find if I yield to temptation and reclaim my place here. None. Sometimes I even go so far that I say, 'What is my grandfather but a glorified bandit?' Only that doesn't help either. Sooner a glorified bandit than a loud-mouthed slave." (14)

Egbo's parents are dead; the story of lineage must skip a beat; and Egbo reads his grandfather, a chief or local big man, as an almost godlike personage. Yet the wider historical rupture between the rural, tribal world of his grandfather—the passage deeply troubles both those assignations—and the modern world of the city is revealed as almost illusory. "What choice, I ask myself, is there between the ugly mudskippers on this creek and the raucous toads of our sewage-ridden ports? What difference?" "None." Yet the metaphor is not innocent. Toads eat mudskippers.

Historical time as it is lived in individual life stories of continuity or rupture has a difficult time getting started in the conversation between Egbo and Kola. This problem is staged in terms of sex and alienated labor. If Egbo "goes back"—reclaims his place there in the world of his grandfather, he will have lots of wives, and, as Kola implies, polygamy is the marker of traditional masculinity, one of the manifestations of the terrifying virility of the grandfather that Egbo feels directly, without the mediation of a female body. Egbo is quick to refute this possibility: "On the contrary. Polygamy is an entirely modern concept. Oh I don't deny the practice is old, but whoever thought it was polygamy then." The idea of return to the old is problematized, because this very notion of tradition is seen as both a production and a function of modernity. The exchange anticipates and qualifies the arguments made in Eric Hobsbawm and Terence Ranger's *The Invention of Tradition* (1983). While arguments about the modern invention of tradition tend to invite debunking, a wholesale acceptance of the invention-of-tradition argument ignores the deep internalization of tradition—the fact on the ground that tradition is a route to subjectivity in decolonization, as Egbo's fantasy makes clear here.

Authenticity or historical truth becomes beside the point. Egbo's shrewd distinction between polygamy as practice and polygamy as category marks the rupture of invention, while noting the sustaining power of authenticity. This distinction also recalls the classic native informant's response to the anthropologist's search for cultural authenticity and difference: I would not have thought about it if you had not brought it up. Egbo, in this scene, is a kind of anthropologist of himself, and the novel once again foregrounds the centrality of questions of interpretation, their historical determinants, their ethical possibilities, and their inseparability from desires. Tradition, invented or not, does not so much dupe as seduce. Egbo will "yield to temptation" to reclaim his place here. The sexual spaces of tradition can be represented only in the mode of speculative fantasy. Egbo does not know how many wives his grandfather has. That the experiences of both grandfather and wives are not represented in *The Interpreters* implies that this world is closed to our urban protagonists, in much the same way that the world of "the exclusive coteries in Lagos and the Emirs and their little boys" will be seen as off-limits to Joe Golder (199). I use a close reading of this exchange to problematize the categories of tradition and modernity—two key terms in the dialectics of colonial and postcolonial studies and in anticolonial nationalisms more generally. My hope is that students can follow the texture of Soyinka's prose to complicate these analytic categories and contest the tradition/modernity binary in a meaningfully historiographic way.

The question of alienated labor—a concept associated with the emergence of capitalism and therefore on the modernity side of the tradition/modernity dyad—in this context pushes the paradox further. Tradition, a set of practices associated with a stultifying sameness; with unreflexive, collective repetition in the developmentalist terms of the tradition/modernity dyad; and in many ways with decolonization understood at least in part as a modernizing project, is seen as more enabling of masculine individualism. The warlord of the creeks is a powerful romantic fantasy in contrast with the homogenizing dull-gray file-cabinet faces of the foreign office. Modernity emasculates through bureaucratization. The old man is a law unto himself, which is why his grandson can call him "a glorified bandit," but this is a modern judgment, an ethnocentric recoding of shifting forms of Egbo sovereignty. In opposition to "the glorified bandit" there are "loud-mouthed slaves" and "cozening half-men who came bloated on empty wind." With whom is Egbo to side? This discussion of the precolonial grandfather can lead to interesting discussions of the nation-state, a formation often utterly naturalized and unquestioned for many of my students when they think about questions of sovereignty and the possibilities of political life.

Egbo sees his Egboness, what he calls his "pride of race," as both something prior and subsequent to his person. He hated those who would "mutilate his beginnings" and claims that "I am after all an Egbo," but what kind of man is he to be after his *beginnings* and before *after all*? Masculine subjectivity caught in the interstitial times of decolonization appears to have nowhere to go, trapped in the revealing phrase "future prospects for the country's traditions." The warlord of the creeks cannot convert the dull-gray file-cabinet faces, never mind the whole world. The satirically rendered fantasy that it is tradition that contains the power of bringing about change in the form of conversion adds complexity to the besieged dynamism experienced by Egbo in working out whether or not his grandfather's life represents possible options for his own life.[2]

I have risked inviting student identification with Egbo here, how the ways they may imagine their grandparents' lives represent possibilities for their own. Usually, I get fairly facile technological triumphalisms, which sometimes can be pushed into speculations on rupture and continuity in the formation of personal and group identity. Postcolonial subjectivity can resonate in national contexts that take modernity as their tradition as well. (I offer a further exploration of this scene in my *African Intimacies.*)

Thinking about African sexuality through the reading of fiction needs to move on two occasionally contradictory strands and to work these strands against each other. The dominant hegemonic understanding of sexuality as a kind of subject-making discourse, increasingly organized around an identitarian homo-hetero binary needs resisting without falling into the historically hegemonic fantasy of Africa as a dark continent of primal, undifferentiated lusts and savage urges. Simultaneously, qualitatively, let it be asserted that African sexuality is as banal, as normative, as unruly, as potentially explosive, and as available for political and civilizational allegorizing as any sexuality.

The task becomes one of how to decenter and recenter Africa simultaneously, recognizing that there is no such thing as a singular African perspective but that there are many ways to see the world from Africa and that a focus on sexuality allows for both African specificities and African universalisms.

Notes

1. The testimony of South Africa's Truth and Reconciliation Commission lends itself to literary reading and adaptation. See, inter alia, Antjie Krog's *Country of My Skull* (1999) for a literary reading, Gillian Slovo's *Red Dust* (2002) for an adaptation.

2. Appiah suggests that Egbo's dilemma may be generalizable to African writers. The cultural-worker milieu of *The Interpreters* may encourage this leap. Subjective identity must negotiate the competing claims and diverging temporalities of race, nation, and ethnicity: "For African writers, the answer is not so easy. They are Asante, Yoruba, Kikuyu, but what does this now mean? They are Ghanaian, Nigerian and Kenyan, but does this yet mean anything? They are black, and what is the worth of the black person?" (102).

Works Cited

Adalla, Carolyne. *Confessions of an AIDS Victim.* Nairobi: Spear, 1993. Print.

Appiah, Kwame Anthony. "Myth, Literature, and the African World." *Wole Soyinka: An Appraisal.* Ed. Adewale Maja-Pearce. Portsmouth: Heinemann, 1994. 98–115. Print.

Arnfred, Signe, ed. *Re-thinking Sexualities in Africa.* Uppsala: Nordiska Afrikainstitutet, 2004. Print.

Behr, Mark. *The Smell of Apples.* New York: Picador, 1995. Print.

Campbell, Catherine. *"Letting Them Die": Why HIV/AIDS Intervention Programmes Fail.* Bloomington: Indiana UP, 2003. Print.

Conrad, Joseph. *Heart of Darkness.* New York: Signet, 1963. Print.

Edelman, Lee. *No Future: Queer Theory and the Death Drive.* Durham: Duke UP, 2004. Print.

Hoad, Neville. *African Intimacies: Race, Homosexuality, and Globalization.* Minneapolis: U of Minnesota P, 2007. Print.

Hobsbawm, Eric, and Terence Ranger, eds. *The Invention of Tradition.* Cambridge: Cambridge UP, 1983. Print.

Jameson, Fredric. "Third World Literature in the Era of Multinational Capitalism." *Social Text* 15 (1986): 65–88. Print.

Kalipeni, Ezekiel, et al., eds. *HIV and AIDS in Africa: Beyond Epidemiology.* Oxford: Blackwell, 2004. Print.

Krog, Antjie. *Country of My Skull: Guilt, Sorrow, and the Limits of Forgiveness in the New South Africa.* New York: Times, 1999. Print.

Martin, William G., and Michael O. West, eds. *Out of One, Many Africas: Reconstructing the Study and Meaning of Africa.* Urbana: U of Illinois P, 1999. Print.

Mbeki, Thabo. *Address by President Thabo Mbeki at the Inaugural Z. K. Matthews Memorial Lecture.* U of Fort Hare, 12 Oct. 2001. African Natl. Congress, n.d. Web. 28 Sept. 2008.

Mbembe, Achille. *Achille Mbembe and the Postcolony.* Interview by Christian Hoeller. Africa Dialogue Ser. 1528. U of Texas, Austin, n.d. Web. 28 Sept. 2008.

Mbodj, Mohamed. "'So Geographers in Africa Maps with Savage Pictures Fill Their Gaps': Representing Africa on Maps." *Contested Terrains and Constructed Categories: Contemporary Africa in Focus.* Ed. George Bond and Nigel Gibson. Boulder: Westview, 2002. 37–58. Print.

Mpe, Phaswane. *Welcome to Our Hillbrow.* Pietermaritzburg: U of Natal P, 2001. Print.

Patton, Cindy. "Inventing African AIDS." *The Gender/Sexuality Reader: Culture, History, Political Economy.* Ed. Roger N. Lancaster and Micaela di Leonardo. New York: Routledge, 1997. 387–405. Print.

Slovo, Gillian. *Red Dust.* New York: Norton, 2002. Print.

Soyinka, Wole. *The Interpreters.* London: Deutsch, 1996. Print.

Spivak, Gayatri Chakravorty. *Death of a Discipline.* New York: Columbia UP, 2003. Print.

Undie, Chi-Chi, and Kabwe Benaya. "The State of Knowledge on Sexuality in Sub-Saharan Africa: A Synthesis of Literature." *Jenda: A Journal of Culture and African Women's Studies* 8 (2006): 1–33. Print.

Wiegman, Robyn. *Women's Studies on Its Own: A Next Wave Reader in Institutional Change.* Durham: Duke UP, 2002. Print.

R. Radhakrishnan

Confessions of a Disinterested Didact: Teaching Nadine Gordimer's *Burger's Daughter*

In this brief essay, I focus on three pedagogical-theoretical issues: the inevitable didacticism of the teacher, the institutional-curricular rubric under which a text is taught in the classroom, and the tension between teaching literature for its own sake and teaching it instrumentally in the name of some other priority. Nadine Gordimer's *Burger's Daughter*, a text that I have now repeated in my syllabus more times than I can remember, becomes the exemplary pre-text for the observations that follow.

Why do I teach *Burger's Daughter*, almost compulsively, in one configuration or another? Of course, it goes without saying that I love the work. It speaks to me in so many ways and on so many registers; offers me new insights into the human condition and the literary condition; and provides me with much to think, say, and write about. I transmit all this to my students, in an attitude that combines the work ethic with the pleasure principle. But such transmission sounds more like self-justification than interest in my students. That is precisely why I used the word *didacticism*—to suggest that teachers are positionally prone to entertain the illusion that what they enjoy will inevitably turn into a source of pleasure and edification for their students as well. There is a dangerous flip side to this illusion: what if, despite my passion for the novel and competence as a teacher, I fail to communicate the value of the text to my class? Therefore I respond candidly to my students when they ask me, Why did you choose *Burger's Daughter*?

I choose *Burger's Daughter* because it is complex and because it is rich in theory.[1] Graduate and undergraduate students, both those who eventually come to love it and those who eventually come to hate it, have told me that this is no easy reading, for a variety of reasons. It is a split narrative. Often it is difficult to tell who is talking and who is listening and who is supposed to overlisten. Rosa Burger is sometimes an "I" and sometimes a "she." There is always an other lurking in the narrative. Fiction and history merge and diverge, even as the "I" and the "we" struggle with each other, sometimes dialectically and at other times differentially. The ethical, the political, and the literary provoke one another into perpetual crisis. To all of which I say yes. I tell my students that complexity and theory are sexy, desirable, and just plain ineluctable. I tell them that our lived life is more complex and complicated than the most avant-garde novel or theory.[2] Part of the reason I teach this text is that it is profoundly and constitutively self-reflexive. When students ask me if the same story could have been rendered justice without any of the formal-narratological virtuosity, I defend Gordimer and tell my class, Absolutely not. Virtuosity becomes a valuable point of entry into a discussion of the ethics of form. When, and on the basis of what demonstrable criteria, does the reader decide that a writer's technical virtuosity is either excessive or organic to the message or the story line? In other words, when is complex form ostentatious, narcissistic, or full of itself, and when is it warranted? But before I begin to respond to these important questions, there is the problem of locating the novel for my students. In this essay, I have in mind an undergraduate class only because any text needs to be explicated more for undergraduates than for graduate students.

What can I assume that my class will know about Africa, South Africa, and the postcolonial human condition? Not a whole lot, really. The challenge here is to historicize the novel for the class without anthropologizing it altogether. The risk of anthropologizing is particularly great with an African novel, for the simple reason that Africa continues to occupy the place of the dangerous and primitive other in the Western sociopolitical imaginary.[3] Consequently, an effort needs to be made to ensure that literary and aesthetic dimensions are not swept aside to make room for the canonical expectation that the natives will serve as acquiescent informants and present Africa to the West as an acceptable item of knowledge.

Gordimer is a white South African woman novelist, and South Africa is a particular kind of Africa. My strategy then is to connect the history of apartheid in South Africa with the problems of settler colonialism in that country and the histories of colonialism and the resistances to it throughout Africa: I speak of Amilcar Cabral, Leopold Senghor, Aimé Césaire, Frantz Fanon, the negritude movement, and the debates over the production of a populist postcolonial national consciousness.[4] Next I move to some critical speculations about the relation between the "I" experience and the "we" experience in the context of the genre called the novel, and I add a rich adjective to the genre: *political.* So is the novel about an individual or a collectivity, or both? Are all novels political because they invoke society at large? Are some novels more intentionally political than others? What is the difference between a novel's being political by default and being political by intention? Furthermore, are all intentionally political novels also didactic? (See Jameson; Ahmad's response to Jameson.)

It is time now to raise, in an interrelated way, two questions that are particularly germane to *Burger's Daughter.* Must a novel from South Africa be political, whereas a contemporary American novel does not face that obligation? How is narrative point of view connected to the realization of political content in a novel? For example, which point of view is better suited to the political novel, first-person or third-person omniscient?

I tell my class that Gordimer's novel represented a major and irreversible change in her career. It landed her in trouble with the apartheid state, which condemned it on two counts: blasphemy against God and sedition against the South African state. Gordimer breaks from her earlier fiction; the break is experiential in a humanistic mode that does not deal head-on with the reality of *apartheid*—as though the author feels that literature can show reality through interpersonal subjectivity and humane empathy, without having to name the political. Raw history enters this novel: one of the characters in the work is based on a historical person,[5] and there are parts of the novel that directly report contemporary events in South Africa: the Sharpeville Massacre, the Soweto Revolt. As in another powerful and poignant work, Ralph Ellison's *Invisible Man*, in Gordimer's work one of the big questions is, How does literature represent history through fictional form?

Why do I choose a novel whose protagonist, Rosa Burger, is filiated with the white minority?[6] Why not go with a narrative where the main character represents a new world order? Would not such a work speak more legitimately about South African reality? I tell my class that though there is what one might call an objective political reality, every human subject has the obligation both to receive that reality as a given and to produce or interpret it from his or her particular location (see Rich). Similarly, the objectivity of history is not a mechanical given; rather, it is a perennial production that is the result of a dialectical interaction between the subjective and the objective poles of experience.[7]

What makes Rosa's subject position profound is its constitutive contradiction. She is a minority within a minority: a white Afrikaner, she is the daughter of a father who is a communist leader and organizer who works with the revolutionary African National Congress and goes to jail as habitually as other people have their morning coffee. Thanks to her politically correct but personally dominant and coercive father, the political has been forced on her as her only mode of personal existence. The very title of the novel says that the only identity she has is as Burger's daughter. To her, the political is a congenital condition, and she is nothing but the didactic instrument of her father's activism. Her very name, Rosa, goes back to the famous international communist activist and organizer Rosa Luxemburg. Rosa's much admired and adulated father, Lionel Burger, is the oppressor and not the capitalists, as far as Rosa is concerned. As a privileged white Afrikaner, she occupies a position of power that guarantees the right to speak and speak for, but as the daughter of Burger, she has been deprived of the right to speak for herself. In a paradoxical way, she is both the beneficiary of a brutal and unconscionable political order and the victim of a progressive but programmatically inflicted politics at home.

Rosa's search is twofold in the novel: Rosa seeks to be a person against the grain, as it were, of her father and also to relate her personal existence to the larger and insufferable reality of South Africa under apartheid. In other words, she must depoliticize herself so that she can repoliticize herself on her own terms. I can also tell the class at this point that even though I am one person, I occupy multiple and contradictory subject positions: a dominant position as a male, a minority position as an Asian American, a feminist position by persuasion. The much celebrated unity of personhood is in fact nothing but the attempt, sometimes successful and sometimes not, to synchronize the many different rhythms and temporalities that make us who we are (see Trinh).

So how does the nature of Rosa's reality dictate the choices that Gordimer makes on her behalf? The first choice is that of the split narrative. Typically, students find this technique frustrating, maddening, often confusing. If I can convince them that there is a necessary and organic relation between Rosa's reality and the way Rosa perceives it, then perhaps they will accept the reading difficulty. There are two kinds of dissonance in the novel: one has to do with the shift between first person and third; the other has to do with Rosa's mode of address. There is always an other to whom her speech is directed; sometimes the other is her father, sometimes her lover, Conrad. These two complications are interrelated. I gently suggest to students that Gordimer is telling the reader that there is always an other within each self, that every speech act, even a soliloquy in the privacy of one's bedroom or bathroom, is still a mode of address to this other. In the confessional privacy of the soliloquy, the speaker is also the listener. It is in the capacity of the other that we listen to ourselves. Of course, the effect of such a realization is disconcerting and denaturalizing. The example I give students is, See yourself in the mirror, or listen to your own taped voice, or see yourself as though in a frame.

It is now easier to tell students that this novel is written in a dialogic mode—it does not use social dialogue extensively; rather, its very conception is dialogic. Using Mikhail Bakhtin's theory of the novel as a dialogic genre, I tell the class that human reality is constituted in and by language; and since language always means the existence of the other in one form or another, all reality is dialogic (see Bakhtin; Vološinov). The presence of the other is always implicit, and the subject, in process, is always in dialogue with several others. By definition, such dialogues are an ongoing part of the production of social reality, of a constant becoming. In other words, the dialogic mode is not a mere instrument or stage to be overcome on the subject's or character's way to a monovocal self-actualization.

It is no surprise that Gordimer, who is interested and invested in language professionally and formally, should use language in such a philosophical manner rather than deploy it as a transparent medium where reality just happens monologically. Her novel is also about feelings and perceptions that are too private for thought, and about historical, objective, and public events of a violent and often repugnant nature. Instead of choosing an either-or strategy of psychological interiority or public transparency, she opts for a narrative method that deconstructs the opposition between the inner and the outer, the personal and the political.[8]

Throughout the novel, Rosa Burger is either seeing as a free subject or is subjected to the perception of others, being seen, objectified as a spectacle. "When they saw me outside the prison, what did they see?" she asks (13). I suggest to the class that this is no neurotic curiosity and refer to R. D. Laing and his book *Self and Others*, which makes the point that all reality is negotiated and interpreted in the dialectical continuum of self and other: the self as the self sees itself, the self as seen by the other, the other as seen by the self, and the other as seen by the other (see also Laing, *Divided Self*). Sure enough, there is a third term functioning as a horizon: society, the nation-state that accommodates the self-other interplay and dialog. A question that would often come up in my classes is, Why is it that most of the novels and characters we are studying seem to live and perform in extreme situations: abnormal, atypical, idiosyncratic, tortured, contradicted, conflicted? One student asked me how normal it was for a person to ponder over the dyadic relation between seeing and being seen. My response, by way of Sigmund Freud, Michel Foucault, and others, is that in general the compartmentalization of lived life into healthy and unhealthy is indeed highly artificial and counter to the flows of empathy and human understanding.[9] I love to demonstrate, through the example of the famous last lines of Ralph Ellison's *Invisible Man*, "Who knows but that, on the lower frequencies, I speak for you?" (581) and of that typically Melvillean subtitle "A Story of Wall-Street" for "Bartleby, the Scrivener," that the so-called extremes bring out what lies latent and disavowed in the so-called normal and well-adjusted human condition.

It is only appropriate for Rosa, who is struggling between objectification by the programmatic political didacticism of her father and her own emerging subjectivity, to view her reality through a double frame.[10] But readers learn from her extreme situation the unfamiliar truth of their own well-adjusted situation. They understand that the unity of subjective interiority and objective exteriority is in fact ideologically constructed and not natural. But whether the human condition being studied is extreme or normal, there is no way to avoid what contemporary film, psychoanalytic, and feminist theorists call the gaze. It is in the context of a particular gaze, the male gaze, the gaze of the family, the gaze of the state, or the gaze as cinematic or televisual apparatus, that realities take shape. The gaze constitutes reality precisely because it is elsewhere: it is the other in whose name reality unfolds. Gordimer's novel demonstrates the gaze at work both in everyday situations and in extraordinary and traumatic situations. See, I tell my students, how reality precedes theory, and not the other way around.

My disinterested didacticism in the classroom, I hope, works to connect theory with literature in a fluid and noncompartmentalizing manner, to connect the world of the text with the textuality of the world, and finally to read a text with care, rigor, and a passion for nuance. With the help of the Gordimer text, I try to demonstrate to my students the salience of literature in the world and show them how this salience can be seen in process in a literary work. Why study literature, goes the often repeated question, when one can study the sciences and history, which are about reality? Literature is fictive, imagined, and imaginary, and as W. H. Auden would have it ironically, in the context of the death of William Butler Yeats, it "makes nothing happen." It is just words, a way of saying, "a mouth": no more, no less (243). I tell my students that great and revolutionary thinkers (e.g., Freud, Marx) often sought examples from literature to make their points about the human condition. It is precisely because literature is just a mouth, a way of seeing, a genre that is only seemingly real that it has the capacity to produce critical knowledge about reality.

Burger's Daughter opens up a fraught space between history and allegory. If history deals with factual, concrete, and specific conditions such as South Africa, the apartheid regime, what took place in which decade, which year, and so on, allegory deals with possibilities of a double coding whereby the truths and values that emerge from a determinate historical condition may also be read as truths and values for all time. Gordimer's novel dwells in the critical tension between the historical and the allegorical. To put it differently, Gordimer uses literature as a way of probing and living in that tension aesthetically and imaginatively, without getting exclusively identified with either pole. She writes not about some nameless, universal human subject but about a specific, gendered Afrikaner, a woman during the apartheid regime. Gordimer historicizes the ontological theme of self and other by creating Rosa Burger, who is a dominant-minority subject hypersaturated with power and privilege on the one hand but terribly underrepresented with reference to her familial location as a dominated daughter.

Readers may ask, What is it like to be a dominant self? a subaltern self? a white self? a black self, a majority or minority self? But Gordimer, in this novel more than in any of her earlier novels, is interested in exploring the ways in which human subjectivity is both untrammeled and a product of what Foucault would term specific regimes and disciplinary truths. Even a reality as basic as suffering is doubly parsed in *Burger's Daughter*: on the one hand, it is a general condition that evokes empathy and calls for ethicopolitical actions of broad human solidarity across denominations and labels; on the other hand, suffering has no historical meaning or relevance unless it is diagnosed, named, and recognized as the suffering of black people under apartheid or the suffering of a hapless donkey at the mercy of a ruthless human holding a whip or the suffering of a woman alienated, exploited, and literally and metaphorically raped by one form of patriarchy or another. Human subjectivity is both general and irreducibly particular. Rosa and her black half brother Baasie, who renames himself Zwalenzeema, despite their condemnation of apartheid cannot and do not experience that regime in the same way. If ethics, spirituality, and literature point toward the nameless and general human subject, politics insists on the importance of naming and historically identifying.

Through the theme of representation, Gordimer dramatizes this push and pull between the general existential and ethical human condition and the highly determinate political human condition. Is representation necessary and unavoidable? Is not all representation inherently violent and invasive insofar as it presumes to speak for the other? But what if the self is already an other? What does it mean to inaugurate a cultural politics of postrepresentation? Gordimer ponders over the role that whites should play in a postapartheid South Africa: Does the politics of representation get played out differentially among the different locations and positions that constitute the totality of the body politic (*Essential Gesture*)? Who is right, the Marx who said that some need to be represented or Foucault and Gilles Deleuze, who claim that representation no longer exists and that the ultimate ignominy and humiliation consist in being represented (Foucault, "Intellectuals")? Is not self-expression itself a form of representation, despite its organic intimacy and insiderliness? To borrow usefully from Edward W. Said, does it or does it not matter who is saying what is being said ("Foucault")? Furthermore, what are some of the commonalities and the differences among different modes of representation: the philosophical, the political, and the aesthetic (Spivak)?

At this point, the agenda can get a bit too thick and profound for students, so my teacherly strategy is to ground these big ideas in the text and indulge in some close readings. I seek a few passages in the novel that act out these ideas experientially, through Rosa's point of view. Thanks to the author, there is no shortage of such passages. I select ones in which the author brings out an issue through narrative technique and rhetorical choice, ones that help students make a meaningful connection between the ethic of a form and what the form is about. In a particularly powerful scene in the novel, a donkey is flayed by a black South African male driving the cart. Rosa, the spectator, is traumatized. Should she act to stop the man from beating the animal? What would her motive be, personal or collective, ethical or political? Would her interference get the black man in trouble? Would it be more than the action of a dominant white subject exercising her privilege to act? Would both the means and the ends of her intervention be beyond reproach and mutually synchronic? What right does she have to stop the man when she knows (and can know) nothing about his existence, his imperatives and exigencies, where he comes from? This moment calls for decision and brings together, in one calamitous precipitation, all her different crises. Since she knows but cannot act—and if she acts, she can act only in bad faith—she cannot bear to live one instant longer in that horrible country called South Africa, a country that she considers Lionel's, her father's. This is the point where the personal, familial, and filial combine with the political, societal, and affiliative to make one suffering.

Why and how does Rosa become aphasic and bereft of all possibility for action? In my book *Theory in an Uneven World*, I show how she suffers a double vision of the scene.[11] On the one hand, the scene is unrelievedly immanent in all its sensory immediacy. The victim, the perpetrator, the hand holding the whip, the agony of the beast—every detail is a form of present history that will not be exorcised in the name of any teleology or eschatology. There is also the logic of substitution that informs this scene: the donkey is to the black man what the black man is to apartheid. On an even deeper level, and this is where the vision becomes allegorical, Rosa is able to see the quintessence of a horrible human drama that gets played out under different circumstances and places and in different dress: "Siberias of snow or sun," as Rosa sees it (*Burger's Daughter* 208). She sees the whip disconnected from any particular hand. The hand is doing its all too human job throughout history. The hand, victim, and whip may change, but the allegorical tableau remains the same; it is transtemporal, omnihistorical. Into a particular moment of historical suffering, oppression, and brutality is condensed the endlessly repetitive drama of all human suffering.

This allegorical vision is possible only to the extent that the specifics of the immediate historical scene are submitted to a double vision. Much like a literary scholar specializing in tropes and figures of speech, Rosa is asking, Which is the tenor, and which the vehicle? The question always comes up, as it should: What is so special about Rosa's dilemma in the larger picture of apartheid and the systematic brutality that South African blacks have been subjected to? At least as a white citizen, she has the luxury of indulging in a dilemma, in postponing her choice, making it only when everything comes together in perfect harmony. To put it more bluntly, why does the author, given the South African situation, choose Rosa Burger as her protagonist?

Writers are free to choose any point of view or character as the basis for their elaboration of the human condition. But it is incumbent on them to show the reader the truth in process as it becomes in the mind, heart, and consciousness of their character. Thus no perspective, subject position, or location can be alien to a writer's imagination. The truths of history as much as the truths of subjectivity need to be produced through a labor of love and conscience. A literary truth has to be something other than a formulaic validation of an a priori principle anchored in the name of some rectitude: political, philosophic, religious, or spiritual.

In *Burger's Daughter*, the perspectival resolution that Rosa finds for herself has something to say to the unexpressed and unexperienced Rosa in each one of us. The allegorical truth that the novel gestures toward is that the condition that we all honor and celebrate as human is never a given. On the contrary, it must be brought into existence by each individual against heavy odds, against the seductions of a variety of bad faiths and complacencies. Rosa Burger can neither prostitute her subjectivity in the name of a formulaic and pregiven political correctness nor honor her existential subjectivity in dialectical separation from its sociopolitical ontology. The choice that she makes eventually to make her life her own and her country her own is one that only she can make. When she rejoins South Africa, she does so as herself, but without privilege as Burger's daughter. Such a choice is simultaneously existential and political; and one is not made at the expense of the other.

The purpose of literature, Gordimer teaches us, is to remind us of our existential obligation to the political as process and not as official orthodoxy. Be true to your self, says literature, but only on the understanding that the self is never your own except as an embodied perspective forever shuttling, with conscience, between the "I" and the "we."

Notes

1. On *Burger's Daughter*, see JanMohamed 79–149; Clingman, *Novels* 170–204; Meese; and Radhakrishnan, "Negotiating."

2. For more on what theory might be made to mean, see my *Diasporic Mediations* xiii–xxix and *Theory* vi–xii.

3. On the relation of Europe to Africa, see Rodney.

4. For easy references to some of the works of Fanon, Césaire, Cabral, and Senghor, see Ashcroft, Griffiths, and Tiffin.

5. See Stephen Clingman's eloquent biography of Bram Fischer, who is the basis for the character of Lionel Burger in *Burger's Daughter*.

6. I use the term *filiation* as developed by Edward Said ("Secular Criticism" 16).

7. For more on debates about the objectivity and subjectivity of history, see Bloch.

8. Early in the novel, Rosa is seen in public as she is menstruating. Gordimer uses this scene emblematically to mark the fragility of the boundary between inside and outside. Meese takes up the question of inadequate feminist charge and valence in *Burger's Daughter*.

9. For classic statements on the nature of the everyday, see Freud's *Psychopathology of Everyday Life*, and for a brilliant reading of how pathology is construed into knowledge by the doctor's gaze, see Foucault's *Birth of the Clinic*. See also the great black South African writer Ndebele on the "everyday" after *apartheid*.

10. See DuBois's *The Souls of Black Folk* for the most poignant and radical articulation of doubleness as it confronts the African American.

11. For an intensive analysis of the donkey scene, see the last chapter.

Works Cited

Ahmad, Aijaz. *In Theory: Classes, Nations, Literatures.* London: Verso, 1992. Print.

Ashcroft, Bill, Gareth Griffiths, and Helen Tiffin, eds. *The Post-colonial Studies Reader.* London: Routledge, 1995. Print.

Auden, W. H. *Collected Poems.* Ed. Edward Mendelson. New York: Random, 1976. Print.

Bakhtin, M. M. *The Dialogic Imagination: Four Essays.* Ed. Michael Holquist. Trans. Caryl Emerson and Holquist. Austin: U of Texas P, 1981. Print.

Bloch, Ernst. *Aesthetics and Politics.* Trans. and ed. Ronald Taylor. London: NLB, 1977. Print.

Clingman, Stephen. *Bram Fischer: Afrikaner Revolutionary.* Amherst: U of Massachusetts P, 2000. Print.

———. *The Novels of Nadine Gordimer: History from the Inside.* London: Allen, 1986. Print.

DuBois, W. E. B. *The Souls of Black Folk.* Oxford: Oxford UP, 2007. Print.

Ellison, Ralph. *Invisible Man.* 2nd ed. New York: Vintage, 1995. Print.

Foucault, Michel. *The Birth of the Clinic: An Archaeology of Medical Perception.* Trans. A. M. Sheridan. New York: Vintage, 1994. Print.

———. "Intellectuals and Power: A Conversation between Michel Foucault and Gilles Deleuze." *Language, Counter-memory, Practice: Selected Essays and Interviews with Foucault.* Ed. Donald F. Bouchard. Trans. Bouchard and Sherry Simon. Ithaca: Cornell UP, 1977. 205–17. Print.

Freud, Sigmund. *The Psychopathology of Everyday Life.* Trans. A. A. Brill. New York: Macmillan, 1914. Print.

Gordimer, Nadine. *Burger's Daughter.* New York: Penguin, 1980. Print.

———. *The Essential Gesture: Writing, Politics, and Places.* New York: Penguin, 1989. Print.

Jameson, Fredric. "Third World Literature in the Era of Multinational Capitalism." *Social Text* 15 (1986): 65–88. Print.

JanMohamed, Abdul R. *Manichean Aesthetics: The Politics of Literature in Colonial Africa.* Amherst: U of Massachusetts P, 1983. Print.

Kauffman, Linda S., ed. *Feminism and Institutions: Dialogues on Feminist Theory.* Oxford: Blackwell, 1989. Print.

Laing, R. D. *The Divided Self.* New York: Pantheon, 1962. Print.

———. *Self and Others.* New York: Pantheon, 1969. Print.

Meese, Elizabeth. "The Political Is the Personal: The Construction of Identity in Nadine Gordimer's *Burger's Daughter.*" Kauffman 253–75.

Melville, Herman. *Bartleby, the Scrivener: A Story of Wall-Street. Bartleby.com.* Bartleby.com, July 1999. Web. 30 Sept. 2008.

Ndebele, Njabulo. *South African Literature and Culture: Rediscovery of the Ordinary.* Manchester: Manchester UP, 1994. Print.

Radhakrishnan, R. *Diasporic Mediations: Between Home and Location.* Minneapolis: U of Minnesota P, 1996. Print.

———. "Negotiating Subject Positions in an Uneven World." Kauffman 276–90.

———. *Theory in an Uneven World.* Malden: Blackwell, 2003. Print.

Rich, Adrienne. "Notes toward a Politics of Location." *Blood, Bread, and Poetry: Selected Prose, 1979–85.* New York: Norton, 1986. 210–32. Print.

Rodney, Walter. *How Europe Underdeveloped Africa.* 1972. Washington: Howard UP, 1981. Print.

Said, Edward. "Foucault and the Imagination of Power." *Foucault: A Critical Reader.* Ed. Couzens David Hoy. Oxford: Blackwell, 1986. 149–56. Print.

———. "Secular Criticism." *The World, the Text, and the Critic.* Cambridge: Harvard UP, 1983. 1–30. Print.

Spivak, Gayatri Chakravorty. "Can the Subaltern Speak?" *Marxism and the Interpretation of Culture.* Ed. Cary Nelson and Lawrence Grossberg. Urbana: U of Illinois P, 1988. 271–316. Print.

Trinh T. Minh-ha. *Woman, Native, Other: Writing Postcoloniality and Feminism.* Bloomington: Indiana UP, 1989. Print.
Vološinov, V. N. *Marxism and the Philosophy of Language.* Trans. Ladislav Matejka and I. R. Titunik. Cambridge: Harvard UP, 2000. Print.

Kimberly Wedeven Segall

Creating Contested Space through the "Nervous Conditions" of Postcolonial Theories

There are several ways to organize a course on African novels. Using postcolonial theory seems logical, since many people assume that the African novel is simply one branch of postcolonial writing. However, there is debate over the theoretical term *postcolonial.* For instance, using this categorization drastically simplifies and reduces the diversity of the continent of Africa with all its varied writing. *Postcolonial* also implies that colonization is the central event of African history and culture. Not only are there conflicts about how *postcolonial* is used, but also there are deeper conflicts among views of what the postcolonial condition looks like. When teachers explore the controversy over *postcolonial* and its varied theories, the classroom becomes a contested space, because many viewpoints are suggested. These postcolonial debates, which help students consider how African novels depict communities and relations of power, reveal varied reading strategies.

Postcolonial theories, focused primarily on how power influences identity, are part of an inherently nervous theoretical condition, since power dynamics includes multiple sites of oppression. This instability also emerges because power resides in dialectics of resistance and changing locations. Intersections of authority and refusal are evident when characters are trapped in the middle of contestations—for instance, when restrictive gender roles become a way to mediate control and avoid the larger issues of cross-cultural conflict and changing traditions. The intersection of multiple hierarchies is also evident in struggles between rural and urban spheres of influence and between Western and local narratives of history.

Ideally, if a class can consider incidents of domination and analyze ways that this power is interrupted, then a contested space both in the text and in varied opinions in the class are recognized. As a postcolonial reading technique, a teacher might ask, "What inhibits this character from achieving her goals?," to establish patterns of domination in the text. To create a sense of the historical location of this domination, a teacher could ask, "How are these inhibiting factors a result of Western colonization? How are these limitations a result of patriarchy, cultural expectations, or modern economic changes?" The uneasy positioning of the past oppression of colonization and modern relocations of power suggest the complexity of postcolonial stories. Then, to provide a counterforce to this focus of domination, a teacher could ask about resistance: "How does this character attempt to resist the roles and restrictions placed on the individual? Does this refusal of expectations interrupt how the character acts? Is this resistance successful? Why or why not?" In the contested space of the text, which is analyzed and placed into questions as a pedagogical strategy, one of the key goals is to find sites of power and resistance. The contestation over power that is presented to the class reveals the shifting of modern identities in response to historical and recent losses. Since students bring with them a host of cultural assumptions, including frozen stereotypes of barbaric rituals and safari panoramas, contested sites of power show modern subjects and heteroglossic voices.

When we begin to situate theory in the classroom, with various definitions and models of the postcolonial, a challenging contact zone can be created. Mary Louise Pratt uses the term *contact zone* "to refer to social spaces where cultures meet, clash, and grapple with each other, often in contexts of highly asymmetrical relations of power, such as colonialism, slavery, or their aftermaths" (586).[1] A text-based cultural zone does not just deal with asymmetrical relations of power; it also exposes how sites of authority in a community and complex forms of collaboration and resistance intertwine in postcolonial stories. Since many students have not studied African literature before, it is important to point out historical distinctions between countries, the diversity and urban hybridity of cultural groups, the entangled relations between urban and rural locations, gender complexities, the relation between colonial and contemporary history, and various forms of protest and community involvement.

Extending Pratt's theory of the asymmetrical clashing and grappling of cross-cultural relations, I want to consider the ethical stakes of choosing to focus on domination or resistance and to argue for classroom spaces that use characters to position layers of power and resistance. Moreover, the African novel as a narrative form also actively refuses cultural domination by writing back to the colonizer's easy narrative, and these texts expand the Western model of the novel with oral stories, African history, syncretic spiritual practices, hybrid identities, and untranslated words in African languages that interrupt Western practices of reading. Thus, in a contested space, the teacher guides the class, exploring cross-cultural power dynamics and intercultural struggles, resistance to injustice, and the tension of informal economies and accomplishments alongside economically debilitating histories of violence and recent losses. The tension that I propose for the classroom is one that considers traumatic loss and historical gains, a weighted view of agency that rejects the simple conclusion of victimization. This approach can be navigated through a survey of the meaning of postcolonialism and its theoretical genealogy.

Ethically, when postcolonial theory is used to create a simple focus on loss after colonization, without noting resistance and gender complexity, it is in danger of repeating the stereotype of the West as agent and of Africa as passive victim—a narrative very different from a description of complex power relations, what I see as convoluted contact zones. In terms of pedagogical practice, this essay contends that creating a contested postcolonial space is a teaching style that reveals the ethical implications of postcolonial reading strategies by rejecting a simplified victimization model. Postcolonial pedagogy can easily fall into the trap of considering solely the colonizers of the past. Considering both the historical past and modern Western interventions reinforces a sense of current political responsibility. By demonstrating Western historical responsibility and analyzing how texts resist oppression, the class rejects the simplified charity complex of the West, which insists on the victim stereotype of Africans.

In short, postcolonial pedagogy should search for multiple sites of agency in a novel. It should show examples of colonial and neocolonial power even as the class considers how characters (and communities) resist that power. A class might also examine the ways the text itself rejects colonization, through its form, aesthetics, and story. Contested postcolonial space, as a classroom and reading strategy, displays complex layers of control and opposition, of historical injury and modern identity, of clashes that are often both cultural and gendered. This strategy can lead to discussions on:

- how stereotypes of Africa require ahistorical understandings of modern African culture and history
- how exotic, stereotypical representations have been used to legitimate Western political intervention
- how African writers resist these representations in their stories by showing local agency, complex characterization, modernity, and hybridity
- how the text reveals instances of shifting power dynamics that are worked out in cross-cultural or gendered roles.

My African novels course exemplifies a pedagogy of contested postcolonial space; it demonstrates the reading strategy of searching for multilayered oppression and resistance, for history and modern identification. I offer here an examination of Tsitsi Dangarembga's *Nervous Conditions*, one of many choices in what Susan Gallagher terms the "canon wars" (56), because it uncovers clashes of culture and gender and resistance. I then suggest pedagogical tactics for teaching postcolonial terminology and theoretical models.

In my course, a few students applauded the way in which roads and schools were brought in by the colonizers; other students, after reading *Nervous Conditions*, argued that English-based education had a negative legacy. To establish a contested space, I ask students to consider a number of questions about both power and resistance: How does learning the English language positively or negatively influence the characters? How do gender roles affect individual perceptions of education? How do oral stories create a counterforce against Western ideas?

Two contrasting viewpoints arise in the novel: that Western education leads to economic prosperity and that Western education is a soul-damaging process, similar to being bewitched. Dangarembga's novel tells how a family unit is fractured when a young boy goes to the mission school and returns, pretending to forget his native Shona language and deriding his family's customs. On the one hand, education is a way for Nhamo to "lift our branch of the family out of the squalor in which we were living" (4). On the other hand, the change in his personality leads his mother to declare him bewitched (53). For many students the accusation of witchcraft will appear barbaric; yet, in many ways, the mother's conclusion is profound.

Students often associate witchcraft with stereotypes of Africa. Yet in southern Africa, witches are known for turning subjects into zombies, people who lose their souls and do the work of others without pay. Education in the English language effectively creates in Nhamo a loss of cultural soul and the feeling of superiority to his family. Indeed, the education in English accomplishes the cultural work of fostering the idea of a complex racist hierarchy: there is division not simply between black and white, Africa and West, but, as the text shows, also among illiterate, rural Africans; the English-speaking Africans (or middle men); and white English speakers.[2]

Approaching the novel as a contested postcolonial space reveals how the oral story of witchcraft creates a subtle challenge to the English narrative that education is simply a path to prosperity. The grandmother views the historical legacy of colonization as a process in which the white wizards, using guns and books, dominated African people. Discussing historical injury, colonization, and the formation of middle men alongside modern identification and education as economic opportunity establishes contested space.

Terminology Debates for Contested Postcolonial Space

Analyzing different definitions of postcoloniality sets up a contested space by calling attention to the ways in which the African novel balances historical wounds, which result from colonization or ethnic conflict, and modern identification, which results from changing cultural traditions and technology. In other words, how we define the postcolonial establishes both a tension between the colonizers of the past and the present state and a time frame.

The *post-* in *postcolonical* refers to countries after they gained national independence, after the historical period of colonization. The breakup of the European empires is generally dated as beginning in 1957. But there was local resistance to colonization much earlier—for example, the massive resistance in the 1940s by the Mau Mau, followed by the eventual independence of Kenya. *Postcolonial* marks the end of colonization and the independence of nation-states.

Yet this terminology ignores the legacy of violence. Disappearances, torture, racist treatment, the destruction of homes, and mass murder leave psychological scars. In teaching African novels, it is important to research the historical violence of the specific country and to consider how a novel inscribes these traumatic events. Also, with its implication of termination, *postcolonial* fails to include the cultural displacement and inferiority complex often created by colonial hierarchy.

These displacements of confidence and restructured authority lines create changing roles and relations in families and larger communities. *Postcolonial* suggests damage to the communities by colonizers but does not recognize the shifting and contested lines of local authority after nation-states receive independence.

Since *postcolonial* suggests a singular stage after colonization, it can reinforce ideas that Africans exist in a timeless zone, where cultures do not change or adapt; therefore the depiction is immutably negative. Static Western stereotypes of Africa are obliterating the historical interactions between the West and Africa. These stereotypes also ignore the shifting identities and relations among urban, rural, migrant, and global African communities. Colonization should be taught as a space of contestation, not just simple domination, and postcolonial space should become a labyrinth of negotiation and challenge, a place for changing and hybrid identifications.

Students, taught the *postcolonial* term, are pressed to reconceive their notions of historical progress. As Anne McClintock argues, the term *postcolonialism* sets up a "crisis" in the concept of linear progression (292). While postcolonial theorists refuse the notion of historical development or a "civilizing influence" from the West, *postcolonial* suggests a movement from precolonial to colonial to postcolonial, figuring Europeans as the center of agency. Indeed, the precolonial world is often ignored, and a certain "Enlightenment trope" shifts from "protest" to "national literature," suggesting a triumphant ending to the story, a story that progresses toward and ends with nationalism (292). Yet a nation-state, as a combination of disparate cultural groups, is often a locus not of resolution but of tension.

The postcolonial nation-state is often a contested space. It inherits a colonial structure whose central purpose was to empty out local resources and place them in the hands of a few. When countries became independent, the newly elected or appointed government inherited a structure designed to make a minority group wealthy. Because of pressures to maintain a capitalist, not socialist structure, the economic divisions of wealth from colonization became fairly fixed and difficult to change. Economic tensions between rich and poor continue in postcolonial spaces. Moreover, simply celebrating nationalism forgets the status of women, especially in cases where the policy makers tend to be male. Thus, postcolonial is not simply a national space but also one that remains subject to gender and class tensions.[3]

That issues of gender are important considerations of the contested postcolonial state is evident in *Nervous Conditions*, when a young girl must decide whether or not to earn money to go to school. Tambu contrasts her mother with her wealthy, educated aunt, Maiguru: "I decided it was better to be like Maiguru, who was not poor and had not been crushed by the weight of womanhood" (16). Education for Tambu offers both hope for prosperity and an escape from some of the rural limitations placed on a Shona woman. At first, education seems to have more advantages for Tambu than for her brother, yet Dangarembga reveals how educated African women face profound cultural challenges and gender conflicts. Tambu's mother, Netsai, fears that with Western education Tambu will become "a stranger full of white ways and ideas" (184). Moreover, Tambu's uncle tells Tambu that she is "an intelligent girl but [she] had also to develop into a good woman, he said, stressing both qualities equally and not seeing any contradiction in this" (88). The contradiction the novel points to is that a good woman must be passive, obedient.

The Shona culture refuses to view women's needs as "legitimate" (12) and restricts individual action (173–74). Yet an intelligent girl educated in a Western paradigm learns to value individual independence over communal actions. The novel reveals both oppressive gender relations and the possible choices of a young woman.

This contestational space of gender and education also sets up tension between social class and urban and rural areas. While Tambu's education is presented as an opportunity for advancement in a career and wealth, it creates a nervous condition as Tambu spends less time with her mother and family in her rural village and more time at the mission school. In Dangarembga's sequel, *The Book of Not*, education is further seen as a sign of collaboration with the white Rhodesians and a sign of inequality with the rural village members. Thus Tambu is viewed as an outsider by her mother, and she is traumatized by the trial of her educated uncle that leads to his beating. At the trial, the accidental injury of her sister devastates her, and the thought of her sister without a leg interrupts her ability to study at the largely white, Rhodesian private school she attends. Not completely accepted by the Rhodesians or the revolutionary members of her family, Tambu, despite her exceptional academic work, finds that she does not belong on either side. *Postcolonial* suggests a power dynamic between colonizer and colonized, but what happens when a liminal character cannot fit into either of these communities? The violence of the Shona resistance movement and the epistemological violations of the white community doubly wound Tambu. This contestation of power has many locations and creates an alienated identity for the protagonist.

Considering these possibilities and pitfalls, perhaps *postcolonial* could be replaced with a word that contains no sense of afterward but rather a sense of aftermath. Or a word that signals points of advancement and hope, not just devastation. But what would the word be? *Colonial aftermath* still positions the colonial period at the heart, forgetting modern imperialism. Arguably, *aftermath* places too much emphasis on the West in relation to Africa. One corrective to this emphasis would to stress local resistance to Western imperialism, thus pointing to African agency, as in a title like "Power and Resistance in African Literature." Unfortunately, the phrase sounds more like a course title than a descriptor for the field.[4] Perhaps your class can come up with a term. As Rajeswari Mohan argues, "Commonwealth Studies" falls into a certain nostalgia for the colonial, and "Third World Studies" implies a certain "monolithic entity" for the non-Western world (264–66).[5] So I return to my initial argument that pedagogically the controversy over the term *postcolonial* can establish an important classroom environment for debate and foreground the active dynamics between (not frozen stereotyped time of) power and resistance.

The debate over postcolonial terminology—how much to focus on the colonizer's legacy—parallels the debates over how to describe the postcolonial condition. By setting up a basic genealogy of postcolonial theories, I recognize the tension between reading for domination and interpreting for resistance. These models for teaching contested postcolonial spaces can be used by students to understand how postcolonial theories evaluate (neo)-colonizing power structures and resistance.

Theoretical Models for Contested Postcolonial Space

In the systems model of exposed domination, readers analyze how imperialism relies on multiple venues to dominate the native inhabitants: for instance, written laws, policing, and court cases all enforced racial injustice. Early writers, such as Sol Plaatje in South Africa (1876–1932), not only described the violence of the European settlers but also showed how the colonizer's laws systematically legislated the removal of land and rights.

Although not often regarded as a theorist per se, Plaatje in his *Native Life in South Africa* gave evidence of both physical violation and legislated economic oppression. By documenting the wide-spread use of economic racism, he placed responsibility on the colonizing state.

In contrast to the systems model, models of oppositional identities trace out how the domination of the colonizers also had a psychological effect. As Frantz Fanon (1925–1961), one of the more famous early theorists, argued, the European colonizers were not content to oppress people and take all their assets and labor; the West then proceeded to distort precolonial history, creating a "perverted logic" that the settlers were rescuing the natives from their barbarian traditions (377). In *Black Skin, White Masks*, Fanon examines the "self-division" created by the oppressive practices of colonizers. He claims that behavior with peers differs from that with a white person, creating a type of split identity (17). This self-division also relies on language, for to speak a certain language is to "assume a culture" with all its presumptions of cultural hierarchy (18). Fanon's language of the "death and burial" of "cultural originality" suggests a violent displacement of cultural confidence in the face of a racist aggressor (18).

Extending this theory, Edward Said argues in *Orientalism* (1978) that the West denigrated Eastern cultures and thus formed a Western identity of superiority, a master persona constructed in part through literature. This literary pattern enhanced the political notions that the West was saving the unenlightened barbarians and served as a rationalization for violence against (so-called) dangerous and exotic foreigners. Echoing the philosopher Hegel's contention that the master required the slave to create a master identity, Said's claim is that literature is part of the power dynamics operating between the imperialist West and the rest of the world.[6]

In contrast to these models of domination, there are models of resistance, such as hybridity and ambivalence. Many postcolonial theories suggest ways that characters interrupt, reject, and imaginatively refuse dominated roles. In *The Location of Culture*, Homi Bhabha, in the resistance vein, suggests that a colonial subject does not merely submit and repeat the master's words but also responds with a "sly civility" that mocks and changes the language between master and servant (132). Arguing for potential hybridity, times when a servant imagines a master role or the Westerner feels lost and uncertain, Bhabha suggests that power-based roles are often interrupted. Instead of focusing on how Europeans dominated others, this form of textual analysis examines the ambivalence between the Westerner and the African. It considers gaps in the text, where relationships seem unfinished and uncertain, or it analyzes how identities become disrupted, fractured, restructured in cross-cultural encounters.

A more global theory of resistance is the model of exchange. Cultures do not simply dominate each other; they also influence each other, adapting and integrating different cultural patterns. The theorist C. L. R. James, born in 1901, could be considered another forefather of theory for his work on the Caribbean leader Toussaint L'Ouverture, known as the black Napoleon. Analyzing the complex identity effects between Europe and its colonies, between the French Jacobins and what James termed the black Jacobins (1963), he argues for cultural exchange of both ideas and identifications between the colonizer and colony. Other theorists continue this line of cultural exchange, movement, diasporic identification, and globalization: Stuart Hall, Paul Gilroy, Arjun Appadurai.

In *The Black Atlantic: Modernity and Double Consciousness*, Gilroy suggests that modernity is a place characterized by cultural hybridity. This framework of postcolonial space as a modern intersection of cultural crossings is a helpful corrective to assumptions of Africa as a place of singular tribal identities and void of temporal change. In *On the Postcolony*, Achille Mbembe considers how territories of influence, not just state or colonial power, are powerful forces of sovereignty in Africa. In his introduction to *Globalization in Public Culture*, Appadurai considers how globalization can be a grassroots force and how global communities do not always fit within national lines. Globalization is often simplistically viewed as a one-way commercial force that destroys local cultures; however, Western products become symbolic of a larger contestation over local and transnational power. Moreover, cultural practices are always changing and marked by traveling communities and ideas—hybrid, not just dominated practices.

Resistance as a reading practice often considers how the postcolonial writer imagines times of empowerment for a character. Models of subaltern voices offer one cautionary note on reading for resistance: some students will think a protagonist is an icon for all African women, for instance. Yet since the African writer usually obtains a position of middle-class privilege in order to have the resources available to publish, the postcolonial theorist Gayatri Spivak argues that the text is not a perfect sample of the lower-class oppressed (what she terms *subaltern*), since most authors are influenced by their middle-to-upper-class status and Western education. Chandra Talpade Mohanty tells us to be careful to situate the woman in the novel in a particular history and locale, avoiding generalizations about all Third World women (262).

How does *Nervous Conditions* balance among theoretical models of domination, or models of resistance, in order to show a complex postcolonial condition? The educated African woman in this novel faces cultural expectations of conformity alongside possibilities for vocational independence and demands for income provision: her postcolonial difficulties are complex. Nyasha returns from her schooling in England and fights with her father, who abhors her refusal to be a submissive daughter (74). Nyasha claims, "I'm not a good girl. I won't be trapped" (201). So even as an intelligent girl who can earn an income is valued, she is also devalued if she does not observe the Shona patriarchal norms. Such devaluation could lead to ostracism from her family and community and even decrease the size of her dowry.

Following a psychological model, Fanon argues for a double consciousness, created here through Shona identity and the Western gaze at identity. Yet many postcolonial feminists argue that women experience a doubled set of gender expectations, both "imperial and patriarchal"—a "double colonization" (Ashcroft, Griffiths, and Tiffin 250). By considering not only cultural loss as a result of colonization but also gender roles, the class can learn how power is structured.[7]

In *The Book of Not*, following a model of globalization and power, the complexity of postcolonial space emerges in power dynamics staged around food. Tambu's mother accuses Tambu of becoming so Western that she cannot even eat village food, and the mother calls her educated daughter a white person: "Can you white people eat mufushwa with peanut butter?" (7). While the mother interprets Tambu's difficulty with eating as a sign of her cultural shift, the narrator suggests that it is not the food but the mother's desire for revenge against her educated uncle that causes the lack of appetite (9). The lines between white and African are sketched onto edible products, even as the food symbolizes a larger contestation over methods of resistance and coercion.

This modern staging of authority through food also occurs at the Rhodesian school, when a white student comments on Tambu's roommate, drawing attention to Ntombi's fingernails as a sign of racial difference, and Ntombi responds by asking for some of her chocolate Nesquik. The chocolate powder becomes a sign of wealth and is described as an "icon" (39).

Ntombi's father, a janitor at the school, does not provide store-bought snacks. Since "consumption proved the consumer was a better being compared with others," this contestation over food is part of "another agenda," a restructuring of power (39). By refusing to give chocolate to Ntombi, the white student could be accused of being stingy or being a racist. So she finds herself in a disempowered position, for a change. In effect, "Ntombi had outmaneuvered one of the white girls" (40). Local food contrasts with global, and food is associated with economic and social symbols. The ownership of purchased chocolate—only accessible to those who have wealth, connections to travel, forms of privilege during the rations of war—influences identifications and gives a sense of self-esteem to the children. That Ntombi resists this delineation of wealth, class, and power with her question but does not dare to take the chocolate powder presents a microcosm of the oppression the Shona students internalize at a largely white Rhodesian school.

This space of resistance and domination through commodities also shows the complicated relationship between Tambu and her roommate. Although they sometimes stand together in solidarity, more often they marginalize each other. Their entangled black-on-black violence mixes the white hierarchical system and desperate attempts at decolonization. Seeing the Nesquik as an icon of power, Tambu is embarrassed, wondering why her roommate has to go "begging," and feels superior to her African colleague (43). She refuses the chocolate powder when it is offered to her. And she rejects an identification with local products and therefore her African identification. This refusal also declares her equality with white students, her participation in the white Rhodesian game of commodity-based superiority. Rejecting the "command to consume," Tambu selects her own "proper sort of personhood" (43). To position her identity within the structures of power, she selects an action different from that of her roommate, suggesting different forms of resistance in this passage.

Despite this double colonization, there is refusal and resistance. Tambu refuses to attend a forced wedding; her cousin Nyasha defies her father by not eating. A starved female body resists patriarchal expectation quite literally: when the menstrual cycle stops, reproduction is not a possibility. It is a limited, dangerous resistance, for the body is threatened by the eating disorder.

Although students experience transference when they identify closely with a protagonist, the text's cultural experience may be alien to them.

Contested space analyzes identification and difference to avoid oversimplified comparison. Again, a postcolonial space sets up dialectical resistance and domination, and the (imagined) position of the author and reader become ingredients in this mixture. Readers should avoid complete transference with a text, which ignores differences between the African self and the student and so constitutes a quiet form of domination over the text.[8]

In setting up a contested space in the classroom, it is critical to create one that recognizes the powerful tensions in novels: a dialectic of historical wounds alongside resistance, present sites of injury and altered identities, hybrid influences and gendered constructions of modern African subjects. Teaching controversy—through postcolonial models and strategies for reading both oppression and its interruption—forces student readers to incorporate the past and the present. Contested space recognizes the ethical imperative of analyzing local African agency and is a reading strategy that avoids simplified models of victimization.

Notes

1. My reading practice extends beyond and varies from Pratt, who defines a contact zone as the way that a variety of texts and a heterogeneous class body would mean that what "one said was going to be systematically received in radically heterogeneous ways that we were neither able nor entitled to prescribe" (596).

2. Mbuya, Nhamo's grandmother, tells the family history with references to the white wizards: both the "black magic" wizards to whom stole the family's land and the "holy wizards," to whom the grandmother brought Babamukuru to be "educated in their wizardry" (19).

3. In Zimbabwe, the war for independence in the 1970s left thousands dead, depleted almost half the state budget, and ended on the condition that one-third of the farmland go to the white minority. Despite the sense that the time of colonization is over, Western countries still desire to influence economically and politically. Note that colonization often granted power to a minority group as a way of maintaining the group's reliance on the West.

4. Postcolonial studies needs to encompass what Spivak calls "epistemic violence" (28), the violations in how Westerners assume to know others.

5. Even a nuanced reading of Third Worldism given by Fredric Jameson contains what Mohan criticizes is a "valorization" of Third World texts as national allegories—a potentially "imperialist argument" that nation-states are a "cultural benefit of imperialism" (267).

6. Williams and Chrisman point out that Said reveals how created cultural knowledge "legitimated" the use of Western power ("Colonial Discourse" 8).

7. Postcolonial theories offer another way to view how cultural conflict centers on women's bodies and identities. Women become the "signifiers of national difference," in a way that is as restrictive as previous tribal expectations for women, according to Deniz Kandiyoti (429). Thus, state policies on the education of women and the control of marriage and reproduction exercised by the family set up dual expectations from a "private and public patriarchy" (430).

8. Positioning the author solely as the resistant voice arising from a subaltern space, as critiqued by Spivak, does not allow for the complexity of multiple authors and their positions.

Works Cited

Appadurai, Arjun. "Grassroots Globalization and the Research Imagination." *Globalization*. Ed. Appadurai. Durham: Duke UP, 2001. 1–21. Print.

Ashcroft, Bill, Gareth Griffiths, Helen Tiffin, eds. *The Postcolonial Studies Reader*. London: Routledge, 1995. Print.

Bhabha, Homi K. *The Location of Culture*. New York: Routledge, 1997. Print.

Dangarembga, Tsitsi. *The Book of Not*. Oxfordshire: Ayebia Clarke, 2006. Print.

———. *Nervous Conditions*. London: Women's, 1992. Print.

Fanon, Frantz. *Black Skin, White Masks*. New York: Grove, 1967. Print.

Gallagher, Susan VanZanten. "Contingencies and Intersections: The Formation of Pedagogical Canons." *Pedagogy* 1.1 (2001): 53–67. Print.

Gilroy, Paul. *The Black Atlantic: Modernity and Double Consciousness*. Cambridge: Harvard UP, 1993. Print.

James, C. L. R. *The Black Jacobins: Toussaint L'Ouverture and the San Domingo Revolution*. 2nd ed. New York: Vintage, 1989. Print.

Kandiyoti, Deniz. "Identity and Its Discontents: Women and the Nation." *Millennium: Journal of International Studies* 20.3 (1991): 429–43. Print.

Mbembe, Achille. *On the Postcolony*. Berkeley: U of California P, 2001. Print.

McClintock, Anne. "The Angel of Progress: Pitfalls of the Term 'Postcolonialism.'" Williams and Chrisman, *Colonial Discourse* 291–304.

Mohan, Rajeswari. "Dodging the Crossfire: Questions for Postcolonial Pedagogy." *Order and Partialities: Theory, Pedagogy, and the "Postcolonial."* Ed. Kostas Myrsiades and Jerry McGuire. Albany: State U of New York P, 1995. 261–83. Print.

Mohanty, Chandra Talpade. "Feminist Scholarship, Colonial Discourses." Ashcroft, Griffiths, and Tiffin 259–63.

Plaatje, Solomon Tshekisho. *Native Life in South Africa, before and since the European War and the Boer Rebellion*. 1922. African Natl. Congress, n.d. Web. 5 Oct. 2008.

Pratt, Mary Louise. "Arts of the Contact Zone." *Reading Context*. Ed. Gail Stygall. Boston: Thomson-Wadsworth, 2005. 585–97. Print.

Said, Edward. *Orientalism*. London: Routledge, 1978. Print.

Spivak, Gayatri Chakravorty. "Can the Subaltern Speak?" Ashcroft, Griffiths, and Tiffin 24–28.

Williams, Patrick, and Laura Chrisman, eds. *Colonial Discourse and Post-colonial Theory: A Reader.* New York: Columbia UP, 1994. Print.

———. "Colonial Discourse and Post-colonial Theory: An Introduction." Williams and Chrisman, *Colonial Discourse* 1–20.

Onookome Okome

Reading the Popular: Onitsha Market Romance and the Practice of Everyday Life

Seeking a Place for the Popular in the North American Classroom

Teaching African literature in a North American university comes with its peculiar problems. It demands creative pedagogical solutions and a versatile engagement with students. The teacher must be innovative and sensitive to ideas of the literature's difference in this learning environment. African literature is surely gaining ground in North American universities and other research institutions, but the need to unpack its texts in different situations must be met if the discipline is to grow.

I find it productive to begin with the obvious. African literature is often regarded as a body of literary expression created by the first generation of African writers who got published in Europe and North America and known to literary pundits and scholars in Europe and North America.[1] This body of literary expression from the continent of Africa was written by African writers who were trained in the West and who wrote in one or more European languages. My contribution to this volume deals not with this kind of literature but with another kind of writing, popular African literature, which I define as the everyday diary of the social and cultural negotiations that take place at the local level. Its writers may not have much contact with the West but are nonetheless aware of the pleasures and contradictions that the West brings to their locality. This tradition of literary expression addresses local concerns and espouses locality. This aspect of creative and literary work is receding further and further into the background as the elite literature of the educated proceeds to occupy the literary schedule of those who teach Africa in Europe and North America. Generally speaking, it comes from the abject of the postcolony. It is an aspect of life in Africa that is worthy of critical literary attention.

In this essay I argue that it is impossible for scholars and teachers of literature in North America to reach any deep understanding of social and cultural existence in contemporary Africa without moving beyond the so-called canonical African writings published by European and American publishing outfits shortly before and after independence. I discuss particular instances of teaching popular writing that excavates the everyday in Africa. I also argue why we should pay heed to the popular as an important sphere of the production, consumption, and circulation of knowledge in Africa today. My goal is not only to foster or rekindle scholarly interest in the ordinary in Africa; it is also to articulate how the ordinary is different and significant to our understanding of the ways of being in contemporary Africa (see Mbembe).

I rely heavily on my classroom experiences at the University of Alberta, Edmonton, and the University of Calabar in Nigeria. I argue that the tendency has been to interpret literary Africa from the perspectives of canonized texts by such writers of early Africa as Chinua Achebe, Wole Soyinka, Ayi Kwei Armah, and their female counterparts, Buchi Emecheta, Nawal El Saadawi, and Tsitsi Dangarembga, but that studying these texts in relation to other forms of writing from the postcolony gives a broader view of Africa. The articulation of life, culture, and philosophy goes beyond what the canon puts forward. Long-neglected, popular literature and its audience are a part of the African episteme. Karin Barber asserts that the "cultural historian seeking to uncover histories of consciousness in African popular genres" ("Preliminary Notes" 347) must pay attention to the social zone inhabited by popular literature and those who produce them. This imperative applies also to the study of popular African literatures.

Critical Strategies of Teaching Popular Literature in an American Classroom

Hired to teach anglophone African literature about four years ago, I was dubbed an Africanist. Although I still do not know what the term means, I knew that being an Africanist entailed being part of a larger construct called postcolonial studies. Although I was part of that construct in my earlier position, which I held at the University of Calabar, where I was a scholar and teacher in African drama and cinema studies, this new position offered me the possibility of using new pedagogical methods and addressing new pedagogical concerns. As an Africanist in a North American classroom, I had to rework my teaching strategies to fit into a larger scholarly map and absorb the politics that assigned to my field an oppositionality to dominant discourse in the West. The problem was that the African postcolonial presence on this map was totally colonized by a set of books that had attained the status of literary canon outside Africa. Not all these books enjoyed that status in Africa. To teach any text outside this canon needed a special mode of speaking. In other words, to teach the popular in Africa, a subject I had been interested in for quite a while, demanded a special appeal, a special pedagogical trust, and a series of negotiations in the classroom. In Edmonton I introduced the Onitsha market pamphlets. Interestingly enough, the library at the University of Alberta has a special-collections section that housed, among other special texts, a large holding of these pamphlets.

To contextualize the problem of teaching popular African literature in this situation is to begin to understand that all may not be well with even Achebe's *Things Fall Apart*, the best known of the African classics in Alberta: one cannot say that this novel has moved outside the fence of what Wole Soyinka describes as the "mystical beast" called "African literature." Questions about the realism of the novel still arise. I refer students to Achebe's essay "Teaching *Things Fall Apart*," calling their attention to the possibility of reading the text as exotic, a problem that Achebe responds to. I quote passages that address issues of the humanity of characters and the historical significance of the text. Achebe makes "one general point that is fundamental and essential to the appreciation of African issues by Americans," that "African people are people in the same way Americans, Europeans, Asians, and other people are" (21). The need to make this point forty years after the publication of this book is spelled out: "The necessity even to say this is a part of the burden imposed on us by the customary denigration of Africa in the popular imagination of the West" (21). Achebe emphasizes the common approach to exoticize his novel in the West and draws our attention to the flaw inherent in that approach (24). Obviously readers should try to identify with the humanity of the text, to see its characters as real social actors and their sociality embedded in a cultural template that is historical. I begin my class from this position but then refer students to Robert Wren's "*Things Fall Apart* in Its Time and Place," which anchors the novel in time. Two passages in Wren's historicization of the novel's events are isolated for further analysis in class. The first is his contention that "the novel seems abstracted in time and place, a mythical Africa, even though Achebe roots his characters and actions in a realistic, if not fictional world" (38). The second passage reads:

> Students and teachers need to look at two larger histories. . . . the familiar and the unexpected reality of life and action among the people of the lands portrayed in the novel. . . . The other history—more familiar, perhaps, yet little known—is the European "scramble for Africa." . . . (39)

This forms the introduction to my course on popular literature in Africa.

First I locate the chosen pamphlets in the context of postcolonial literature, because the course falls under the rubric of postcolonial studies and because students are already familiar with the idea of the postcolonial. I proceed indirectly, introducing the debates by having students read two essays instead of explaining to them why popular literature should be an essential aspect of the curriculum of postcolonial literature dealing with Africa. I begin with Kwame Anthony Appiah's "Is the Post- in Postmodern the Post- in Postcolonial?" Stripping the argument to its essence, I point to his definition of *postcoloniality* as "what we might call a comprador intelligentsia: a relatively small, Western styled, Western trained group of writers and thinkers, who mediate the trade in cultural commodities of world capitalism at the periphery" (348). I ask the students to turn this statement over in their minds. What does it mean for the condition of the postcolonial? I urge them to look at this small group that mediates Africa in the West and at "the Africa [the members of the group] offer," the "Africa they invent for the world, for each other, and for Africa."

Predictably, not all aspects of the cultural life of Africa are interesting to this group of mediators. In the selection of what to present to the world, aspects of Africa that are considered unpalatable are consciously left out of the picture, even when it is obvious that some of these aspects "have been influenced, often powerfully, by the transition of African societies through colonization," as Appiah notes. This exclusion is necessary, because popular arts "are not all in the relevant sense postcolonial" (348), for "the *post-* in postcolonial, like the *post-* in postmodern, is the *post-* of the space-clearing gesture I characterize earlier" (349). I ask my students to look closely at some of the contradictions in Appiah's position. If African popular culture grows apace and if there is no lack of interest among those who produce and consume it, why then is its usefulness in question? Why can't we study it as a site of knowledge that would enrich our understanding of contemporary Africa?

One hurdle we must overcome is to rethink the role of the comprador bourgeoisie as legislating and legitimizing canonical African texts. We need to understand why it excludes popular texts. Appiah seems to validate the position of this class of cultural mediators. In other words, he acknowledges his own legislative intent or at least supports the notion that all postcolonial African writing must speak directly to the colonial narrative one way or another, which popular texts do not seem to do. Popular arts are concerned with other things, as Barber points out ("Popular Arts"). I tease out the contradictions embedded in this selective notion of Africa's epistemic framework and direct my students to the possibility that this act of snobbery for everyday popular expression on the continent may have a history in the school system bequeathed to the colonized in Africa. The scholarly history of cultural production and reception is implicated in this colonial heritage, and the sharp divide between what is popular, rustic, and uncouth and what is refined, polished, and aesthetically palatable is part of this history. But does this invented dichotomy matter to the social significance of popular expression? When I ask my classes to debate this question, the answer is usually a loud no.

Accepting the mediatory status of this group of comprador bourgeoisie, Appiah's essay dismisses popular culture as uncritical, arguing that it cannot provide a critical platform for an understanding of contemporary Africa: "Indeed, it might be said to be a mark of popular culture that borrowings from international cultural forms are remarkably insensitive to, not so much dismissive of, or as blind to, the essence of . . . cultural imperialism." Just before this assertion, he writes, "[W]hat has come to be theorized as popular culture . . . [is not] concerned with transcending, with going beyond coloniality" (348). I encourage my students to read against the grain here, to provide an alternative reading that sees our critical engagement with a text, whether elite or popular, as determined by what we bring to it. Appiah's position signals an important aspect of the debate about the social relevance of popular culture in Africa, because the popular Onitsha market pamphlet helped create the African popular culture that Appiah addresses.

Barber's position in this debate is on the opposite side. I summarize it from her essays (Introduction, "Popular Arts," and "Preliminary Notes"). The crucial question for Barber is, Why do we apply the elite/popular model to the evaluation of African popular art? This model in scholarship has now "dominated the study of African cultures" and given to the study of African art and by extension African popular culture "a spurious solidity" (Introduction 1). This dichotomy is complicated by the activities of the first-wave African elite after independence in the 1960s, which recognized "the traditional" as "an affirmation of self-worth, an assertion of African civilization," and then sought to showcase this dimension of African culture to the world. Barber cautions that this scholarly binary and the work of African elites have obscured "the cultural activities, procedures, and products of the majority of people in present-day Africa" (1–2). What results is "the work of local cultural producers speaking to local audiences about pressing concerns, experiences and struggles that they share." I tell my students that popular Onitsha market literature is deeply implicated in this debate. Barber writes that "this old paradigm is beginning to break up" (1), but I have reason to disagree. I am now ready to take my students to the Bruce Peele Special Collections section of the University of Alberta's massive Rutherford Library, to study the pamphlets.

Reading Onitsha, Unpacking a Colonial Local

A brief introduction to Onitsha, a town by the legendary River Niger, is necessary at this point so that students can locate the Onitsha market pamphlets geographically. It is not always easy to convince students that reading the pamphlets is worthwhile and that they will slide easily into the world of Onitsha of the 1940s, 1950s, and 1960s. To begin, I select two of my favorites, *Veronica My Daughter* (Ogali) and *Mabel the Sweet Honey That Poured Away* (Speedy Eric).[2] I introduce them as belonging to the "romance genre," as Emmanuel Obiechina puts it (46). I provide their economic and cultural context and reinforce the point that the

Onitsha market literary ferment was a typical example of colonial locality that consciously invested in the eccentric current of global flow (Comaroff and Comaroff). I tell my students that the production of these pamphlets did not arise out of what Max Gluckman describes as "the magic of despair," as happened in similar circumstances in other dislocated colonial stations.

Instead, the production of Onitsha pamphlets and its readers proceeded from a historical moment expressed more by a desire than a want, a desire for the high life, which was a synthesis of the local and the global. The global is quickly captured in its concrete (printing technology) and ephemeral senses (scribal narrative). It is the inscription of locality that I dwell on, by drawing attention to how the global is appropriated and reassigned, how local cultural vestiges of life are preferred and how adoption of the global is never wholesale. I show my students how the narrative structures of the pamphlets defy the assumptions of colonization and create a critical window that allows us to peek into the mind of this local globality. I remind my students of Achebe's wish that the characters in *Things Fall Apart* be seen as "normal people and their events as real human events" ("Teaching" 22). Can the characters in the pamphets be seen in the same way? I ask students to post their preliminary ideas on the WebCT, a university-based learning scheme on the Internet that allows the less vocal in class to be part of the conversation. I have students address these issues in *Veronica My Daughter* and *Mabel the Sweet Honey That Poured Away:* locality, women, and high life. The result is often stunning.

Two Pamphlets

When I assign the reading of the first two pamphlets, I suggest that students look beneath the veneer of simplicity that *Veronica* presents to literary students stuffed with grand literary theories. I ask them to place the stories in context and locate the modernity I refer to as highlife. I warn them that the Onitsha pamphleteering tradition does not observe the strict literary categories as we have them today. Indeed, authors crisscross genre boundaries so frequently in their narratives that it is difficult to assign the symbols or codes of a particular genre to any pamphlet. I urge students to pay special attention to narrative surpluses, passages that may have slipped out of the author's control, allowing us to see the flip side of the privileged story. Reading the paratexts also helps. The covers of *Veronica My Daughter* and *Mabel the Sweet Honey That Poured Away* eloquently tell about the drama of highlife modernity, which this locality designed for itself at this point in its history. I introduce the texts by providing synopses, which I relate to the issues of locality, women, and the highlife. I inform students that both pamphlets were highly regarded by Onitsha market readers for more than twenty years after publication.

Veronica My Daughter

Veronica My Daughter sold over sixty thousand copies and went through a number of reprints.[3] It is written in a variety of Nigerian Englishes, the pidgin being the most obvious. That the plot is thin does not detract from its robustness. The story makes no pretense to any social or cultural idyll; at its core is the dissent that Veronica proposes and abides by in the course of the narrative. Her dissent is to the luring presence of the opportunities that highlife presents to women, perhaps for the first time, in the Onitsha postcolony in transition. Veronica tells her father, Chief Jombo, in clear and unambiguous terms that she will not marry Chief Bassey, the rich local man her father has chosen for her. Chief Bassey is not literate, a point that Veronica repeatedly makes. She prefers Mike, a young man who is poor but educated and writes brilliant essays for the local newspaper. Mike demonstrates in his writing, which is often bombastic, a knowledge of both the local and the outside. He is a man very well located in the highlife of the time. He is serious, goal-driven, and upwardly mobile but sometimes overly involved with the outside.

Although the narrative focuses on the choice of Mike, I ask my students to consider why Veronica's dissent troubles the masculinity not only of her father but also of all the men in the community. I ask them to see the boldness of the dissent, which is supported by Veronica's mother, Paulina, who recounts her own experiences on the matter of forced and arranged marriage. The stories of Veronica and Paulina point to the subservient position of women before the wind of highlife blew over the Onitsha region. Even before Veronica's dissent, Paulina regrets her early marriage to the chief and talks about how her dream of education was cut short, something she does not want for her daughter. She tells her husband, "Mike has even been encouraging her to read harder and has on many occasions bought her new and interesting books" (7). But Paulina does not share Veronica's fervor; her attitude toward the youth of the period is ambiguous. She supports Veronica's wish to marry Mike but describes young men "of nowdays" as "generally mad with girls at first sight" (17). In this statement, Paulina shows insight into this brave new world. She has doubts about highlife but at the same time recognizes its benefits, which she didn't enjoy as a girl. Her support is cautious, because "appearance may deceive you" (17), as she puts it.

The family trouble caused by Veronica's dissent leads to a communal meeting. The meeting itself is a signal that the traditional values are not all gone, despite the highlife that threatens them. The meeting is a move taken by Chief Jombo in exasperation: "well send Tom to call all my friends and neighbours and dem headman say make them come tomorrow evening" (30). All the important people of the community assemble, including proponents of highlife modernity, whose presence foregrounds the cultural and economic changes taking place. Mark Johnson, the school headmaster, introduces the matter of Veronica's dissent, making it absolutely clear that the position he takes with her father is the sign of the times. "Remember what I told you when you first reported the matter to me," he tells Chief Jombo and the gathered crowd. That he is the head of the local school defines him as an important figure in the community. Momo, a neighbor, sides with Paulina and Veronica. Bomber Billy sides with Chief Jombo and Chief Bassey, but he is not taken seriously. Paulina refers to him as a "pocket radio," who does not mean anything (28). Ogali positions him as the parrot of the empire. Bomber Billy is fond of expressing mundane issues in grandiose, incomprehensible words. He loves the empire without understanding it. Simply put, he is in love with the English language. Paulina sides with the headmaster, the brilliant representive of the new world, the mediator between the local and the global flow of new ideas. He is, after all, the new man. Exasperated, Chief Jumbo can only ask, "Oh! Na the thing wey dey for country?" (31); a tough translation is, "Is this what is happening in the country?"

The communal gathering turns out right for Mike and Veronica: Chief Jumbo is forced to accept the marriage, and there is the image of a wonderful future for the couple. Chief Jumbo and Chief Bassey are dislodged from their position of authority, and their masculine egos are badly shaken. Veronica's dissent, with its support by the school headmaster, is a crucial first step to the emancipation of women in the public space of the highlife tradition, yet we must not forget that the options open to Veronica are still limited. The freedom she has is not to refuse to marry but simply to marry the person of her choice. This freedom is a big step, and if we accept that Veronica speaks for a younger generation of women in this region, it is no longer difficult to see the emancipatory spirit embedded in her defiance of patriarchy. But I remind my students that her highlife is a tame expression of the freedom that modernity offers. It is still confined to what Elaine Showalter calls the "women's sphere" (198), which is acceptable to the patriarchy of Onitsha modernity. Certainly, there is no *prise de la parole* ("gaining access to speech," "insisting on being heard") in what Veronica does before and after her marriage. Rather, we see and feel her acknowledgment of a limited selfhood that disturbs the authority of men in the female sphere. It is not an assertion of equal rights with men.

By the end of our study of *Veronica*, my students realize that what they take for granted was not taken for granted by women in the culture of the Onitsha market. Chosing one's love partner in that culture was a far more serious affair than students can ever imagine. The rather simple expression of dissent by Veronica therefore points to a profound cultural problem. My students are puzzled that Veronica suffers so much because she wants to be with "whosoever," as a student put it in one of my classes.

Mabel the Sweet Honey That Poured Away

Mabel the Sweet Honey That Poured Away stirs the most debate in all my classes dealing with popular literature in Africa. In the last four years during which I taught these pamphlets in postcolonial writing classes and independent popular literature courses, this one generated the greatest number of postings on the WebCt.

The title of this pamphlet is not only telling and dramatic but also descriptive. The cover suggests the content yet also diverts attention from it. I tell my students that cover design of Onitsha market pamphlets reveals the mind-set of the pamphleteers and marketers; it also speaks about the culture of this literary tradition as well as about its audience. The cover copy of *Mabel* presents Mabel as a sweet local girl, but the cover image shows the face of a European woman who gazes straight at the camera. Her eyes are not innocent but somewhat wild, wise, and open to the world. The pose is self-conscious. The dress she is wearing suggests that she comes from elsewhere. She knows that she is beautiful. My students point to the incongruity between copy and image. I ask them to think why a dramatic Caucasian woman is on the cover and not the local girl we meet in the text. There is often intense debate on this question.

I suggest that the appeal of this cover girl may be located in the exotic that the Onitsha community invested in its choice of highlife and glitter. If the cover girl is a form of advertisement for the pamphlet, it is also the trope of the exotic, the exquisite outside, a reversal of the rending of the exotic in colonial discourse as the other. I refer my students to the essays of Veena Das and of Lila Abu-Lughod, which make the point that the local does not always kneel down in abject surrender to the visible and invisible current of global tide. This cover girl is a telling example of how a local community reconstitutes the global in its own image.

The deft and dramatic arrangement of the words on the cover is also eloquent. "Mabel the Sweet Honey" is boldly printed at the top, close to the edge of the page, and just below the hips of the worldly cover girl are the words "That Poured Away." The second part of the title competes with the first, to make one of the most stylistically daring covers in the romance subgenre of the Onitsha market pamphlets. Another line follows, in a less bold and smaller font; "Her skin would make your blood flow in the wrong direction. She was so sweet and sexy, knew how to romance. She married at sixteen, but she wanted more fun. Yet it ended at seventeen. And what an end? So thrilling."

My students find the style of writing very Western. I agree with them but stress the point that Speedy Eric, obviously the pseudonym of an author who does not want to be identified, infuses a certain morality into the sexually promiscuous activities of the local girl, Mabel, and her sex tutor, Margie. Essentially *Mabel* is a story for men written by a man and describes the obnoxious masculinity enacted by the men in Mrs. Ojina's Pleasure Home. The male sexual exploits take place entirely in the Pleasure Home, a quasi-restaurant operated by Mabel's mother. The story is about the tutorship that Mabel goes through as she discovers her body and puts it to use. The narrative reads like an airport pornographic paperback. Once Mabel finds the pleasures that her body can generate, she goes from one man to another at the Pleasure Home. Early in her career, she comes into contact with Gilbert, whom she marries. She soon tires of him, packs her clothes, and tells him she wants to visit her mother. Unsuspecting, Gil lets her return to the Pleasure Home. Back with her mother, Mabel goes wild. Her sexual activities take a new turn: she begins to demand money for her services. Her libidinous activities convert the restaurant into a brothel.

Tired of waiting, Gil comes to the Pleasure Home to seek Mabel. She refuses to go back with him. In another visit, he actually sees her making love with one of the customers, Mr. Eze, the "juicy ebony man" (52). Margie admonishes Mabel. The mother also admonishes her. But this time Gil has had enough. Exasperated, Mabel leaves Onitsha for Port Harcourt, lodges in the Palace Hotel, and continues her sexual escapades as a mere prostitute. It is the "terrible desire to taste a young man" (4) that finally leads this beautiful young girl of seventeen to her infamous end. The narrative focuses attention on this inordinate desire, a desire that is harmful to the community and that marks a girl out of tune with local morality. We are reminded of the oral tale of the beautiful maiden who will not listen to the ancient wisdom of her community and ends up marrying a spirit because she refused all the local suitors. The sexual excess of Mabel provides an example of what women in this community should not be. She is an example of how not to be a young girl. She typifies highlife culture gone totally awry.

There are many similarities between the two pamphlets. Their images of highlife modernity may differ, but the expression of its values does not. In *Veronica*, that modernity is a culture that liberates, that uses the English language, the language of the colonized, as an icon of a new life. Veronica's agency depends on it. In *Mabel*, the untamed and insistent desire to take control of the traditionally fractured female body goes far beyond making a choice about a life partner. That the moral boundaries of female sexuality are ignored leads to, as Speedy Eric puts it, a "predisposition to corruption." Mabel has "an unhealthy desire for sexual matter" (23).

Gilbert says to Mabel's mother, "I go to school at C.K.C." (26), which is Christ the King College, a famous missionary school established in Onitsha in the 1940s, and Mike in *Veronica* has an intermediate BA. These pieces of information tell the reader that modernity is linked to the global current of change. All the Onitsha pamphlets, including the political and do-it-yourself genres, oppose the modern to the traditional. While they voice a grassroots revolution and may constitute an early "vernacular discourse about the global" (Appadurai 2), they also show the anxiety of males in the Onitsha community of the 1940s and 1950s. Dissenting women are given a little space to demonstrate agency but only enough to make them think of a new world. If they push their freedom from patriarchal masculinity too far, the authors of the pamphlets put a check on their activities.

Mabel oversteps the boundary marked by the highlife tradition of the Onitsha market and is viciously punished at the end of her tale of excesses.

Predictably, it is not the escapades of Gilbert, who is "an experienced young man with women" (46), that the narrative foregrounds but Mabel's sexuality. On Mabel's chastity, Speedy Eric writes, "[T]he boy was tired of begging. But he also knew he was standing with a complete virgin. That made him resolve to take her in, even if he had to die after" (47). The idea of conquering a woman's body by force is clear here, and it is likely that the author approves of this idea. The objectification of a woman is heightened when Gilbert, the future husband of Mabel, "*carried his meat* into his room and then put it down, locking the door immediately." That it is "no simple matter to BREAK a virgin" (47) presents a challenge to the male spirit. My students often take issue with this part of the pamphlet, "breaking a virgin." I explain that this attitude comes from a traditional belief in female chastity.

Mabel dies a lonesome death, in a hotel bathroom in the big city of Port Harcourt:

> She took her contraceptives and in overdose too. The next day the result came. In the middle of the day the abortion took place, but a hell of blood followed. There was no mother or sister to help. No friend like Margie to come and carry her to the hospital. No one even took notice of her agony. . . . The blood flowed freely unchecked, by about four thirty the last drop that held her life together flowed away. And she collapsed and died. (69–70)

Mabel obviously depicts the evil side of highlife modernity—a depraved, isolated, and extremely insecure existence. But if she is the errant child of this modernity, Veronica is not. Veronica stays within the space that the patriarchy has allowed for women in the new world.

Another key point of debate for my students is the notion of a local modernity. The highlife, I reiterate at the end of the class, is the cultural and political upheaval that a community experiences when it comes into contact with the global. This contact is marked by shifting allegiances. In the Onitsha community, these shifting allegiances were located in the eroding masculine power base and the presence of women willing to assume agency. The complexity of highlife modernity is expressed most clearly in the simultaneous acceptance and denial of female agency. European modernity is obviously a source of anxiety in the local patriarchy. The pamphlets, an expression of this anxiety and communal upheaval, also give insight into the local femininity that the patriarchy disapproves of. But Onitsha modernity is only one among many in colonial West Africa.

In my classes, I end with another reference to Achebe, this time to his early "*The Sacrificial Egg*" *and Other Stories*, a collection that is rarely mentioned by scholars. It validates my attempt to relocate popular thoughts and sentiments to the front burner of study and also gives additional evidence of the similarity between elite and popular writing from the post-colony. This collection of stories is, after all, published as an Onitsha market pamphlet. Its content expresses the modernity of the Onitsha market community.

What I emphasize in my teaching popular Onitsha market literature in the North American classroom depends on the composition of the class. However, one thing remains unchanged in all my classes on popular arts in Africa: the humanization of the text. When teaching at the University of Calabar in Nigeria, I did not need to state the obvious about these pamphlets. The experiences of the characters in them may have been unfamiliar to some of my Calabar students, but they were not remote to them. Onitsha still exists as a city where, according to Achebe, the bizarre meets the sane and the sinner mingles with the preacher (Obiechina ix). My Calabar students could relate to that mixture perfectly. In Edmonton, contextualizing the social and cultural essentials is imperative. The best way to put in context these pamphlets is to bring students to understand what Achebe states in his essay "Teaching *Things Fall Apart*," that the fictional world of its characters must be given human attention. I make the same appeal for the popular Onitsha market pamphlets. Because they are written by people who see themselves as part of the highlife culture that the pamphlets describe, they provide a valuable social history of this locality under colonialism.

Veronica My Daughter and *Mabel the Sweet Honey That Poured Away* are two of the most popular expressions of highlife culture, but I also teach the politically inspired pamphlets and the do-it-yourself manuals that tell young men and women how to win the love of the opposite sex or how to pass an examination. This eclectic method of unpacking the popular text has worked very well with my Edmonton classes on popular Onitsha market literature and popular Nigerian film.

Notes

This essay is the summation of four classes I taught dealing with popular literature and culture in Africa. In one of the classes, I also taught popular videos, using such films as *Living in Bondage 1 and 2* and *Rituals*, both considered classics of popular art in Nigeria since the demise of the Onitsha market pamphlets after the Nigerian civil war. I teach popular African literature and culture under the rubric of postcolonial studies at the Department of English and Film Studies in the University of Alberta, Edmonton.

1. Soyinka relays to us the rejection of what is now described as African literature in the early 1970s in England, as "the dilemma of the English Literature traditionalists" (vii).

2. I am using versions of *Veronica My Daughter* and *Mabel the Sweet Honey That Poured Away* deposited at the Special Collections Library of the University of Alberta Rutherford Libraries. I quote from them without emendation.

3. There is conflict about the sales figures of this pamphlet. Obiechina tells us that "Ogali A. Ogali's play *Veronica My Daughter* has recorded a sale of 60,000 copies" (4). But Sanders and Ayers record a sales figure of 250,000 in their 1980 published anthology of Ogali A. Ogali's works (ix). In either case, the work is obviously a classic of the Onitsha market tradition.

Works Cited

Abu-Lughod, Lila. "The Objects of Soap Opera: Egyptian Television and the Global Politics of Modernity." Miller 190–210.

Achebe, Chinua. *"The Sacrificial Egg" and Other Stories.* Onitsha: Etudo, 1962. Print.

———. "Teaching *Things Fall Apart.*" Lindfors 20–24.

———. *Things Fall Apart.* Expanded ed. London: Heinemann, 2000. Print.

Appadurai, Arjun. "Grassroots Globalization and Research Imagination." *Public Culture* 12.1 (2000): 1–10. Print.

Appiah, Kwame Anthony. "Is the Post- in Postmodern the Post- in Postcolonial?" *Critical Inquiry* 17 (1991): 336–57. Print.

Barber, Karin. Introduction. *Readings in African Popular Culture.* Ed. Barber. Bloomington: Indiana UP, 1997. 1–11. Print.

———. "Popular Arts in Africa." *African Studies Review* 30.3 (1987): 1–78. Print.

———. "Preliminary Notes on Audience in Africa." *Africa* 67.3 (1997): 347–62. Print.

Comaroff, Jean, and John L. Comaroff. "Millennial Capitalism: First Thoughts on a Second Coming." *Public Culture* 12.2 (2000): 291–343. Print.

Das, Veena. "On Soap Opera: What Kind of Anthropological Object Is This?" Miller 168–89.

Gluckman, Max. "The Magic of Despair." 1954. *Order and Rebellion in Tribal Africa: Collected Essays with an Autobiographical Introduction.* London: Routledge, 2004. 137–45. Print.

Lindfors, Bernth, ed. *Approaches to Teaching Achebe's* Things Fall Apart. New York: MLA, 1991. Print.

Mbembe, Achille. "African Modes of Self-Writing." *Public Culture* 14.1 (2002): 239–73. Print.

Miller, Daniel, ed. *Worlds Apart: Modernity through the Prism of the Local.* London: Routledge, 1995. Print.

Obiechina, Emmanuel. *Literature for the Masses: An Analytical Study of Popular Pamphleteering in Nigeria*. Enugu: Nwankwo-Ifejika, 1971. Print.

Ogali, A. Ogali. *Veronica My Daughter: A Drama*. Onitsha: Appolos, n.d. Print.

Sanders, Reinhard W., and Peter K. Ayers, eds. Veronica My Daughter *and Other Onitsha Plays and Stories*. Washington: Three Continents, 1980. Print.

Showalter. Elaine. "Feminist Criticism in the Wilderness." *Critical Inquiry* 8.2 (1981): 179–205. Print.

Soyinka, Wole. *Myth, Literature and the African World*. Cambridge: Cambridge UP, 1976. Print.

Speedy Eric. *Mabel the Sweet Honey That Poured Away*. Onitsha: Onwudiwe, n.d. Print.

Wren, Robert M. "*Things Fall Apart* in Its Time and Place." Lindfors 38–44.

Part IV

Resources

Further Resources for Teaching the African Novel

Since the amount of scholarly literature on African literature in general and the African novel in particular has now reached gargantuan proportions, it seems advisable to present a recommended list of additional readings rather than attempt a comprehensive bibliography. What follows is a list of print readings based more on an assessment of the particular value of a work to the immediate concerns of a potential teacher. Many fine studies that would be required reading for a doctoral dissertation are left out, because they are too specialized. While I include a list of representative single-author studies, readers interested in critical analysis of individual authors and texts will be best served by doing a keyword search on the MLA's online bibliography. There are also a growing number of Web sites dedicated to African literature, but the usual caveats on carefully determining the source and credibility of the material they present apply here.

To make the lists more manageable, I have focused on full-length books and edited collections rather than articles. In addition to the works listed here (and those appearing in the works-cited lists of the individual essays of this book), readers will find it useful to browse through previous issues of the *ALA Bulletin* and the journals *African Literature Today* and

Research in African Literatures. The *ALA Bulletin* is the news bulletin of the African Literature Association, the largest professional organization in North America dedicated to the study and teaching of African literatures. The bulletin chronicles the growth of the discipline, has provided a stage for some of its debates, and helps scholars keep abreast of new scholarship and new works. The bibliography compiled in this bulletin has been an important point of reference to scholars in the field. The journal *African Literature Today,* founded by Eldred Durosimi Jones in Sierra Leone, has been one of the most respected avenues for the publication of critical essays on African literatures. In the North American context, the journal *Research in African Literatures* is considered the preeminent journal in the field. A systematic browse through the journal from its inception in 1970 to the present provides an excellent overview of the debates and movements in the field. Particularly useful are the book reviews in this journal, which provide readers with an assessment of the critical apparatus being published as the field has developed. Lastly, those interested in a historical understanding of the field may also find it useful to read through the volumes of selected conference papers published each year by the African Literature Association.

Reference Books, Interviews, and Bibliographies on African Literatures

Cox, Brian, ed. *African Writers.* 2 vols. New York: Scribner's, 1997.

Gerard, Albert. *African Language Literatures: An Introduction to the Literary History of Sub-Saharan Africa.* Washington: Three Continents, 1981.

———, ed. *European Language Writing in Sub-Saharan Africa.* 2 vols. Budapest: Akadémiai Kiadó, 1986.

Gikandi, Simon, ed. *Encyclopedia of African Literature.* New York: Routledge, 2003.

Irele, F. Abiola, and Simon Gikandi, eds. *The Cambridge History of African and Caribbean Literature.* 2 vols. Cambridge: Cambridge UP, 2004.

James, Adeola. *In Their Own Voices: African Women Writers Talk.* Portsmouth: Heinemann, 1990.

Killam, Douglas, and Ruth Rowe, eds. *The Companion to African Literatures.* Bloomington: Indiana UP, 2000.

Lindfors, Bernth, ed. *Africa Talks Back: Interviews with Anglophone African Writers.* Trenton: Africa World, 2004.

———. *Black African Literatures in English: A Guide to Information Sources.* Detroit: Gale Research, 1979. This bibliographic guide has been supplemented over the years by additional volumes by Lindfors covering the critical literature until 1999.

Olaniyan, Tejumola, and Ato Quayson, eds. *African Literature: An Anthology of Criticism and Theory.* Oxford: Blackwell, 2007.

Owomoyela, Oyekan, ed. *A History of Twentieth-Century African Literatures.* Lincoln: U of Nebraska P, 1993.

Parekh, Pushpa Naidu, and Siga Fatima Jagne, eds. *Postcolonial African Writers: A Bio-bibliographical Critical Sourcebook.* Westport: Greenwood, 1998.

Zell, Hans, Carol Bundy, and Virginia Coulon, eds. *A New Reader's Guide to African Literature.* 2nd ed. New York: Africana, 1983.

Contexts for Studying the African Novel

Listed here are works that provide a larger frame for the study of the African novel. Some are concerned with the legacy of colonial discourse and its postcolonial manifestations. Others are interested in reading African literatures across genres for thematic continuities. Yet others bring into focus a regional frame for the reading of African texts. These texts are deemed to be of particular interest to teachers of the African novel and do not include studies primarily dedicated to African theater and performance, poetry, or film.

Achebe, Chinua. *Hopes and Impediments: Selected Essays.* New York: Doubleday, 1988.

———. *Morning Yet on Creation Day: Essays.* New York: Anchor, 1975.

Afolabi, Niyi. *The Golden Cage: Regeneration in Lusophone African Literature and Culture.* Trenton: Africa World, 2001.

Allan, Tuzyline Jita. *Womanist and Feminist Aesthetics.* Athens: Ohio UP, 1995.

Almeida, Irene Asssiba. *Francophone African Women Writers: Destroying the Emptiness of Silence.* Gainesville: UP of Florida, 1994.

Amuta, Chidi. *The Theory of African Literature: Implications for Practical Criticism.* London: Zed, 1989.

Appiah, Anthony. *In My Father's House: Africa in the Philosophy of Culture.* New York: Oxford UP, 1992.

Arnaud, Jacqueline. *La littérature maghrebine de langue francaise.* Paris: Publisud, 1986.

Arndt, Susan. *The Dynamics of African Feminism: Defining and Classifying African-Feminist Literatures.* Trenton: Africa World, 2002.

Bethlehem, Louise. *Skin Tight: Apartheid Literary Culture and Its Aftermath.* Boston: Brill Academic, 2006.

Bishop, Rand. *African Literature, African Critics: The Forming of Critical Standards, 1947–1966.* New York: Greenwood, 1988.

Bjornson, Richard. *The African Quest for Freedom: Cameroonian Writing and the National Experience.* Bloomington: Indiana UP, 1991.

Burness, Donald, ed. *Critical Perspectives on Lusophone African Literatures.* Washington: Three Continents, 1981.

Cazenave, Odile. *Rebellious Women: The New Generation of Female African Novelists.* Boulder: Rienner, 1999.

Chabal, Patrick. *The Post-colonial Literature of Lusophone Africa.* Evanston: Northwestern UP, 1996.

Chapman, Michael. *Southern African Literatures.* New York: Longman, 1996.

Chinweizu, Onwuchekwa Jemie, and Ihechukwu Madubuike. *African Fiction and Poetry and Their Critics.* Washington: Howard UP, 1983. Vol. 1 of *Toward the Decolonization of African Literature.*

Coetzee, J. M. *White Writing: On the Culture of Letters in South Africa.* New Haven: Yale UP, 1988.

Davies, Carole Boyce, and Anne Adams Graves, eds. *Ngambika: Studies of Women in African Literature.* Trenton: Africa World, 1986.

Desai, Gaurav. *Subject to Colonialism: African Self-Fashioning and the Colonial Library.* Durham: Duke UP, 2001.

Fanon, Frantz. *The Wretched of the Earth.* Trans. Constance Farrington. New York: Grove, 1968.

George, Olakunle. *Relocating Agency: Modernity and African Letters.* Albany: State U of New York P, 2003.

Gikandi, Simon. *Maps of Englishness: Writing Identity in the Culture of Colonialism.* New York: Columbia UP, 1996.

Gray, Stephen. *South African Literature: An Introduction.* Cape Town: Philip, 1979.

Gugelberger, Georg, ed. *Marxism and African Literature.* Trenton: Africa World, 1986.

Hamilton, Russell. *Voices from an Empire: A History of Afro-Portuguese Literature.* Minneapolis: U of Minnesota P, 1975.

Harrow, Kenneth, ed. *Faces of Islam in African Literature.* Portsmouth: Heinemann, 1991.

———. *Less than One and Double: A Feminist Reading of African Women's Writing.* Portsmouth: Heinemann, 2002.

———, ed. *The Marabout and the Muse: New Approaches to Islam in African Literature.* Portsmouth: Heinemann, 1996.

———. *Thresholds of Change in African Literature: The Emergence of a Tradition.* Portsmouth: Heinemann, 1994.

Hayes, Jarrod. *Queer Nations: Marginal Sexualities in the Maghreb*. Chicago: U of Chicago P, 2000.

Hoad, Neville. *African Intimacies: Race, Homosexuality, and Globalization*. Minneapolis: U of Minnesota P, 2007.

Hountondji, Paulin. *African Philosophy: Myth and Reality*. Bloomington: Indiana UP, 1983.

Irele, Abiola. *The African Experience in Literature and Ideology*. London: Heinemann, 1981.

———. *The African Imagination: Literature in Africa and the Black Diaspora*. New York: Oxford UP, 2001.

Jack, Belinda Elizabeth. *Negritude and Literary Criticism: The History and Theory of Negro-African Literature in French*. Westport: Greenwood, 1996.

Jules-Rosette, Bennetta. *Black Paris: The African Writer's Landscape*. Urbana: U of Illinois P, 1998.

Kesteloot, Lilyan. *Black Writers in French: A Literary History of Negritude*. Philadelphia: Temple UP, 1974.

Lindfors, Bernth. *"The Blind Men and the Elephant" and Other Essays in Biographical Criticism*. 2nd ed. Trenton: Africa World, 1999.

Magubane, Zine, ed. *Postmodernism, Postcoloniality, and African Studies*. Trenton: Africa World, 2003.

Mbembe, Achille. *On the Postcolony*. Berkeley: U of California P, 2001.

McNee, Lisa. *Selfish Gifts: Senegalese Women's Autobiographical Discourses*. Albany: State U of New York P, 2000.

Miller, Christopher. *Blank Darkness: Africanist Discourse in French*. Chicago: U of Chicago P, 1985.

———. *Nationalists and Nomads: Essays on Francophone African Literature and Culture*. Chicago: U of Chicago P, 1998.

———. *Theories of Africans: Francophone Literature and Ideology in Africa*. Chicago: U of Chicago P, 1990.

Mortimer, Mildred, ed. *Maghrebian Mosaic: A Literature in Transition*. Boulder: Rienner, 2000.

Mudimbe, V. Y. *The Invention of Africa: Gnosis, Philosophy, and the Order of Knowledge*. Bloomington: Indiana UP, 1988.

Ndebele, Njabulo. *South African Literature and Culture: Rediscovery of the Ordinary*. Manchester: Manchester UP, 1994.

Newell, Stephanie. *Literary Culture in Colonial Ghana: How to Play the Game of Life*. Bloomington: Indiana UP, 2002.

———, ed. *Writing African Women: Gender, Popular Culture and Literature in West Africa*. London: Zed, 1997.

Nfah-Abbenyi, Juliana Makuchi. *Gender in African Women's Writing: Identity, Sexuality, and Difference*. Bloomington: Indiana UP, 1997.

Ngũgĩ wa Thiong'o. *Decolonising the Mind: The Politics of Language in African Literature*. Portsmouth: Heinemann, 1986.

———. *Moving the Centre: The Struggle for Cultural Freedoms*. Portsmouth: Heinemann, 1992.

Nnaemeka, Obioma. *The Politics of (M)Othering: Womenhood, Identity, and Resistance in African Literature*. New York: Routledge, 1997.

Obiechina, Emmanuel. *An African Popular Literature: A Study of the Onitsha Market Pamphlets*. Cambridge: Cambridge UP, 1973.

Peterson, Kirsten Holst, ed. *Criticism and Ideology: Second African Writers' Conference, Stockholm 1986*. Uppsala: Scandanavian Inst. of African Studies, 1988.

Priebe, Richard. *Myth, Realism, and the West African Writer*. Trenton: Africa World, 1988.

Quayson, Ato. *Calibrations: Reading for the Social*. Minneapolis: U of Minnesota P, 2003.

———. *Strategic Transformations in Nigerian Writing*. Bloomington: Indiana UP, 1997.

Ricard, Alain. *Languages and Literatures of Africa*. Trenton: Africa World, 2004.

Soyinka, Wole. *Art, Dialogue, and Outrage: Essays on Literature and Culture*. New York: Pantheon, 1993.

———. *Myth, Literature and the African World*. Cambridge: Cambridge UP, 1976.

Stratton, Florence. *Contemporary African Literature and the Politics of Gender*. New York: Routledge, 1994.

Thomas, Dominic. *Nation-Building, Propaganda, and Literature in Francophone Africa*. Bloomington: Indiana UP, 2002.

Veit-Wild, Flora. *Teachers, Preachers, and Non-believers: A Social History of Zimbabwean Literature*. New York: Zell, 1992.

Wise, Christopher, ed. *The Desert Shore: Literatures of the Sahel*. Boulder: Rienner, 2001.

Studies of the African Novel

These texts take the genre of the African novel, sometimes in explicit relation to the European novel, as a particular focus of study.

Allen, Roger. *The Arabic Novel: An Historical and Critical Introduction*. 2nd ed. Syracuse: Syracuse UP, 1995.

Booker, Keith. *The African Novel in English: An Introduction*. Portsmouth: Heinemann, 1998.

Brown, Nicholas. *Utopian Generations: The Political Horizon of Twentieth-Century Literature*. Princeton: Princeton UP, 2005

Cooper, Brenda. *Magical Realism in West African Fiction: Seeing with a Third Eye.* New York: Routledge, 1998.

Coundouriotis, Eleni. *Claiming History: Colonialism, Ethnography, and the Novel.* New York: Columbia UP, 1999.

Gakwandi, Shatto Arthur. *The Novel and Contemporary Experience in Africa.* New York: Africana, 1977.

Gikandi, Simon. *Reading the African Novel.* Portsmouth: Heinemann, 1987.

Green, Michael. *Novel Histories: Past, Present and Future in South African Fiction.* Johannesburg: U of Witwatersrand P, 1997.

JanMohamed, Abdul. *Manichean Aesthetics: The Politics of Literature in Colonial Africa.* Amherst: U of Massachusetts P, 1983.

Julien, Eileen. *African Novels and the Question of Orality.* Bloomington: Indiana UP, 1992.

Kane, Mohamadou. *Roman africain et traditions.* Dakar: Nouvelles Editions Africaines, 1982.

Ker, David. *The African Novel and the Modernist Tradition.* New York: Lang, 1997.

Kurtz, John Roger. *Urban Obsessions, Urban Fears: The Postcolonial Kenyan Novel.* Trenton: Africa World, 1998.

Mortimer, Mildred. *Journeys through the French African Novel.* Portsmouth: Heinemann, 1990.

Ngara, Emmanuel. *Art and Ideology in the African Novel: A Study of the Influence of Marxism on African Writing.* London: Heinemann, 1985.

Ngate, Jonathan. *Francophone African Fiction: Reading a Literary Tradition.* Trenton: Africa World, 1988.

Obiechina, Emmanuel N. *Culture, Tradition and Society in the West African Novel.* Cambridge: Cambridge UP, 1975.

Ogunyemi, Chikwenye. *African Wo/Man Palava: The Nigerian Novel by Women.* Chicago: U of Chicago P, 1996.

Palmer, Eustace. *The Growth of the African Novel.* London: Heinemann, 1979.

Wehrs, Donald. *African Feminist Fiction and Indigenous Values.* Gainesville: UP of Florida, 2001.

Wright, Derek. *New Directions in African Fiction.* New York: Twayne, 1997.

Studies of Individual Authors

These texts are representative of the many excellent studies of the oeuvre of individual African writers. I do not include studies of authors such as Wole Soyinka, whose work in genres other than the novel (in Soyinka's case, theater) is the primary focus of critics.

Abrahams, Cecil. *Alex La Guma*. Boston: Twayne, 1985.

Attwell, David. *J. M. Coetzee: South Africa and the Politics of Writing*. Berkeley: U of California P, 1993.

Azodo, Ada Uzoamaka, ed. *Emerging Perspectives on Mariama Bâ: Postcolonialism, Feminism, and Postmodernism*. Trenton: Africa World, 2003.

Azodo, Ada Uzoamaka, and Gay Alden Wilentz, eds. *Emerging Perspectives on Ama Ata Aidoo*. Trenton: Africa World, 1999.

Chennells, A. J., and Flora Veit-Wild, eds. *Emerging Perspectives on Dambudzo Marechera*. Trenton: Africa World, 1999.

Emenyonu, Ernest, and Iniobong I. Uko, eds. *Emerging Perspectives on Chinua Achebe*. Trenton: Africa World, 2004.

Gikandi, Simon. *Ngugi wa Thiong'o*. Cambridge: Cambridge UP, 2000.

———. *Reading Chinua Achebe: Language and Ideology in Fiction*. Portsmouth: Heinemann, 1991.

Head, Dominic. *Nadine Gordimer*. Cambridge: Cambridge UP, 1994.

Ibrahim, Huma. *Bessie Head: Subversive Identities in Exile*. Charlottesville: UP of Virginia, 1996.

Lazarus, Neil. *Resistance in Postcolonial African Fiction*. New Haven: Yale UP, 1990.

Malti-Douglas, Fedwa. *Men, Women, and God(s): Nawal El Saadawi and Arab Feminist Politics*. Berkeley: U of California P, 1995.

Muponde, Robert, and Mandivavarira Maodzwa-Taruvinga, eds. *Sign and Taboo: Perspectives on the Poetic Fiction of Yvonne Vera*. Harare: Weaver, 2003.

Okome, Onookome. *Before I Am Hanged: Ken Saro-Wiwa: Literature, Politics, and Dissent*. Trenton: Africa World, 1999.

Sougou, Omar. *Writing across Cultures: Gender Politics and Difference in the Fiction of Buchi Emecheta*. Amsterdam: Rodopi, 2002.

Umeh, Marie, ed. *Emerging Perspectives on Flora Nwapa: Critical and Theoretical Essays*. Trenton: Africa World, 1998.

Willey, Ann Elizabeth, and Jeanette Trieber, eds. *Negotiating the Postcolonial: Emerging Perspectives on Tsitsi Dangarembga*. Trenton: Africa World, 2002.

Wise, Christopher, ed. *Yambo Ouologuem: Postcolonial Writer, Islamic Militant*. Boulder: Rienner, 1999.

Wright, Derek, ed. *Emerging Perspectives on Nuruddin Farah*. Trenton: Africa World, 2002.

The Teaching of African Literatures

Teachers of African literature have long been concerned with sharing useful and appropriate pedagogical strategies. In that sense, this volume adds to an already existing legacy that is rich with insights. Here are some of the texts on pedagogy that precede this volume.

Allan, Tuzyline Jita, ed. *Teaching African Literatures in a Global Literary Economy.* Spec. issue of *Women's Studies Quarterly.* 25.3–4 (1997): 1–248.

Hale, Thomas, and Richard Priebe, eds. *The Teaching of African Literature.* 2nd ed. Washington: Three Continents, 1989.

Hay, Margaret Jean, ed. *African Novels in the Classroom.* Boulder: Rienner, 2000.

Lindfors, Bernth, ed. *Approaches to Teaching Achebe's* Things Fall Apart. New York: MLA, 1991.

———. *Long Drums and Canons: Teaching and Researching African Literatures.* Trenton: Africa World, 1995.

Notes on Contributors

Cora Agatucci is professor of English at Central Oregon Community College, Bend. She has published articles on African, African Caribbean, and African American writers. Her African culture and literature instructional Web materials have earned international recognition, wide educational use, and print publication. She teaches writing, world literature, and film.

Fernando Arenas is associate professor of lusophone African, Brazilian, and Portuguese studies in the Department of Spanish and Portuguese Studies at the University of Minnesota. He is the author of *Utopias of Otherness: Nationhood and Subjectivity in Portugal and Brazil* (2003) and co-editor with Susan C. Quinlan of *Lusosex: Gender and Sexuality in the Portuguese-Speaking World* (2002). His book "Beyond Independence: Globalization, Postcolonialism, and the Cultures of Lusophone Africa" is forthcoming.

Louise Bethlehem is a senior lecturer in the Department of English at the Hebrew University of Jerusalem, where she currently heads the Program in Cultural Studies. She has published on J. M. Coetzee as well as on South African literary history more generally, including the recent volume *Skin Tight: Apartheid Literary Culture and Its Aftermath* (2006).

Nicholas Brown is associate professor of English and African American studies at the University of Illinois, Chicago. His book *Utopian Generations: The Political Horizon of Twentieth-Century Literature* (2005) examines the relation between African literature and European modernism and the relation of each to continuing crises in the global economic system.

Odile Cazenave is professor of French at Boston University, where she teaches francophone literature and cinema. She is the author of *Femmes rebelles: Naissance d'un nouveau roman africain au féminin* (1996; trans. as *Rebellious Women* by Lynne Rienner [1999]) and *Afrique sur Seine: Une nouvelle génération de romanciers africains à Paris* (2003; *Afrique sur Seine: A New Generation of African Writers in Paris* [2005]). She guest-edited, with Tanella Boni, a special issue, "L'engagement au féminin," for *Cultures Sud*.

Brenda Cooper is director of the Centre for African Studies (CAS) at the University of Cape Town and professor in the Department of English Language and Literature. At the center, she teaches issues of African knowledge production; in the English department, she teaches African literature and postcolonial theory. Her most recent work is *A New Generation of African Writers: Migration, Material Culture and Language* (2008).

Eleni Coundouriotis is associate professor of English and associate director of the Human Rights Institute at the University of Connecticut. In addition to her work on the African novel, she has written on the relation between human rights and literature (e.g., *Claiming History: Colonialism, Ethnography, and the Novel* [1999]). Her forthcoming work is on African war fiction.

Gaurav Desai is chair of the Department of English at Tulane University and has served as codirector of its African and African Diaspora Studies Program. He is the author of *Subject to Colonialism: African Self-Fashioning and the Colonial Library* (2001) and has coedited *Postcolonialisms: An Anthology of Cultural Theory* (2005). His articles have appeared in journals such as *Cultural Critique*, *Genders*, *Research in African Literatures*, and *Representations*.

Shirin Edwin is assistant professor of French at Sam Houston State University. Her articles on African Islam and Islamic feminism have appeared in *Research in African Literatures*, *Frontiers: A Journal of Women Studies*, and *Third World Quarterly*. She is the author of *L'islam mis en relation: Le roman francophone de l'Afrique de l'Ouest* (2009).

Dosinda García-Alvite is assistant professor of Spanish at Denison University. Her teaching and research interests focus on migration, historical memory, and gender as manifested in the literature, film, and music of contemporary Spain. She has published in *Arizona Journal of Hispanic Cultural Studies*, *Hispania*, *Bulletin of Spanish Studies*. Her current project is a book on literature from Equatorial Guinea written in exile in Spain.

Harry Garuba is associate professor at the Centre for African Studies, University of Cape Town, with a joint appointment in the Department of English Language and Literature. He is widely published in the field of African and postcolonial literatures. His essays have appeared in *Public Culture*, *PMLA*, and *Research in African Literatures*.

Olakunle George is associate professor in the Department of English at Brown University. He is author of *Relocating Agency: Modernity and African Letters*, selected as a CHOICE Outstanding Academic Title in 2003. His articles have appeared in *Comparative Literature*, *Diacritics*, *Novel: A Forum on Fiction*, *Research in African Literatures*, and *Representations*.

Jarrod Hayes is associate professor of French and francophone studies at the University of Michigan. He is the author of *Queer Nations: Marginal Sexualities in the Maghreb* (2000) and works at the intersection of queer theory and postcolonial studies. His current project is a book entitled "Queer Roots for the Diaspora: Ghosts in the Family Tree."

Neville Hoad is associate professor of English at the University of Texas, Austin. He is the author of *African Intimacies: Race, Homosexuality, and Globalization* (2007) and coeditor, with Karen Martin and Graeme Reid, of *Sex and Politics in South Africa: Equality / Gay and Lesbian Movement? The Anti-apartheid Struggle* (2005). He is currently working on a manuscript on the literary and cultural representations of the HIV/AIDS pandemic in sub-Saharan Africa.

Peter Kalliney is associate professor of English at the University of Kentucky. He is the author of *Cities of Affluence and Anger: A Literary Geography of Modern Englishness* (2006). His essays have appeared in *Modern Fiction Studies*, *PMLA*, and *Research in African Literatures.*

Mohamed Kamara, associate professor of French at Washington and Lee University, has published articles on Sierra Leonean literature, Leopold Sédar Senghor and human rights, and French colonial education. He is currently working on a book-length study of French colonial education and the making of the African bourgeoisie.

Lisa McNee is assistant professor in the French Studies Department at Queen's University. She is author of *Selfish Gifts: Senegalese Women's Autobiographical Discourses* (2000) and studies the influence of diaspora on contemporary African literatures and cultural forms (musical and other) and on the construction of childhood through children's literatures.

Onookome Okome is professor of African literature and cinema at the University of Alberta, Edmonton. A leading scholar in the study of popular arts in Africa, he has edited books of essays on leading Nigerian writers, including *Before I Am Hanged: Ken Saro-Wiwa, Literature, Politics, and Dissent* (1999) and *Ogun's Children: The Literature and Politics of Wole Soyinka since the Nobel* (2004).

Tejumola Olaniyan is Louise Durham Mead Professor of English at the University of Wisconsin, Madison. He is author of *Scars of Conquest / Masks of Resistance* (1995) and *Arrest the Music! Fela and His Rebel Art and Politics* (2004) and coeditor with Ato Quayson of *African Literature: An Anthology of Criticism and Theory* (2007), with John Conteh-Morgan of *African Drama and Performance* (2004), and with James H. Sweet of *African Diaspora and the Disciplines* (forthcoming).

R. Radhakrishnan is professor of English and comparative literature at the University of California, Irvine. He is author of *History, the Human, and the World Between* (2008), *Theory in an Uneven World* (2003), and *Diasporic Meditations* (1996); editor of *Theory as Variation* (2007); and coeditor of *Transnational South Asians: The Making of a Neo-diaspora* (2008), and *Theory after Derrida* (2009).

Kimberly Wedeven Segall is associate professor of English at Seattle Pacific University and director of the South Africa Study Abroad Program. She has recently published in *Comparative Studies of South Asia, Africa, and the Middle East* and *Research in African Literatures.* She teaches postcolonial literature and theory and is an affiliate faculty member at the University of Washington in women's studies.

S. Shankar is a novelist, cultural critic, and translator. He is the author of the novel *No End to the Journey* (2005) and the volume of criticism *Textual Traffic: Colonialism, Modernity, and the Economy of the Text* (2001). He is professor in the Department of English and director of the Center for South Asian Studies at the University of Hawai'i, Manoa.

Zahr Said Stauffer is visiting professor of law at the University of Virginia School of Law. She has published articles on Arabic literature and the significance of postcolonial rewriting for intellectual property law. She teaches law and literature.

Christopher Wise is professor of English and comparative literature at Western Washington University. His books include *Derrida, Africa, and the Middle East* (2009), *The Yambo Ouologuem Reader* (2008), *The Desert Shore: Literatures of the Sahel* (2001), and *Yambo Ouologuem: Postcolonial Writer, Islamic Militant* (1999).

Index

Modern Language Association of America
Options for Teaching

Teaching the African Novel. Ed. Gaurav Desai. 2009.

Teaching World Literature. Ed. David Damrosch. 2009.

Teaching North American Environmental Literature. Ed. Laird Christensen, Mark C. Long, and Fred Waage. 2008.

Teaching Life Writing Texts. Ed. Miriam Fuchs and Craig Howes. 2008.

Teaching Nineteenth-Century American Poetry. Ed. Paula Bernat Bennett, Karen L. Kilcup, and Philipp Schweighauser. 2007.

Teaching Representations of the Spanish Civil War. Ed. Noël Valis. 2006.

Teaching the Representation of the Holocaust. Ed. Marianne Hirsch and Irene Kacandes. 2004.

Teaching Tudor and Stuart Women Writers. Ed. Susanne Woods and Margaret P. Hannay. 2000.

Teaching Literature and Medicine. Ed. Anne Hunsaker Hawkins and Marilyn Chandler McEntyre. 1999.

Teaching the Literatures of Early America. Ed. Carla Mulford. 1999.

Teaching Shakespeare through Performance. Ed. Milla C. Riggio. 1999.

Teaching Oral Traditions. Ed. John Miles Foley. 1998.

Teaching Contemporary Theory to Undergraduates. Ed. Dianne F. Sadoff and William E. Cain. 1994.

Teaching Children's Literature: Issues, Pedagogy, Resources. Ed. Glenn Edward Sadler. 1992.

Teaching Literature and Other Arts. Ed. Jean-Pierre Barricelli, Joseph Gibaldi, and Estella Lauter. 1990.

New Methods in College Writing Programs: Theories in Practice. Ed. Paul Connolly and Teresa Vilardi. 1986.

School-College Collaborative Programs in English. Ed. Ron Fortune. 1986.

Teaching Environmental Literature: Materials, Methods, Resources. Ed. Frederick O. Waage. 1985.

Part-Time Academic Employment in the Humanities: A Sourcebook for Just Policy. Ed. Elizabeth M. Wallace. 1984.

Film Study in the Undergraduate Curriculum. Ed. Barry K. Grant. 1983.

The Teaching Apprentice Program in Language and Literature. Ed. Joseph Gibaldi and James V. Mirollo. 1981.

Options for Undergraduate Foreign Language Programs: Four-Year and Two-Year Colleges. Ed. Renate A. Schulz. 1979.

Options for the Teaching of English: Freshman Composition. Ed. Jasper P. Neel. 1978.

Options for the Teaching of English: The Undergraduate Curriculum. Ed. Elizabeth Wooten Cowan. 1975